Japan Real Estate Appraisal in a Global Context

不動産鑑定評価の国際化

JAPAN REAL ESTATE INSTITUTE
編著 (財)日本不動産研究所
執筆 国際業務担当上席主幹, CRE(USA), FRICS(UK)
渡辺 卓美 (TAKUMI WATANABE)

住宅新報社

Japan Real Estate Appraisal in a Global Context

不動産鑑定評価の国際化

Remarks upon the publication of *Japan Real Estate Appraisal in a Global Context*

Kenji Igarashi, President
Japan Real Estate Institute

1. In the past, real estate appraisal operations in Japan belonged to a world that was far removed from the themes of globalization and information technology. With an enormous domestic real estate market and unique market practices, this was an area of domestic operations with little connection to the English language as a means of communicating information across borders. Also, real estate information was closely tied to individual interests, and it was difficult to obtain access to valuable information. These trends applied to appraisal operations elsewhere in the world as well, not only in Japan. For a long time, appraisal was considered to be more of an art than a science.

   But today, appraisal is one of the fields experiencing the fastest progress in globalization and the adoption of information technologies. As the spread of securitization adds liquidity to real estate, the real estate markets of all countries are in a relationship of international competition through the real estate financial market, and vast amounts of global investment capital are being moved around the world in search of the most advantageous investment opportunities. Potential investors increasingly need accurate evaluations of market values based on the earnings potential of the properties. Not only within Japan but from an international standpoint as well, appraisal operations have entered a new stage of heightened transparency and reliability. This trend applies both to appraisal operations within Japan and to appraisal operations in other countries; however, it seems to be progressing more rapidly in the U.S., U.K., and Australia. Scientific data is playing an increasingly important role in the field of appraisal.

2. In 2003, the Japan Real Estate Institute (JREI) published an English translation of the book Japanese Real Estate Appraisal Standards. This step was taken in response to the 2002 revision of the Japanese appraisal standards that continued the emphasis on profitability in the appraisal process, that was begun with the 2001 start of real estate securitization and the adoption of market price-based appraisal in corporate accounting. The writing and editing of the English translation of the standards involved trips overseas for repeated discussions with appraisers, investors, and other experts, in order to ensure that the translation would accurately convey the content of the standards to real estate professionals who are native speakers of English. That book was only a first endeavor to communicate the Japanese standards internationally, but it has been well received by persons engaged in cross-border valuation and investment; and it has fulfilled the preliminary role of informing persons in other countries concerning the fact that appraisals in Japan are performed on the basis of unified stan-

『不動産鑑定評価の国際化』刊行にあたって

財団法人日本不動産研究所
理事長　五十嵐　健之

1．日本の不動産鑑定評価業務は、かつて、グローバル化やIT化とは最も縁の遠い業界に属していました。巨大な国内不動産市場や独特な市場取引慣行を背景にして、国境を越えた情報伝達手段としての英語とはあまり縁のないドメスティックな業務でした。また、不動産情報は個別の利害と密接に結びついていて、情報へのアクセスが難しい業務でした。こうした傾向は、日本の鑑定評価業務だけでなく、海外の鑑定評価業務でも同様であったと言っていいでしょう。鑑定評価は、長い間、サイエンスというよりアート（技術）であると言われてきました。

　現在、鑑定評価業務は、グローバル化とIT化が最も急速に進んでいる業界に属しています。不動産が証券化によって流動性を増し、各国の不動産市場は不動産金融市場を通して国際的な競合関係に立ち、グローバルな巨額の投資資金は最も有利な投資機会を求めて世界中を動き回っています。そして、投資判断に先立って、収益性に基づく不動産の的確な市場価値の把握が問われています。鑑定評価業務も、国内だけでなく国際的視点に立って、透明性と信頼性の中身を充実させる段階に入っています。こうした方向は日本の鑑定評価業務も海外の鑑定評価業務も同様ですが、米国、英国、オーストラリアではさらに急速に進んでいると言っていいでしょう。鑑定評価にも、客観的データに基づくサイエンスの要素が増えています。

2．当研究所は、2001年に開始された不動産証券化の伸展や、企業会計における時価評価等にみられる収益性を重視する方向での鑑定評価の確立を目指して2002年に改正された鑑定評価基準に対応して、2003年に『英語で読む不動産鑑定評価基準』を刊行しました。鑑定評価基準の英訳に際しては、英語を母国語とする不動産の実務家に基準の内容が正確に伝わるように、海外に出向いて現地の鑑定人や投資家等の専門家と議論を重ね、編集・執筆をしました。日本の基準を海外に発信する初の試みでしたが、クロス・ボーダーの評価や投資に関わる方々から一定の評価をいただき、日本では収益性を重視する統一基準に基づいて鑑定評価が行われていることを海外に伝える役割は、ひとまず果たせたと考えています。

dards focusing on profitability.

Since then, the real estate securitization market has been expanding remarkably. Japan's appraisal process plays an important role in the securitization market. The appraisal standards were revised in 2007 (Discussion Sections, Chapter 3) to ensure greater transparency and reliability. Also, the guidelines for the appraisal of overseas investment properties, which were introduced in 2008, state that licensed real estate appraisers may engage in joint work with local appraisers in other countries and submit appraisal documents to clients on that basis. Clearly, an understanding of the differences among the appraisal standards of other countries has become indispensable in appraisal operations.

From these situations, JREI has acquired extensive experience in the valuation business for clients at home and overseas. However, as more detailed knowledge concerning appraisal operations in various countries is obtained, it has become apparent that a mere English translation of the standards does not necessarily communicate the characteristic attributes and aims of Japanese appraisals. Although the appraisal standards of all countries are themselves based on economic theory and basically share many points in common, major differences emerge at the stage of their practical application, since their application is based on the respective systems and markets which reflect each country's historical, cultural, and political uniqueness. Although it may seem at first glance that each country uses similar appraisal terminology and methodology, prior to investing, investors should be sure to ascertain whether there are differences in content depending on the country, find out what those differences are, and determine the scope of responsibility assumed by the person conducting the appraisal. It is not possible to obtain this information just by reading the appraisal standards. It has become essential to make a comparison study of the institutional framework related to appraisal, including the Japanese appraisal standards as well as the historical development and characteristic attributes of these standards, within a global context. This is base upon which to convey the content of the appraisal standards.

3. Consequently, we decided to publish this book on a new concept, based on practical experience in international valuation services in other countries, as well as a comparative verification of Japanese appraisals with appraisals in other countries on the basis of common measures. This book, like the previous one, was written, based on discussions at international conferences and with appraisers, investors, and other experts in foreign countries, by Takumi Watanabe, Managing Director, Global Valuation Group, who has experience in the valuation of real estate located in U.S., Europe, Asia, and Oceania for domestic clients, in addition to international valuation services within Japan.

The authors have benefited from discussions with many appraisers, investors, and

その後、不動産証券化市場はめざましい拡大基調を続け、諸制度が整備されています。証券化市場で重要な役割を担う鑑定評価においては、2007年に鑑定評価基準が改正され（各論第3章の新設）、鑑定評価におけるより高度の透明性と信頼性が要求されるようになりました。さらに、2008年に導入された「海外投資不動産鑑定評価ガイドライン」では、不動産鑑定士が海外現地の鑑定人と共同して業務を進め、依頼者に鑑定評価書を提出するものとされましたが、鑑定評価では彼我の鑑定評価基準の差異性を理解することが不可欠となりました。

　こうした中で、当研究所は国内外の国際評価業務の実務経験を重ねてきましたが、各国の鑑定評価業務の詳しい実態がわかるようになるにつれて、鑑定評価基準の英訳だけでは日本の鑑定評価の特質や趣旨が必ずしも伝わらないことが明らかになりました。各国の鑑定評価基準は、経済理論をベースにしていて、基本的な点において共通しています。しかし、基準を現実に適用する段になると、それぞれの国の歴史的・文化的・政策的な独自性を有する制度や市場によって大きな違いが出てきます。投資家も、投資に先立って、一見したところ似たような鑑定評価の用語や手法を用いているが、国によって内容に違いがあるのか、違いがあるとすれば何故か、鑑定評価を行う者はどの業務範囲まで責任を負うのか、こうした点を確認したいところですが、鑑定評価基準を読むだけではわかりません。日本の鑑定評価基準の歴史的展開と特質及び鑑定評価基準を含めて鑑定評価に関わる制度的な大枠を、グローバルな文脈の中で比較検証し、そのうえで鑑定評価基準の内容を伝えていくことが必要でした。

3．そこで、海外における国際評価業務の実務経験と、日本の鑑定評価と海外諸国における鑑定評価について共通のモノサシによる比較検証を踏まえて、新たなコンセプトで本書を刊行するに至りました。国内の国際評価業務案件のほか、米国、欧州、アジア、オセアニアに所在する不動産の評価を行ってきた当研究所国際評価業務担当の渡辺卓美上席主幹が、国際会議や現地の鑑定人や投資家等の専門家の方々との議論を踏まえて執筆しています。

　執筆者は、本書の企画・執筆・編集の各段階で、現地鑑定人や投資家など多数の専門家の方々

other experts around the world. After a draft of the book was completed, we sent out copies individually to obtain their suggestions and messages, and this book includes some of messages received from contributors including Mr. R. Wayne Pugh MAI, President Appraisal Institute ; Mr. Bruce A. Kellogg MAI, FRICS, Past President Appraisal Institute, Past Member of the Board of Trustees, Appraisal Foundation ; Mr. Steve Williams FRICS, MAI, Past President RICS ; Mr. Nicolas Brooke FRICS, Past President RICS ; Mr. David Faulkner BSc(Hons)FRICS, FHKIS, RPS MAE ; Mr. John K. Rutledge CRE, FRICS ; Mr. Howard Gelbtuch MAI, CRE, FRICS ; Mr. Jonathan Avery MAI, CRE, FRICS Past Chairman CRE ; Mr. Jon Fumio Yamaguchi, CRE, FRICS, SRPA, SRA ; Mr. A.C. Schwethelm, CRE, FRICS ; Mr. Bill Ramseyer CRE ; Dr. Marc Louargand, CRE and other professional experts.

Dr. Michael Milgrim, who was involved in the compilation of the respective appraisal standards of the (U.S.) Appraisal Institute, the International Valuation Standards Committee, and the (U.S.) Appraisal Foundation, has provided detailed advice and suggestions for this book directly as well as through Kazuhiko Fujiki, JREI's North America Associate. We would like to thank Dr. Milgrim again for his valuable guidance and cooperation.

4. Of course, there are still many points that should be given a fuller explanation, but this book is just a beginning which summarizes our work up to the present time. Readers are invited to visit the website of JREI (www.reinet.or.jp) which will provide a place to deepen our mutual understanding through the further exchange of information, opinions, and questions.

と議論を重ね、さらに出来上がったドラフトを個別にお送りして改めてご意見を頂きましたが、その際に頂いたメッセージの一部を掲載させていただきました。米国鑑定協会会長 R. Wayne Pugh 氏（MAI）；同協会前会長 Bruce Kellogg 氏（MAI, FRICS）；英国立勅認サーベイヤー協会（RICS）前会長 Steve Williams 氏（FRICS, MAI）；RICS 元会長 Nicolas Brooke 氏（FRICS, CRE）；David Faulkner 氏（BSc（Hons）FRICS, FHKIS, RPS MAE）；John K. Rutledge 氏（CRE, FRICS）；Howard Gelbtuch 氏（MAI, CRE, FRICS）；米国 CRE 前会長 Jonathan Avery 氏（MAI, CRE, FRICS）；Jon Fumio Yamaguchi 氏（CRE, FRICS, SRPA, SRA）；A.C. Schwethelm 氏（CRE, FRICS）；Bill L. Ramseyer 氏（CRE）；Marc Louargand 博士（CRE）ほかの方々です。

　執筆者は、米国鑑定協会、国際評価基準委員会及び鑑定財団の各鑑定評価基準の編集を務められましたマイケル・ミルグリム（Michael Milgrim）博士に、細部にわたって、直接あるいは当研究所北米駐在の藤木一彦を通じて、助言・提案を頂きました。ここに改めて、ご指導とご協力に厚く御礼申し上げます。

4．当然のことながら解明すべきことがまだ多く残されていますが、ひとまずこの本に成果をまとめると同時に、当研究所のホームページ（www.reinet.or.jp）上に、情報、意見、質疑の交換の場を設けて、相互の理解をさらに深めていきたいと思いますので、よろしくお願い申し上げます。

Forward to Japan Real Estate Appraisal in a Global Context

Institutional investors continue to pour billions of dollars into real estate. They are basing their investment decisions on market analysis and projected cash flows. The Appraisal Institute and the Japanese Real Estate Institute have been working together for over twenty years to make sure that Japanese appraisers have access to advanced knowledge in these areas. We have been exchanging expertise to let these multinational corporate players know that appraisers in both countries have the analytical tools necessary to provide valuation services to meet their needs.

Capital is flowing around the world including developing markets in Eastern Europe and Southeast Asia. Recognizing this trend, Japanese laws were recently changed to allow J–REITs — Japanese Real Estate Investment Trusts — to invest in properties outside Japan. These markets have evolved to the point that the exchange between the Appraisal Institute and the Japanese Real Estate Institute includes not only information about the markets and practices in each country, but information about global standards and practices.

The Appraisal Institute is pleased to see this latest addition to the international valuer's body of knowledge. We look forward to the continued success and advancement of the real estate valuation profession around the world and the further integration of cross–border practices.

R. Wayne Pugh, MAI
2008 Appraisal Institute President

Foreword to *Japan Real Estate Appraisal in a Global Context*

The importance of developing a guideline for global appraisal practice is being realized today more than ever. Today there are numerous individual, national requirements that must be followed by an appraiser who is working within his or her specific borders, but, more frequently, we are experiencing cross–border valuation requirements that must consider professional standards, requirements and procedures that address needs beyond the scope of any single nation or professional standard. We have seen the emergence of the International Valuation Standards as an example of this quest for standardization, which is clearly explained within these pages.

The author, himself a knowledgeable and conscientious valuer who recognized the need for further articulation and clarification of our current global requirements, clearly and carefully explains for the reader the various major requirements found within our world today, and proceeds to integrate them into a thoughtful and thorough discussion of what is occurring within our shrinking world. Without such a text, valuers who find themselves involved in a global assignment will become bewildered and perplexed about the manner in which this work should be completed to meet the needs of appraisals today for multi–national clients seeking to invest beyond the borders normally considered too risky and complex to consider.

The depth of discussion found within these pages appropriately focuses on all the major players within the valuation and investment marketplaces today. While some may feel there are others, the text appropriately reflects those standards and guidelines that have led to the adoption of the most universal of all: the International Valuation Standards. While acknowledging that all nations have their specific standards and guidelines for domestic requirements, there is no doubt that the global marketplace has asked for this analysis to be written due to the increasing needs addressed above.

Thank you for giving us this text and for making it clear that the world is changing. To ignore this change would be unfortunate and irresponsible. Having become acquainted with the author and JREI in 2004 while attending a conference with ARGUS Software, I recognized their dedication and professionalism, evident within the pages that follow.

Bruce A. Kellogg, MAI, FRICS

2008 Chair, OSCRE Americas

2005 President, Appraisal Institute

1999–2002 Member of the Board of Trustees, The Appraisal Foundation

Senior Vice President, ARGUS Software, Industry Relations, Research

FOREWORD

The appraisal profession in Japan and indeed across the world is fortunate indeed that Takumi Watanabe has summoned the patience and commitment to provide us with this landmark work. By sheer hard work, diligent research and an extraordinary gift for interpreting the technical nuances of at least two languages, he provides a remarkably clear insight into Japanese appraisal methodology.

Moving rapidly towards financial convergence, the financial world's need for joined – up appraisal processes to serve both its home and its the cross – border investment markets has never been more urgent. In this context, Mr. Watanabe's comparative study of standards and methods integrates precisely into the move towards more consistent global valuation standards.

While valuation organizations in many countries are debating how to achieve this with a minimum of toe – treading, Mr. Watanabe takes a bold step towards outlining the thought processes that lie behind the valuation cultures of the developed world.

His work is not perfect. In a world of fast – moving financial creativity and changing real estate markets both in developed and emerging nations, how could it be ? Nevertheless it forms a firm platform on which to build the mutual understanding so necessary for a joined up profession.

If while reading it, we expose methodological flaws, or if we have a moment of agony about the inconsistencies of the various appraisal cultures described, then Mr. Watanabe will have done his job. He will have succeeded in moving the valuation profession a little further forward in today's shrinking world.

Globalization is not going away any more than is urbanization. Private equity, debt finance and listed funds are not retiring to the isolation of their own national markets nor is there any slowing of the revolution in transportation and communications technologies. Indeed, it is against this background of accelerating technology that Mr. Watanabe provides a clear view of a Japanese appraisal culture that, until recently, had been maligned as opaque and misunderstood.

To this end, he addresses Japan's gradual shift from a reliance on underlying land values to the DCF – driven investment valuations of the Japan's 21st century JREIT culture; and the current move to bring greater transparency to Japan's transactional data. Until recently, property data was carefully filtered in the interests of confidentiality and strict privacy legislation. This text applauds the new moves by an enlightened Ministry of Land, Infrastructure, Transport and Tourism to promulgate transparent and publicly available data as a catalytic force for inward investment in Japan.

Throughout his writings, Mr. Watanabe is quick to point out that, like every other developed country, a prerequisite to a healthy Japanese real estate market is a credible and unbiased global valuation profession. I commend his work to you. It is a clear lens through which others view our profession and through which should take time to view ourselves.

Steve Williams FRICS, MAI
Past President, Royal Institution of Chartered Surveyors
Global Advisor to Real Capital Analytics
Founding Partner, Williams – Murdoch (NY) Inc.

It is a great pleasure to recognise and endorse the contribution that the research undertaken by Watanabe-san will make to a better understanding of the characteristics and structure of Japan's real estate appraisal system. As Japan becomes an increasing focus for overseas investment in real estate, the alignment with international valuation standards will grow in importance and it is encouraging to see the progress that is being made in relation to the mechanisms to support transparency and reliability in appraisal, such as more general access to market data and the creation of independent commercial property investment indices. I envisage that this publication will become an essential and long lasting source of reference and information for all those operating in the real estate sector in Japan.

Nicholas Brooke
FRICS
Past President RICS

This book forms an important addition to the body of knowledge in regard to the use and application of valuation standards. As the markets become more global and cross – border investment increases, investors, financiers and valuation practitioners need to have a good knowledge of how valuations standards are applied in the key markets. This book provides a detailed comparison of the main standards adopted around the world and explains the key differences between these and those used in Japan.

For those who are investing in real estate in Japan, or Japanese investors who are buying real estate overseas, this book will be essential reading, but for those interested in cross – border real estate valuation in any form, this book will be a useful reference, proving a lot of information in one volume.

David Faulkner BSc (Hon)FRICS FHKIS RPS MAE

As a consumer of appraisal services for many decades, I have come to greatly respect the wisdom and judgment demonstrated by professional appraisers. It is their task to estimate the price at which buyer and seller will reach a meeting of the minds so that a transaction can occur. Their opinions of value can only be as good as the available market data and the consistency and logic of their analytical processes.

All three approaches to value rely on market data. The income approach depends on market rents and expenses as well as capitalization rates determined in the marketplace. The cost approach requires market data on land sales and on construction costs negotiated in the marketplace as well as depreciation rates as reflected in the prices of properties of various ages actually sold. And the comparative sales approach obviously relies on market data regarding similar properties actually sold.

A serious problem arises, however. Although all of the market data considered by the appraiser is historical, the appraiser is asked to estimate the value of an asset as of a current date, later than the transactions from which market data are drawn but excluding data from subsequent transactions. At times of increased market volatility, the risk is even greater that historical data will be misleading as to current and future conditions. Yet suppliers of capital require valuation guidance in making investment decisions.

When the property, seller, buyer, and lender were local, values were more easily understood. In recent decades, though, new money has arrived as institutional investors (both domestic and international) have discovered the opportunity to improve portfolio performance by investing in real estate. Most market participants welcome the increased capital availability and the lower capitalization rates and higher values resulting from this new capital.

To satisfy the demands of this new capital for useful market information, it is imperative that we standardize appraisal practices and terminology, nationally and internationally, so that we are communicating effectively about property values despite different languages and markets. Only then can capital flow freely to the best opportunities anywhere in the world.

Takumi Watanabe is a dedicated student of these difficult questions. His insightful work is a welcome contribution to efficient real estate capital markets.

John K Rutledge, CRE, FRICS
President, Rutledge Company LLC
Wheaton IL USA

Japan is a major economic power. As of this writing, it ranks second of all countries in the world in Gross Domestic Product, fourth in terms of exports, fifth in defense budgets, and sixth in imports. It is, of course, also a world leader in technological innovations. Nearly two percent of the world's population lives in Japan, making it the tenth-most populous country on the planet.

Yet, to many real estate appraisers, consultants, and potential investors, Japan remains a mystery. The real estate community is thus indebted to Takumi Watanabe, LREA, CRE, FRICS, for authoring this book. Concisely and clearly written, and published in both Japanese and English, readers will benefit from his unique background as Managing Director of the Japan Real Estate Institute's Global Valuation Group.

"Tak," whom I have had the honor of knowing for many years, logically begins with the evolution of the appraisal process in Japan, and eloquently takes us on a journey detailing economic conditions around the globe, and how they influenced the appraisal process in Japan. Based on his personal interviews with valuers in numerous countries, it concludes with an explanation of the latest guidelines for valuing overseas properties by Japanese Licensed Real Estate Appraisers.

Whether you are based in Japan, or are a valuer with a global practice interested in the valuation process there, this reference book is required reading. It is an invaluable guide for all real estate professionals wishing to gain a better understanding of the real estate appraisal process in one of the world's most important countries, Japan.

Howard Gelbtuch, MAI, CRE, FRICS
Principal
Greenwich Realty Advisors Incorporated
New York, New York

Comment By : Jonathan H. Avery, MAI, CRE, FRICS

Takumi Watanabe has written a timely and definitive book which will be invaluable not only to the real estate appraiser practitioner in Japan but also government officials, investors and lenders. He provides a history of the development of appraisal theory together with the economic and political events which have brought about major changes in the practice of appraisal. This book examines carefully the trend towards global standardization of appraisal standards with emphasis on the important differences in how appraisals are prepared and reported in different countries. I recommend it not only to readers in Japan but also to all those with an interest in global real estate investment and valuation.

Congratulations on your new book entitled "Japan Real Estate Appraisal in a Global Context". This book is a timely text that will help solve some of the global valuation problems facing us now and in the future. The cross securitization of real estate properties globally has produced a complex myriad of varying assets in a world of diverse cultures.

Every country and locale contains varying aspects of unique culture, land tenure, governmental regulations, population, economics, demand and supply. Accurate valuation and evaluation of securitized assets are essential not only for Japan but for the global economy. Your professional effort is a large step in the right direction and I am honored to have been a part of your professional real estate team. Also, as Vice Chairman of the Counselors of Real Estate's International Steering Committee I would like to thank you for your contribution to our International Organization.

Sincerely yours,
Yamaguchi & Yamaguchi Incorporated

雄文口山

Jon Fumio Yamaguchi CRE, FRICS, SRPA, SRA
President/CEO

As a real estate appraisal practitioner for over forty years, and as a college real estate appraisal instructor I have accumulated a large library of real estate appraisal related books. I find, however, that "Japan Real Estate Appraisal in A Global Context" to be unique.

It provides a concise history of the evolution of real estate appraisal and describes the current importance of appraisal in finance, syndication, and marketing of real estate.

It is The source of legal requirements for real estate appraisal in the jurisdictions where it applies.

It provides instruction on how to comply with the requirements, including the three approaches to value with all of its variations, sources and application of market research, and use of sophisticated techniques such as discounted cash flow.

This book is appropriate for the real estate practitioner, or any one for that matter, interested in learning more about appraisal and how it relates to all of the other real estate disciplines.

It is ideal for the beginning real estate appraiser seeking to begin practice with confidence in knowing the requirements and procedures for complying with them.

Furthermore, it is a constant reference source for the experienced practicing appraiser for legal requirements as well as refreshing memory regarding appropriate, but perhaps seldom used techniques.

Congratulations, my dear friend Takumi, on producing a very valuable tool for so many people that will use this book. You should feel gratification in knowing that you have contributed so valuably.

    A. C. Schwethelm, CRE, FRICS
    President, A. C. Schwethelm & Associates, Inc.
    Comfort, Texas, USA, 78013-0248

Tak, You have been particularly effective in putting the new regulatory environment in Japan in context of the experience and practice in other developed countries as the real estate community converges on some form of International Valuation Standards. While the importance of full and timely disclosure of all relevant data for properties engaged in some form of transaction cannot be overemphasized, the real estate valuation and investment management sectors do require some form of regulatory oversight. From your writing, it appears that Japan has given the valuation topic very serious thought, particularly as it relates to the capital market implications of what you describe as the inevitable tsunami of capital flows and the resulting volatility in market price. Certainly the LREA will benefit from such guidance and your writing on the topic.

Congratulations on your fine contribution to our real estate investment business.

Bill L. Ramseyer, CRE
Pension Fund / Institutional Advisor

Tak Watanabe has created a comprehensive view of valuation that will be a valuable
addition to a rapidly globalizing property market. I expect that any valuer, investor or other professional will want to add this work to their library.

Marc Louargand, Ph.D., CRE, FRICS
Immediate Past President, American Real Estate Society, and
Principal
Saltash Partners LLC
Investing in American Ingenuity

Foreword to *Japanese Real Estate Appraisal in a Global Context*

The Japanese regard real estate appraisal practice in their country as a national system of appraisal. The Japanese government assumes ultimate responsibility for the functioning of the appraisal system, thereby ensuring confidence in the reliability of appraisals and safeguarding the interests of the general public of property owners, underwriters, landlords, tenants and investors. The two pillars of this system are the *Real Estate Appraisal Act* (promulgated in 1963 and most recently revised in 2006) and the *Japanese Real Estate Appraisal Standards* (first published in 1964 and most recently revised in 2007; the 2002 edition of the *Standards* appeared in a bilingual Japanese – English format).

Both the *Real Estate Appraisal Act* and *Real Estate Appraisal Standards* were drawn up by the Ministry of Land, Infrastructure, Transport and Tourism on the basis of advice provided by the National Land Development Council and the Japanese Association of Real Estate Appraisal (JAREA). All professional appraisers in Japan belong to this Association, which requires its members, Licensed Real Estate Appraisers or LREAs, and LREA candidates to observe the above corpus of appraisal – specific legislation and standards. Indeed, under the *Appraisal Act*, in Japan appraisals done for a fee may only be performed by LREAs in compliance with the *Standards*. No other appraisals are permitted.

Real estate markets around the world are steadily being transformed by globalization, securitization and an increase in cross – border transactions. Since 2001, J – REITs have been listed on the Tokyo Stock Exchange, and in 2007 measures were taken to authorize the acquisition by J – REITs of overseas investment properties for inclusion among their holdings. Appraisal is the cornerstone of decision – making for real estate investment, whether domestic or foreign. To facilitate an understanding of appraisal practice in Japan, this book provides an indispensable service by making available to Japanese and English – reading real estate professionals the most up – to – date documents that form the foundation of the Japanese appraisal system.

In an introductory overview, Takumi Watanabe, LREA, CRE, and FRICS, traces recent real estate cycles in Japan and elsewhere, and the accelerating momentum toward the adoption of national and international appraisal standards. Mr. Watanabe then presents a comparative survey of the appraisal standards, valuation bases, and other features of professional practice in five countries – – Japan, the US, the UK, Australia, and China – and also the characteristics of appraisals performed under the *International Valuation Standards*. Mr. Watanabe, who has played an important role in preparing the revision of the *Japanese Real Estate Appraisal Standards*, especially the guidelines for Japanese appraisers on the appraisal of overseas investment properties to be acquired by J – REITs, gives special attention to how the various Standards documents deal with the issue of securitization.

The two most salient features of the 2007 revision of the *Japanese Real Estate Appraisal Standards* are the introduction of a new chapter in the Detailed Standards section (the former Discussion section) on the appraisal of real estate subject to securitization (along with a new guidance note to supplement this new chapter), and the guidelines for Japanese appraisers on carrying out collaborative assignments with foreign appraisers in valuing overseas investment properties. The new chapter on the appraisal of property subject to securitization identifies the various Japanese legislation, dealing with securitization property; outlines the detailed work plan for the appraisal of such property with an emphasis on data verification; explains the investigation of property–specific influences on the subject property as well as the rigorous standards required of the property inspection and engineering report; and examines each of the line items that enter a discounted cash flow analysis of a property.

Although no Japanese law ever prohibited J–REITs from acquiring overseas investment properties, the Tokyo Stock Exchange did establish special criteria, governing the appraisal of real estate backing any listed security. Therefore, the move by the Tokyo Stock Exchange to authorize the acquisition by J–REITs of overseas investment properties for inclusion among their holdings necessitated the drafting of guidelines for Japanese appraisers on undertaking appraisals of properties abroad. Because in most circumstances, it is reasonable and realistic to anticipate that a Japanese appraiser, appraising properties abroad, will enter into a collaborative effort with a professional appraiser in the overseas country, the new guidelines set out the procedures for engaging foreign colleagues, and provide directives on the division of labor and the ultimate assumption of responsibility for verifying an appraisal and signing off on its conclusions.

With the special attention given to the appraisal of securitization properties and overseas investment properties, the 2007 edition of the *Japanese Real Estate Appraisal Standards* should prove highly effective in preventing the recurrence of price run–ups and contribute to a smoother and sounder functioning of real estate markets, both in Japan and elsewhere.

Michael Milgrim, PhD
   Formerly, Technical Writer, Appraisal Institute &
   International Valuation Standards Committee

Foreword to the English – Language Translation of the Japanese *Real Estate Appraisal Standards*

Thomas A. Motta, MAI
Appraisal Institute President 2002

The English-language translation of the Japanese *Valuation Standards* (JVS) is a welcome addition to the global literature on valuation standards. The Japanese *Valuation Standards* reflect both the sophistication and maturity of the appraisal profession in Japan, and a significant degree of convergence with the principles enunciated in other prominent Standards documents, including the *Uniform Standards of Professional Appraisal Practice* (USPAP) of the Appraisal Foundation in the United States, and the *International Valuation Standards* (IVS) of the International Valuation Standards Committee….(The rest is omitted)

The Globalization of Real Estate Valuation

John A. Edge, FRICS
IVSC Chairman 2002 – 2005

Real estate is a significant factor in global business. Investors, regulators, and users of valuation require consistency, clarity, reliability, and transparency in valuation reporting worldwide. The IVSC objective is to produce one set of high quality, global valuation standards. Valuation rules are no longer national standards existing in isolation. The standards of various countries have to harmonize with each other, and to do that there must be a strong, single benchmark of common standards to which all our states can relate. This is the role that the IVSC fulfills.

International Valuation Standards (IVS) were initiated and first published in 1985. The Japanese Association of Real Estate Appraisal has been a member of the IVSC since the early 1980s and involved in the development of the IVS. One of the key early successes of the IVSC has been developing a common definition of market value accepted in most of the world and I am pleased that definition of market value in the Japanese Valuation Standards is compatible with the IVSC definition. The IVS have been extended and developed over the years, and the publication of the 2003 edition of the IVS in April this year is the culmination of a three year 'Standards Project' to produce a set of comprehensive standards. An important objective of the Project was to ensure that the IVS complement the standards of other international bodies, most notably the International Accounting Standards Board (IASB)….(The rest is omitted)

Globalization and Reliable Valuation Standards

Howard C. Gelbtuch, CRE, MAI
Principal
Greenwich Realty Advisors, Incorporated

As we enter the 21st century, Japan and the United States, some 6,000 miles apart, are both caught in the same tsunami wave of globalization. The advent of the Internet has made communication instantaneous, cost-effective, and commonplace. International travel is more frequent. Goods and services produced in one part of the world are increasingly marketed overseas, not just domestically.

Real estate professionals around the globe are more closely connected to each other than ever before. Money to acquire, finance, and dispose of land and buildings is rapidly transferred around the world, often more quickly than ever, seeking the highest rate of return for the least amount of risk. Decisions concerning where to invest, how much to pay, when to sell and to whom, are increasingly made in countries other than where a property is located....(The rest is omitted)

On the Publishing of "Japanese *Real Estate Appraisal Standards*"

Hiroyuki Ito, President
Japan Real Estate Institute

The Japanese *Real Estate Appraisal Standards* was revised in 2002, twelve years after the last revision, in order to cope with the changes in the socioeconomic situation with respect to real estate. Since the "burst of the bubble economy," in the stream of economic globalization, what is called the "myth of land" has come to an end, and at the same time, the concept of the value of real estate has greatly changed from putting emphasis on capital gain to placing emphasis on income flow.

It is no exaggeration to say that of the principal points in the revision of the standard, the ideas of the capitalization approach, the market analysis, the close investigation for property, etc. constitute parts of internationalization. In addition, if we look at the trend in foreign countries, representatives of the leading countries have been exchanging opinions actively, especially on international standards for real estate estimation during the past few years. Foreign countries have been interested in the standard of estimation for appraisal of real estate of our country, but no books written in English have been available with only some fragmentary introductions on the Japanese Standards made available on a haphazard basis.

It is my great pleasure to see this booklet published, and I am convinced that informing the whole world of the Japanese Standards is really significant for all those concerned. As you see in the title of this booklet, this is not merely an English translation of some Japanese booklet. Our concept was to make the content of this booklet fully understandable to those in the business of real estate who use English as their mother tongue....(The rest is omitted)

Table of Contents

PART 1: Evolution and Characteristics of Japan Real Estate Appraisal 1

PART 2: Real Estate Appraisal Act 109

PART 3: Real Estate Appraisal Standards 133
    General Standards (GS) 138
    Specific Standards (SS) 232

PART 4: Guidance Notes on the Real Estate Appraisal Standards (GN) 279

PART 5: Guidelines for the Appraisal of Overseas Investment Properties (GL) 347

INDEX (English-Japanese) 388
INDEX (Japanese-English) 398

総　目　次

**第1編：日本の不動産鑑定評価の
　　　　　展開と特質** ……………………… 1

**第2編：不動産の鑑定評価
　　　　　に関する法律** ………………… 109

第3編：不動産鑑定評価基準 ………… 133
　総論(GS) ……………………………… 139
　各論(SS) ……………………………… 233

**第4編：不動産鑑定評価基準
　　　　　運用上の留意事項(GN)** …… 279

**第5編：海外投資不動産
　　　　　鑑定評価ガイドライン(GL)** … 347

英和索引 …………………………………… 388

和英索引 …………………………………… 398

PART1

Evolution and Characteristics of Japan Real Estate Appraisal

Takumi WATANABE:LREA(Japan), CRE(US), FRICS(UK)

第1編

日本の不動産鑑定評価の展開と特質

渡辺卓美　不動産鑑定士、CRE(米国)、FRICS(英国)

Table of Contents

Chapter 1. Evolution and Characteristics of Japan Real Estate Appraisal ··· 4
   1. Uniformity of Real Estate Appraisal Standards ·· 4
   2. Transparency and Reliability in Appraisal ··· 8
   3. Revision of the Real Estate Appraisal Standards in 2007 ···························· 10
   4. Globalization of Real Estate Appraisal Standards ·· 12
   5. Role of and Responsibility for the Appraisal System ···································· 16

Chapter 2. Comparison of Appraisal / Valuation Standards ···················· 20
   Ⅰ. Japan : Real Estate Appraisal Standards ··· 20
   Ⅱ. USA : Uniform Standards of Professional Appraisal Practice (USPAP) ······ 36
   Ⅲ. UK : RICS Valuation Standards (Red Book) ··· 50
   Ⅳ. Australia : API Valuation Standards ··· 66
   Ⅴ. The People's Republic of China : Appraisal Standards ································· 82
   Ⅵ. International Valuation Standards (IVS) ··· 94

目　次

第1章　日本の不動産鑑定評価の展開と特質 …………………………………………5
　1．不動産鑑定評価基準の統一 ………………………………………………………5
　2．鑑定評価の透明性と信頼性 ………………………………………………………9
　3．2007年の鑑定評価基準改正 ……………………………………………………11
　4．鑑定評価の国際化 …………………………………………………………………13
　5．鑑定評価の役割と責任 ……………………………………………………………17

第2章　各国の不動産鑑定評価の比較 ……………………………………………………21
　Ⅰ．日本：不動産鑑定評価基準 ………………………………………………………21
　Ⅱ．米国：鑑定評価業務統一基準（USPAP） ………………………………………37
　Ⅲ．英国：RICS 鑑定評価業務基準（Red Book） …………………………………51
　Ⅳ．オーストラリア：API 鑑定評価業務基準 ………………………………………67
　Ⅴ．中華人民共和国：鑑定評価基準 …………………………………………………83
　Ⅵ．国際評価基準（IVS） ……………………………………………………………95

Chapter 1. Evolution and Characteristics of Japan Real Estate Appraisal

CHAPTER 1. EVOLUTION AND CHARACTERISTICS OF JAPAN REAL ESTATE APPRAISAL

The social and economic environment in which real estate appraisal is performed is undergoing major changes, including real estate securitization, increasing cross-border transaction, and development of a two-tier market （large, centrally located class A properties are strong, while the lower class B and C properties face continuing price declines）. And the public-interests objectives and operation of Japan's real estate appraisal system are being reexamined and reassessed to meet new challenges through improved transparency and reliability in appraisal. In addition to fulfilling the conventional task of ensuring appropriate pricing for real estate, Japan's appraisal system must provide an infrastructure to protect clients and investors, and must also promote efficiency in the marketplace.

To assist in identifying the characteristics of the existing laws, appraisal standards, guidance notes, and guidelines which underlines Japan's real estate appraisal system, this introductory part describes the evolution of the Japan appraisal system in relation to the real estate market in a global context, specifically the US, the UK, Australia, China and IVS and the progress being made toward the developing mechanisms that supports transparency and reliability in appraisal, such as access to market data.

1. Uniformity of Real Estate Appraisal Standards

It is generally recognized in developed countries that the uniformity of real estate appraisal standards is very important in terms of the infrastructure supporting real estate markets, a lesson that has been learned through severe market cycles including bubbles and subsequent bursting of the bubbles.

UK

From the early to mid-1970s, the UK experienced a sudden rise and fall in real estate prices. It has been pointed out that "the collapse exposed a wide variation in the approach to property valuation, which had thrown up vastly different — and often completely unrealistic — figures for properties with similar value factors"*. Appraisal practice came under harsh criticism.

The Royal Institution of Chartered Surveyors （RICS, founded in 1881）, which plays a central role in appraisal in the UK, responded in 1976 by developing and publishing a set of uniform appraisal standards generally known as the "The Red Book" with the objectives of unifying the approaches to and techniques of appraisal, which had been variously interpreted and applied up to that time; of establishing a code of conduct regarding the independence, objectivity, and accountability of surveyors, the professionals involved in appraising real estate, and the transparency of their reports; and of strengthening regulations concerning conflicts of interest.（see Part 1 Chap.2, Ⅲ. UK - 1）

*Michael Brett, *Valuation Standards for the Global Market* （RICS Leading Edge Series 2002）

第1章 日本の不動産鑑定評価の展開と特質

不動産の証券化、不動産金融市場のグローバル化、地価動向の二極化・個別化と、鑑定評価をめぐる社会経済環境は大きく変化をしている。その中で、日本の不動産鑑定評価制度は、鑑定評価の透明性と信頼性を高めることによって、その公共の目的や機能について、従来の"適正な地価の形成に資する"視点からだけでなく、"依頼者・投資家の信頼を保護する"及び"不動産市場の整備・活性化のためのインフラ基盤である"との視点からも議論され、施策が講じられている。

そこで、日本の不動産鑑定評価制度の骨格を構成する現行の法律、鑑定評価基準、留意事項及びガイドラインの趣旨と方向性を理解するために、鑑定評価制度が不動産市場及び不動産金融市場とどのような関わりをもって展開してきたのか、市場データへのアクセス環境など鑑定評価の透明性と信頼性を支える仕組みはどのように展開してきたのか、第2章のグローバルな鑑定評価（特に米国、英国、オーストラリア、中国の鑑定評価基準及び国際評価基準）の文脈での検証を踏まえて述べる。

1. 不動産鑑定評価基準の統一

不動産の鑑定評価の基準を統一することが不動産市場のインフラ基盤として重要であるとの認識は、数度の不動産バブルの発生と崩壊から得た教訓として、先進諸国にほぼ共通している。

英 国

英国は1970年代初めから半ばにかけて不動産価格の急騰と急落を経験した。その際、価格形成要因が同じであるにもかかわらず、掛け離れた鑑定評価額がついたり、非現実的な鑑定評価額がついたりして、鑑定評価は厳しい社会批判に晒された＊。

英国の鑑定評価の中心的な役割を担っている王立勅認サーベイヤー協会（The Royal Institution of Chartered Surveyors: RICS。1881年設立）は、これに応えて、それまでバラバラに解釈・運用されていた鑑定評価の基準を一本化し、それに携わる専門鑑定人（上級会員FRICSと一般会員MRICSからなるチャータード・サーベイヤー）に対する独立・中立性、客観性、説明責任、透明性等の行為規範及び利益相反に関する規制を強化して、通称「Red Book」と呼ばれる統一鑑定評価基準を策定した（1976年）。（第1編第2章Ⅲ．英国 - 1参照）

　＊Michael Brett, *Valuation Standards for the Global Market*（RICS Leading Edge Series 2002）

US

The experience of the US has been similar to that of the UK. In the first half of the 1980s, financial deregulation (resulting from the Depository Institutions Deregulation and Monetary Control Act of 1980), rising inflation and the adoption in 1981 of tax incentives for real estate investment led to huge amounts of capital being shifted into the real estate market, as seen in the expanded investment activity of commercial banks and savings and loan institutions (S&Ls). This brought about a real estate boom, and real estate prices soared. However, prices dropped sharply in the late 1980s and early 1990s due to excess supply, which arose from the boom, along with declining demand caused by an economic recession and changes in the law that eliminated many tax incentives for real estate investment.

Excessive financing, related to unrealistically high valuations during the boom period in an environment where uniform valuation standards were sorely lacking, came under severe criticism; and there were calls such as the feature article in the *New York Times* on October 21, 1990 for fair and impartial appraisal standards that would be free from external pressures. The Appraisal Foundation, a private nonprofit corporation composed of eight major appraisal organizations including the Appraisal Institute, was established in 1987. The foundation has developed and administered uniform appraisal standards called the Uniform Standards of Professional Appraisal Practice (USPAP). These standards apply to appraisal services to be performed with professionalism, independence, fairness, and objectivity on the part of appraisers. Title XI of the Financial Institutions Reform, Recovery and Enforcement Act of 1989 (FIRREA) provided recognition and authorized financial institution regulatory agencies to reference USPAP in their regulations. The standards gain legal force when they are invoked in federal and state legislation and administrative matters, and in private appraisal contracts. (see Part 1 Chap.2, II. US - 1)

Japan

Japan has also experienced three land price bubbles over the half-century period from the completion of its post-World War II economic recovery to the present. Except for Tokyo and other large urban areas, land prices have continued to decline over the sixteen years since the third bubble burst. By analyzing the characteristics of each of these bubbles, it is possible to gain useful insights regarding the direction to be taken in the development of future appraisal standards.

(a) High Economic Growth

During the period of high economic growth, which began in the mid-1950s and lasted about 20 years until it was brought to an end by the oil crisis, real GDP rose at an average of 10% per year, and land prices soared two during two different periods peaking in 1961 and again in 1973. The fundamental reason for these sudden land price increases was rapid economic growth, combined with an imbalance in housing supply and demand as industry and population became concentrated in urban areas. However, public confusion regarding land prices——due to the lack of a system for the rational pricing of land——was recognized as an additional reason.

The Real Estate Appraisal Act of 1963 (see Part 2 of this book) established a

第1章　日本の不動産鑑定評価の展開と特質

米 国

米国でも、英国と類似した経過をたどって鑑定評価基準の統一が進んだ。1980年代前半、インフレ懸念の高まりと81年の不動産投資優遇税制によって、商業銀行や貯蓄貸付組合（S&L）のシェア拡大に示される大量の投資資金が不動産市場に流れ込んで不動産ブームを引き起こし、不動産価格が急騰した。80年代末から90年代初めにかけての不動産価格の急落は、このブーム期の供給過剰に加えて、不動産投資優遇税制改正や経済不況による需要減退が重なったことに起因するが、ブーム期にバラバラな基準によって過大評価と過剰融資が行われていたことが指弾され、外部からの圧力を受けない独立・中立な鑑定評価制度が要望された。

これに応えて、1987年、不動産鑑定協会（Appraisal Institute）など主要評価団体8機関から構成される、民間非営利の鑑定財団（Appraisal Foundation）が発足し、鑑定評価業務統一基準（Uniform Standards of Professional Appraisal Practice：USPAP）を策定・運用することになった。USPAPが対象とする評価業務は、鑑定人として独立・中立性、客観性をもって行う鑑定評価業務である。1989年に金融機関改革・再生・執行法（FIRREA）が制定され、同法第11章が、連邦金融機関に対して、USPAPを評価基準とすることを認めている。同基準は、連邦及び州の立法や行政部門による援用又は民間の鑑定評価委託契約での援用によって法的強制力を得る。（第1編第2章Ⅱ.米国‐1参照）

日 本

日本でも、第2次大戦後の経済復興が完了した年から現在までに地価バブルを3回経験し、3回目のバブルの崩壊から16年を超える地価下落が続いた。それぞれの地価バブルの特徴を分析すると、鑑定評価のあり方について手がかりが得られる。

(a) 高度経済成長期

1950年代半ばからの高度経済成長が石油危機によって終了するまでの約20年間、実質経済成長率GDPは年平均10％で上昇し、この間に地価は2回急騰している。この地価急騰は、根本的には急速な経済成長及び産業と人口の都市集中による宅地需給の不均衡に起因するが、これに加えて、合理的な地価形成を図るための制度が欠如していることが地価の混乱を引き起こしていると総括された。

そこで、専門家による合理的な価格情報を不動産市場に提供することを通じて、市場における"適正な地価の形成に資する"役割を担う国家制度として、鑑定評価が位置づけられ（本書第2編「不動産の鑑定評価に関する法律」。1963年）、それまでバラバラだった基準を一本化して鑑定評価基準が策定された（本書第3編「不動産鑑定評価基準」及びその適用に関わる本書第4編

legal and administrative framework for appraisal, which plays an important role in contributing to appropriate pricing in the real estate market by providing the market with information about property values by authorized professionals such as Licensed Real Estate Appraisers (LREAs). In addition, various standards were unified in the Japanese Real Estate Appraisal Standards of 1964 (see Part 3 General Standards (GS) / Specific Standards (SS) and Part 4: Guidance Notes (GN). In Japan, only appraisals performed by an LREA in accordance with the Japanese Real Estate Appraisal Standards are permitted. (see Part 1 Chap.2, Ⅰ. Japan - 6)

(b) **Excessive liquidity**

The oil crisis was overcome through cost-cutting measures based on belt-tightening energy-management and the development of energy-saving technologies. GDP growth recovered to around 5% in the latter half of the 1980s. Land prices then soared for the third time. Unlike the rapid increases in land prices during the previous period of high economic growth, this rise in land prices occurred during a period of great credit availability, which grew at a rate exceeding the rate of GDP growth. Excessive liquidity led to huge amounts of capital flowing into the real estate market, which was essentially local in nature. The imbalance between the capital market and the real estate market, was then suddenly corrected through a precipitous fall in sale prices at the beginning of the 1990s.

The appraisal system at that time was not capable of functioning properly in response to the sudden rise in sale prices during the late 1980s. In a market of soaring land prices, the reversion generated by selling a property was much more significant than the annual cash flow generated by the management and operation of real estate. Prices indicated by comparable sales data played the decisive role in appraisal values, while values indicated by the income approach were only used for verification. Nevertheless, because there was no adequate mechanism in place for appraisers to obtain the latest detailed market data, it was difficult to analyze the impact of excess liquidity and the sustainability of market prices by verifying sale prices based on income-earning capabilities and the like. With such limitations on access to market data, appraisal values were led higher and higher by a scanty amount of sales data and asking prices, until the rug was pulled out by a sudden bursting of this bubble.

2. Transparency and Reliability in Appraisal

In Japan, during the long-term decline in land prices since the bursting of three land price bubbles, people's sense of value regarding real estate has shifted away from simple ownership of real estate to the improvement of cash flow, which is one aspect of land ownership. As illustrated by advances in real estate securitization and the momentum toward the full-scale introduction of "mark-to-market" valuation of real estate in corporate accounting, there is a growing demand for detailed explanation of the cash flow generated by land together with buildings as combined real estate products, and for the income-earning capabilities of that real estate to be accurately reflected in its pricing and reporting.

「同基準運用上の留意事項」。1964年)。不動産鑑定士による鑑定評価基準に準拠した鑑定評価以外の鑑定評価に類似した行為は禁止されている。(第1編第2章Ⅰ.日本-6参照)

(b) 過剰流動性

石油危機を減量経営、省エネ技術の開発によるコストダウンなどによって乗り越えると、GDPは80年代後半に5％前後まで持ち直してきたが、ここで3回目の地価急騰を経験した。このときの地価バブルは、それまでの高度経済成長期の地価バブルと違って、GDPの伸びを上回る金融超緩和を背景として「不動産金融市場（資本市場）」に堆積した大量の資金が過剰流動性となって、本来はローカルな「不動産市場」に流れ込み、両市場のバランスが崩壊したものといえる。

この急激な過剰流動性に対して、鑑定評価は、鑑定士の行為規範や個々の評価技術の改善だけでは期待された役割を果たせなかった。地価が右肩上がりで急騰する市場では、不動産の賃貸によって毎年発生するキャッシュフローと比べて、転売によって発生するキャッシュフローが圧倒的なウエートを占めた。したがって、取引事例価格が市場価値の決め手になり、収益価格は実質的な規範性を持たず、鑑定評価基準の実効性が問われるに至った。しかし、取引事例も収益事例も、鑑定士が市場から最新の詳細なデータを入手できる仕組みが整備されていなかったので、取得能力や収益比率などから取引価格を検証して過剰流動性の影響と市場価値の持続可能性を分析することは困難であった。市場データへのアクセスが限られている中で、鑑定評価額は数少ない取引事例や呼び値に引っ張られて急騰を続けた後、突如バブル崩壊に足をすくわれた。

2. 鑑定評価の透明性と信頼性

日本では、3回目の地価バブル崩壊後、地価の長期下落を背景にして、不動産市場における人々の価値観は、不動産を単に「所有」することから、その特質である「キャッシュフロー向上」を実現する方向に重心を移している。特に不動産の証券化や企業不動産に着目した経営戦略（CRE）では、土地・建物一体の複合不動産から生み出されるキャッシュフローを予測・検証して、市場価値を的確に把握するニーズが高まっている。

その一方で、他の先進諸国と同様に金融やITなど成長分野への産業構造の転換過程にある日本では、それに伴う過剰流動性が依然として顕著である。加えて国際的にも不動産金融市場のグローバル化が加速している。その結果、内外の巨額な投資資金が不動産市場に流れ込んで両市場のバラ

Chapter 1. Evolution and Characteristics of Japan Real Estate Appraisal

Meanwhile, like other advanced countries, Japan is in the process of transforming its industrial structure in the direction of finance, IT, and other growth areas, and is still experiencing a high level of excess liquidity, which tends to accompany such a transformation. In addition, the globalization of the real estate market is accelerating around the world. As a result, it is likely that enormous amounts of both domestic and foreign investment capital will be directed to the real estate market, and that this will include some sale prices which are unreasonably high in terms of income-producing capabilities of a property. The ability to procure investment capital at a low cost, a result of excess liquidity, is one of the reasons why investors are eager to invest, even at high prices, along with their high expectations for future cash flow and the dispersion of investment risk through real estate securitization.

In response to the major changes in the social and economic environment such as real estate securitization, increasing cross-border investment, and the two-tier market, concrete steps are being taken to create mechanisms for an infrastructure to improve transparency and reliability in appraisals. For example, the Japanese Real Estate Appraisal Standards were totally revised in 2007 (see Part 3 Specific Standards Chapter 3 (SS. Chap.3)). Collaboration between the government and private sectors in establishing a database to improve access to market data is now progressing. Beginning in 2008, appraisals are monitored by a third-party committee established by the regulatory authorities. (see Part 1 Chap.2, Ⅰ. Japan - 6,7)

In the US and other countries besides Japan, much energy is being devoted to efforts to improve access to market data, to heighten the transparency and reliability of appraisals, and to increase the effectiveness of uniform appraisal standards. For a long time, appraisal has been said to be more of an art than a science. However, the current appraisal environment may be characterized by the creation of a data management process to acquire, monitor, and store market data and increasing competition in terms of the quality and speed of data analysis. (see Part 1 Chap.2, Ⅱ. US - 7, Ⅲ. UK - 7, Ⅳ. Australia - 7)

3. Revision of the Real Estate Appraisal Standards in 2007

Appraisals by LREAs, who are responsible for conducting an objective, highly precise appraisal from an independent and impartial standpoint, reflecting an absence of any conflict of interest with regard to investors and market participants, are becoming increasingly important in ensuring the sound development and transparency of the real estate securitization market.

The 2007 revision of the Japanese Real estate Appraisal Standards goes beyond a mere revision of the existing standards and incorporates additional content (Part 3 Specific Standards Chapter 3 (SS. Chap.3)). The main content of this new chapter is summarized below.

① The scope of securitization-properties requiring real estate appraisal should first be clarified. It includes real estate, which is subject to, or under consideration for, several types of transactions (including transactions involving trust beneficiary rights) under various legislation such as the *Asset Liquidation Law, the Investment*

ンスが崩れる可能性はあり、中には収益性にふさわしくない高い取引価格も見受けられる。投資家がそうした高い価格でも積極的な投資姿勢を見せている原因として、将来キャッシュフローへの強い期待感及び不動産の証券化による投資リスクの分散に加えて、過剰流動性を背景とする低コストの投資資金調達が指摘されている。

そこで、不動産の証券化、不動産金融市場のグローバル化、地価動向の二極化・個別化など社会経済環境の変化に対して、鑑定評価の透明性と信頼性を支える基盤の仕組みづくりが具体化している。官民協働の市場データベース構築による情報アクセス環境の強化、不動産の証券化に対応する鑑定評価基準改正、2008年から実施の第三者委員会による鑑定評価の監視検証(monitoring)などである。(第1編第2章Ⅰ.日本-6、7参照)

米国など日本以外の国でも、市場データへのアクセス環境を強化して鑑定評価の透明性と信頼性を高め、統一鑑定評価基準の実効性を上げる動きが急ピッチで進んでいる。鑑定評価は、長い間、サイエンスというよりアートであると言われてきたが、現在はデータ管理システム(data management system)を構築して、客観的な市場データ分析の質とスピードを競う時代に入っている。(第1編第2章Ⅱ.米国-7、Ⅲ.英国-7、Ⅳ.オーストラリア-7参照)

3.2007年の鑑定評価基準改正

不動産証券化市場の健全な発展と透明性の確保のために、証券化市場で重要な役割を担う鑑定評価において、より高度の透明性と信頼性が要求されるようになっている。

2007年の鑑定評価基準改正は、従来基準の修正を超えて、従来基準の各論編に新たに第3章を追加する構成として、次の内容を組み入れている(本書第3編「基準各論」第3章)。

①不動産鑑定評価が必要とされる「証券化対象不動産」の適用範囲を明確にする。資産流動化法及び投信法のほかに、不動産特定共同事業法及び金融商品取引法に該当する不動産取引の目的である不動産又はその見込みのある不動産(信託受益権の取引も含まれる)が該当するが、これ以外の不動産であっても投資用不動産の評価においては、投資家及び購入者の保護の観点から各論第3章を準用する。(同各論第3章第1節)

②証券化対象不動産については、関係者が多岐にわたり利害関係が複雑である場合が多いことから、依頼者と証券化対象不動産や証券化関係者との利害関係について鑑定評価書に記載する。(同各論第3章第2節Ⅲ)

③鑑定評価の依頼を受ける場合、依頼目的・背景、想定される証券化スキーム、依頼者と証券化

Chapter 1. Evolution and Characteristics of Japan Real Estate Appraisal

Trust and Investment Corporation Law, the Real Estate Syndication Act (Fudosan Tokutei Kyodo Jigyo Ho), or the Financial Instruments Trading Law. The provisions of Chapter 3 of the Specific Standards apply to the valuation of other types of investment properties for the protection of investors and buyers. (SS. Chap.3 Sec.1)

② Since, in many cases, a wide variety of parties may be involved and hold complex interests in a securitized property, the appraisal report must indicate the interests of the client with regard to the property and the parties involved in the securitization. (SS. Chap.3 Sec.2Ⅲ)

③ When accepting a request to perform an appraisal, the LREA must determine the purpose and background of the appraisal request, the anticipated securitization plan, and the relationship between the client and parties involved in the securitization; the LREA must also draft a reasonable and reliable plan for how to proceed. (SS. Chap.3 Sec.2Ⅰ)

④ In an appraisal of a securitization property, the LREA must ask the client to submit the engineering report required for that appraisal, and provided the report is submitted and its content meets the needs of the appraisal, the LREA must use such report in the appraisal. (If the engineering report is incomplete, the LREA must clarify those areas needing further explanation on the basis of his own knowledge or another expert's advice.) Whether or not an engineering report is utilized, the use of a uniform format is required. (SS. Chap.3 Sec.3Ⅲ)

⑤ To improve the accuracy of an appraisal of a securitization property and to enhance the comparability of the report, the value indicated by the income approach must be calculated by both direct capitalization and DCF analysis. In the application of DCF analysis, steps are taken to allow comparisons of net operating income (NOI) over intervals, which unifies the income and expense items and makes the market data more easily understandable. The use of a uniform format is required. (SS. Chap.3 Sec.4Ⅱ)

4. Globalization of Real Estate Appraisal Standards

The real estate markets of all countries stand in a relationship of international competition by way of the real estate financial market. In the real estate financial market, vast amounts of accumulated excess capital are moved around the world in search of the most advantageous investment opportunities, just as Tokyo Bay, Hudson River, the Thames River, and Victoria Harbor are all linked by the waterway that covers the earth. When all goes well, this can contribute to global economic growth. However, investment capital sometimes pours in too rapidly, like a *tsunami*, followed by an outflow or capital flight.

As investment capital becomes increasingly global in nature, it is necessary to ensure the transparency and reliability in appraisals from an international perspective in addition to a national one. Here, I will consider two approaches to studying the appraisal standards of individual countries : the top-down approach, which is based on the ideal of unified international appraisal standards; and the bottom-up approach, which is based on the reality of how appraisals are actually conducted in each country.

関係者の関係等を把握して、円滑かつ確実な処理計画を策定する。(同各論第3章第2節Ⅰ)
④証券化対象不動産の鑑定評価においては、不動産鑑定士は依頼者に対して鑑定評価に必要なエンジニアリング・レポートの提出を求め、その内容を鑑定評価に活用しなければならない。活用したか否かについて、統一形式の様式の採用を義務づける。(同各論第3章第3節Ⅲ)
⑤説明責任と比較可能性の向上によって鑑定評価の精度を上げるために、証券化対象不動産の鑑定評価においては、収益価格は、直接還元法のほかに、DCF法によって求める。DCF法適用においては、収益費用項目を統一し、市場データのとりやすい運営純収益(NOI)ベースの比較を途中段階でできるようにし、統一形式の様式の採用を義務づける。(同各論第3章第4節Ⅱ)

4. 鑑定評価の国際化

　各国の不動産市場は不動産金融市場を通して国際的な競合関係に立っている。不動産金融市場は、地球を覆う水のように、東京湾、ハドソン川、テムズ川、ビクトリア港とつながっていて、過剰に蓄積された巨額な投資資金は最も有利な投資機会を求めて世界中を動き回っている。うまく循環すれば世界の経済成長に貢献するが、ときには"津波"となって襲ったり、逆流する(capital flight)こともある。
　資本のグローバル化の加速に対して、鑑定評価も国内だけでなく国際的視点に立って、透明性と信頼性の中身を充実させる必要がある。ここでは、各国で適用されるべき鑑定評価のモノサシについて、国際評価基準による統一の「理念」からトップダウンでアプローチする視点と、現に各国で行われている鑑定評価の「現実」からボトムアップでアプローチする視点の2つの方向から検討する。

Chapter 1. Evolution and Characteristics of Japan Real Estate Appraisal

(a) **International Valuation Standards**

In cross-border transactions, it is essential to recognize the principle-based International Valuation Standards (IVS), which should be commonly understood, relied upon, and applied by all countries. In recent years, the International Accounting Standards Board (IASB) has accelerated its efforts for the adoption of International Financial Reporting Standards (IFRS) which are principle-based and focus on reporting at Fair Value rather than historical cost. IASB continues the convergence with national accounting standards, with than 120 countries adopting IFRS. The International Valuation Standards (IVS) role in support of IFRS and other valuation and practice standards continues to grow. The standards of individual countries are also being developed in relation to globalization, either adopting IVS, converging with IVS or incorporating them in some form as a path to future convergence or adoption. (see Part 1 Chap.2, Ⅵ. IVS - 1)

For example, the fifth edition of the RICS appraisal standards generally referred to as the Red Book distinguishes between national standards applicable only in the UK, and global standards applicable both in the UK and abroad. The global standards in the Red Book are adopted from the appropriate IVS standards. (see Part1 Chap.2, Ⅵ. IVS - 1)

In the US, in response to the strong demands of global finance, the appraisal standards and business models have been changed to facilitate the prompt and flexible handling of appraisals. For example, since July 2006, the "departure rule", which applied to exceptions to compliance with USPAP, has been removed; and the "scope of work rule", which is considered as a contractual arrangement for other professionals including lawyers, has been recognized outright as the basis of appraisal assignments. (see Part1 Chap.2, Ⅱ. USA - 2) This represents an alignment with the approach taken by the US Financial Accounting Standards Board (FASB), which with a litigious society in mind had based its standards on a strictly rule-based approach, but is now moving toward the principle-based approach taken by the International Accounting Standards Board (IASB), as part of the IASB/FASB convergence project. The US appraisal standards are to be brought into convergence with the International Valuation Standards under the Madison Agreement of 2006.

In Japan as well, the green light has just been given in 2008 for cross-border appraisals according to overseas standards (or IVS, if the overseas country standards has adopted the IVS), based on the concept of "When in Rome, do as the Romans do". However, LREAs who engage in collaboration or joint work with overseas appraisers are to report the matters required under Japan's appraisal standards to the extent possible; and if some items are not customarily taken into consideration under the overseas standards, a note should be included to this effect. (see Part 1 Chap.2, Ⅰ. Japan - 5, Part 5 Guidelines for the Appraisal of Overseas Investment Properties (GL))

(b) **Cross-border valuation**

In each country, the appraisal standards which are based on economic theory have many basic aspects in common. However, significant differences appear at the stage of practical application of those standards, since their application is based on systems and markets which reflect the unique historical, cultural, and political nature of each country. Thus, IVS, which has no enforcing power, must rely on the national standard setter or

第 1 章　日本の不動産鑑定評価の展開と特質

(a)　国際評価基準（IVS）
　まず、国境を超えた取引では、どこの国であっても共通に理解され、信頼され、適用されるべき鑑定評価基準の統一が進むことが重要である。その役割は、細目を偏重せず基本ルールを定めて実務的な運用を行うべしとする原則主義に立つ国際評価基準（IVS）に期待されてきている。特に近年、国際会計基準審議会（IASB）が、同じく原則主義に立って、取得原価ではなく、公正価値に基づく財務報告を内容とする国際財務報告基準（IFRS　通称「国際会計基準」）の採択に向けて動きを加速させていて（120カ国以上が採択）、IFRS及びそれに基づく実務基準による数値計上の基準として、IVSの役割が大きくなっている。各国の鑑定評価基準も、IVSをそのまま採用したり、IVSと収斂させたり、又は何らかの形でIVSを取り込んで、グローバル化に対応する方向に進んでいる。（第1編第2章Ⅵ. 国際評価基準 - 1参照）
　例えば、英国の鑑定評価業務基準（Red Book）第5版は、イギリス国内のみで適用される国内基準（national standards）に先立って、イギリス国内外を問わず適用になる国際基準（global standards）を規定し、国外についてはIVSから適切な基準を引用している。（第1編第2章Ⅲ. 英国 - 1参照）
　米国でも、不動産金融市場のグローバル化に対して、鑑定評価が素早くかつ柔軟に対応できるように、自らの基準やビジネスモデルを変更している。例えば、2006年7月から、「基準の例外ルール（Departure Rule）」に代わって、他の専門職業では当たり前の「業務範囲ルール（Scope of Work Rule）」を正面から認めている。（第1編第2章Ⅱ. 米国 - 2参照）また、細目まで細かく決めて実務を積み上げてきた規則主義の米国財務会計基準（FASB）が、原則主義に立つ国際会計基準（IASB）へと収斂する方向にあるのと軌を一にして、米国の鑑定評価業務基準も国際評価基準と共同歩調をとるようになっている（The Madison Agreement.2006年）。
　日本でも2008年、「郷に入っては郷に従え」として海外現地基準（海外現地基準がIVSを援用している場合にはIVS基準）によるクロス・ボーダーな鑑定評価に道を開いたが、海外鑑定人と連携・協同する不動産鑑定士は日本の鑑定評価基準に照らして必要な事項はできる限り記載するものとし、海外現地基準では記載しないことが通常である場合にはその旨記載するものとしている（第1編第2章Ⅰ. 日本 - 5及び第5編「海外投資不動産鑑定評価ガイドライン」）。

(b)　クロス・ボーダー評価の現実
　各国の鑑定評価は、経済理論をベースとする鑑定評価基準自体については基本的には共通するところが多い。しかし、そのモノサシを現実に適用する段階となると、各国の歴史的・文化的・政策的な独自性を反映した制度や市場によって大きな違いが出てくる。しかも、国際評価基準IVSの導入は、各国鑑定評価基準の策定主体次第であり、強制（enforce）する機関はない。
　したがって、クロス・ボーダーな鑑定評価を行うには、各国の鑑定評価基準、市場データへの

regulators to ensure consistent application and enforcement of IVS.

Therefore, in cross-border appraisal, it is necessary to obtain a thorough understanding of the differences that characterize each country with regard to appraisal standards, concepts of property rights, the environment of access to market data and verification, and other basic matters, and to make these matters clear to the client and investor in each appraisal report. Disclosure as to the level of compliance with IVS and reasons behind any departures must be clear and prominent. Before making an investment, investors want to know the reasons for any substantive differences that may exist among the terms and techniques used in market and appraisals, even when they seem similar at first glance, so that this information can be used to analyze investment risk.

To introduce Japan real estate appraisal standards in a global context and discuss the differences among the appraisal standards of these countries, the author has compared appraisal standards in Japan with appraisal standards of US, the UK, Australia, China and IVS with regard to the following fundamental points at Chapter 2:

① Framework of Appraisal Standards (Who writes appraisal standards? For whom appraisal standards are written? Who must abide by and what services must comply?)
② Fundamentals for Appraisals (Real Property ownership and interest, Scope of work, Assumptions, Appraisal reviews)
③ General Concepts & Principles (Market value, Value other than market value)
④ Approaches to Value
⑤ Appraisal Report
⑥ Implementation of Appraisal Standards
⑦ Availability of Data
⑧ Specific Appraisal Standards for Securitization Purposes

The following parts are based on the author's understanding of the discussions and his appraisal practices conducted in these countries.

5. Role of and Responsibility for the Appraisal System

In order to convert the wave of rapid globalization in the real estate market into energy that leads to efficient land use and sound capital formation, instead of a *tsunami* which results in the formation and collapse of bubbles, there is a need for coordinated efforts in a wide range of fields, including real estate securitization schemes and urban planning. Although the roles that can be played by appraisals are limited, it is more important than ever to accurately estimate market values through the analysis of verified market data and macroeconomic data, including the objectives, motives, and characteristics transactions of investors. Compared to the time of Japan's economic bubble, today there is much greater access to market data, which is indispensable for this kind of detailed analysis.

In addition, the national government in Japan is considered to bear ultimate responsibility for the appraisal system on behalf of the general public, and this attribution of responsibility is clearly specified. The conception of appraisal as a national system underlies many differences between Japan and other countries in aspects such as the scope of appraisal work, assumptions, appraisal reports, responsibilities of appraisers, and standards

アクセス環境と検証、財産権と権利保全の内容等の基本的な事柄の差異性について十分理解を深めておき、個々の鑑定評価書の中で依頼者・投資家に対して差異性の内容やその理由を明らかにする必要がある。投資家も、投資に先立って、一見したところ似たような鑑定評価の用語や手法を用いているが、国によって内容に違いがあるのか、違いがあるとすればなぜか、海外現地基準の適用に当たってどのような不確定リスクがあるのか、是非確認したいところである。

そこで、日本の不動産鑑定評価をグローバルな視点に立って紹介し、各国の鑑定評価との差異性を理解する手がかりとして、第2章では日本、米国、英国、オーストラリア、中国の各基準と運用及び国際評価基準について、以下の共通項目について比較を行い、その要旨を示す。

① 制度的枠組み（鑑定評価基準の策定主体、目的、対象となる財産権と権利保全の内容）
② 鑑定評価の前提（鑑定評価の業務範囲、前提条件、審査）
③ 鑑定評価の基礎（市場価値、市場価値以外の価値）
④ 鑑定評価の方式
⑤ 鑑定評価報告書（記載事項、依頼者、利用目的、利用者）
⑥ 鑑定評価基準の履行（鑑定士又は鑑定人の責任）
⑦ 市場データへのアクセス環境
⑧ 不動産証券化に関する基準

本書第2編以下も、こうした国際比較の議論及び具体的評価実務経験を踏まえた対訳としている。

5．鑑定評価の役割と責任

不動産金融市場の急速なグローバル化の波を、バブルの発生や崩壊を引き起こす"津波"ではなく、魅力ある土地利用や堅実な資産形成を実現するためのエネルギーに変換していくには、不動産の証券化や都市計画を含めて幅広い分野での連携した取り組みが必要である。鑑定評価が果たせる役割は限られているが、投資家の取引の対象、動機、手段まで踏み込んで客観的な市場データやマクロデータを分析して市場価値を的確に把握することが、これまで以上に重要になっているし、そうした詳しい分析に不可欠な市場データへのアクセス環境は過去のバブル時と比べて格段に整備されてきている。

日本では、さらに、鑑定評価を国家が国民に対して責任を持つ制度として位置づけている。国家制度としての位置づけは、鑑定評価の業務範囲（scope of work）、前提条件、鑑定評価報告書の記載内容、鑑定士又は鑑定人の責任、不動産証券化に関する基準などの個々の実務分野で、多くの海外諸国と様々な違いをもたらしている。

現在、米国の低所得者向け（サブプライム）住宅ローン問題を契機として、流動性危機が国際金融市場さらには不動産市場へと拡がっているが、そこでは情報の開示と責任の明確化（traceability：追及可能性）による投資家及び公共の信頼回復が問われている。国によって対応は異なるが、

relating to real estate securitization. Currently, the problem of sub-prime home mortgages aimed at low-income earners in the US, has led to a liquidity crisis, which is adversely affecting the global securitization and real estate markets, and this has raised the issue of restoring the confidence of investors and the general public through the disclosure of information and clarification of responsibilities. Countries vary in their responses, but Japan's real estate appraisal system meets the call for responsibility regarding transparency and reliability in appraisals not only with regard to appraisal clients but also with regard to the general public. (see Part 1 Chap.2, Ⅰ. Japan - 6,7)

日本の不動産鑑定評価制度は、依頼者だけでなく公共に対しても、鑑定評価の透明性と信頼性の責任を担うものとして、この問いかけに応えるものである。（第1編第2章Ⅰ．日本‐6、7参照）

CHAPTER 2. COMPARISON OF APPRAISAL/VALUATION STANDARDS

I. Japan : Real Estate Appraisal Standards

1. Framework of Appraisal Standards

(a) **Who writes Appraisal Standards?**
The Ministry of Land, Infrastructure, Transport and Tourism

(b) **For whom Appraisal Standards are written? (Principal purposes of appraisal standards)**
The purpose of the Real Estate Appraisal Act is to prescribe the necessary matters regarding licensed real estate appraisers (LREAs) and real estate appraisal firms, and thereby to contribute to the formation of appropriate pricing in the real estate market. (see Part2 Article 1) This concept of a national system for public benefit has required the LREA to set up and maintain high standards of professional practices. Also, under this system, the appraiser may be held liable for improper or illegal appraisal practices.

(c) **Who must abide by the Standards and what services must comply? (Compliance with appraisal standards)**
Real estate appraisal services and consulting services regarding land use, transactions, and investment, using the name of LREA. (Real Estate Appraisal Act Article 3)
The organization of the standards follows;

General Standards (GS)
 Chap. 1 Foundation of Real Estate Appraisal
 Chap. 2 Use Categories and Physical Development &Title Categories of Real Estate
 Chap. 3 Influences on Real Estate Value
 Chap. 4 Principles of Real Estate Value
 Chap. 5 Basic Appraisal Problem
 Chap. 6 Market Area Analysis and Property Analysis
 Chap. 7 Appraisal Methods
 Chap. 8 Appraisal Process
 Chap. 9 Appraisal Report

Specific Standards (SS)
 Chap. 1 Appraisal of Real Estate Value
 Chap. 2 Appraisal of Real Estate Rental Value
 Chap. 3 Appraisal of Real Estate Value Subject to Securitization

Guidance Notes (GN)
 GN I on GS. Chap.2 Use Categories and Physical Development &

第2章　各国の不動産鑑定評価の比較

Ⅰ．日本：不動産鑑定評価基準

1．鑑定評価基準の制度枠組み

(a) 基準の策定主体
国土交通省

(b) 基準の目的
不動産の鑑定評価に関する法律（以下「鑑定評価法」という）は、不動産の鑑定評価に関して、不動産鑑定士及び不動産鑑定業について国家資格等の事項を定めることによって、土地等の適正な価格の形成に資することを目的とする（⇒第2編「鑑定評価法」第1条）。国土交通省が国家制度として策定した鑑定評価制度は、不動産鑑定士が専門家として鑑定評価を行うに当たっての拠り所となるとともに、不正又は著しく不当な鑑定評価に対する懲戒処分の判断根拠となる。

(c) 基準の対象
不動産鑑定士及び不動産鑑定業者による不動産鑑定評価業務、及び不動産鑑定士の名称を用いて行う調査・コンサルティング業務。基準の構成は以下のとおりである。

総論（General Standards：GS）
　　第1章　不動産の鑑定評価に関する基本的考察
　　第2章　不動産の種類及び類型
　　第3章　不動産の価格を形成する要因
　　第4章　不動産の価格に関する諸法則
　　第5章　鑑定評価の基本的事項
　　第6章　地域分析及び個別分析
　　第7章　鑑定評価の方式
　　第8章　鑑定評価の手順
　　第9章　鑑定評価報告書

各論（Specific Standards：SS）
　　第1章　価格に関する鑑定評価
　　第2章　賃料に関する鑑定評価
　　第3章　証券化対象不動産の価格に関する鑑定評価

留意事項（Guidance Notes：GN）
　　Ⅰ　「総論第2章　不動産の種類及び類型」について
　　Ⅱ　「総論第3章　不動産の価格を形成する要因」について
　　Ⅲ　「総論第5章　鑑定評価の基本的事項」について
　　Ⅳ　「総論第6章　地域分析及び個別分析」について

Chapter 2. Ⅰ. Japan : Real Estate Appraisal Standards

	Title Categories of Real Estate
GN Ⅱ on GS. Chap.3	Influences on Real Estate Value
GN Ⅲ on GS. Chap.5	Basic Appraisal Problem
GN Ⅳ on GS. Chap.6	Market Area and Subject Property Analysis
GN Ⅴ on GS. Chap.7	Appraisal Method
GN Ⅵ on GS. Chap.8	Appraisal Process
GN Ⅶ on SS. Chap.1	Appraisal of Real Estate Value
GN Ⅷ on SS. Chap.2	Appraisal of Real Estate Rental Value
GN Ⅸ on SS. Chap.3	Appraisal of Real Estate Value Subject to Securitization

Guideline for the Appraisal of Overseas Investment Properties （GL）

(d) **Licensing**

Licensed Real Estate Appraiser （LREA, Real Estate Appraisal Act Article 3）

2. Fundamentals for Appraisal

(a) **Real Property Rights and Interests to be Appraised**

Appraisal is applicable to the real estate ownership （"ownership" means the right to freely use, operate, and dispose of one's property within legal limits）, leasing rights, and other rights and economic interests. "Real estate" is defined as an identified parcel of land and a building. Among items fixed to the land, buildings remain separate from the land as independent real estate （unlike the principle of *superficies solo credit* in Europe, Australia and North America, in which structures on the land belong to land）, but other fixtures are considered to be part of land. The "one real estate for one registry" has been adopted for the registration, and buildings are registered separately from land.

(b) **Terms of Engagement**

In the last decade, USPAP has evolved from a document that listed a series of "musts" for the appraiser to apply in the appraisal process, to one that emphasizes the appraiser's application of sound judgement in solving the problem at hand. The newly adopted concept of "Scope of Work" provides the appraiser the flexibility to perform a variety of appraisal services and describes how those services can be performed without compromising objectivity and impartiality. Appraisal is to be proceeded in a similar manner with other professional services.

On the other hand, the Japanese government has established the appraisal system as a national system and writes the appraisal standard to establish a legal and administrative framework for appraisal, which plays an important role in contributing to appropriate pricing in the real estate market by providing the market with information about property values exclusively by LREAs. A LREA must meet all the requirements of the Appraisal Standards established by the government. Japan has not adopted the concept of Scope of Work.

Therefore, terms of engagement with the client are dealt with in the mandatory standards of Part 3 General Standards. Chapter 5. Chapter 8. Chapter 9. Specific Standards. Chapter 3. and Part 5 Guideline for the Appraisal of Overseas Investment Properties.

(c) **Assumptions**

Ⅴ 「総論第7章　鑑定評価の方式」について
Ⅵ 「総論第8章　鑑定評価の手順」について
Ⅶ 「各論第1章　価格に関する鑑定評価」について
Ⅷ 「各論第2章　賃料に関する鑑定評価」について
Ⅸ 「各論第3章　証券化対象不動産の価格に関する鑑定評価」について

海外投資不動産鑑定評価ガイドライン（Guideline：GL）

(d)　資格
不動産鑑定士（⇒第2編「鑑定評価法」第3条）

2．鑑定評価の前提

(a)　鑑定評価の対象となる権利・利益
鑑定評価の対象は、不動産に対する所有権（ownership＝法令の制限内において、自由にその所有物の使用、収益及び処分をする権利）、賃借権等の権利又は経済的利益である。「不動産」とは、「土地」と「建物」である。土地の定着物のうち、建物は常に土地とは別の独立の不動産となり（欧米の「地上物は土地に属する（superficies solo credit）」の原則とは異なる）、登記も土地とは別個となる。その他の定着物は土地の一部となる。登記は一個の不動産ごとに独立の一個の登記用紙を備える物的編成主義による。

(b)　業務の範囲
米国の不動産鑑定評価基準は、従来は日本と同様に、評価において最低限遵守すべき強制的な基準を列挙する考え方をとっていた。しかし2006年7月、不動産証券化や経済活動のグローバル化による評価業務に対する要請に対応して、弁護士等の専門職業と同様に評価業務の内容を依頼者との間で柔軟に定めて、依頼者にとってさしあたり不要なところを業務範囲からはずし、コストも節約できる「業務範囲のルール（Scope of Work Rule）」を導入した。鑑定人は、依頼目的に基づいて対象とする鑑定評価上の問題が何であるかを明確にし、それに対して信頼できる結論を下すのに必要な範囲を、依頼者との間で取り決める。信頼できる結論を導けないような業務範囲に絞ることは許されない。依頼者と鑑定人との間で、評価上の不確定要因に伴うリスクを分けあうことになるから、鑑定人は業務範囲について報告書の中で詳細な情報開示が要請される（Scope Disclosure）。

一方、日本の鑑定評価は、専門家による合理的な価格情報を不動産市場に提供することを通じて、市場における"適正な地価の形成に資する"役割を担う国家制度として位置づけられ、鑑定評価基準が策定されている。鑑定士は、法律上、依頼者のみならず第三者に対しても評価上の責任を負っていて、米国USPAPの業務範囲（scope of work）のように依頼者と鑑定人間の合意によって業務範囲を柔軟に定められる規定はない。以下で解説する、「3．鑑定評価の基礎」、「4．鑑定評価の方式・手順」及び「5．鑑定評価報告書」は、鑑定評価業務の範囲を依頼者と合意する際に遵守すべき内容となる。

(c)　評価の前提条件

Although there are cases where a client may request the appraiser to make certain assumptions or limiting conditions with respect to the effect of market-specific or property-specific value influences on the subject property, such assumptions and limiting conditions imposed by a client must be reasonable, realistic, and legitimate. The appraiser will proceed objectively whether or not the results of the valuation jeopardize the benefits of an involved party (i.e., the client) or third party.

In cases where the effect of influences on the value of the subject property cannot be clearly estimated despite the appraiser's having undertaken all the required research, it may be necessary to rely on the results of the investigation of another professional. Sometimes, because of restrictions resulting from the client's request, the appraiser will only be able to perform the appraisal by imposing additional assumptions or limiting conditions with the consent of the client. In other cases, the appraiser will have to estimate the effect of value influences on the subject property based on his / her own investigative and analytical capabilities. In such situations, it is necessary to report all additional assumptions imposed to perform the appraisal assignment and to arrive at the value estimate (see Part 3 GS. Chap. 8).

(d) **Appraisal Reviews**

No description of appraisal reviews exist under the law and Standards.

3. General Concepts and Principles (Valuation Bases)

(a) **Market Value (MV)**

Market value refers to the probable value that would be formed for the marketable real estate in a market that satisfies conditions associated with a rational market under actual socio-economic circumstances. (see Part 3 GS. Chap.5 Sec.3, Part 4 GN.Ⅲ) The basis of MV is fully compatible with the definition of MV found in USPAP, the Red Book and the IVS. When value other than MV is reported, it should always be clearly distinguished from MV. Items related to MV are as follows:

① Highest and Best Use (HABU)

The market value of real estate is analyzed on the premise of the potential best use of the real estate, i.e., the use under which the real estate will achieve its maximal utility. (see Part 3 GS. Chap.6 Sec.2)

② Market Exposure Time

The subject property must be exposed in the market for an appropriate period of time before the date of value opinion. (see Part 4 GN.Ⅲ)

③ Value for Regulated Purposes (VRP)

Value for Regulated Purposes may be divided into two categories : market value and value other than market value. (see Part 3 GS. Chap.5 Sec.3, Part 3 SS. Chap.3 Sec.1 , Part 4 GN.Ⅲ) The value under the Asset Liquidation Law and the Investment Corporation law, is the market value assuming an operation management scheme which reflects the expectation of a typical investor. It refers to the investment profitability value of the subject property under the securitization regulation, but represents those of a typical investor rather than a specific investor in the market.

対象不動産について、依頼目的に応じて対象不動産に係る価格形成要因のうち地域要因又は個別的要因について想定上の条件を付加する場合があるが、この場合には、想定上の条件が実現性、合法性、関係当事者及び第三者の利益を害するおそれがないか等の観点から妥当なものでなければならない。

価格形成要因について、専門職業家としての注意を尽くしても、なお対象不動産の価格形成に重大な影響を与える要因が明らかでない場合には、原則として他の専門家が行った調査結果等を活用する。ただし、依頼目的や依頼条件による制約がある場合には、依頼者の同意を得て、想定上の条件を付加して鑑定評価を行うこと又は自己の調査分析能力の範囲内で当該要因に係る価格形成上の影響の程度を推定して鑑定評価を行うことができる（⇒第3編「基準総論」第8章）。

(d) 評価の審査
鑑定評価基準に規定はない。

3．鑑定評価の基礎（価値の種類）

(a) 正常価格（Market Value）
正常価格は、市場性を有する不動産について、現実の社会経済情勢の下で合理的と考えられる条件を満たす市場で形成されるであろう市場価値を表示する適正な価格である（⇒第3編「基準総論」第5章第3節、第4編「留意事項」Ⅲ）。正常価格は、米国の鑑定業務統一基準（USPAP）、英国の評価基準（Red Book）、国際評価基準（IVS）における「市場価値（Market Value）」と要件及び実体が共通である。鑑定士が、この要件を満たさない価格（Value other than MV）を求められることがあるが、正常価格とは厳格に区別する。正常価値に関連する項目は以下の通りである。

①**最有効使用**（Highest and Best Use ⇒第3編「基準総論」第6章第2章）
不動産の価格は、その不動産の効用が最高度に発揮される可能性に最も富む使用を前提として把握される価格を標準として形成される。その場合、現実の社会経済情勢の下で客観的に見て、良識と通常の使用能力を持つ人による合理的かつ合法的な最高最善の使用方法に基づくものである。

②**市場公開期間**（Market Exposure Time ⇒第4編「基準留意事項」Ⅲ）
価格時点に先立って、すでに相当の期間市場に公開されていること。

③**特定価格**（Value for Regulated Purpose ⇒第3編「基準総論」第5章第3節、「基準各論」第3章第1節、第4編「基準留意事項」Ⅲ）
特定価格とは、市場性を有する不動産について、法令等による社会的要請を背景とする評価目的の下で、不動産の経済価値を適正に表示する価格をいう。法令等に基づく対象不動産の運用方法等について市場の典型的な投資家を前提とする投資採算価値の場合には正常価格（Market Value）と一致し、特定の投資家を前提とする場合には正常価格以外の価格（Value Other Than Market Value）となる。

1) The value under the Asset Liquidation Law and the Investment Corporation Law, is the market value assuming an operation management scheme which reflects the expectation of a typical investor. It refers to the investment profitability value of the subject property under the securitization regulations, but represents those of a typical investor rather than a specific investor in the market.

2) The value under the Civil Rehabilitation law is the value of the marketable property assuming that it is estimated in circumstances where a proper marketing period is not available.

3) The value under the Corporation Reorganization Law and the Civil Rehabilitation Law is the value of the marketable property assuming that the particular property is estimated as a part of the entity's continuing business.

(b) **Value Other Than Market Value**

①Special Value

Special Value includes "synergistic value or plottage value" and "component value" of the limited-market property which has relatively few potential buyers and sellers as a result of assemblage or, subdivision of real property.(see Part 3 GS. Chap.5 Sec.3)

②Value of Special-Purpose Property

Non-market value refers to the appropriate economic value of specialized real estate such as cultural assets that typically are not marketable. Non-market value is premised on the continuation of the current use of the real estate. (see Part 3 GS. Chap.5 Sec.3)

③Investment Value

In the US, the UK, Australia add IVS, the investment value is defined as the value of an income-producing property to a specific investor, while there is no particular description exists under the Appraisal Act and the Real Estate Appraisal Standards in Japan.

4. Approaches to Value

(a) The appraisal method applied should be appropriate to the subject property and the problem of the appraisal. As a general rule, all three methods, i. e., the cost approach, sales comparison approach, and income capitalization approach, should be employed. Where the type of subject property or circumstances involving the property's location or reliability of the data make it difficult to apply each of the three approaches, every possible effort should be made to incorporate concepts from all approaches. The method being applied to estimate real estate value is as follows (see Part 3 GS. Chap.7 Sec.1). The three methods are also applied to estimate real estate rental value (see Part 3 GS. Chap.7 Sec.2).

①Cost Approach :

The cost approach to value first estimates the reproduction cost of the subject property on the date of value opinion. Then, an estimate of accrued depreciation must be deducted from the reproduction cost.

②Sales Comparison Approach :

特定価格を求める場合を列挙すれば、次のとおりである。
1) 資産の流動化に関する法律又は投資信託及び投資法人に関する法律に基づく評価目的の下で、投資家に示すための投資採算価値を表す価格を求める場合
2) 民事再生法に基づく評価目的の下で、早期売却を前提とした価格を求める場合
3) 会社更生法又は民事再生法に基づく評価目的の下で、事業の継続を前提とした価格を求める場合

(b) **正常価格以外の価格**（Value Other Than Market Value）
①**限定価格**（Special Value ⇒第3編「基準総論」第5章第3節）
市場性を有する不動産について、不動産と取得する他の不動産との併合又は不動産の一部を取得する際の分割等に基づき市場価値と乖離することにより、市場が相対的に限定される場合における取得部分の当該市場限定に基づく価値。
②**特殊価格**（Value of Special-Purpose Property ⇒第3編「基準総論」第5章第3節）
特殊価格とは、文化財等の一般的に市場性を有しない不動産について、その利用現況等を前提とした不動産の経済価値を適正に表示する価格。
③**投資価値**（Investment Value）
米国では、特定の投資家を前提として、融資手段、税法上の特典、投資リスクの認識の違い等を反映したキャッシュフローと収益率による価値を投資価値というが、日本の鑑定評価基準には規定がない。

4．鑑定評価の方式・手順

(a) 鑑定評価方式の適用に当たっては、鑑定評価法方式を当該案件に即して適切に適用すべきである。この場合、原則として、原価方式、比較方式及び収益方式の3方式を併用すべきであり、対象不動産の種類、所在地の実情、資料の信頼性等により3方式の併用が困難な場合においても、その考え方をできるだけ参酌するように努める。
以下は価格を求める場合の3方式であるが（⇒第3編「基準総論」第7章第1節）、賃料を求める場合もこれに準じる（⇒第3編「基準総論」第7章第2節）。
①**原価方式**：原価法は、価格時点における対象不動産の再調達原価を求め、この再調達原価について減価修正を行って対象不動産の積算価格を求める手法である。
②**比較方式**：比較方式は、最近の取引事例について、比較要因を、対象物件に即した市場での比較単位によって比較し、補正を行って比準価格を求める手法である。
③**収益方式**：収益方式は、不動産から生み出される収益（NCF又は資本的支出を控除した修正後運営純収益NOI）に着目し、直接還元法又はDCF法によって収益価格を求める手法である。

The sales comparison approach estimates value by comparing the subject property with other comparables properties that recently have sold. The sales price of comparables must be adjusted for elements of comparison through units of comparison which differ for different property type.

③Income Capitalization Approach :

The income capitalization approach estimates the present value of the Net Cash Flow (or Adjusted Net Operating Income considering a capital expenditures and operating profit on lump-sum payments) that the subject property is expected to generate in a future period, through the direct capitalization method or the DCF method.

(b) **Appraisal of Securitization-Properties**

When appraising the value of a securitization-property by the income capitalization approach, DCF methods must be applied. Then, it is appropriate to apply direct capitalization method for verification. The appraiser must form a final opinion of value after reexamining a relationship between the value indicated by the Income approach and the indicated value by the cost approach and sales comparison approach. and meaningfully and defensibly state the reconciliation grounds for the final opinion in the appraisal report. (see Part 3 GS. Chap.3 Sec. 4)

(c) **Appraisal of Overseas Investment Properties**

The licensed real estate appraiser (LREA) may conduct an appraisal according to the approved or officially authorized real estate appraisal standards of a specific overseas country in collaboration with an approved or officially authorized professional real estate appraiser of the overseas country (see Part 5 GL. I (2)).

5. Appraisal Reports

(a) **Minimum content of reports**

The document used by an LREA who has performed an appraisal when reporting the appraisal results to his/her real estate appraisal firm is called an "appraisal report". The standards specify how this report is to be prepared and what information it is to contain (see Part 3 GS. Chap.9 Sec.2). Using the appraisal report as a draft, the real estate appraisal firm must issue to the client an "appraisal document" containing the final opinion of value and other required matters (see Part 2 Article 39).

The report must clearly indicate how matters were handled that could not be clarified because of limitations on, or insufficiency of, data at any stage of the appraisal process (e.g., in identifying the subject property, reviewing the data compiled, or analyzing value influences). LREAs must describe the scope and content of the investigations they themselves conducted, and when they made use of investigations conducted by other professionals, the scope and content of those investigations must be clearly indicated (see Part 3 GS. Chap.9).

(b) **Appraisal of Securitization- Properties**

The LREA must take care as to the way information is presented in the appraisal report in order to make the content of the appraisal report easier for the client, persons holding interests in the securitization–property, and others to understand and use in compari-

(b) 証券化対象不動産の鑑定評価

証券化対象不動産の鑑定評価では、DCF法を適用しなければならない。この場合、併せて直接還元法によって検証する。さらに、収益価格を原価法及び取引事例比較法で求めた試算価格との関係について明確にして、鑑定評価額を決定する（⇒第3編「基準各論」第3章第4節）。

(c) 海外投資不動産の鑑定評価

海外投資不動産の鑑定評価では、不動産鑑定士が、海外現地において専門職業家として認定又は公認された鑑定人との連携・共同作業によって、海外現地において認定又は公認された鑑定評価基準に基づいて鑑定評価を行う（⇒第5編「ガイドライン」Ⅰ(2)）。

5．鑑定評価報告書

(a) 必要的記載事項

鑑定評価を行った不動産鑑定士が、自らが所属する不動産鑑定業者に対して報告する鑑定評価の成果を記載した文書を「鑑定評価報告書」といい、作成方針や記載事項については基準に定める（⇒第3編「基準総論」第9章第2節）。不動産鑑定業者は、鑑定評価報告書を素案として、依頼者に対し、鑑定評価額その他別に定める事項を記載した「鑑定評価書」を交付しなければならない（⇒第2編「鑑定評価法」第39条）。

鑑定評価の手順の各段階において、資料収集の限界、資料の不備等によって明らかにすることができない事項が存する場合には、不動産鑑定士が自ら行った調査の範囲及び内容を明確にするとともに、他の専門家が行った調査結果等を活用した場合において、当該専門家が調査した範囲及び内容を明確にする（⇒第3編「基準総論」第9章）。

(b) 証券化対象不動産の鑑定評価

証券化対象不動産の鑑定評価書については、依頼者及び証券化対象不動産に係る利害関係者その他の者がその内容を容易に把握・比較することができるようにするため、鑑定評価報告書の記載方法等を工夫し、及び鑑定評価書に活用した資料等を明示することができるようにするなど説明

Chapter 2. I. Japan : Real Estate Appraisal Standards

son with reports on other properties. The LREA must be fully accountable, ensuring that the following data and other informational materials used in the appraisal are available for disclosure. (see Part 3 SS. Chap.3 Sec.1)

①Records of verified information (see Part 3 SS. Chap.3 Sec.2 II)
②Purpose of the request for the appraisal, and the relationship between the client and the parties involved in the securitization of the property (see Part 3 SS. Chap.3 Sec.2 III)
③Property inspection (see Part 3 SS. Chap.3 Sec.3 II)
④Engineering report and the property investigation by the LREA (see Part 3 SS. Chap.3 Sec.3 III)
⑤Clarifying the procedure for applying DCF analysis (see Part 3 SS. Chap.3 Sec.4 I)
⑥Uniformity in income and expense items in DCF analysis (see Part 3 SS.Chap.3 Sec.4 II)

When using DCF analysis to estimate the value by the income approach, the income and expense items must be entered in the appraisal report for each of several continuous time periods, classified according to the items shown in the attached table (see attached table at page). Each of the income and expense items should be accompanied by a breakdown of how the figures were calculated. When entering this data in the appraisal report, each item of the attached table should be defined as specified in the table.

(c) **Appraisal of Overseas Investment Properties**

According to the Part 5 Guideline for the Appraisal of Overseas Investment Properties, an effort should be made to include all items that are required by the Japanese Standards. If there are items that are considered necessary for inclusion under the Japanese Standards, but which are not considered essential in the real estate market of the overseas country and are not ordinarily included in appraisal reports by local appraisers, it is then acceptable to omit these items. However, in this case the reasons for their omission must be stated.

(d) **Verbal report**

No description of verbal reports exist under the law and Standards.

6. Implementation of Appraisal Standards

(a) The Real Estate Appraisal Act provides that a licensed real estate appraiser (LREA) has an exclusive status to perform appraisals which play an important role in contributing to the public good, namely appropriate price setting in the real estate market.

At the same time the appraiser may be held liable for breach of the standards and administrative sanctions may be imposed for improper or illegal appraisal practices.

①Revocation of LREA Registration or suspension of Appraisal practice, for improper practice including intentional unjust or improper practice (Article 40 - I) or illegal practice including breach of confidentiality (Article 6) or violation of registered operation (Article 33).

②Reprimand or suspension of appraisal practice, for illegal or improper practice in a

責任が十分に果たされるものとする（⇒第3編「基準各論」第3章第1節）。
①確認事項の記録（⇒第3編「基準各論」第3章第2節Ⅱ）
②鑑定評価の依頼目的及び依頼者の証券化関係者との関係（⇒第3編「基準各論」第3章第2節Ⅲ）
③実地調査（⇒第3編「基準各論」第3章第3節Ⅱ）
④エンジニアリング・レポート（⇒第3編「基準各論」第3章第3節Ⅲ）
⑤DCF法の適用過程等の明細化（⇒第3編「基準各論」第3章第4節Ⅰ）
⑥DCF法の収益費用項目の統一等（⇒第3編「基準各論」第3章第4節Ⅱ）
　DCF法の適用により収益価格を求めるに当たっては、証券化対象不動産に係る収益又は費用の額につき、連続する複数の期間ごとに、一定の収益費用項目に区分して鑑定評価報告書に記載する。また、収益費用項目及びその定義について依頼者に提示・説明したうえで必要な資料を入手するとともに、収益費用項目ごとに定められた定義に該当していることを確認する。

(c) 海外投資不動産の鑑定評価

　第5編「海外投資不動産鑑定評価ガイドライン」によると、鑑定評価基準で必要な記載事項とされている内容は、できる限り記載する。ただし、海外現地の不動産市場においては重視されず、現地鑑定評価報告書に記載されないことが通常である場合には記載しないこととして差し支えないが、その合理的理由を記載する。また、①不動産鑑定士及び現地鑑定人の連携・共同作業の役割分担、②海外現地の不動産市場の動向に関する事項等、③現地鑑定検証方式における検証内容等について追加的に記載する。

(d) 口頭の報告

　鑑定評価基準に規定はなく、認められない。

6．鑑定評価基準の履行

(a)　不動産鑑定士は、不動産の鑑定評価を通じて土地等の適正な価格形成という公共の福祉に重大な関係を有することから、鑑定評価業務に関して独占的地位を与えられるとともに、法及び基準に定める行政上の責務を負う。すなわち、不動産鑑定士が、①故意に不正又は著しく不当な鑑定評価等業務を行ったとき（⇒第2編「鑑定評価法」第40条1項前段）並びに第6条の守秘義務違反及び第33条の無登録業務を行ったとき（同法第40条1項後段）は懲戒処分（鑑定士の登録消除又は業務禁止）、②相当な注意を怠って不正又は著しく不当な鑑定評価等業務を行ったとき（同法第40条2項）は懲戒処分（戒告又は業務禁止）となる。また、不動産鑑定士が不正又は著しく不当な鑑定評価等を行ったことを疑うに足りる事実があるときは、何人も、国土交通大臣又は都道府県知事に対し、資料を添えてその事実を報告し、適当な措置をとるべきことを求めることができる（同法第42条）。不動産鑑定士でない者による鑑定評価は禁止する（同法第36条）。

negligence manner (Article 40 - Ⅱ).

If there are grounds for reasonable suspicion that the LREA has committed an improper practice, any person may claim those matters to the Minister of Land, Infrastructure, Transport and Tourism or the governor of the prefecture in which the LREA is registered, appending documentation: and may request that the appropriate disciplinary measures be taken (Article 42). A person who is not designated as a LREA shall not perform real estate appraisal (Article 36).

(b) **Monitoring**

To determine and verify adherence to appraisal standards in the performance of appraisal duties, as well as to ensure the positive impact of appraisal on real estate securitization, the market for real estate sales, etc., appraisals are monitored by means of the following:

①On-site inspection of real estate firms, and the submission of appraisal reports (Vol. 2, Appraisal Act, Article 45, Paragraph 1).

②Investigation of documentation regarding the organization and business situation of real estate firms.

③Interviews with appraisal clients and so on.

The results of such monitoring are utilized in the everyday efforts of appraisal firms and appraisers, in resolving practical issues of the Japanese Association of Real Estate Appraisal, and in issuing guidance and taking disciplinary measures for appraisal firms and appraisers, in order to build an environment for conducting appropriate appraisals, and to maintain and improve the reliability of the real estate appraisal system.

7. Availability of Data

(a) **Specific Data (Primary Data)**

Since 2006, it has been possible to search for sale price information, published land prices, and researched land prices using Information of Land Synthesis System run by the Ministry of Land, Infrastructure, Transport and Tourism (www.tochi.mlit.go.jp). The sale price information includes survey responses from participants in transactions and sales data cards from appraisers.

Home and building agents (real estate agents) can search for actual prices and other transaction information for properties that have been sold (REINS market information) within a Real Estate Information Network System (REINS), of which there are four for the nation's regions (www.contract.reins.or.jp). Information on properties for sale or lease can be found at Real Estate Japan, which is operated by the Real Estate Transaction Modernization Center (www.fudousan.or.jp) and Home Navi, which is operated by the Association of Real Estate Agents of Japan (www.homenavi.or.jp).

(b) **General Data (Secondary Data)**

Considerable demographic and economic data are collected centrally and at the local government level. General data on real estate is also available from the private sector including the Japan Real Estate Institute (www.reinet.or.jp). Members of the Association for Real Estate Securitization can obtain information on the J-REIT market and in-

(b) 証券化対象不動産の鑑定評価に係る監視検証（Monitoring）

鑑定評価のモニタリングは、①鑑定業者への立入検査と鑑定評価書の提出（⇒第2編「鑑定評価法」第45条1項）、②鑑定業者の体制・受注状況等に関する書面調査、③鑑定評価の依頼者等からのヒアリング等によって、鑑定評価業務における鑑定評価基準の適用状況や、鑑定評価が不動産証券化や不動産取引市場などに及ぼす影響等について把握・検証する。その結果を、鑑定業者や鑑定士の日頃の取り組み、鑑定協会における実務の課題の解決、鑑定業者や鑑定士の処分・指導に反映させて、適正な鑑定評価が実施される環境を整備し、不動産鑑定評価制度の信頼性の維持・向上の実現を図る。

7. 鑑定評価に利用するデータ

(a) 個別データ（Specific Data）

2006年以降、国土交通省による土地総合情報システム（Information of Land Synthesis System）から、「取引価格情報」、「地価公示価格」、「地価調査価格」を検索できる（www.tochi.mlit.go.jp）。このうち「取引価格情報」は、取引当事者からの調査回答及び鑑定士から提供される取引事例カード等から構成されている。

なお、宅地建物取引業者（不動産業者）間では、全国で地域ごとに4つ指定された指定流通機構（REINS: Real Estate Information Network System）が保有している実際に売買が行われた成約物件の価格等の取引情報（REINS Market Information）を検索できる（www.contract.reins.or.jp）。また、売り出し物件・貸し出し物件等に関する情報は、㈶不動産流通近代化センターが運営する総合不動産情報サイト「不動産ジャパン」（www.fudousan.or.jp）、㈳不動産流通経営協会が運営する「Home Navi」（www.homenavi.or.jp）から検索できる。

(b) 一般データ（General Data）

㈶日本不動産研究所（www.reinet.or.jp）ほか、ネットを通じて多くの情報にアクセスが可能である。不動産証券化に関しては、㈳不動産証券化協会（ARES）の会員は、J-REIT市場の概況や各投資法人に関する情報（J-REIT View）のほか、J-REITの保有物件に関する情報（ARES J-REIT Property Database）を検索できる（www.ares.or.jp）。

vestment corporations (J-REIT View) as well as information on the properties held by J-REITs (ARES J-REIT Property Database) at the association's website (www. ares. or.jp).

8. Specific Appraisal Standards for Securitization Purposes

According to Part 3 Specific Standards. Chapter 3., the term "securitization-properties" refers to properties (including those held under trust beneficiary rights), which are subject to or likely to become subject to a real estate transaction under the certain regulations including the Asset Liquidation Law and the Investment Trust and Investment Corporation Law The appraisal of securitization properties must be conducted as is prescribed in this chapter. A statement to this effect must be included in the appraisal report.

When J-REITs include overseas investment properties in their asset portfolios, the appraisal procedures and principles specified at Part 5 GL will be applied and be subject to guidance and supervision under the Real Estate Appraisal Act.

8．証券化に関する基準

「資産流動化法（改正 SPC 法）」及び「投信法」のほかに、「不動産特定共同事業法」及び「金融商品取引法」に該当する不動産取引の目的である不動産又はその見込みのある不動産（信託受益権の取引も含まれる）の取引には、不動産の鑑定評価が必要である。J-REIT が海外不動産を組み入れる場合に要請される不動産鑑定士による鑑定評価については、「海外投資不動産鑑定評価ガイドライン」を逸脱することにより不当な鑑定評価が行われた場合には、鑑定評価法に基づく指導監督が行われるものとしている（⇒第 5 編「ガイドライン」XII）。

Chapter 2. II. USA (USPAP)

II. USA : *Uniform Standards of Professional Appraisal Practice (USPAP)*

For the purpose of introducing Japan Real Estate Appraisal System in a global context, The author has often referred to Uniform Standards of Professional Appraisal Practice (USPAP) 2007 published by the Appraisal Foundation that holds the copyrights. No responsibility is accepted by the RICS for the accuracy of the author's understanding contained in the text. The full text of USPAQP may be obtained from the Appraisal Foundation, 1155 15th Street, NW, Suite 1111, Washington, DC 200005 US. http://www.appraisalfoundation.org.

1. Framework of Appraisal Standards

(a) **Who Writes Appraisal Standards?**

①Appraisal Foundation

The Appraisal Foundation, a private nonprofit corporation composed of eight major appraisal organizations including the Appraisal Institute, was established in 1987. The foundation has developed and administered uniform appraisal standards called the Uniform Standards of Professional Appraisal Practice (USPAP). These standards apply to appraisal services to be performed with professionalism, independence, fairness, and objectivity on the part of appraisers. Title XI of the Financial Institutions Reform, Recovery and Enforcement Act of 1989 (FIRREA) provided recognition and authorized financial institution regulatory agencies to reference USPAP in their regulations.

②Appraisal Institute

The Appraisal Institute, an appraisal sponsor of The Appraisal Foundation, has developed and published the Standards of Professional Appraisal Practice. It is composed of the USPAP and the Certification Standards of the AI ; the IVS applicable national Standards, and the Certificate Standards of the AI. AI has also adopted the Guidance Note to the Standards of Professional Appraisal Practice to provide members with guidance as to how the requirements of the Standards may apply in specific situations.

(b) **For whom Appraisal Standards are written ? (Principal purposes of appraisal standards)**

The first paragraph of the preamble of USPAP states: The purpose of USPAP is to promote and maintain a high level of public trust in appraisal practice by establishing requirements for appraisers. It is essential that appraisers develop and communicate their analyses, opinions, and conclusions to intended users of their services in a manner that is meaningful and not misleading.

Although the main function of USPAP is not to protect appraisers, appraisers who comply with USPAP are viewed as unbiased professionals whose work is worthy of public trust.

(c) **Who must abide by the Standards and what services must comply? (Compliance with appraisal standards)**

Ⅱ．米国：鑑定評価業務統一基準（USPAP）

日本の不動産鑑定評価基準を国際的文脈から検証するために、米国鑑定財団が著作権を有し発行している米国鑑定評価業務統一基準（USPAP）を、執筆者による同基準の理解と責任で引用している。同鑑定評価業務統一基準の全文は、「The Appraisal Foundation, 1155 15th Street, NW, Suite 1111, Washington, DC 200005 US.」から入手できる。http://www.appraisalfoundation.org.

1．鑑定評価の制度枠組み

(a) 鑑定評価基準の策定主体
民間の鑑定評価団体が自主規制として鑑定評価基準を策定している。

①鑑定財団（Appraisal Foundation）
1987年、不動産鑑定協会（Appraisal Institute）など主要評価団体8機関から構成する、民間非営利の鑑定財団（Appraisal Foundation）が発足し、鑑定評価業務統一基準（Uniform Standards of Professional Appraisal Practice：USPAP）を策定・運用することになった。USPAPが対象とする評価業務は、鑑定人として独立・中立性、客観性をもって行う鑑定評価業務である。1989年、金融機関改革・再生・執行法（FIRREA）が制定され、同法第11章が、連邦金融機関に対して、USPAPを評価基準とすることを認めている。

②不動産鑑定協会（Appraisal Institute）
鑑定財団の主要スポンサーである不動産鑑定協会は、会員に対して、倫理規程（Code of Professional Ethics）及び「鑑定評価基準（Standards of Professional Appraisal Practice）」を策定している。同基準は、USPAP及びAI認証基準又は国際評価基準準用及びAI認証基準からなる。また、基準の適用に当たっての留意事項（Guidance Note）を策定している。

(b) 基準の目的
鑑定評価業務統一基準は、鑑定人に求められる要件を規定し、鑑定業務に対する社会の信頼を高いレベルに向上、維持することを目的とする。鑑定人は、鑑定評価の利用者に対して、誤解を与えない方法で、自分の分析と結論を伝えなくてはならない。基準は鑑定人を保護することを主たる目的とするものではないが、基準を遵守する鑑定人は社会の信頼を担う専門職とみられる。

(c) 基準の対象
不動産、動産、企業（business）を対象とする鑑定評価（appraisal）の実施及び報告。不動産の

Chapter 2. Ⅱ. USA (USPAP)

The third paragraph of the preamble of USPAP states: USPAP does not establish who or which assignments must comply. Neither The Appraisal Foundation nor its ASB is a government entity with the power to make, judge, or enforce law. Compliance with USPAP is required when either the service or the appraiser is obligated to comply by law or regulation, or by agreement with the client or intended users. When not obligated, individuals may still choose to comply.

USPAP clarifies the difference between valuation services, which are performed by many professionals, including appraiser, and appraisal practice, which pertains solely to those valuation services performed only by appraisers and requiring independence, impartiality, and objectivity. This distinction rests on whether the practitioner is functioning in the role of an appraiser. USPAP contains the recognized standards of practice for real estate, personal and business appraisal. The organization of the USPAP follows:

①Ethic Rule: Conduct, Management, Confidentiality, Record Keeping
    Competency Rule
    Scope of Work Rule
    Jurisdictional Exception Rule
    Supplemental Standards Rule
    Standards and Standards Rule:

Standard 1	Real Property Appraisal, Development
Standard 2	Real Property Appraisal, Reporting
Standard 3	Appraisal Review, Development and Reporting
Standard 4	Real Property Appraisal Consulting, Development
Standard 5	Real Property Appraisal, Reporting
Standard 6	Mass Appraisal, Development and Reporting
Standard 7	Personal Property Appraisal, Development
Standard 8	Personal Property Appraisal, Reporting
Standard 9	Business Appraisal, Development
Standard10	Business Appraisal, Reporting

②Statements on Appraisal Standards (SMT)

SMT-1	Appraisal Review -Retired
SMT-2	Discounted Cash Flow Analysis
SMT-3	Retrospective Value Opinion
SMT-4	Prospective Value Opinion
SMT-5	Confidentiality Section of the Ethics Rule-Retired
SMT-6	Reasonable Exposure Time in Real Property and Personal Property Market Value Opinion
SMT-7	Permitted Departure from Specific Requirements in Real Property and Personal Property Appraisal Assignments-Retired
SMT-8	Electronic Transmission of Reports -Retired
SMT-9	Identification of Intended Use and Intended User
SMT-10	Assignments fo Use by a Federally Insured Depository Institution in a Federally Related Transaction-Retired

評価は鑑定人（appraiser）以外の者によっても広く行われているが、USPAP が対象とする鑑定評価（appraisal）は、このうち、鑑定人として、すなわち、専門能力に基づいて（competently）、外部から独立して（independent）、公正中立に（impartial）、客観的事実に基づいて（objective）評価を行うものと期待される。鑑定評価は、狭義の鑑定評価（appraisal：価値の判断）、鑑定評価コンサルティング（appraisal consulting：問題解決のための分析・意見）、審査（appraisal review）に三分されるが、相互に重なることもある。

　USPAP の構成は次のとおりである。まず、基準で使用する用語の「定義」、「序文」、「倫理規定（Rule）」、「能力規定」、「業務範囲規定」、「裁判管轄例外規定」、「補足基準規定」を規定する。そのうえで、①基準（Standards）、②基準規定（Standards Rules）、③留意事項（Statement、SMT）、④参考意見（Advisory Opinion）を置いている。基準の解釈、詳述を内容とする留意事項は基準規定と同様の重要性を持つが、参考意見は鑑定基準委員会の参考意見、助言を提案するものである。
（基準・基準規定、留意事項、意見留意事項）

①基準・基準規定
　　　　基準1　　　不動産鑑定の実施
　　　　基準2　　　不動産鑑定の報告
　　　　基準3　　　鑑定の審査
　　　　基準4　　　鑑定コンサルティングの実施
　　　　基準5　　　鑑定コンサルティングの報告
　　　　基準6　　　大量評価の実施
　　　　基準7　　　動産鑑定の実施
　　　　基準8　　　動産鑑定の報告
　　　　基準9　　　企業評価の実施
　　　　基準10　　企業評価の報告

②留意事項（SMT）
　　　　SMT-1　　　鑑定の審査―削除
　　　　SMT-2　　　DCF 法
　　　　SMT-3　　　過去時点の評価
　　　　SMT-4　　　将来時点の評価
　　　　SMT-5　　　倫理規定のうちの守秘義務-削除
　　　　SMT-6　　　Reasonable Exposure Time in Real Property and Personal Property Market Value Opinion
　　　　SMT-7　　　Permitted Departure from Specific Requirements in Real Property and Personal Property Appraisal Assignments―削除
　　　　SMT-8　　　Electronic Transmission of Reports―削除
　　　　SMT-9　　　利用者及び利用目的
　　　　SMT-10　　Assignments for Use by a Federally Insured Depository Institution in a Federally Related Transaction―削除

③参考意見

③Advisory Opinions
(d) **Licensing / Certification**
①State Licensed or Certified Real Estate Appraiser

The power of regulation currently rests with the individual states and territories that issue licenses and certificates to real property appraisers. FIRREA requires that real estate appraisal developed by a state licensed or certified real estate appraiser in conjunction with federally-related transactions (FIRREA Chapter 10. Article 1121) be performed in advance with USPAP. More than 80,000 state certified and licensed appraisers are currently required to adhere to USPAP.

②Designation

An appraisal designation is awarded by one of many professional organizations including Appraisal Institute. A professional organization provides appraisers with the opportunity to network with other professionals, to keep abreast of pertinent issues such as regulatory changes, and to receive continuing education. Other distinguished organization includes the Counselor of Real Estate (CRE) for real estate counseling and the American Society of Appraisers (ASA) for personal and business appraisals.

2. Fundamentals for Appraisal

(a) **Real Property Rights and Interests to be Appraised**

"Land" is legally defined in the same way as "real estate", encompassing the surface, the ground underneath the surface, and the space immediately above it. Further, items fixed to the land (such as buildings) are treated as part of the land. Ownership (exclusive control) of the land can be either a freehold (fee simple), in which no time limit is established; or a leasehold, in which a time limit is specified. However, this is simply a distinction in terms of the amount of time; and there is no essential difference.

The acquisition and preservation of ownership follows the process of first signing a sales contract, followed by a due diligence period and then the transferal procedures. At the stage of transferal procedures, the escrow company submits a transferal certificate to the registry office. The registry office does not gather records together for each individual property, but files copies of the transferal certificates for each title transfer in the order that they were received, and only adjusts the ledger of conveyors and recipients (personal basis of organization). (However, in a few states including Hawaii and New York, records are compiled for each individual property according to a physical basis of organization, and these records can be accessed online.) The buildings are considered as a part of the land, and buildings are not registered independently of land.

(b) **Scope of Work**

An appraiser must identify the problem to be solved; determine and perform the scope of work necessary to develop credible assignment results; and disclose the scope of work in the report. Therefore, an appraiser must not allow assignment conditions to limit the scope of work to such a degree that the assignment results are not credible in

(d) ライセンス・会員

①ライセンス

1989年、金融機関改革・再生執行法（FIRREA）によって、連邦政府が関わる一定の不動産金融取引には州のライセンスを持つ鑑定人の評価が必要。同法に基づく金融機関審議会・鑑定評価委員会（Appraisal Subcommittee）が、各州の評価を統括し、現在は民間8評価団体から構成される鑑定財団を監督・支援。

②資格称号

不動産の鑑定評価については不動産鑑定協会のMAI、SRPA、SRA、動産・企業の鑑定評価についてはASA（American Society of Appraisers）、コンサルティングについてはカウンセラー協会（The Counselors of Real Estate: CRE）。

2. 鑑定評価の前提

(a) 鑑定評価の対象となる権利・利益

「土地（land）」は、「不動産（real estate）」と同義で、法的には土地の表面、その地下、その真上の空間を含む。さらに、土地に付着している定着物（例えば建物）も土地の一部となる。土地に対する「保有権（ownership：排他的支配を内容とする）」は、期限が不確定のフリーホールド（freehold／fee simple）と期限が確定しているリースホールド（leasehold）に分類されるが、単なる期間という量の差であり本質的な差異はない。保有権の取得及び保全は、売買契約締結→デューディリ→譲渡手続きのプロセスの順に進む。譲渡手続きの段階では、エスクロー会社が譲渡証書を登記所に提出する。登記所は、個々の不動産ごとに登記を編成することをせず、個々の権利変動の譲渡証書のコピーを受付順にファイルし、譲渡人及び譲受人の名簿を備えるだけである（人的編成主義。ただし、ハワイ、ニューヨークなど少数の州では、個々の土地ごとの物的編成主義で、ネットで検索が可能である（www.nyc.gov））。建物は土地と一体とされ、独立した建物登記はない。

(b) 業務の範囲（Scope of Work）

鑑定人は、鑑定評価の利用目的に基づいて対象とする問題が何であるかを明確にし、それに対して信頼できる回答を下すのに必要な業務の範囲を依頼者との間で取り決めて、その具体的内容を報告書の中で開示しなくてはならない。したがって、鑑定評価の利用目的に対して信頼できる結論を導けないような業務の範囲に絞ることは許されない。米国鑑定評価業務統一基準（USPAP）

Chapter 2. II. USA (USPAP)

the context of the intended use. A appraiser must withdraw from the assignment.

Starting in 2006/7, the "departure rule", which permits deviation from certain standards, was abolished and the "scope of work rule" was adopted, defining the scope of appraisal work broadly and flexibly, in a similar manner to the work of attorneys and other legal professions. (The distinction between "complete appraisal" and "limited appraisal" was abandoned.) As a result, risk is shared between the appraiser and the client; so reports are now required to disclose detailed information (Scope Disclosure).

(c) **Assumptions**

"General assumption and limiting condition" must be reasonable and supportable in the context of the appraisal and must not conflict with the appraiser's other responsibilities such as extraordinary assumptions and hypothetical conditions; "extraordinary assumptions" presume uncertain information to be factual and if found to be false these assumptions could alter the appraiser's opinions or conclusions; "hypothetical conditions" are contrary to what exists, but the conditions are asserted by the appraiser for the purpose of analysis.

(d) **Appraisal Reviews**

In performing an appraisal review assignment, an appraiser acting as a reviewer must develop and report a credible opinion as to the quality of another appraiser's work and must disclose the scope of work performed (Standard 3). When the reviewer's scope of work includes expressing his or her own opinion of value, that opinion is an appraisal (Standards Rule 3-1(a)). The reviewer may include his or her own value opinion within the appraisal review report itself without preparing a separate appraisal report (Standards Rule 3-2).

3. General Concepts and Principles (Valuation Bases)

(a) **Market Value**

Market value is a value estimate made as of a specific date that represents the most probable price that a seller could expect to command for a specific interest in real property, assuming a typical, knowledgeable investor, a reasonable marketing time, and a sale made in cash or its equivalent.

①Highest and Best Use (HABU)

Highest and best use is defined as the reasonable and probable use that results in the highest present value of the land or property after considering all legally permissible, physically possible, and financially feasible. In appraisal practice, the concept of HABU represents the premise on which value is based. The test of HABU must be applied first to the land as if vacant and then to the property as improved. The HABU for the property as improved may be the same or different from the HABU of the land as if vacant. If the HABU for the property is not the same as the land as if vacant, the HABU as improved is referred to as the Highest and Best Interim Use.

②Exposure time

The reasonable exposure time inherent in the market value concept is always presumed to precede the effective date of the appraisal.

は、2006年7月から、基準からの一定の逸脱を内容とする「Departure Rule」を撤廃し、弁護士等の専門職業と同様に柔軟に鑑定評価業務の内容を決め、余計なコストも減る「業務の範囲ルール（Scope of Work Rule）」を採用している。これによって、鑑定人と依頼者の間で評価上の不確定要因に伴うリスクを分けあうことになるから、業務の範囲については、報告書の中で詳細な情報開示が要請される（Scope Disclosure）。

(c) 評価の前提条件

鑑定評価の前提となる条件には、特別な想定条件（extraordinary assumption）、仮定条件（hypothetical condition）がある。特別な想定条件は、対象不動産の物的、法的又は経済的要因について、あるいは対象不動産に外在する要因について、不確かな内容の情報を事実と想定する条件である。例えば、鑑定人が土壌汚染について不明である、確信がもてない場合、汚染がないものと想定して評価する。汚染の存在について認識した場合は、この想定で評価はできない。ただし、汚染を原因とする価値の減価を示すための汚染前後の分析など一定の場合、汚染の事実に反する条件（仮定条件）の下で評価は可能である。

(d) 評価の審査（Review）

審査（レビュー）は、他の鑑定人が行った鑑定評価、鑑定審査、鑑定コンサルティングの全部又は一部について、レビュー業務の範囲を特定し明示したうえで、意見を報告する業務である。依頼人がレビューを行う鑑定人に対して、レビュー業務の範囲を拡大して鑑定評価額について意見（opinion of value）を求める場合もある。鑑定評価額に同意するかどうか、同意できないとすれば鑑定評価額はいくらかを示す（これも鑑定評価（appraisal）になる）。この場合、レビューの対象となる鑑定評価の手順を繰り返す必要はない。信頼できると判断した項目に基づく価値の判断であるという条件をつけて鑑定評価額について意見を報告する。

3．鑑定評価の基礎（価値の種類）

(a) 市場価値（Market Value）

特定の不動産について、マーケティングのための合理的期間（exposure time）、公開の競争市場、現金ないしそれと同等のファイナンス条件を前提に、典型的な投資家が投資（購入）するとした場合に、売主が見込むことができる最も確からしい価格である。鑑定人が求める価値は、原則として市場価値である。市場価値以外の価値を評価することもあるが、その場合は市場価値と峻別する。

①最有効使用（Highest and Best Use）

最有効使用とは、土地又は土地・建物一体としての不動産について、法的に許容され、物的に可能で、採算的に実現可能な選択肢のうちで、最高の現在価値をもたらす使用である。最有効使用は市場価値の前提にあり、まず「更地としての最有効使用」、次に「土地と建物を一体とした複合不動産としての最有効使用」の二面から判定する。両者が一致しないときには、暫定的最有効使用がありうる。

②市場公開期間（Exposure time）

市場公開期間は、価格時点の市場価値の実現に先立って市場に公開している期間。これに対して、マーケティング期間（marketing time）は価格時点後に市場で売却に要する期間。

(b) **Value Other Than Market Value**
①Investment Value
Investment value is the value of an income-producing property to a specific investor. If the return requirements of the investment mirror those of the typical buyer in the marketplace or dominate the marketplace, investment value and market value are identical. Otherwise, there could be a significant difference in the two values.
②Value in Use (Use Value)
The value of a real property as it is currently used, not its use considering alternative uses. Value in use is similar to investment value in that it reflects the requirements of a specific investor, Value in use differs from investment value, however, in representing the value of a real property to its current user.
③Plottage Value
Plottage value is an increment of value that results when two or more sites are combined to produce a larger site with greater utility.
④Value of Special-Purpose property
Limited -market property with a unique physical design, special construction materials, or a layout that restricts its utility to the use for which it was built.

4. Approaches to Value

In developing a real property appraisal, an appraiser must collect, verify, and analyze all information necessary for credible assignment results.

(a) **Cost Approach**
In this approach, value is based on adding the contributing value of any improvements (after deduction for accrued depreciation) to the value of the land as if it were vacant based on its highest and best use. When the existing improvements and land have the same highest and best use and the improvements have suffered little loss in value (depreciation) due to age, wear and tear functional problem, or external market problems, the cost approach is relatively reliable in estimating the value. When the site and improvements have a different HABU, when the improvements are older, or when market conditions are adverse, the cost approach would be suspect.

(b) **Sales Comparison Approach**
In this approach, value is estimated by comparing similar properties that have sold recently to the subject property. The reliability of an indication found by this approach depends on the quality of the comparable data found in the market place and the ability of the appraiser to make reasonable and supportable adjustments.

(c) **Income Capitalization Approach**
In this approach a property is viewed through the eyes of a typical investor, whose primary objective is to earn a profit on the investment principally through the receipt of expected income generated form operation and the ultimate resale of the property at the end of a holding period.

(b) 市場価値以外の価値（Value Other Than Market Value）
①投資価値（Investment Value）
投資価値は、特定の投資家を前提として、融資手段、税法上の特典、投資リスクの認識の違い等を反映したキャッシュフローと収益率による価値である。前提要件が典型的な投資家を反映する場合（または、特定の投資家が市場を支配（dominate）している場合）には、投資価値は市場価値と同じになる。
②使用価値（Use Value）
使用価値は、特定の投資家の要求を反映する点では投資価値と似ているが、現在の使用者による特定の使用を前提にする点で投資価値とは異なる。対象不動産は、そのスペースの現在の使用者にとって価値があるかもしれないが、別の使用者にとっては何ら付加価値を生じないものかもしれない。
③併合価値 （Plottage Value）
複数の不動産の併合によるシナジー効果を生み出す価値。
④特殊価値（Value of Special-Purpose Property）
特殊なデザイン、建築資材、レイアウトのために用途が限定されている価値。

4．鑑定評価の方式・手順

鑑定評価は、商業不動産では主として投資又は融資の過程で実施され、取引事例比較法及び収益還元法（新築の場合は、さらに原価法）を採用する。住宅では主として融資の過程で実施され、取引事例比較法（新築の場合は、さらに原価法）を採用する。

(a) 原価法（Cost Approach）
現存する建物等（発生した減価控除後の）の価値を、最有効使用をベースとした更地を想定した土地の価値に加算することを基礎として価値を求める方式。土地建物一体の複合不動産の最有効使用が更地の最有効使用と合致し、経過年数、損傷、機能性、市場性による建物価値の減少がほとんどない場合には、原価法は比較的高い信頼性を有する。

(b) 取引事例比較法（Sales Comparison Approach）
対象不動産を最近売買された類似の不動産と比較して価値を求める方式。この方式の信頼性は、取引事例データの質及び鑑定人がデータの格差修正を的確に行えるかどうかに依存する。

(c) 収益還元法（Income Capitalization Approach）
対象不動産から生み出されるキャッシュフロー、すなわち賃貸運営から生まれる期待収益及び投資期間の終了期の転売によって生まれる転売利益を、現在価値に還元して価値を導く方式。この方式の信頼性はデータの質と還元方式の適正な適用に依存する。取引事例比較法の格差修正にも収益還元法を利用する。

Chapter 2. Ⅱ. USA (USPAP)

5. Appraisal Reports

(a) **Minimum content of reports**

Each written appraisal report must be prepared under one of the following three options and prominently state which option is used:

①Self-Contained Appraisal Report

Client and any intended user, intended use, property interest, value, effective date and date of report, information analyzed, appraisal methods and techniques employed, reasoning that supports the analyses, opinions and conclusions.

②Summary Appraisal Report

③Restricted Use Appraisal Report

(b) **Intended User**

The client and any other party as identified, by name or type, as users of the appraisal, appraisal review, or appraisal consulting report by the appraiser on the basis of communication with the client at the time of the assignment. A restricted use appraisal report may only be used when the client is the only intended user. Eventual receipt of a copy of an appraisal, appraisal review, or appraisal consulting report does not make the recipient an intended user. To be an intended user the recipient must have been identified as such by the appraiser. Without clear knowledge of the intended users in an assignment, an appraiser cannot be certain that the report content is appropriate. (SMT-9)

(c) **Oral reports**

To the extent that it is both possible and appropriate, an oral real property appraisal report must address the substantive matters ser forth in Standards Rule 2.2. (SR.2.4)

6. Implementation of Appraisal Standards

(a) **Appraisal Foundation**

The foundation accomplishes its mission through the work of two independent Boards :

Appraisal Standards Boards (ASB) — It sets forth the rules for developing an appraisal and reporting its results. In addition, it promotes the use, understanding and enforcement of the USPAP.

Appraiser Qualifications Boards (AQB) — It establish the qualification criteria for state licensing, certification and recertification of appraisers.

(b) **Appraisal Institute**

Every member agrees to conduct his or her professional activities in accordance with the Code of Professional Ethics and Standards of Professional Appraisal Practice. In addition, the Appraisal Institute has developed a sophisticated peer review system through which it enforces Its Code of Professional Ethics and Standards of Professional Appraisal Practice. Violations of the Code of Ethics or Standards can result in remedial

5．鑑定評価報告書

(a) 必要的記載事項

鑑定評価報告書は、依頼者及び利用者、利用目的、評価対象不動産の確定、評価対象不動産の不動産権、価値の種類、価格時点、業務の範囲、鑑定評価の方式、条件、鑑定人署名を含み、3つのタイプがある。

① 完結型鑑定評価報告書（Self-Contained Appraisal Report）
② 要約型鑑定評価報告書（Summary Appraisal Report）
③ 利用制限付鑑定評価報告書（Restricted Use Appraisal Report）：利用者は依頼者のみであり、したがって評価についての十分な情報を得ている場合である。

(b) 鑑定評価の依頼者、利用目的及び利用者

依頼者（client）は、鑑定人との間の、特定の鑑定評価に関する契約当事者。契約では、鑑定評価の利用目的（intended use）を特定して、鑑定人の責任範囲を限定する。また、鑑定評価の利用者（intended user）を特定する（通常は依頼者であるが、依頼者以外の者が利用者となるケースもある）。

(c) 口頭の報告（Oral report）

口頭の報告も可能であるが、書面の報告と同様に、作業ファイルに記載する。

6．鑑定評価基準の履行

(a) 鑑定財団（Appraisal Foundation）

鑑定財団が二つの独立した委員会を設けて鑑定評価基準の履行をはかっている。鑑定基準委員会（Appraisal Standards Board：ASB）は、USPAPの利用、理解、及び実施を担当し、鑑定評価の実施及び鑑定評価書に関するルールづくりを行う委員会である。鑑定評価業務統一基準（USPAP）は、鑑定評価の基準（standards）とともに、基準に基づいて鑑定評価を実施する際に適用される倫理、職務資格、業務範囲等に関する規定（rule）も定めている。また、鑑定人資格委員会（Appraiser Qualification Board：AQB）は、課題となっている各州実施の鑑定評価のライセンス制度の充実を担当する委員会である。

(b) 不動産鑑定協会（Appraisal Institute）

不動産鑑定協会は、会員に対して、倫理規程（鑑定人の利益と依頼人の利益の衝突回避、依頼人の秘密遵守等）及び鑑定評価業務統一基準（USPAP補充項目及び留意事項）並びにそれらの遵守を担保する自主規制を定めている。鑑定評価を信頼した結果として損害が発生した場合、鑑定人は、契約関係（privity）がない第三者に対しても、報告書の不実記載、重過失、fraud（不正行為）を理由とする民事責任が生じる。そのため、鑑定評価の利用者の範囲を記載、第三者に開示されることを予想して免責条件記載、損害賠償保険、業務の範囲（Scope of Work）の限定を行う。業務の内容の正当化根拠は、市場データの正確性と分析に十分に注意を尽くしているかど

or disciplinary actions.

7. Availability of Data

(a) **Specific Data (Primary Data)**

In general, data collected by other survey organizations is obtained on a regular basis, not data personally collected by appraisers for each property. In addition to data from government agencies and nonprofit organizations (such as "www.reiac.org" and "www.ncreif.com"), data is also obtained for a fee from real estate investment related information service companies, which have shown rapid growth since the 1980s. Each of these information service companies collects data independently and uses it to create databases. This saves data purchasers the time and expense of collecting the data themselves. In addition to supply/demand data and market data for each city, each submarket, and each type of property, in some cases it is also possible to obtain sales data on individual properties. Although their data has a high level of market credibility, the information service companies do not guarantee the accuracy of their data, and verification is the responsibility of the appraisers who purchase and use this data.

Direct contact with participants in a transaction can not only lead to confirmation of information available in public records but may disclose information not otherwise known or available. Rental data is difficult to obtain, compared with sales data.

(b) **General Data (Secondary Data)**

General data are not gathered for a specific study at hand but are gathered by other sources and published typically on a periodic basis. In addition to government or nonprofit organization data (e.g., www.reiac.or.jp/ www. ncreif.com), private companies offer services that supply historical, current, and projected future forecast based on market area, and type of property.

8. Specific Appraisal Standards for Securitization Purposes

Not specifically referenced at the USPAP.
REIT companies perform internal assessments for business reasons. There are no rules requiring external assessments when acquiring, holding, or disposing of real estate. The reason is that purchasers (investors) of REIT shares make their investment decisions based both on how well the REIT company operates its properties as a portfolio, including cash flow, and on how the REIT company is valued by the stock market (share price), rather than on details about the individual properties owned by the company. Meanwhile nonpublic, privately-subscribed funds must explain investment performance to investors on the basis of the Global Investment Performance Standards (GIPS). Since the compensation of management companies is based on performance, explanations to investors must be based on external appraisal in addition to internal appraisal.

うかである。

7. 鑑定評価に利用するデータ

(a) 個別データ（Specific Data）

鑑定人が直接収集するデータには、事実関係に関する資料と数値に関する資料がある。1980年代以降急拡大している不動産投資関連情報サービス企業から、有料で個別データが入手できる。情報サービス企業はそれぞれ独自にデータを収集しデータベース化していて、データ購入者はデータ収集の費用と時間を節約できる。都市別・サブマーケット別・物件タイプ別の需給データ・市場データのほか、個別取引のデータ入手も可能である。賃貸事例データは、取引事例データと違って、入手は一般的に難しい。データの信頼性については、市場から高い評価を得ているものもあるが、情報サービス企業が信頼性を保証することはなく、データを購入して利用する鑑定人に検証責任がある。取引事例に関わった当事者に直接当たってみることは、公表されているデータの裏付けを取ることに留まらず、一般には明らかにされていない事実を見出す可能性がある。

(b) 一般データ（General Data）

鑑定人が個別案件のたびに独自に収集するデータではなく、他の調査主体が集めたデータを、通常は定期的に入手するものである。官庁・非営利団体データ（例えば、www.reiac.org や www.ncreif.com）の他に、民間から様々な経済データ及び人口データが入手できる。

8. 証券化に関する基準

USPAP（2007年）では特に規定はない。REIT 会社は、経営上の必要性から不動産の内部評価は行っているが、不動産を取得・保有・処分する際に外部評価が要求されるというルールはない。REIT 会社の株式の購入者（投資家）は、REIT 会社が保有する個別の不動産の内容よりも、ポートフォリオとしていかに管理運営してキャッシュフローの実績を与えるか、及びそれを株式市場がどのように評価しているか（株価）の双方に着目して投資を決定するからである。非公開の私募型ファンドの場合は GIPS（グローバル投資実績基準）に準拠して投資家に投資実績を説明する必要があり、さらに運用会社の受け取る報酬は実績を基準とする。したがって、内部評価のほかに外部評価によって投資家に説明する必要がある。

Chapter 2.Ⅲ. UK (RICS Valuation Standards)

Ⅲ. *UK : RICS Valuation Standards (Red Book)*

For the purpose of introducing Japan Real Estate Appraisal System in a global context, the author has often referred to the corresponding Valuation Standards (Red Book) 6th edition published by the Royal Institution of Chartered Surveyors (RICS) that holds the copyrights. No responsibility is accepted by the RICS for the accuracy of the author's understanding contained in the text. The full text of the official version of the Valuation Standards may be obtained from the RICS, Surveyor Court, Westwood Business Park, Coventry CV4 8JE UK. http://www.ricsbooks.com

1. Framework of Valuation Standards

(a) **Who writes Valuation Standards?**
The Royal Institution of Chartered Surveyors (RICS) has published valuation standards since 1974, which have colloquially become known as the "Red Book".

(b) **For whom Valuation Standards are written? (Principal purposes of valuation standards)**
The role of the RICS Valuation Standards is to provide an effective regulatory framework, within the Rules of Conducts, so that users of valuation services can have confidence that a valuation provided by an RICS member is not only in accordance with internationally recognized standards but that there is an obligation placed on the individual valuer or firm to follow these standards, and an effective sanction in the case of a material breach.

The Red book quotes large section of the Rules of Conduct to ensure that valuations produced by members achieve high standards of integrity, clarity and objectivity, and are reported in accordance with recognized bases that are appropriate for the purpose.

(c) **Who must abide by the Standards and what services must comply? (Compliance with valuation standards)**
The Red Book is to be applied by members in whatever state they operate. RICS recognizes that the member may be requested to provide a report that complies with valuation standards other than the RICS standards. Before treating such a request as a *departure* the member should establish if the RICS standards impose the same, or higher, standard and if so should include the following statement in the terms of engagement and the report: that the RICS standards impose the same or higher standard as the named standard and will therefore be compliant with those standards.

The subject of valuations includes real property, trade property including assets other than land and buildings, plants and equipments including tangible assets other than land and buildings, business, and financial interests.

The Red Book is divided into practice statement (PS) which have mandatory status, appendices (Appendix) which amplify the practice statement are only advisory, and the guidance notes (GN) which explain how the practice statement should be applied in particular situations and are not mandatory.

A significant change in the Red Book 5th Edition is that it distinguishes between

Ⅲ. 英国：RICS鑑定評価業務基準（Red Book）

日本の不動産鑑定評価基準を国際的文脈から検証するために、王立勅認サーベイヤー協会が著作権を有し発行している鑑定評価業務基準（Red Book）を、執筆者の同基準の理解と責任で引用している。同鑑定評価基準の全文は、「The RICS, Surveyor Court, Westwood Business Park, Coventry CV4 8JE UK」から入手できる。
http://www.ricsbooks.com

1．鑑定評価の制度枠組み

(a) 鑑定評価基準の策定主体
王立勅認サーベイヤー協会（The Royal Institution of Chartered Surveyors：RICS．1881年設立）

(b) 基準の目的
英国鑑定評価の中心的な役割を担う王立勅認サーベイヤー協会は、様々に解釈・運用されていた鑑定評価の考え方や手法を統一し、それに携わる専門家であるサーベイヤー（鑑定人）に対する独立性・客観性、説明責任、透明性等の行為規範及び利益相反に関する規制を強化して、通称「Red Book」と呼ばれる鑑定評価基準（RICS Valuation Standards）を策定している（1976年）。会員が行う評価が、高度の信頼性、明快性、客観性を備え、鑑定評価の目的に適った基礎（価値の種類）に則って実行されるようにする。

(c) 基準の対象
RICS基準（Red Book）第5版は、国内外を問わず適用される国際基準（global standards）と、国内のみで適用される国内基準（national standards）とに分けて規定する。どちらも、会員に対する強制力を持つ「実務指針（practical statement：以下PS又はUKPS）」、各実務基準を補うアドバイスを内容とする「付則（appendix：以下APP又はUKAPP）」及び各実務基準の適用に関する「留意事項（guidance notes：以下GN又はUKGN）」から構成されている。

RICSは国際評価基準（IVS）策定の推進母体であるが、RICS基準はIVSより詳細かつ厳格な内容になっていて、RICS基準に準拠していればIVSにも準拠したものとしている。RICS基準は、会員のサーベイヤーが何処の国で評価業務を行おうと適用される。会員がRICS基準以外の現地評価基準による評価を求められる場合は、RICS基準が認める例外（departure）として扱われるが、会員はその評価が現地基準を満たしていることを確認しなければならない。

基準の対象は、不動産、不動産以外の資産を含む事業用資産、不動産以外の機械及び工場を対象として書面（鑑定評価書）を発行する行為である。会員が行うアドバイスなどは対象とならない。

（一般規定）
（基準・付則・留意事項）
①国際実務基準（Practical Statement：PS）

global standards that apply to chartered surveyors undertaking valuations anywhere in the world and the national standards. The organization of the Red Book follows:

①Practical Statement (PS):
- PS1　　Compliance and ethical requirements
- PS2　　Agreements of terms of engagement
- PS3　　Basis of Value
- PS4　　Applications
- PS5　　Investigations
- PS6　　Valuation reports

②Guidance Notes (GN):
- GN1　　Trade related property valuations
- GN2　　Plant & equipment
- GN3　　Valuations of portfolios and groups of properties
- GN4　　Mineral-bearing land and waste management
- GN5　　Valuation uncertainty

③UK Practical Statement (UKPS):
- UKPS1　Valuations for financial statements
- UKPS2　Valuations fro financial statements-specific applications
- UKPS3　Valuations for loan facilities
- UKPS4　Residential property valuations (other than for mortgage purpose)
- UKPS5　Regulated purpose valuations

④UK Guidance Notes (UKGN):
- UKGN1　Inspection and material consideration
- UKGN2　Shared ownership of residential property
- UKGN3　Valuations for capital gain tax, inheritance tax and stamp duty land tax
- UKGN4　Valuation for charities
- UKGN5　Local authority disposed of land for less than best consideration

(d) **Licensing / Designation**

There are no license requirements in the UK so anyone can be called a valuer. In practice, most valuation work is undertaken by the chartered surveyors designated as FRICS or MRICS.

2. Fundamentals for Valuation

(a) **Real Property Rights and Interests to be Valued**

"Land" is legally defined in the same way as "real estate", encompassing the surface, the ground underneath the surface, and the space immediately above it. Further, items fixed to the land (such as buildings) are treated as part of the land. Ownership (exclusive control) of the land can be either a freehold (fee simple), in which no time limit is established; or a leasehold, in which a time limit is specified. However, this is simply a distinction in terms of the amount of time; and there is no essential difference. If leaseholders erect buildings on land, then at the time when the lease period expires, the

実務基準1	（PS1）	基準の遵守と倫理の要請
実務基準2	（PS2）	評価業務契約
実務基準3	（PS3）	評価の基礎（価値の種類）
実務基準4	（PS4）	評価基準の適用
実務基準5	（PS5）	実地調査
実務基準6	（PS6）	鑑定評価書

②国際実務基準留意事項（Guidance Notes : GN）

留意事項1	（GN1）	事業用不動産の評価
留意事項2	（GN2）	工場及び機械設備
留意事項3	（GN3）	ポートフォリオ及び複数不動産の一括評価
留意事項4	（GN4）	鉱物包蔵地及び廃棄物処理場
留意事項5	（GN5）	不確定要因

③国内実務基準（UK Practical Statement : UKPS）

国内実務基準1	（UKPS1）	財務報告のための評価
国内実務基準2	（UKPS2）	財務報告のための評価—具体的適用
国内実務基準3	（UKPS3）	融資のための評価
国内実務基準4	（UKPS4）	住宅の評価（融資以外のための評価）

④国内実務基準留意事項（UK Guidance Notes : UKGN）

留意事項1	（GN1）	実費及び重要な検討事項
留意事項2	（GN2）	住宅持分権
留意事項3	（GN3）	キャピタルゲイン税、相続税、印紙地租のための評価
留意事項4	（GN4）	慈善団体のための評価
留意事項5	（GN5）	最善の対価を下回る地方行政体の土地処分

(d) ライセンス・認定

RICSの会員のうち勅認サーベイヤーとは、MRICS及びFRICS（MRICS取得後、5年間のキャリアを経たシニア鑑定人）の資格称号を有する者をいう。

2．鑑定評価の前提

(a) 鑑定評価の対象となる権利・利益

「土地（land）」は、法的には、その土地の表面、その地下、その真上の空間を含む。さらに、土地に付着している定着物（例えば建物）も「土地」の一部となる。登記上も、建物は土地と一体とされ、独立した建物登記はない。土地（又は土地及び建物）に対する「保有権（包括的な排他的支配を内容とし、ownershipと総称）」は、日本法の所有権に相当する不確定期限のフリーホールド（freehold／fee simple）と、日本には相当するものがない確定期限のリースホールド（leasehold）に大別されるが（日本法の賃借権は契約による債権）、両者には本質的な差異はなく単なる期間という量の差である。土地のリースホールドを取得した者が土地上に建物を建て

leasehold ends and the land reverts to its freeholder, and the buildings are absorbed into land of the freeholder.

The records of the Land Registry office (one Land Registry in England and Wales with 24 regional offices) and are organized by each individual parcel of land, not by transferal certificate for each transfer as in the case of France and most states of the U.S. These records are computerized and can be accessed on the Internet (www.landregistry.gov.uk). The registry records consist of property registers, title registers, and tax liability registers. Records showing sales prices are included, in addition to ordnance survey maps showing the locations of sites and buildings. The buildings are considered as a part of the land, and buildings are not registered independently of land.

(b) **Terms of Engagement**

It is the written contact between the valuer and the client. The practice statement lists the following minimum mandatory requirements and the lists can be extended to suite the particular instruction. (PS2) :

(a) identification of the client, (b) the purpose of the valuation, (c) the subject of the valuation, (d) the interests to be valued, (e) the type of property and how it is used or classified by the client, (f) the basis or bases of valuation, (g) the date of valuation, (h) disclosure of any of material involvement, or a statement that there has not been any previous material involvement, (i) if require, a statement of the status of the valuer, (j) where appropriate, the currency to adopted, (k) any assumptions, reservation, any special instructions or departures, (l) the extent of the member's investigation, (m) the nature and source of information To be relied on the member, (n) any consent to, or restrictions on, publication, (o) any limits or exclusion of liability to parties other than the client, (p) confirmation that the valuation will be undertake in accordance with theses standards, (q) the basis on which the fee will be calculated, (r) the member's, or firm's complaints handling procedure with a copy available on request, (s) a statement that the valuation may be subject to monitoring under the institution's conduct and disciplinary regulations.

A clear statement in writing of any departure from a specified practice statement, together with details of, and reasons for it, and confirmation of the client's agreement must be given in the report. (PS1.3)

(c) **Assumptions**

Any assumptions, special assumptions, reservations, any special instructions or departures (Appendix 2.2)

An assumption is a supposition that is taken to be true. Assumptions are made where it is reasonable for the valuer to accept that something is true without the need for specific investigation. Many of the assumptions are made to limit the valuer's liability where full investigation has been impossible, or impractical within the context of the instruction

(see App0.2.2). A special assumption is an assumption that either require the valuation to be based on facts that differ materially from those that exist at the date of valuation or an assumption that a prospective purchaser could not reasonably be expected to make at the date of valuation. Appendix 2.3 gives several examples. It is essential that any special assumptions must be agreed with the client and be made if they can reasonably be regarded as realistic, relevant and valid in connection with the particular circum-

場合、リース期間満了によってリースホールドが消滅し、フリーホールド所有者に復帰（reversion）する時点で、建物はフリーホールドの中に吸収される。

登記所（Land Registry）の登記は、米国の多くの州やフランスのような人名別ではなく土地別であり、コンピューター化されていてインターネットでアクセスが可能である（www.landregistry.gov.uk）。登記記録は、表示簿・権利簿・負担簿の構成で、敷地又は建物配置図（ordnance survey map）のほかに、1995年から住宅の取引価格の情報も入手できる。

(b) 業務の範囲（Terms of Engagement）

鑑定人は依頼者と評価業務に関する条項を書面で確認しなければならない。最小限必要な確認事項として、依頼者、評価の目的、評価の対象、評価する権利、不動産の種類、価格の種類と属性、価格時点、利害関係の開示、外部・内部の評価人、通貨単位、評価の想定条件・特別想定条件・基準からの逸脱（departure）、現地調査の程度、評価の基礎とする情報の源と性格、報告内容の公表に関する同意・制限、依頼者以外の第三者に対する法的責任の制限と免責、本基準準拠の評価であることの確認、報酬、クレームへの対応、モニタリングの対象となりうる旨（PS2-2.1）。

(c) 評価の前提条件

想定条件（assumption）は、その内容について特別な調査をしなくても事実として想定することに合理性がある場合に設定され、その多くは依頼の諸事情から十分な調査を行うことが不可能又は非現実的な場合に、鑑定人の責任を限定するためにつけられる（App2.2）。特別な想定条件（special assumption）は、事実と著しく異なる事実を前提としたり、一般的な市場環境では想定しえない事実を前提として想定する場合である。この場合は、依頼者と同意が必要であり、かつ、その内容が現実性、関連性、及び有効性がなければならない（App2.3）。

stances of the valuation (see App. 2.3).

(d) **Valuation Reviews**

A member must not undertake a critical review of a valuation prepared by another valuer that is intended for disclosure or publication unless the member is in possession of all the facts and information on which the first valuer relied.

3. General Concepts and Principles (Valuation Bases)

(a) **Market Value**

The estimated amount for which a property should exchange on the date of valuation between a willing buyer and a willing seller in an arms-length transaction after proper marketing wherein the parties had each acted knowledgeably, prudently and without compulsion. "In an arms-length transaction" means that there is no particular or special relationship between the parties that could lead to an inflated value because of an element of special value. (PS3.2)

①Highest and Best Use

Not specifically referenced

②Marketing Period

The hypothetical marketing period takes place before the valuation date and should be appropriate for the type of property.

③Fair Value

Fair value represents the price that would be reasonably agreed between two specific parties for the exchange of an asset. Although the parties may be unconnected and negotiating at arm's length, the asset is not necessarily exposed in the market and the price agreed may be one that reflects the specific advantages (or disadvantages) of ownership to the parties involved rather than the market at large. (PS3.5)

(b) **Value Other Than Market Value**

①Existing Use Value (EUV)

EUV is the Market Value with one additional assumption that the buyer is granted vacant possession of all parts of the property and disregarding potential alternative uses. EUV is to be used only for valuing property that is owner-occupied by a business, or other entity, for inclusion in financial statement. (UKPS1.3)

②Depreciated Replacement Cost (DRC)

The current cost of reproduction or replacement of an asset less deductions for physical deterioration and all relevant forms of obsolescence and optimization. As a part of the process of valuing any property, the valuer needs to consider if there is potential

(d) 評価の審査

会員は、他の鑑定人が行った評価について批判的レビューを依頼されたとき、公に審議申し立てする目的で依頼された場合には、その鑑定人が評価の基礎にしたすべての事実関係や情報を知り得ない限り、依頼を受けてはならない（PS2-2.6）。

3．鑑定評価の基礎（価値の種類）

(a) 市場価値（Market Value）

市場価値は、価格時点において、売買の意欲のある売主と買主が、各々市場と資産に関する十分な情報を持ち、慎重にかつ強制されずに行動し、適切なマーケティング活動を経て、独立した取引当事者としての取引（arm's length transaction）として最も実現可能性が高いと判定される価格である（PS3-3.2）。公開市場価値（open market value）と呼ばれたが、国際評価基準が市場価値を定義して以降は、単に市場価値という。

①最有効使用

最有効使用について特に規定はないが、市場価値は最有効使用に基づく価値といえる。

②市場公開期間（Marketing period）

価格時点における市場価値の実現に先立って市場に公開している期間。

③公正価値（Fair Value）

公正価値は特定の当事者間で公正（fairness）と考えられる価格である。多くの場合、当事者にとって公正価値は市場価値であるが、市場価値以外の価値の場合もある。例えば、取引当事者が独立した当事者間であっても、必ずしも広い市場に公開されるとは限らないし、当事者の有する特定の事情を考慮に入れるべき場合もある（例えば、特殊価値で市場価値ではない）。公正価値を求められる場合として、賃貸借当事者間での立ち退きや契約延長の対価、財務報告、企業譲渡などの場合である（PS3-3.5）。

　国際会計基準によると、財務諸表のための評価は国際評価基準（IVS）に準拠するものとし（PS4.1）、国際評価基準は財務報告のための評価は「市場価値」を評価するものとしているが（RICS基準でも、求める価値は市場価値である）、他方で企業は国際会計基準に従って「公正価値」による会計処理を要求される。そこで鑑定人は、企業を支援して会計基準による開示を可能にするために、評価書に一定の情報（例えば、外部評価人による評価、市場価値査定の手法や想定条件、市場での独立当事者間の取引に基づく評価、市場における根拠に立脚など）を記載しなくてはならない（PS4-4.1）。

(b) 市場価値以外の価値（Value Other Than Market Value）

①現行用途前提の市場価値（Existing Use Value：EUV）

市場での交換価値であるが、現存する用途を前提にして（潜在的用途を考慮外として）かつ不動産を物的及び法的に占有できる保有権（ただし、第三者が占有している場合は、その占有状態を前提にして）が取引によって移転するという想定の下で求める価値である。市場価値とほぼ同じであるが、現存するという用途という非市場要因が追加されている。国内基準であり、企業又はその他の団体が自用資産を財務諸表に計上する目的で評価する場合にのみ用いる。

②特別な積算価格（Depreciated Replacement Cost：DRC）

土地の現行用途に基づく市場価値に、構築物の価格時点での再調達原価を加え、物理的劣化と陳腐化による減価を差し引いて査定する。「特殊不動産（specialized property：公共部門の施

for an alternative use that would be reflected in the Market Value. In the case of specialized property that can be valued using the DRC method, any alternative use value is likely only to relate to the land because the building s or other improvements may be incapable of alternative use. (PS6)

③Special Value
An amount above the Market Value that reflects particular attributes of an asset that only of value to a special purchaser. It includes synergistic value (known as marriage value). (PS3.2)

④Investment Value/Worth
The value of a property to a particular investor, or a class of investors, for identified investment objectives. This subjective concept relates specific property to a specific investor, group of investors, or entity with identified investment or operational objectives and/or criteria. (PS3.4)

⑤Value in Use
Value in use is the present value of the future cash flows obtainable as a result of an asset's continued use, including those resulting from its ultimate disposal. (UKPS Appendix1.1)

4. Approaches to Value

Valuers in the UK use five traditional methods for market valuation. Since the Red Book does not deal with valuation techniques or methodology, the following description is mainly based on "Property Valuation Principles" by David Issac and interview with valuers.

(a) **Capital Value and Rental Value**
　①Comparison Method
　　The comparison method compares the capital values and rental values of properties that have recently been sold or let with the subject property. It is the simplest and most direct method. As property is unique, the problem lies in the adjustment to be made to the comparables o fit the subject property.
　②Investment method (corresponding to Income Approach in Japan)
　　Most investors seek to obtain a return on their invested money either as an annual income or a capital gain, but the investment method for a market valuation is traditionally concerned with the former. Valuers in the U.K. are reluctant to use DCF for valuation as these techniques are not thought to reflect market behavior. In addition, market evidence has illustrated how volatile the rental market can be over the critical first 10yeara of the holding period.

　　However, it has been pointed out that the property crash in the early 1970s focused attention on valuation methods used in the profession ; investment advisers are looking for more analysis in the valuations ; clients are demanding that the valuation

設、特殊な生産施設、教会、博物館など、資産の特質・構造・立地・その他の特殊性のために、事業の構成要素として一括して取引される以外に、市場で取引されることがほとんどない資産)」の市場価値を示す数値として、償却後取替原価による積算価格は、財務報告での評価に利用される価値又は手法である。この価値と事業を廃止して他の用途に転用する場合の価値は大きく異なるので、これに関する記述が必要になる。詳しくは、"財務報告のための特別な積算価格の評価（VIP No.10を参照）。

英国会計基準では、長い間、特殊不動産の価値の査定は市場資料の裏づけがないため信頼性が劣るとして、財務諸表上、評価とは別扱いされてきた。しかし、国際会計基準ではそのような区別はなく、資産の公正価値は、市場資料に基づいても、あるいは収益や積算に基づいてもよしとしている。信頼性の問題は資料・手法の開示によって対応する。

③**特殊価値（Special Value）**
特定の買主に対して市場価値を上回る価値を生じる属性（物的、地理的、経済的、又は法律的属性）を備えた不動産の価値である。複数の資産を組み合わせた相乗効果によって個別の資産の合計価値を上回る価値が生じる併合価値（marriage value）も、特殊価値に属する。

④**投資価値（Investment Value／Worth）**
明確な投資又は管理上の目的を有する特定の投資家や所有者を前提とする不動産の価値である。例えば、市場の客観的な収益率とは別の独自の収益率などに基づいて投資不動産に対して認める価値である。

⑤**使用価値（Value in Use）**
資産の継続使用を前提として、将来発生する管理運用によるキャッシュフロー及び転売によるキャッシュフローの現在価値（UK App.2.1）。

4．鑑定評価の方式・手順

RICS鑑定評価業務基準には評価技術や手法についての記述はないが、英国の鑑定人は次の5つの伝統的な鑑定評価の手法を用いる。以下は、David Issac氏の「鑑定評価の原則（Property Valuation Principles）」及び鑑定人からの取材による。

⒜ 価格・賃料を求める方式

①**比較方式（Comparison Method）**
対象物件と類似した取引事例又は賃貸事例から、市場での価値（capital value）又は賃料（rental value）を求める。最も単純で直接的な方式であるが、不動産の個別性ゆえ、各事例の修正がポイントになる。

②**投資方式（Investment Method）**
ⓐ純収益、ⓑ賃貸期間、ⓒ利回りに関する市場データⓐとⓑは賃貸市場、ⓒは投資市場）によって、実際の賃貸又は想定上の賃貸に基づく年間収益を資本還元して市場での価値（capital value）を求める。

さらに1970年代のバブルを経て、鑑定の依頼者及び投資家から鑑定人に対して、評価の前提を明確にしたうえで、将来の収益及び価格、リスク要因、経済的要因についての専門的な分析（analysis）の結果を、「投資」の分野だけではなく「評価（valuation）」の分野でも、反映させるべきであるとの要請が高まり、将来の収益及び費用を割引いて市場での価値を求める手法（DCF）が提唱され（"Commercial Investment Property: Valuation Methods", Information Paper, RICS 1997）、適用されてきている。

③**残余方式（Residual Method）**

professional should not just act as an agent but provide some idea of the forecast of income arising from the investment in the future ; there should be more comments on valuation risk force, price trends and economic factors, and the use of more refined discounted cash flow techniques ("Commercial Investment Property: Valuation Methods", Information Paper, RICS 1997).

In the present U.K. market, the principal application of the DCF has been in the analysis of the worth of an investment (investment value).

③Residual Method (corresponding to Development Approach in Japan)

The residual method is a calculation that estimates the completed development Value and deducts costs and profits to arrive at a residual land value. A more suitable method would be the use of Comparison Method, but the problem relates to the fact that the end value of the development will determine the land value. Developers will envisage different development proposals and thus the end values will vary, making direct comparison of projects and thus land values difficult.

(b) **Profits Method (corresponding to Income Approach for an owner-occupied property for business operation in Japan)**

The profits Method is used where the property value is based on the profit produced by the business operation in the property (GN1: Trade Related Property Valuations). Those properties are generally sold as operational entities, e.g., hotels, restaurants, theatres or cinemas, fuel stations, and care homes.

The calculation is shown as follows:

Gross earning − cost of purchases (direct cost) = Gross Profit
Gross Profit − expenses (indirect cost) = Net profit
Net profit − return on capital for business (goodwill) = Annual rental value
Annual rental value ÷ cap rate (or multiplier) = Capital Value

(c) **Cost of Replacement Method (corresponding to Cost Approach in Japan)**

The method is based on the cost of building less obsolescence and depreciation plus the site value. In the U.K. Cost Approach is not generally used because cost rarely equates with value and the market will provide little evidence. It is used for rating and compulsory purchase.

Replacement cost
<u>Less Depreciation + Obsolescence</u>
Building Value
<u>Plus Site Value</u>
Value of Property

5. Valuation Reports

(a) **Minimum content of reports**

The report must deal with all the matters agreed between the client and the member in terms of engagement and include the following information (PS6.1) :

(a) identification of the client, (b) the purpose of the valuation, (c) the subject of the valuation, (d) the interest to be valued, (e) the type of property and how it is used or classified

開発（又は再開発）素地の評価は、適切な比較事例が入手できれば比較法による。しかし、それぞれの開発（又は再開発）後の価値が立地条件や都市計画上の許可いかんによって様々であるから、比較は一般に困難である。そこで、開発（又は再開発）後の価値を査定し、それから開発費用等を控除して素地の価値（capital value）を求める。日本の鑑定評価基準の「開発法」に相当する。

(b) 利益に基づいて価格を求める方式（Profit Method）

ホテル、レストラン、劇場や映画館、ガソリンスタンド、介護施設などの事業用不動産は、特定の目的に合わせて設計・適合され、通常はひとつの事業体の価値（capital value of business）を構成するものとして取引されるのが通常である。運営から発生する総収益を分析し、利益（profit）から価値（capital value）を求めるが、運営には家具什器備品と「のれん」など非不動産要素が不可欠である（GN1 Trade Related Property Valuations）。

売上高（Gross earning）－売上原価（cost of purchases）＝売上総利益（Gross Profit）
売上総利益（Gross Profit）－販売費及び一般管理費（expenses）＝営業利益（Net profit）
営業利益（Net profit）－経営帰属分（return on capital for business）＝収益（Rental value）
収益（Rental value）÷還元利回り cap rate（or×multiplier）＝価格（Capital Value）

(c) コストに基づいて価値を求める方式（Cost of Replacement Method）

特殊不動産は、市場で取引されることがほとんどないので、その価値は同等の機能を持つ不動産の建設コストに基づく（敷地は市場からの事例による）。

再調達原価
－物的劣化・陳腐化
建物価格
＋土地価格
不動産価格

5．鑑定評価報告書

(a) 必要的記載事項

報告書には、契約で鑑定人が依頼者と合意した事項を記載しなければならない。最小限必要な事項として、依頼者、評価の目的、評価の対象、評価する権利、価格の種類、価格時点、利害関係の開示、通貨単位、評価の想定条件・特別想定条件・基準逸脱、現地調査の程度、評価の基礎とする情報の源と性格、報告内容の公表に関する同意・制限、依頼者以外の第三者に対する法的責

by the client, (f) the basis or bases of the valuation, (g) the date of valuation, (h) disclosure of any material involvement or a statement that there has not been any previous material involvement, (i) if required, a statement of the status of the valuer, (j) where appropriate, the currency that has been adopted, (k) any assumptions, special assumptions, reservations, any special instructions or departures, (l) the extent of the member's investigation, (m) the nature and source of information relied on by the member, (n) any consent to restrictions on, publication, (o) any limits or exclusion of liability to parties other than the client, (p) confirmation that the valuation accords with these Standards, (q) a statement of the valuation approach, (r) the opinions of value in figures and words, (s) signature and the date of the report. (PS6)

(b) **Verbal report**
In the main body of the report the opinion of value is required in words, as well as in figures.

6. Implementation of Valuation Standards

In its valuation standards, RICS establishes rules of conduct for surveyors who are its members, and creates a regulatory framework to ensure that these rules are implemented. Its aim is to ensure that the users of valuations can be confident that surveyors are held to internationally recognized standards and will be sanctioned if they violate these standards. As an independent organization, RICS establishes its own fundamental organizational rules, takes steps to ensure that it can obtain information from its members, monitors for adherence to its standards, and publishes the specific results of its investigations on the Internet.

7. Availability of Data

(a) **Specific Data (Primary Data)**
A clear distinction is made between the advice rendered by an agent / broker on sale price and the work of professional surveyor designated as FRICS or MRICS. However, major brokerage / consulting companies which have their own professional valuation section hold much of the sales and rental data in their own file and increasingly share these date on the internet.

The member must take reasonable steps to verify the information relied upon in the preparation of the valuation and clarify with the client any necessary assumptions that well be relied upon. (PS5.2) Some of information service companies are listed below :

Estate Gazette : Subscribers of Estate Gazzette are given access to www.egi.co.uk.
Focus   : CoStar Group in the UK , providing information services to commercial real estate professionals in the US. www.costar.co.uk
PMA   : Commercial property research including the Property Market Information Service. www. pma. co.uk

(b) **General Data (Secondary Data)**
There are a number of useful website for valuers: some of them are listed below:

任、基準準拠の評価であることの確認、評価方法、評価額の文字及び数字による記載、署名。たとえ依頼者が報告書を読まずに評価額を見るだけであっても、対象物件について知識がなくても内容が明確でなくてはならない。

　鑑定評価書には、①担保や売買の参考にする通常の長い評価書と、②財務諸表の数値計上又は不動産ファンド又は CMBS の証券市場上場の際の目論見書に含まれる鑑定評価書（Valuation report/certificate）がある。

(b)　口頭の報告
　RICS 基準は、訴訟手続き中の助言、仲裁、交渉中又はその準備中の助言、内部評価等の場合は適用されない。

6. 鑑定評価基準の履行

RICS は、評価基準の中に、会員である鑑定人（surveyors）の行為規範（Rules of Conducts）を定め、それが有効に履行されるように規制する枠組みを整備し、鑑定人が基準遵守義務に違反した場合には制裁があるものとして利用者が確信できるようにしている。自律団体としての根本規則を定め、基準遵守のモニタリングを実施して、具体的な調査結果をネット上に公開している。

7. 鑑定評価に利用するデータ

(a)　個別データ（Specific Data）
　鑑定業者の多くが取引仲介業を兼業しているために、事例は詳細に把握されていて、売買事例及び賃貸事例の共有化が進んでいる。ただし、鑑定人は個別データがどの程度信頼できるか検証しなければならない。信頼性の乏しいデータを利用せざるを得ないときには、契約条項で適切な想定条件を設定する（PS5-5.2）以下は、データ提供会社の例示である。

Estate Gazette　：不動産専門情報会社であり、EGi はオンラインでデータ提供。www.egi.co.uk
Focus　　　　　：米国商業不動産情報提供会社 CoStar グループ。www.costar.co.uk
PMA　　　　　：不動産調査会社で、PROMISE は地域の市場レポート提供。www. pma.co.uk

(b)　一般データ（General Data）
　ネットを通じて多くの情報にアクセスが可能である。例えば、RICS：マクロ情報「Global Real

RICS : Global Real Estate Weekly (www.rics.org.uk), BCIS: Details of construction costs (www.bcis.org.uk)

8. Specific Valuation Standards for Securitization Purposes

The British REIT (UK-REIT) market was created in January 2007. It was begun through conversion from major real estate corporations, so the market expanded rapidly. UK-REITs are capable of development operations and real estate agency operations in addition to real estate leasing operations. Their leasing operations are exempt from corporate tax if they meet the following conditions as a conduit; however, corporate tax applies normally to their other operations.

① A UK-REIT business entity must be a domestic corporation, listed on a stock exchange, and a public company.

② A non-profit UK-REIT must own more than three properties; no property can account for more than 30% of its total assets; and it must distribute at least 90% of its profits from leasing operations.

③ Regarding business proportions, at least 75% of total revenues must be from tax-exempt leasing operations, and asset values must be based on a fair valuation according to the International Accounting Standards.

Estate Weekly」（www.rics.org.uk）、BCIS：建物建設コストの情報提供（www.bcis.org.uk）。

8．証券化に関する基準

英国のリート「UK-REIT」市場の創設は2007年1月であるが、大手不動産株式会社からの転換による発足で市場規模は急拡大している。不動産賃貸業務のほかに開発業務や仲介業務もできるが、賃貸業務は導管性用件を満たせば法人税非課税、その他の業務は通常の法人税がかかる。①事業主体要件：内国法人、証券取引所に上場、公開会社であること等、②非課税事業要件：3つ以上の不動産を所有、1つの不動産が総資産額の30％を超えない、賃貸事業に係る利益の90％以上を配当する等、③事業比率要件：総収益の75％以上が非課税の賃貸事業によるもの、資産価値は国際会計基準による公正価値による。

Chapter 2.Ⅳ. AUSTRALIA : API Valuation Standards

Ⅳ. *AUSTRALIA : API Valuation Standards*

Originally drafted by Mr. Bevan Richardson, MRICS API, and edited by the author.

For the purpose of introducing Japan Real Estate Appraisal System in a global context, the author has often referred to the Professional Practice 5th Edition published by the Australian Property Institute (API) that holds the copyrights. The full text of the valuation standards may be obtained from The API, 6 Campion Street, Deakin ACT 2600 Australia. http://www.api.org.au

1. Framework of Valuation Standards

(a) **Who writes Valuation Standards?**

Valuation standards are produced in Australia by the Australian Valuation and Property Standards Boards (AV&PSB). The standards are contained in the Australian Property Institute's (API) Professional Practice guide. The Australian Property Institute (API) is the leading property professional organization in Australia with 7,500 members. Members include residential, commercial and plant and machinery valuers, property advisers, property analysts and fund managers, property lawyers, and property researchers and academics. The fifth edition of the guide is the most current version (as at March 2008). The fifth edition of this manual is the second stage toward the harmonization of valuation and property standards within Australia and New Zealand. The manual adopts the International Standards and Guidance Notes of the International Valuation Standards Committee in their entirety. Areas not covered by IVSC standards are covered by Australian and New Zealand standards and guidance notes.

(b) **For whom Valuation Standards are written? (Principal purposes of valuation standards)**

The principal aim of the API and PINZ is to set and maintain high standard of professional practice (through adoption of the IVSC standards), education, ethics and discipline. Members of these bodies include experts in property such as valuers, property advisors, property managers, property analysts and facilitators. (API-Introduction to Professional Practice Fifth Edition-1.0)

(c) **Who must abide by the Standards and what services must comply? (Compliance with valuation standards)**

The API's professional practice manual sets out the duties, responsibilities and professional standards required to be followed by members of the API and of the PINZ. (API-Introduction to Professional Practice Fifth Edition-2.0)

The organization of the standards follows:
- Code of Ethics and Rules of Conduct
- International Valuation Standards
  (Code of conduct, General Valuation Concepts and Principles, Property Type)
  (Standards / Applications / Guidance Notes)
- National Standards (API&PINZ)

Ⅳ. オーストラリア：API鑑定評価業務基準

Mr. Bevan Richardson（MRICS API）による原文に執筆者加筆
日本の不動産鑑定評価基準を国際的文脈から検証するために、オーストラリア・プロパティ協会（API）が著作権を有し発行している鑑定評価業務基準を、執筆者の同基準の理解と責任で引用している。同鑑定評価基準の全文は、「The API, 6 Campion Street, Deakin ACT 2600 Australia」から入手できる。http://www.api.org.au

1．鑑定評価の制度枠組み

(a) 鑑定評価基準の策定主体

オーストラリアの「鑑定評価業務基準及び留意事項（API ＆ PINZ Valuation Standards, Guidance notes）」は、オーストラリア・プロパティ協会（API：Australian Property Institute）及びニュージーランド・プロパティ協会（PINZ）が共同で策定したものである。APIは、1926年設立の英連邦評価人協会（Commonwealth Institute of Valuers）を前身とし、現在は評価人のほかに不動産関連のアドバイザー、アナリスト、アセット・マネージャー、法律家、学者等の専門家約7,500人から構成されている。

(b) 基準の目的

APIの役割は、不動産の専門家としての「実務基準（Professional Practice Standards）」、「倫理規定（A Code of Ethics）」及び「行為規定（Rules of Conducts）」を策定して実施することである。上記評価基準及び留意事項は、API「専門実務ガイド（Professional Practice Guide）」の項目に編纂されている。2008年3月刊行の最新ガイド（第5版）は、オーストラリアとニュージーランドの評価基準の調和と国際評価基準委員会策定の国際評価基準（IVS）及び留意事項の尊重を強く打ち出している。IVSが決めていない事項をオーストラリア及びニュージーランド評価基準及び留意事項が規定する。

(c) 基準の対象

APIのメンバーが依頼者に提供する各分野の業務について、API専門実務ガイドは、会員が遵守すべき義務、責任、専門基準を規定している。すなわち、居住用不動産、商業用不動産、工場及び機械の評価、アドバイス、売却、取得、リース、リーガル・アドバイス、投資分析及びリサーチ、資産運用である。

評価基準は、次のように構成されている。まず、基準全体に関係する法的及び経済的な概念及び原則として、「倫理規範」及び「行為規定」を置く。そのうえで、国内基準に先行して、国際評価基準を挙げる。その内容は、本章Ⅵ．国際評価基準（IVS）の内容と同じで、「評価の一般概念と原則」「行為規範」「評価の対象となる権利・利益」及び「評価基準（Standards）」「適用（Applications）」「留意事項（Guidance Note）」である。次に、国内基準として、「①評価基準

① **API&PINZ Valuation Standards**
    ANZPS 1   Valuations for Compulsory Acquisitions
② **API&PINZ Valuation Guidance Notes**
    ANZVGN 1   Valuation Procedures-Real Property
    ANZVGN 2   Valuation for Mortgage and Loan Security Purpose
    ANZVGN 3   Valuation for Mortgage and Loan Security Purpose (Forced Sale)
    ANZVGN 4   Valuation for Rating and Taxing
    ANZVGN 5   Valuation for Compulsory Acquisitions
    ANZVGN 6   Valuations of Accommodation Hotels
    ANZVGN 7   Valuation of Partial Interests held within Co-Ownership Structure
    ANZVGN 8   Prospectus Valuations
③ **API Valuation Guidance Notes**
    ANGN 1   Valuations for use in Australian Financial Reports
    ANGN 2   Valuations for Insurance Purposes
④ **API&PINZ Real Property Guidance Note**
    ANZRPGN 1   Disclaimer Clauses and Qualification Statements
    ANZRPGN 2   Acting as an Expert Witness, Advocate or Arbitrator
    ANZRPGN 3   Leasing Incentives
    ANZRPGN 4   Methods of Measurement
    ANZRPGN 5   Feasibility Studies
    ANZRPGN 6   Due Diligence
    ANZRPGN 7   Property Insurance Management
    ANZRPGN 8   Preparing Property for Sale
    ANZRPGN 9   Property Development Management and Terms of Appointment
    ANZRPGN10   Leasing Agent Service
    ARPGN 1   Land Contaminated Issues
    ARPGN 2   Native Title Issues

(d) **Licensing / Designation**

The certification of Certified Practicing Valuer (CPV) is available only to the membership classes of the Life Fellow, Fellow or Associate.

2. Fundamentals for Valuation

(a) **Real Property Rights and Interests to be Valued**

"Land" is legally defined in the same way as "real estate", encompassing the surface, the ground underneath the surface, and the space immediately above it. Further, items

（Valuation Standards）」「②留意事項（Guidance Notes）」「③不動産留意事項（Real Property Guidance Notes）」を置いている。

- 倫理規範及び行為規定
- 国際評価基準（IVS）
  （一般規定）
  （基準・適用・留意事項）
- 国内基準（API＆PINZ）

①基準（API＆PINZ Standards）
  ANZPS 1 強制収用目的の評価

②留意事項（API＆PINZ Valuation Guidance Notes）
  ANZVGN 1 不動産評価手続
  ANZVGN 2 担保目的の評価
  ANZVGN 3 早期売却目的の評価
  ANZVGN 4 課税目的の評価
  ANZVGN 5 強制収用目的の評価
  ANZVGN 6 ホテル評価
  ANZVGN 7 共有権評価
  ANZVGN 8 目論見書に記載する不動産評価

③評価留意事項（API Valuation Guidance Notes）
  ANGN 1 財務報告のための評価
  ANGN 2 保険目的の評価

④不動産留意事項（API＆PINZ Real Property Guidance Note）
  ANZRPGN 1 責任排除・限定条項
  ANZRPGN 2 専門家証人・弁護士・仲裁人の司法及び準司法業務
  ANZRPGN 3 賃料及び価値評価における誘因（leasing incentives）
  ANZRPGN 4 計測単位
  ANZRPGN 5 投資採算分析
  ANZRPGN 6 デューディリジェンス
  ANZRPGN 7 保険管理
  ANZRPGN 8 不動産売却業務
  ANZRPGN 9 不動産開発管理及び業務委託契約
  ANZRPGN 10 不動産仲介業務
  ARPGN 1 土壌汚染
  ARPGN 2 原住民権限

(d) ライセンス・認定

「認定評価人（CPV：Certified Practising Valuer）」の認定資格は、会員のうち特定の者（Life Fellow、Fellow or Associate）に限られている（By Law 19.3）。

2．鑑定評価の前提

(a) 鑑定評価の対象となる権利・利益

「土地（land）」は「不動産（real estate）」と同義で（日本では、「土地」と「建物」が「不動産」）、法的には土地の表面、その地下、その真上の空間を含む。さらに、土地に付着している定着物

attached to the land (such as buildings) are treated as part of the land. Ownership (exclusive control) of the land can be either a freehold (fee simple), in which no time limit is established; or a leasehold, in which a time limit is specified. However, this is simply a distinction in terms of the amount of time; and there is no essential difference.

The acquisition and preservation of the land ownership follows the process of first signing a sales contract, followed by a due diligence period and then the transferal procedures. At the stage of transferal procedures, a lawyer submits a title deed to the Land Registry (for example, Department of Natural Resources, Mines and Water at the state of QLD). The buildings are considered as a part of the land, and buildings are not registered independently of land). The registry office retains the original title paper (not on paper but in electronic form, computerized Automated Titles System) ; and the applicant is issued a certificate of title which states the content of the title rights. At the registry office, the records are organized by each individual property (physical basis of organization), and a third party can access the registry records online (for example, www.nrm.qld.gov.au)

(b) **Terms of Engagement (Scope of Work)**

Before commencing any valuation it is important to clarify with the client what is to be included in the scope of work. The valuer is responsible for determining the appropriate scope of work in the valuation assignment, given the client's intended use and the nature of the problem to be solved (API-ANZVGN1-3.1). Instructions should be confirmed in writing and include details regarding access arrangement, identification, ownership, agreed fee (or basis for it calculation) and, if applicable, the purchase price and the selling agent. The instructions should also list the parties intended to rely on the valuation, the purpose of the valuation and agreed time for completion of the report. (API-ANZGN1-2.1).

(c) **Assumptions, Hypothetical Conditions and Limiting Conditions**

Assumptions are suppositions taken to be true. Assumptions involve facts, conditions, or situations affecting the subject of, or approach to a valuation but which may not be capable or worthy of verification. They are matters that, once declared, are to be accepted in understanding the valuation. All assumptions underlying a valuation should be reasonable (API-ANZGN1-3.1). Assumptions presume uncertain information to be factual. If found to be false, these assumptions could alter the valuer's opinions or conclusions. For example, consider a valuation of an ex-warehouse that may be subject to environmental contamination. Even though the presence of contamination is suspected, it is possible for the valuation to be based on the assumption that the property is not contaminated.

Hypothetical conditions are contrary to what exists, but the conditions are asserted by the valuer for the purposes of analysis. For example, in the case of a manufacturing plant that is known to be subject to environmental contamination, it is possible for the valuation to be based on the hypothetical condition that is not contaminated.

Limiting conditions are constraints imposed on valuations. Limiting conditions may be imposed by clients, by the Valuer or by local statutory law. (API-ANZGN.1-3.2). Statements of Limiting Conditions are included in the report to help protect both the valua-

(例えば建物) も土地の一部となる。土地に対する「保有権 (ownership：排他的支配を内容とする)」は、期限が不確定のフリーホールド (freehold／fee simple) と期限が確定しているリースホールド (leasehold) に分類されるが、単なる期間という量の差であり本質的な差異はない。

保有権の取得及び保全は、売買契約締結→デューディリ期間→譲渡手続きのプロセスの順に進む。譲渡手続きの段階では、弁護士が譲渡証書を登記所 (Land Registry：クイーンズランド州では天然資源・水資源省土地局) に申請する。登記の対象は土地のみであり、登記所は譲渡証書の原本 (original title paper) を保管し (文書ではなく電磁的記録として、コンピューター管理：ATS)、権限の内容を示す権限証明書 (certificate of title) を申請者に発行する。登記所では個々の土地ごとに登記が編成されていて (物的編成主義)、第三者でもオンラインで登記記録の情報を入手することが可能である (例えば、www.nrm.qld.gov.au)。

(b) 業務範囲

評価実務に先だって、依頼者の目的や解決すべき問題の性質に基づいて、評価業務の範囲 (Scope of Work) を取り決める。

(c) 評価の前提条件

想定条件 (assumptions) は、事実かどうか不確定な情報を、事実として想定するものである。不確定な情報は対象不動産又は評価手法に影響を与える要因であるが、それが事実であることの検証が著しく難しい又は意味が認められず、想定条件を設けることに合理性がある場合でなくてはならない (API-ANZGN 3.1)。もし、想定した事実が存在しないことが明らかになった場合、評価人の意見や評価額は違ったものになる。例えば、環境が汚染されているかもしれない倉庫跡地の評価で、汚染の疑いはあるが、それが無いものと想定して評価する場合である。

仮定条件 (hypothetical conditions) は、事実に反する仮定を内容とするが、評価人が分析の目的であることを明らかにして評価する条件である。例えば、環境汚染が明白な工場の評価で、汚染の影響を分析する目的で、汚染がないものとしての評価を求める場合である。

限定条件 (limiting conditions) は、依頼者、評価人又は法令によって付け加えられる、評価を行う上の制約である。限定条件も評価書の中に記載され、評価及び依頼者に対して免責条項となり、依頼者及び鑑定評価の利用者にそれに伴うリスクを知らせることになる。例えば、対象不動産への十分な立ち入りが許可されていない場合である。

tion and the client and to inform the client and other users of the report about limitations on the use of the valuation. For example, where the valuer is not permitted to investigate fully.

(d) **Valuation Reviews**

Valuation covers a range of types and purposes. The principal characteristics all valuation reviews have in common is that one valuer exercises impartial judgment in considering the work of another valuer. Valuations reviews have become an integral part of professional practice. In a valuation review, the correctness, consistency, reasonableness, and completeness of the valuation are considered (API -International Valuation Guidance Notes 11-1.2).

3. General Concepts and Principles (Valuation Bases)

(a) **Market Value**

Market value is defined as "the estimated amount for which a property should exchange on the date of valuation between a willing buyer and a willing seller in an arm's-length transaction after proper marketing wherein the parties had each acted knowledgeably, prudently, and without compulsion". Implicit within this definition is the concept of a general market comprising the activity and motivation of many participants rather than the preconceived view or vested interest of a particular individual (API-General Valuation Concepts and Principles-5.2).

①Highest and Best Use (HABU)

Highest and Best Use is defined as "the most probable use of a property which is physically possible, appropriately justified, legally permissible, financially feasible, and which results in the highest value of the property being valued". Market value of land based upon the "highest and best use" concept reflects the utility and the permanence of land in the context of a market, with improvements constituting the difference between land value alone and total market value as improved (API-General Valuation Concepts and Principles-6.3).

Highest and Best Use of Land as though vacant and Highest and Best Use of Property as Improved

The unique characteristics of land determine its optimal utility. When improved land is valued separately from improvements to or upon the land, economic principles require that improvements to or on the land be valued as they contribute to or detract from the total value of the property. Thus, the Market Value of land based upon the "highest and best use" concept reflects the utility and the permanence of land in the context of a Market, with improvements constituting the difference between land value alone and total. Market value as improved. Most properties are valued as a combination of land and improvements. In such cases, the Valuer will normally estimate market value by considering the highest use of the property as improved (General Valuation Concepts and Principles-6.1.1, 6.2).

②Marketing Period

Conceptually, this period is envisaged as having preceded the date of valuation. It

(d) 評価の審査

評価業務は多様であるが、「審査」に共通している点は、別の評価人が行った業務を中立の立場で判断することである。審査は、専門業務では不可欠である。評価の審査では、内容が正確であること、論理が一貫していること、合理性があること及び必要な内容を全部備えていることが審査される。

3．鑑定評価の基礎（価値の種類）

(a) 市場価値（Market Value）

国際評価基準（IVS）による市場価値を採択し、特定の不動産について、マーケティングのための合理的期間（exposure time）、公開の競争市場、現金ないしそれと同等のファイナンス条件を前提に、典型的な投資家が投資（購入）するとした場合に、売主が見込むことができる最も確からしい価格である。鑑定人が求める価値は原則として市場価値である。市場価値以外の価値を評価することもあるが、その場合は市場価値と峻別する。

①**最有効使用（Highest and Best Use）**

最有効使用とは、法的に許容され、物的に可能で、採算的に実現可能な選択肢のうちで、最高の収益性を持つ使用である。最有効使用は市場価値の前提にあり、「更地としての最有効使用（HABU of land as though vacant）」と「土地と建物を一体とした複合不動産としての最有効使用（HABU of property as improved）」の二面から判定する。両者が一致しないときには暫定的最有効使用がありうる。

②**市場公開期間（Marketing Period）**

市場公開期間は、価格時点に先だって市場価値の実現に必要なマーケティング期間。

③**公正価値（Fair Value）**

公正価値は国際会計基準で使われる会計上の概念であり、取引に必要な情報を十分に有している売主と買主が独立の取引当事者として（at arm's length）締結するものと推定する価値ではあるが、これ以外の要件も加わって、市場価値と同じ場合もあるし、市場価値以外の価値の場合もある。

should reflect a typical marketing period for the class of property in the then current market conditions. Conceptually this period is envisaged as having preceded the date of valuation (API-ANZVGN1-7.6).

③Fair Value

Fair value is not necessarily synonymous with Market Value. It is used throughout International Financial Reporting Standards (IFRSs). Fair value, an accounting concept, is defined in IFRSs and other accounting standards as the amount for which an asset could be exchanged, or a liability settled, between knowledgeable, willing parties in an arm's' length transaction. Fair value is generally used for both Market and Non-Market Values in financial statement (API-AVGN1-2.2).

(b) **Value Other Than Market Value**

①Existing Use Value (EUV) or Value in Use

The value a specific property has for a specific use to a specific user and therefore non-market related. In estimating existing use value, the valuer focuses on the value the property contributes to the enterprise of which it is a part, without regard to the highest and best use of the property or the monetary amount that might be realized from sale. Existing use value may vary depending on the management of the property and economic conditions such as changes in business operation. Real property may have an existing use value and a market value. An older industrial building that is still used by the original firm may have considerable existing use value to that firm but only a nominal market value for another. Existing use valuation assignments may be performed to value real property for mergers, acquisition, or refinancing purposes. (IVS2-3.1)

②Investment Value / Worth

Value in Use focuses on the specific use of a property ; investment value represents the value of a specific property to a particular investors, or a class of investors, for identified investment objectives. In contrast to market value, investment value is value to an individual, not necessarily value in the market place. It differs in concept to market value, although investment value and market value amounts sometimes may be similar. If the investor's requirements are typical of the market, investment value will be the same as market value. (IVS2-3.2)

③Special Value

Special value may accrue to a property by reason of a unique location, unique designs, special construction materials, or layouts that restrict their utility to the user, or premium payable by a purchaser having a special interest. Marriage value, the value increment resulting from the merger of two or more interests in a property, represents a special example of special value. Special value could be associated with investment value. (IVS2-3.8)

④Reproduction Cost / Replacement Cost

A cost estimate for a property may be based on either an estimate of reproduction cost or replacement cost. Reproduction cost is the cost to create a virtual replica of the existing structure as of the effective valuation date, employing the same design and similar building materials. A replacement cost estimate is the cost to construct, as

(b) **市場価値以外の価値**(Value Other Than Market Value)
①現行用途前提価値(EUV)又は使用価値(Value in Use)
　不動産が最有効使用かどうか、最も収益があがる使用かどうかに関わりなく、特定の使用を前提とし(したがって、特定の使用者を前提とするから市場価値ではない)、かつ第三者の占有があるときには、それを前提として譲渡契約によって物的及び法的権限が移転する(vacant possession)前提の下で、取引に必要な情報を十分に有している売主と買主が独立の取引当事者として(at arm's length)合意するものと推定する価値である。例えば、古い工場建物を評価する場合、市場から見れば価値がないかもしれないが、その工場主にとってはその建物は使用価値がある。この価値がM&Aや財務諸表では求められる。

②投資価値(Investment Value/Worth)
　使用価値が特定の使用を前提とする価値であるのに対して、投資価値は特定の投資家を前提とする価値である。投資価値は特定の投資家を前提とする点で市場価値と異なるが、市場での典型的な投資家を前提とする場合には市場価値と同じになる。

③特殊価値(Special Value)
　特殊な立地・デザイン・資材・用途などを前提とする価値である。複数の不動産の併合を前提としてプレミアムが生ずる限定価格(Marriage value)もこれに属する。投資価値として特殊価値を求めることもありうる。

④再調達価格・置換価格(Reproduction Cost/Replacement Cost)
　不動産の積算価格を、対象不動産と同じ設計と建設資材を用いて再調達することを想定して査定する再調達価格(identical or reproduction cost)から求める方法と比べて、対象不動産と同等の効用を持つ不動産を新たに調達する置換価格(replacement cost)から求める方法は、機能的要因による減価修正の多くを不要にするため、一般的に採用される。

of the effective valuation date, a building with utility equivalent to the building being valued using contemporary materials, standards, design and layout. The use of replacement cost can eliminate the need to measure many, but not all, forms of functional obsolescence. The replacement cost is commonly used because it may be easier to obtain and can reduce the complexity of depreciation analysis.

4. Valuation Approaches

(a) **Cost Approach**

This comparative approach considers the possibility that, as a substitute for the purchase of a given property, one could construct another property that is either a replica of the original or one that could furnish equal utility. In a real estate context, one would normally not be justified in paying more for a given property than the cost of acquiring equivalent land and constructing an alternative structure, unless undue time, inconvenience and risk are involved. (API-General Valuation Concepts and Principles-9.2.1.3)

(b) **Sales Comparison Approach**

This comparative approach considers the sales of similar properties and related market data, and establishes a value estimate by processes involving comparison. (API-General Valuation Concepts and Principles-9.2.1.1)

(c) **Income Capitalization Approach**

This comparative approach considers income and expense data relating to the property being valued and estimates value through a capitalisation process. Capitalisation relates to income (usually a net income figure) and a defined value type by converting an income amount into a value amount. This process may consider direct relationships, yield or discount rates, or both. In general, the principle of substitution holds that the income stream which produces the highest return commensurate with a given level of risk leads to the most probable value figure. (API-General Valuation Concepts and Principles-9.2.1.2)

5. Valuation Reports

(a) **Minimum content of reports**

The result of a valuation is communicated to a client in writing, which includes electronic communication. Written communications prepared under one of the three reporting options (1. self contained valuation reports, 2. summary valuation reports, 3. restricted valuation reports) may be form or narratives. Even if a client asks for a report that does not include detailed documentation, the valuer can undertake the analysis required by an assignment in accordance with the scope of work. In such a case all material, data, and working papers used to prepare the valuation are kept in the valuer's work file.

4. 鑑定評価の方式・手順

(a) 原価法（Cost Approach）

原価法は、一定の不動産を購入する代わりに、その不動産とそっくり同じ不動産又は同じ効用を有する不動産を建築するとしたらいくらかかるか、との考え方に立つ方式である。建築に時間が余分にかかったりすることがなく、面倒なことや不都合なことが起きないのであれば、土地を購入し建物を建築するのに必要となるコストを超えて購入代金を支払うことは考えられない。実務では、新築価格から建物の老朽化及び機能的陳腐化による減価修正をして不動産価格を査定する。（API 一般規定9.2.1.3）

(b) 取引事例比較法（Sales Comparison Approach）

取引事例比較法は、類似の取引事例及び関連する市場データから見るといくらかかるか、との考え方に立つ方式である。（API 一般規定9.2.1.1）

(c) 収益還元法（Income Capitalization Approach）

収益還元法は、対象不動産に関わる収益・費用データから資本還元した価値はいくらかかるか、との考え方に立つ方式である。資本還元には還元、割引、及び両方があり、最大の収益は、最大のリスク負担によって定まるとの代替の原則に基づく。（API 一般規定9.2.1.2）

5. 鑑定評価報告書

(a) 必要的記載事項

評価リポートには、完結型リポート（self-contained or comprehensive style）、要約型リポート（summary or short form-style）、及び書式型リポート（restricted or pro-forma style）がある。電子ファイルによる提供も可能である。

完結型リポートの構成は次のとおり。

① 要約
② 依頼者：依頼者名称、依頼目的、想定、仮定、限定条件
③ 対象物件（Property）：権利利益、計画規制、立地条件、画地、公共サービス、建物
④ 市場分析（Market Analysis）：取引及び賃貸市場の動向、市場データ
⑤ 評価：取引事例比較法、収益還元法、積算法、開発法、ファイナンシャル分析（DCF）
⑥ 結論

(b) **Verbal report**
A report communicated orally to a client must be supported by a work file and at a minimum followed up by a written summary of the valuation (IVS3-3.2).

6. Implementation of Valuation Standards

As the valuation industry strives for greater professionalism, the scope of valuer responsibility and potential liability grows. Valuers may be held liable for negligence, breach of contract, or lack of compliance with the standards imposed by the API or other professional bodies. Continuing Professional Development (CPD), backup review, sanctions including reprimand, publicly admonishing, counseling, payment to the institute of up to $5,000 (By Law 23 Complaints Procedure). Professional indemnity insurance is available and required by many lenders.

7. Availability of Data

(a) **Specific Data (Primary Data)**
Specific property data is available from both Government and Private Sector sources:
①Government Data
Each State has a land title registry charged with providing accurate, secure and readily accessible registers for the recording of ownership and other interests and transactions relating to freehold land. The various State registry record land sales. Sales information is available to the public on line (for a fee), but in some cases the sales price may be overstated because of sales tax reductions or overstated because of financing. The transparency of the property market has improved because of many factors including laws requiring disclosure of information. Also it has been pointed out that independence of valuation advice is an assistance to the market.

Buildings are considered as a part of the land (development) and little is recorded about the buildings which is readily available to interested stakeholders. No tax records are available concerning buildings. The only way to view drawings and other building information is to obtain a letter of mandate from the owner and apply to the relevant local authority for permission to view the approved "as constructed" building plans.

②Private Sector Data
Sales and income data can be obtained (for a fee) from third party information companies. RP Data, for example, gathers its data from various sources, including the land registry office in most States. Information is also available via various publications (e.g., Commercial Property Monitor). Verification is the appraiser's responsibility.

(b) **General Data (Secondary Data)**
General property data is available from bodies such as:

⑦　アドバイス
⑧　付属資料

(b) 口頭の報告
依頼者に対して評価についてのリポートを口頭で行うときには、その根拠となる作業シートを備え付けておき、少なくとも後でサマリーを提供する。

6．鑑定評価基準の履行

鑑定評価の専門性が深まるとともに、鑑定人が責任を負う範囲も拡がっている。鑑定人は、過失、契約違反、APIから示される評価基準違反などによる責任を負う。これに対してAPIは、継続義務研修（CPD: Continuing Professional Development）、鑑定審査によるバックアップ、懲罰、訓戒、カウンセリング、義務研修、5,000豪ドル以下の支払いを伴う不服審査手続き（By Law 23 Complaints Procedure）などを定めているが、評価分野でも他の専門職業分野と同様に法的紛争が増えている。融資サイドからは、専門職業保険を求められる。

7．鑑定評価で利用するデータ

(a) 個別データ（Specific Data）

①官庁データ
各州の登記所の登記記録には、所有者、土地の明細、実測図番号その他の保有権に関する情報が記載されているが、建物は土地の一部とされ、記載はない。課税対象も土地のみであるから建物に関する課税資料もなく、建物図面等は所有者の委任状を得て開発許可担当部局へ閲覧申請するほかない。対象物件及び比較物件の取引情報にオンラインでアクセス可能（有料）であるが、取引価格について取得税軽減のための過小申告、ファイナンスを受けるための過大申告のケースもあるといわれる。データの整備が進んでいる理由は、法律上の要請のほかに、データに依拠する評価の独立性が市場の機能を支援する点が指摘されている。

②民間データ
RP Data、Residexなどの不動産投資関連情報サービス企業のデータベースから詳細な情報も入手可能（有料）であるが、内容の信頼性を保証するものではなく検証は鑑定人の責任。

(b) 一般データ（General Data）
ネットを通じて多くの情報にアクセスが可能である。

Australian Property Institute (www.prres.net),
Property Council of Australia (www.propertyoz.com.au),
Real Estate Institute of Australia (www.reia.com.au),
The Royal Institute of Chartered Surveyors (www.rics.org), and
Housing Industry Association (www.hia.com.au).

8. Specific Valuation Standards for Securitization Purposes

A listed property trust (LPT) is a closed-end fund. There are traditional externally operated trusts which are run by an external responsible entity (RE), and "stapled securities" which are internally operated. In one type of trust, only passive investment in rental properties is allowed, and the goal is stable income. In another type, the trust's units (trust beneficiary rights broken down into units) are listed on an exchange. In the stapled securities approach, a unit of a trust which holds real estate is combined with a share of the trust's asset management company (or its parent company) and listed together as a single share; this approach is conducive to active business endeavors that include development projects. It is high-yield but also extremely high-risk. In externally operated trusts, conflicts of interest could be a potential problem. However, the leading major firms such as the Westfield Group, Macquarie Goodman Group, Stockland Trust Group, and Centro Properties Group use the stapled securities approach in a structure that resembles U.S. REITs, and there are no particular statements concerning real estate appraisal.

Australian Property Institute（www.prres.net）
Property Council of Australia（www.propertyoz.com.au）
Real Estate Institute of Australia（www.reia.com.au）
The Royal Institute of Chartered Surveyors（www.rics.org）
Housing Industry of Association（www.hia.com.au）

8．証券化に関する基準

　LPT（Listed Property Trust）は、クローズドエンドのファンドであり、外部運用会社（RE: responsible entity）による伝統的な外部運用型トラストと内部運用型のステープル証券（stapled securities）がある。トラスト型は賃貸不動産へのパッシブな投資のみ可能で安定収益を目指し、トラストのユニット（unit：細分化された信託受益権）が上場されるタイプであり、ステープル証券型は不動産を保有するトラストのユニットのユニット及び資産運用会社（又はその親会社）の株式を抱き合わせて一体の株式として上場されるタイプで、開発案件を組み入れた積極的な事業を可能とする。高利回りであるが、リスクははるかに高い。

　外部運用では「利益相反」が問題となり得るが、Wested Group、Macquarie Goodman Group、Stockland Trust Group、Centro Properties Group を初めとする上位大手はステープル証券型で、米国 REIT と類似したストラクチャであり、鑑定評価基準でも取り立てていうほどの記述はない。

V. The People's Republic of China : Appraisal Standards

Originally drafted by Ms.Chie Hishimura,
Senior Asset Manager, Asian Asset Research Co., Ltd., and edited by the author.

1. Framework of Appraisal Standards

(a) **Who writes Appraisal Standards?**
①Land Appraisal : The Ministry of Land and Resources
②Real Estate Appraisal : The Ministry of Construction

(b) **For whom Appraisal Standards are written? (Principal purposes of appraisal standards)**
①Land Appraisal :
a. Appraiser and Appraisal Organization: The qualifications to license a land appraisal company to conduct appraisal, rate appraisers, and bear responsibility for reporting to land administrative departments are prescribed by the Land Appraisal Organization Provisional Act (1993).
b. Appraisal standards: As for the appraisal of land in urban areas, general standards, principles of appraisal, value influences, appraisal method and procedures are prescribed by the Town and City Appraisal Standards (2001).
c. The standards state that the purpose of land valuation is; 1.To improve land asset management by realizing the use which yields the highest economic value of land under effective government control, 2. To promote the disposal of publicly–owned lands and their resale to realize efficient governmental management of lands and fair transactions in the market place, 3. to make use of standards to realize comprehensive, scientific and rational land use in urban areas.

②Real Estate Appraisal :
a. Appraiser and Appraisal Organization: The qualifications to license a real estate appraisal company to conduct appraisals, rate appraisers, and bear legal responsibility are prescribed by the Real Estate Appraisal Organization Management Act (2005). Supplementary Real Estate Appraisal Management Act (2006) requires a systematic registration of real estate appraisers. As a result, the systemization of the real estate appraisal licensees has clearly been established clearly. Nowadays, only a qualified and registered real estate appraiser is able to use the name "real estate appraiser" and conduct property appraisal by affiliating with an authorized real estate appraisal organization.
b. Appraisal Standards: The People's Republic of China issued the National Standards for Real Estate Appraisal (1999) which prescribes the standards to unify the procedure of real estate appraisal, thereby establishing objectivity, fairness, and rationality as fundamental of valuation conclusion. It also provides definitions of the value, valuation principles, the procedures, the methods, additional guidance notes for the various purposes of appraisals, a prescribed form of appraisal report, and professional

Ⅴ．中華人民共和国：鑑定評価基準

原文は菱村千枝氏（株式会社アジアン・アセットリサーチ、シニアアドバイザー）による原文に執筆者加筆

1．鑑定評価基準の制度枠組み

(a) 基準の策定主体
①土地評価：国土資源部
②不動産評価：建設部

(b) 基準の目的
①土地評価 ── 対象は土地にかかる各種の経済価値
a．鑑定業法に該当するもの：『土地評価機構管理暫定規定（1993年）』
土地評価を行う業者のライセンス認定基準、等級認定、土地監督行政部門への報告義務内容等が規定されている。
b．評価基準に該当するもの：『城鎮土地評価規定（2001年）』
都市部の土地の評価をその範囲として、総則、評価原則、価格影響要因、基本的評価方法について規定している。また、『土地評価報告の規範様式（1996年）』では、土地評価報告書が備えるべき記述内容について規定されている。
c．上記土地評価規定では、土地評価の目的は「①国家の土地所有権の経済的実現と経済的手段を強化して土地資産管理を強化すること。②土地使用制度改革、つまり国有土地使用権の払い下げと転売制度を促進し、国家による土地市場管理を強化し、正常な取引を促進すること。③全面的、科学的、合理的に都市の土地を利用するための根拠とする」という目的が明記され、社会主義国のイデオロギーが強く現れた文言となっている。

②不動産評価 ── 対象は土地、建築物及び地上定着物
a．鑑定業法に該当するもの：『不動産評価機構管理弁法（2005年）』
不動産評価を行う業者のライセンス認定基準、等級認定、業者の法律責任等が規定されている。また、『注冊不動産評価師管理弁法（2006年）』では、不動産評価師登録制度が義務化され、不動産評価業務の就業資格制度が確立された。就業資格登録を行った者のみが「登録不動産評価師」という名称を使用し、評価機関において評価業務を行うことができる。
b．評価基準に該当するもの：『中華人民共和国国家標準不動産評価規範（1999年）』
不動産評価行為における統一的な規範を定め、評価結果の客観性、公正性、合理性を確立するために規定された。価値の定義、評価原則、手順、評価手法、目的別の評価における留意事項、報告書様式、職業倫理について記載がある。

③基準地価制度の存在とその評価への影響
公的地価評価制度として、全国の都市において「基準地価」制度が普及している。路線評価に近い考え方で都市の各地域を地価水準で等級分類したマトリックス形式のものである。土地の評価を行う際に、評価人は原則としてこの「基準地価評価」を用いた方法を採用することとなっており、政府が公布する基準地価制度の、中国の不動産評価全般への影響度は大きい。

ethics.
③Standard Land Value system and its impact on valuation
Standard Land Value exists for all cities and districts in China. This is a matrix system, which is very similar to a rating or classifying method used for land assessments like a street value methods. In land appraisals, the appraiser must apply this standard land value, which means the standards provided by the government have a huge impact on overall real estate valuation in China.

(c) **Who must abide by the Standards and what services must comply? (Compliance with appraisal standards / Licensing)**
①Land Appraisal : Licensed as Land Appraiser, to conduct appraisal of various kinds of land
②Real Estate Appraisal : Licensed as Real Estate Appraiser, to conduct appraisal of subject sites, buildings and other developments.
In practice, most of real estate companies in China acquire both licenses for the appraisal assignment. Individual appraiser is not allowed to conduct an appraisal as a fee appraiser, but allowed to conduct an appraisal as an institutionally employed appraiser (Mostly formed as corporation)
③Authorized Property Appraiser for business valuation
In addition to land appraisal and real estate appraisal, general property appraisal businesses and license exist in China. Property appraisers are authorized to appraise an unincorporated or incorporated business entity such as operating company. They are experts both at accounting and property appraisal. To pass the certifying examination to become an authorized property appraiser is much more difficult than to become a regular real estate or land appraiser. The Ministry of Finance of the People's Republic of China has jurisdiction over this position.
In 2006, the Chinese government revoked the 2002 deregulation of real estate holdings by foreign investors and curtailed the foreign investment in mainland China. If a foreign company wishes to acquire a right to real estate, there is only one method, which is to purchase the whole company, which occupies the real estate. In these circumstances authorized property appraisers play a significant role in conducting the valuation.

2. Fundamentals for Appraisal

(a) **Real Property Rights and Interests to be Appraised**
According to Article 10 of the Constitution, land in cities (land for construction) is state-owned, and land in rural villages and suburbs are owned by agricultural collectives (essentially state-owned) unless specified by law as state-owned. Therefore, to enhance their liquidity for developments, it is necessary to establish land usage rights (in effect, leasehold) other than ownership. Land usage rights are of the following two types, and land usage certificates are issued by the authorities.
①Government sale of land usage rights
Usage rights are sold for a fee (lump sum payment), for a limited period of time, restricted to private use. The land usage rights could be transferred to a third party by

(c) ライセンス
　①土地（使用権）の評価：国土資源部が所管、国家資格名は「公認土地評価師」
　②不動産（土地及び建物）の評価：建設部が所管、国家資格名は「公認不動産評価師」
　　不動産評価業に従事する会社の大半が「土地評価会社」のライセンスと「不動産評価会社」のライセンスの両方を取得して業務を行っている。資格者は、個人では評価業務を行うことはできず、評価業の営業ライセンスを保有する評価機関（ほとんどが有限会社形式である）に所属して初めて評価業務を行うことができる。
　③中国ではこのほかに、土地、建物を含む企業を評価する国家資格である「公認資産評価師」という資格がある。公認会計士と有形資産の評価の双方の知識を有する専門家であり、試験の難度は不動産評価師以上である。財政部（日本の財務省に相当）が管轄する。

　なお、中国では2006年、2002年以来継続してきた外資導入政策を方向転換して不動産取引規制を導入している。すなわち、外国企業（中国において法人を設立していない外国の法人）は、投資用の不動産単体（プロジェクトカンパニーでなく不動産そのもの）を買い、登記移転を受けることはできない。外国企業が、投資目的で不動産の支配権を取得できる可能性があるとすれば（それも許認可が必要だが）、不動産をまるごと含む企業（株式）を買収する方法しかない。

2．鑑定評価の前提

(a) 鑑定評価の対象となる権利・利益

憲法第10条により、都市の土地（建設用地）は国有、農村及び都市近郊の土地は法律で国有の旨の規定がない限り農民集団所有（実質的には国有）である。したがって、土地を流動化（権利移転）させるには、所有権以外の土地使用権を認める必要がある。土地使用権には次の二種類があり、当局発行の土地使用証が発給される。

①払い下げ式の土地使用権（出譲）
　有償取得（一括払い）、期間制限、民間使用を前提とし、土地使用権の転売・賃貸は可能である。使用権の最長期間は用途によって決められている（例えば、住宅用地70年、商業用地40年、工業用地50年）。2007年の人民代会議で物権法が改正され、住宅用地の使用権期間満了後の自動継続が認められている。住宅用地以外の使用権は、これまでどおり、使用権期間満了の1年

resale or leasing. The longest time period of the usage rights is determined according to the purpose of use (e.g., 70 years for housing, 40 years for commercial use, and 50 years for industrial use). The Realty Law was revised by the Congress of People's Deputies in 2007, allowing automatic renewal after expiration of the usage rights period in the case of land used for housing. For land used for other purposes than housing, it is still necessary to apply for renewal to the national government one year before expiration of the usage rights period, and to enter into a new rights issuance contract if approval is granted.

②Special grant of land usage rights

Usage rights are also granted free of charge or for a nominal fee, for an unlimited period of time, restricted to purposes such as state-run businesses, the military, roads, and public works projects.

However, private ownership of buildings is recognized. In rural villages, most housing is owned by individual residents. In cities as well, many homes are owned by individuals.

(b) **Scope of Work**

Before conducting an appraisal, the client and the appraisal company must sign an engagement contract for an appraisal. The subject of the appraisal and the interest to be valued, the basis on which the subject will be appraised, and rights and liabilities between the parties must be specified in the terms of engagement. In addition, a clause about a breach of contract will be included in the terms.

(c) **Assumptions and Limiting Conditions**

A statement of assumptions and limiting conditions is often included in the premise of the appraisal for an appraiser's protection as well as for the information and protection of the client and others using the report:

Assumptions presume as fact otherwise uncertain information about the physical, legal, or economic characteristics of the subject property or about conditions external to the subject property such as market conditions at the date of value. When used in performing an appraisal they become part of the givens in the appraisal and have an effect on the appraiser's opinions and conclusions.

Limiting conditions deals with special conditions such as ①whether the value estimate in the report applies only for the stated data, ②the use of an appraisal is limited by specifying the intended use, intended user, or intended period of the appraisal report.

(d) **Appraisal Reviews**

There is no specific description about reviewing valuations within the law, regulations, or provisions above.

3. *General Concepts and Principles (Valuation Bases)*

(a) **Market Value**

①Open Market Value

On the market, with the intention of assuring maximum profit for both willing seller and willing buyer, the value is estimated for which an asset property will exchange af-

前に国に継続申請し、許可されれば新たに使用権払い下げ契約を結ぶことになる。
②割り当て式の土地使用権
　無償又は格安取得、期間制限なし、国営企業、軍事、道路、公益事業など用途が制限されている。
　なお、建物は私有が認められていて、農村では住宅はほとんど農民個人の所有、都市部でも相当数が個人所有といわれる。

(b)　業務の範囲
　不動産評価着手前に、依頼者と評価会社の間で「不動産評価業務委託契約」を締結する。当該契約において、対象不動産、評価の基本的事項が明記され、相互の義務と権利が明記される。違約の場合の規定も盛り込まれる。

(c)　評価の前提条件
　後述の必要記載事項に含まれる「⑯評価の仮定と限定条件」には、2つの概念が含まれる。ひとつには評価の仮定条件である。つまり、価格時点において不動産市場の状況と評価対象物件の状況において不確定な要因であるが、価値に影響のある要因について仮定を置いて評価を行う場合の条件である。もうひとつは評価の制限条件で、これには、①評価結果が制約あるいは影響を受ける制限条件（資料の出所など）、②評価報告の使用範囲、使用できる場合、使用期限などの制約条件である。

(d)　評価の審査
　前記の不動産評価関連法律・法規及び評価規範・規定に記述がない。

3．鑑定評価の基礎（価値の種類）

(a)　**市場価値**（Market Value）
　①公開市場価値
　　市場において、取引双方が取引における最大利益の追求を目的として、必要な市場情報と取引のための十分な時間的余裕を持ち、取引対象についての必要な専門知識を備え、取引条件が公

ter proper marketing wherein the parties had each acted knowledgably, prudently and without compulsion. Additionally, the terms of sale must be made prior to the conclusion of the sales contract.

②Highest and Best use

The most probable use of land or improved property that is legally possible, physically possible, financially feasible and appropriately supported by the market, and which results in maximum profitability.

(b) **Value Other Than Market Value**

The lowest bid which is determined with the assumption of an open market and under circumstances where some legal process must be carried out in a short term.

4. Approaches to Value

(a) **Approaches to Value**

In the valuation process, more than one approach to value must be applied to develop final value opinion.
① Sales Comparison Approach
② Income Approach
③ Cost Approach
④ Hypothetical Development Method
⑤ Standard Land Value Adjustment Method

(b) **Valuation Procedure**

The valuation procedure is as follows: ①Clarify principal items of valuation ; purpose, subject, the date of valuation, ②Settle on a plan for the valuation process, ③Gather necessary information, data, and materials for the valuation, ④Confirm the subject property by site inspection, ⑤Select valuation methods and applications, ⑥Conclude the result of the valuation, ⑦Draw up the valuation report, ⑧Organize and preserve the information, data, and materials.

5. Appraisal Reports

(a) **Contents**

　a. Entire Structure:
　Ⅰ. Introduction
　Ⅱ. Statements of the purpose of the appraisal, description of the property and interest to be valued, lists of names of the people who conduct the inspection
　Ⅲ. Assumptions and Limiting conditions
　Ⅳ. Valuation conclusion
　Ⅴ. Valuation Technical Report (This does not have to be given to the client. The purpose for which it is prepared is for the inspection by the appraisal organization or by the competent authorities.)
　Ⅵ. Appendixes

開され排他性がない条件下で成立する可能性が最も高い価格。
②最高最佳使用（Highest and Best Use）
法律上許容され、技術的に可能で、経済的に実現可能性の高い十分な合理性の検証が行われた、評価対象に最も高い価値を実現させうる使用方法。

(b) **市場価値以外の価値**（Value Other Than Market Value）
・拍売底価（競売最低価格）
公開市場価値を前提として、短期的な強制処分による影響を考慮した価格。

4．鑑定評価の方式・手順

(a) **鑑定評価の方式**
評価では、下記のうち2種類以上の評価方法を併用して行うべきこととされている。
① 市場比較法
② 収益法
③ 成本法
④ 剰余法
⑤ 基準地価修正法

(b) **不動産鑑定評価の手順**
① 評価の基本的事項の明確化（評価目的、対象、価格時点）
② 評価作業計画の策定
③ 評価に必要な資料の収集
④ 現地踏査による対象不動産の確認
⑤ 評価方法の選択と適用
⑥ 評価結果の確定
⑦ 評価報告書の記述
⑧ 評価資料の整理と保存

5．鑑定評価報告書

(a) **必要的記載事項**
　a．**全体構成**
・依頼者に対する前言
・評価人による声明（真実性、利害関係なし、実地踏査人員氏名等宣誓事項）
・評価の仮定と制限条件
・評価結果報告
・評価技術報告（依頼者に提供しないことができる。評価機関の保存及び監督行政部門の査閲のために作成する）
・付属書類
　b．**記載事項**
①評価対象プロジェクトの名称、②依頼者の名称と住所、③不動産評価会社の名称と住所、

b. Minimum requirements for appraisal report

①Identification of the subject property and location, ②Client's name and address, ③The appraisal company's name and address, ④Information about the subject property; the site: name, location, area, shape, circumstance、adjoining land, environment, view, infrastructure, condition, topography, geological features, town planning and regulation, current utilization, title and tenure.

the building: name, location, area, stories, structure, interior, facilities, arrangement, operation quality, age, repair and maintenance, infrastructure, current utilization, title and tenure.

⑤The purpose of the valuation, ⑥The date of the value opinion, ⑦The value definition, ⑧ Sources of information and data used for the valuation; real estate appraisal standards, laws and ordinances etc., ⑨Valuation rules, ⑩Valuation Technical Procedure: methods and calculations, ⑪Valuation Conclusion and Reasons, ⑫Valuation date, ⑬The effective period of validity of the appraisal report, ⑭Appraiser's name, ⑮Registered appraiser's name, signature, and stamps, ⑯Assumptions and limiting conditions, ⑰Map, photos, copy of the title for the subject property, copy of the licenses for the appraisal company, and copy of appraiser's licenses

(b) **Verbal Report**

There are no provisions or allowances for making an oral report.

6. Implementation of Appraisal Standards

Article 25 of the Supplementary Real Estate Appraisal Management Act of 2006 prescribes the items a registered real estate appraiser must fulfill:

①Compliance with the law, administrative regulations, morals, and ethics, ②Compliance with the appraisal standards, ③Responsibility for objectivity and fairness in developing value opinions, ④Confidentiality of information classified as confidential by applicable laws or identified as confidential when given to the appraiser, ⑤Avoiding conflicts of interest, ⑥Continuing education requirements to enhance professional knowledge and experience, ⑦Assisting the registration organization in carrying out its responsibilities.

Also, registered real estate appraisers must refrain from the following conduct: ①Not carrying out the contracted or provisioned items which must be executed, ②Demanding /accepting bribes or other economic benefits, ③Making false and/ or misleading statements and/or omissions, ④Concealing facts or distorting, ⑤Lending their name to someone else to conduct the appraisal, ⑥Working for two or more appraisal companies at the same time, ⑦Conducting real estate appraisal without belonging to a registered appraisal company, ⑧To use license or certification for real estate appraiser illegally, and ⑨Conducting outside the scope of the contract or rules of the appraisal company to which he/she belongs.

If a registered real estate appraiser has performed an improper appraisal, the department of real estate administration at the place the violation occurs must investigate the facts.

④評価対象（土地：名称、所在地、面積、形状、四囲隣接、周辺環境、景観、インフラ設備程度、整地程度、地勢、地質、計画規制内容、現状利用、権利の状況。
建物：名称、所在地、面積、階層、構造、内装、設備の程度、平面配置、施工の質、建築年、維持補修の程度、インフラの程度、現状利用、権利の状況）、⑤評価目的、⑥価格時点、⑦価値の定義、⑧評価に用いた根拠文献（不動産評価規範、各種法令等）、⑨評価原則、⑩評価技術方針・方法と計算、⑪評価の結果とその理由、⑫評価の決定日時、⑬評価報告書の有効期限、⑭評価人氏名、⑮登録不動産評価師の署名と捺印、⑯評価の仮定と限定条件、⑰地図、写真、対象不動産の権利の証明書コピー、評価機関のライセンス及び評価人の資格証明書コピー

(b) 口頭の報告

上記関連法律法規や不動産評価規範に規定がなく、認められない。

6. 鑑定評価基準の履行

注冊不動産評価師管理弁法第25条で、登録不動産評価師の履行すべき事項として以下の事項が定められた。
① 法律法規、行政管理規定、職業道徳の遵守
② 標準不動産評価規範の実行
③ 評価結果の客観公正性に相応の責任を負う
④ 就業中に知り得た国家機密と他社の商業・技術機密の守秘
⑤ 当事者との利害関係がある場合は評価を回避する
⑥ 継続教育を受け資質向上に努める
⑦ 登録管理団体に協力する

また、登録不動産評価師は以下のことを行ってはならない。
① 登録不動産評価師の履行すべき事項を履行しない
② 就業中の収賄、収賄要求、契約報酬以外の経済利益の要求行為
③ 虚偽、誤解を招く記述、重大な遺漏のある報告書の記載
④ 報告における事実の隠蔽又は歪曲
⑤ 他人に自己の名義で評価業務を行わせる
⑥ 同時に2社以上の評価会社において就業する
⑦ 個人名義で評価業務を行う
⑧ 非合法に登録証書を利用する
⑨ 就業評価会社の業務範囲を超えた業務を行う

Chapter 2.Ⅴ. The People's Republic of China : Appraisal Standards

The result will be reported to the department where the appraiser has registered. The appraiser will probably have his or her license or certificate revoked.

7. Availability of Data

In the case that the appraiser collects sales data, the following procedures are used. There is no single data base for the collection and preparation of sales data.
① Collecting advertised sale and rental prices, actual subdivision sale prices, and the like by visiting Internet websites for end users. (The largest such website is Soufun, followed by Sofu, Sina, Google, etc.)
② Visiting subdivision sales centers and real estate agencies in the area where the subject property is located and asking for sales data. (The basic approach is to use connections by way of acquaintances.)
③ Visiting real estate trade centers in various localities and asking for sales data, etc. through acquaintances.
④ Collecting pamphlets and other information issued by public organizations in various localities.

8. Specific Appraisal Standards for Securitization Purposes

There is no specific appraisal standard for real estate securitization purposes. Global REITs including properties in China as a portfolio exists in Singapore, Hong Kong, and others.

登録不動産評価師が違法に評価活動に従事した場合、違法行為発生地の不動産管理部門は、事実関係を調査し、かつ、その結果を当該登録評価師の登録地の不動産管理部門に通知して、法律に従いその登録を抹消することができる。

7．鑑定評価に利用するデータ

評価人が取引事例等を収集する場合には、以下のような手段を用いる。評価のための組織的な事例作成や収集といった仕組みはない。
① 売却募集事例、賃貸募集事例、分譲実績価格などは、インターネット上のエンドユーザー向けのウェブサイトを閲覧して収集する（最大規模のウェブサイトは「中国捜房網」、その他「SOFU」、「SINA」、「GOOGLE」など各サイトがある）。
② 評価対象不動産が存在する地域の分譲販売センターや仲介会社を訪問して、取引事例等を紹介してもらう（知人を通じた人脈が基本）。
③ 各地の「不動産交易センター」へ行き、知人を通じて取引事例等を紹介してもらう。
④ 各地の公的機関が発行する冊子や情報を収集する。

8．証券化に関する基準

現在、中国において不動産の証券化の制度は実現していない。中国本土の不動産を証券化商品として取り込んだ外国のREITは存在する（シンガポール、香港等）。

Ⅵ. International Valuation Standards (IVS)

Extracts from the International Valuation Standards (Eighth Edition) 2007 are reproduced with the permission of the International Valuation Standards Council that holds the copyright. No responsibility is accepted by the IVSC for the accuracy of information contained in the text as republished or translated, the English version of the IVSC Standards as published by the IVSC from time to time being the only official version of the IVSC Standards. The full text of the official version may be obtained from the IVSC International Headquarters, 12 Great George Street, London SW1P 3AD, UK. http://www.ivsc.org

1. Framework for Valuation Standards

(a) **Who write Valuation Standards?**

The International Valuation Standards Committee (IVSC) was established in 1981 originally between UK and US real estate professional valuation organizations. IVSC has widen its pursuits and today develops and promulgates international valuation standards for all asset classes. These include real estate, plant and machinery, business valuations, and intangible assets. Guidance is provided for secured lending, financial reporting including public sector reporting and valuation for a variety of uses such as litigation and tax matters. At present, 52 countries (from the initial 20 in 1984) are members of the IVSC. The IVSC continues to build relationships with the users and prepares of valuations throughout the world in addition to furthering mutual collaboration with other standards setters including the International Accounting Standards Board (IASB). As part of this process and IVSC's evolution, it is completing an organizational restructuring started in 2006 to make its membership open to a wider group of stakeholders, much like the restructure IASC embarked on in the late 1990s. The new organization know as the International Valuation Standards Council (IVSC) will have an fully independent Standards Board, as well as a Professional Board. The Professional Board will provide practitioners assistance (in some cases extensive) in the form of implementation guidance, advice and continuing education specific to IVS. It will also provide a set of quality control measures and a model code of ethics for professional valuers.

(b) **For whom Valuation Standards are written? (Principal aim and purposes of valuation standards)**

IVS has been guided by three principal objectives:

① To facilitate cross-border transactions and contribute to the viability of international property markets by promoting transparency in financial reporting as well as the reliability of valuations performed to secure loans and mortgages, for transactions involving transfers of ownership, and for settlements in litigation or tax matters;

② To serve as a professional benchmark, or beacon, for Valuers around the world, thereby enabling them to respond to the demands of international property markets for reliable valuations and to meet the financial reporting requirements of the global business community; and

Ⅵ. 国際評価基準（IVS）

国際評価基準委員会が発行する2007年国際評価基準（英文）からの抜粋は、著作権を有する同委員会の許可を得て、執筆者の理解とを責任で行われている。国際評価基準の全文は、国際評価基準委員会の「International Headquarters, 12 Great George Street, London SW1P 3AD, UK」から入手できる。http://www.ivsc.org

1．鑑定評価の制度枠組み

(a) 鑑定評価基準の策定主体

1981年、英国及び米国の不動産鑑定評価団体が、国際評価基準委員会（IVSC）を設立した（両国の基準を調整する趣旨も指摘されている）。同委員会は次第に活動を拡げてきて、現在では全ての資産について鑑定評価基準を策定し公表している。すなわち、不動産、工場及び機械設備、企業及び無形資産を対象とし、担保融資、公的部門によるものを含めて財務報告、訴訟や税務など多様な目的のための鑑定評価の指針を提供している。同委員会は、現在、52カ国のメンバーから構成され（1984年当初は20カ国）、鑑定人と鑑定評価の利用者との関係の構築に努め、また国際会計基準委員会（IASB）をはじめとする他の基準策定団体と相互の連携を強めている。同委員会は、さらに活動を強化するために、かつて国際会計基準委員会が1990年代後半に始めたように、メンバー資格を鑑定評価に利害関係を有する広範囲のグループまで開放して、2006年開始の組織再編の仕上げ段階に入っている。新しい組織は、国際評価協議会（International Valuation Standards Council（IVSC））の下に、常設の専門家委員会（Professional Board）及び独立した基準委員会（Standards Board）を設置している。専門委員会は、鑑定評価の留意事項、助言、IVS継続研修などの実務家研修（さらに広範囲に及ぶ研修もある）を提供し、品質管理及び専門職業たる鑑定人の倫理規定モデルも提供する。

(b) 基準の目的

国際評価基準は次の3つの目的を有する。
① 所有権移転等の取引及び紛争や税務の解決のために、ローンや担保の確保に係る評価の信頼性及び財務報告における透明性を高めて、クロス・ボーダー取引を推進し国際資産市場の活性化に貢献する。
② 世界中の鑑定人に対して、国際資産市場の信頼できる評価への要請に応え、グローバルな企業の財務報告の要請に応えられる基準を提供する。
③ 新興及び新たに工業化された国々の需要に応じられる評価及び財務報告の基準を提供する。

Chapter 2.Ⅵ. International Valuation Standards (IVS)

③ To provide Standards of valuation and financial reporting that meet the needs of emerging and newly industrialized countries.

(c) **Who must abide by the Standards and what services must comply? (Compliance with valuation standards)**

The organization of the standards follows.
1. Introduction
2. Concepts Fundamental to Generally Accepted Valuation Principles (GAVP)
3. Code of Conduct (CC)
4. Property Types
5. Standards / Applications / Guidance Notes
  ①Standards :
    IVS 1   Market Value Basis of valuation
    IVS 2   Bases Other Than Market Value
    IVS 3   Valuation Reporting
  ②Applications :
    IVA 1   Valuation for Financial Reporting
    IVA 2   Valuation for Secured Lending Purposes
    IVA 3   Valuation of Public Sector Assets for Financial Reporting
  ③Guidance Note :
    GN 1   Real Property Valuation
    GN 2   Valuation of Lease Interests
    GN 3   Valuation of Plant and Equipment
    GN 4   Valuation of Intangible Assets
    GN 5   Valuation of Personal Property
    GN 6   Business Valuation
    GN 7   Consideration of Hazardous and Toxic Substances in Valuation
    GN 8   The Cost Approach for Financial Reporting- (DRC)
    GN 9   Discounted Cash Flow Analysis for Market Valuation and Investment Analyses
    GN10   Valuation of Agricultural Properties
    GN11   Reviewing Valuations
    GN12   Valuation of Trade Related Property
    GN13   Mass Appraisal for Property Taxation
    GN14   Valuation of Properties in the Extractive Industries
    GN15   Valuation of Historic Property

(d) **Licensing / Designation**

A Valuer is a person of who possesses the necessary qualifications, ability, and experience to execute a valuation. In some States, licensing is required before a person can act as a Valuer.

(c) 基準の対象

　国際評価基準は、次のように構成されている。まず、基準全体に関係する法的及び経済的な概念及び原則として、評価の一般概念、行為規範、評価の対等となる権利・利益の規定を置いている。そのうえで、①評価基準、②適用、③留意事項を規定するが、いずれも重要性は同じであり、IVS に準拠したというためには、そのすべてを満たすものでなくてはならない。

（一般規定）

評価の一般概念と原則：GAVP（Concepts Fundamental to Generally Accepted Valuation Principles）

行為規範：CC（Code of Conduct）

評価の対象となる財産権：PT、不動産（real property）、動産（personal property）、企業（businesses）、及び金融商品（financial interests）

（基準・適用・留意事項）

①評価基準（Standards）
　　基準 1 （S1）　　市場価値
　　基準 2 （S2）　　市場価値以外の価値
　　基準 3 （S3）　　評価書

②適用（Applications）
　　適用 1 （IVA1）財務報告のための評価
　　適用 2 （IVA2）担保融資のための評価
　　適用 3 （IVA3）公的部門における財務報告のための評価

③留意事項（Guidance Note）
　　ガイダンスノート 1 （GN1）　　不動産の評価
　　ガイダンスノート 2 （GN2）　　リースホールドの評価
　　ガイダンスノート 3 （GN3）　　工場及び機械設備の評価
　　ガイダンスノート 4 （GN4）　　無形資産の評価
　　ガイダンスノート 5 （GN5）　　動産の評価
　　ガイダンスノート 6 （GN6）　　企業の評価
　　ガイダンスノート 7 （GN7）　　評価における危険物質
　　ガイダンスノート 8 （GN8）　　財務報告のための原価法
　　ガイダンスノート 9 （GN9）　　市場分析及び投資分析のための DCF
　　ガイダンスノート10 （GN10）　農業用不動産の評価
　　ガイダンスノート11 （GN11）　評価の審査
　　ガイダンスノート12 （GN12）　事業用資産の評価
　　ガイダンスノート13 （GN13）　財産税課税標準のための大量評価
　　ガイダンスノート14 （GN14）　鉱物・石油資源関連産業の財産権の評価
　　ガイダンスノート15 （GN15）　歴史的建造物の評価

(d) ライセンス・認定

　評価人（valuer）は、評価、すなわち最も確からしい資産価値判断を行う資質、能力、経験を有する者をいい、国によってはさらに一定の資格を要する。

2. Fundamentals for Valuation

(a) **Real Property Rights and Interests to be Valued**
IVS contains the recognized standards of practice for real estate, personal and business valuation.

(b) **Scope of work**
A valuer ensures that the analyses, information and conclusions presented in the report fit the specifications for the assignment. The specifications for the valuation assignment include the following seven elements: ① an identification of the real, personal, business or other property subject to the valuation; ② an justification of the property rights (solo proprietorship, partnership, or partial interest) to be valued; ③ the intended use of the valuation and any related limitation; and the identification of any subcontractors or a-gents and their contribution; ④ a definition of the basis of value sought; ⑤ the date as of which the value estimate applies and the date of the intended report; ⑥ an identification of the scope / extent of the valuation and of the report; and ⑦ an identification of any contingent and limiting conditions upon which the valuation is based.
(IVS3-3.4)

(c) **Assumptions**
Assumptions are suppositions taken to be true. Assumptions involve facts, conditions, or situations affecting the subject of, or approach to, a valuation but which may not be capable or worthy of verification. They are matters that, once declared, are to be accepted in understanding the valuation. All assumptions underlying a valuation should be reasonable. (CC-3.0)

(d) **Appraisal Reviews**
A valuation review is a review of a valuer's work undertaken by another valuer exercising impartial judgment. Because of the need to ensure the accuracy, appropriateness, and quality of valuation report, valuation reviews have become an integral part of professional practice. Reasons for agreement or disagreement with the conclusions of a valuation report should be fully explained and disclosed. Where the review valuer is not in possession of all the facts and information on which the valuer relied, the review valuer must disclose the limitations of his or her conclusions. Where the scope of the work undertaken is sufficient to constitute a new valuation, such valuation must conform to the requirements of the IVS Standards and Code of Conduct. (CN11)

3. General Concepts and Principles (Basis of Value)

(a) **Market Value**
Market Value is the estimated amount for which a property should exchange on the date of valuation between a willing buyer and a willing seller in an arm's length transaction after proper marketing wherein the parties had each acted knowledgeably, prudently, and without compulsion. (IVS1-3.0) The IVSC position is that the term Market Value never requires further qualification and that all States should move toward compliance with this usage. To estimate Market Value, a valuer must first determine highest and

2. 鑑定評価の前提

(a) 鑑定評価の対象となる権利・利益
評価の対象とする資産は、不動産、動産、企業（business／going concern）、金融上の権利（financial interest）。

このうち、不動産（real estate）とは、土地及びその定着物（例えば建物）をいう。不動産に対する権利を不動産権（real property）といい、フリーホールド（freehold／fee simple）とリースホールド（leasehold）に大別される。

(b) 業務の範囲（Specification for the Valuation Assignment）
評価の内容と範囲を定め、評価にまつわる問題に曖昧な部分があれば解決する。次の7項目が含まれる（S3-3.4）。対象となる不動産・動産・企業ほか、権利（単独所有、共有、部分的権利）、利用目的、価値の種類、価格時点、業務の範囲・限度、想定条件。

(c) 評価の前提条件
想定条件（assumption）は、事実とみなされる前提条件である。内容は評価の対象や手法に影響を及ぼす事実・条件・状況であるが、事実であることの確認が不可能であったり検証に値しないものである。評価の前提となる想定は、合理性がなくてはならない（CC-3.0）。

(d) 評価の審査
鑑定評価の審査は、鑑定評価人の業務について、他の鑑定評価人が公平な判断をもって吟味して意見を報告することである。鑑定評価書の正確性・妥当性・高品質を確保するうえで重要な専門領域となっている。審査した者が評価書の結論に同意する場合も同意しない場合も、その理由を十分に説明し開示する。評価人が依拠した事実関係や情報を入手していない場合には、その結論の限界を開示する。審査した者の業務範囲が評価に該当するに至った時は、評価に関する基準の適用を受ける（GN11）。

3. 鑑定評価の基礎（価値の種類）

(a) 市場価値（Market Value）
市場価値は、交換価値（value in exchange／not value in use）、すなわち価格時点において、買う意欲のある買主と売る意欲のある売主が各自資産及び市場に関する十分な情報を持ち、慎重にかつ強制されないで行動し、適切なマーケティングを経て、独立した取引当事者としての取引（arm's length transaction）において交換される価格である（S1-3.0）。市場価値の定義は、更なる制限は一切不要であり、すべての国がこの用法に従うようにすべきとするのがIVSCの立場である。

best use (HABU). That use may be for continuation of a property's existing use or for some alternative use. Theses determinations are made from market evidence. (IVS1-1.1)

①Highest and Best Use (HABU)

The most probable use of a property which is physically possible, appropriately justified, legally permissible, financially feasible, and which results in the highest value of the property being valued. (GAVP6.3) In markets characterized by extreme volatility or severe disequilibrium between supply and demand, the HABU of a property may be a holding for future use. In other situations, where several types of potential HABU are identifiable, the valuer should discuss such alternative uses and anticipated future income and expense levels. Where land use and zoning are in a state of change, the immediate HABU of a property may be an interim use. (GAVP6.6) The concept of HABU is fundamental and integral part of Market Value estimates. The valuer considers both the HABU of land as though vacant and the HABU of a property as improved. (GN5.8)

②Exposure Time

It means that the property would be exposed to the market in the most appropriate manner to effect its disposal at the best price reasonably obtainable in accordance. The length of exposure time may vary with market conditions, but must be sufficient to allow the property to be brought to the attention of an adequate number of potential purchasers. The exposure period occurs prior to the valuation date. (IVS1-3.27)

③Fair Value

Fair Value is a broader concept than Market Value. Although in many cases the price that is fair between two parties will equate to that obtainable in the general market, i.e., Market Value, there will be cases where the assessment of Fair Value will involve taking into account matters that have to be disregarded in the assessment of Market Value. (IVS2-6.4) When the Market Value of an asset can be established this will equate to Fair Value.

(b) **Value Other Than Market Value**

①Value in use

The present value of estimated future cash flows expected to arise from the continuing use of an asset and from its disposal at the end of its useful life. It should be noted that the above definition, which applies to financial reporting, considers the value of an asset at the end of its useful life. This meaning differs from the way the term is commonly used in valuation practice. (Glossary of Terms)

②Depreciated Replacement Cost (DRC)

An application of the cost approach used in assessing the value of specialized assets for financial reporting purposes, where direct market evidence is limited or unavailable. The current cost of replacing an asset with its modern equivalent asset less deductions for physical deterioration and all relevant forms of obsolescence and optimization. (GN8-3.0)

③Special value

市場価値を評価するには、鑑定人はまず最有効使用が何であるかを判定しなければならない。最有効使用は現行用途（existing use）を継続する場合もあるし、違う用途（alternative use）の場合もある。判定は市場から得られる資料（evidence）に基づいて行われる（S1-1.2）。

① **最有効使用（Highest and Best Use）**

最有効使用とは、物的に可能で、適切妥当で、法的に許容され、経済的に採算がとれ、最高の価値が実現されるような最も確からしい使用である（GAVP-6.3）。乱高下又は需給の著しい不均衡が見られる市場にあっては、最有効使用は、将来使用のため当面そのまま持っていることであるかもしれない。また、いくつかの潜在的な最有効使用が考えられる場合は、鑑定人は、種々の代替用途と予想される将来の収益と費用の水準を検討すべきである（GAVP-6.6）。最有効使用の概念は、市場価値の評価に当たって、基礎的で不可欠な部分である（GAVP-6.7）。鑑定人は更地の最有効使用と土地建物一体の複合不動産の最有効使用の両方を分析して判定する（GN1-5.8）。

② **市場公開期間（Exposure Time）**

不動産を最高の価格で売却できるように、最も適当な方法で市場に公開することを想定するが、公開期間の長さは市場の状態によって流動的である。潜在的な相当数の買い希望者の注意を引くに足るだけの十分な長さが必要である。公開期間は価格時点より前に設定される（S1-3.2.7）。

③ **公正価値（Fair Value）**

会計基準で使われる公正価値は、市場価値についても市場価値以外の価値についても使われるが（GAVP-8.1）、通常は市場価値と一致する。公正価値は、国際会計基準によると、買う意欲のある買主と売る意欲のある売主が各自資産及び市場に関する十分な情報を持って独立した取引当事者としての取引（arm's length transaction）において交換されるであろう価格である。国際評価基準は、鑑定人が財務報告のための評価を行う場合は市場価値を報告すべしとしている。企業が国際会計基準にそって公正価値を開示する場合には、鑑定人は市場価値の判定に使われた想定や限定条件をすべて開示する（IVA1-5.4）。

(b) **市場価値以外の価値（Value Other Than Market Value）**

① **使用価値（Value in Use）**

企業（going concern）の評価は、一般に使用価値に基づく（PT-4.6）。国際会計基準では、資産の継続的使用とその耐用年数の終了時における処分によって生じると予測される、見積もり将来キャッシュフローの現在価値と定義している。なお、英国のRed Bookの「現在用途を前提とする市場価値*」とは、最有効使用を必ずしも前提としない点では共通であるが、現行用途での売却取引を想定していない点で異なる。

＊IVSは、かつては現行用途を前提とする市場価値（EUV: Existing Use value、Market Value for the Existing Use）の概念を基準の中に入れていたが、1998年に基準から削除している。取引価格を前提とする公正価値の概念と矛盾するためである（すなわち、公正価値は売却取引を想定するが、取引においては、取引当事者は多様な見解を持つのであり、現在用途を前提とするとか他の用途を前提とするとはいえないからである）旨、説明されている（IVS 2000）。

② **特別な積算価格（Depreciated Replacement Cost: DRC）**

土地の現行用途に基づく市場価値に、構築物の価格時点での再調達原価を加え、物理的劣化と

Special Value can arise where an asset has attributes that make it more attractive to a particular buyer, to a limited category of buyers, than to the general body of buyers in a market. These attributes can include the physical, geographic, economic or legal characteristics of an asset. Market value requires the disregard of any element of special value because at any given date it is only assumed that there is a willing buyer, not a particular buyer. (IVS2-6.6) When special value is reported, it should always be clearly distinguished from Market Value. (IVS2-6.8)

④Synergistic Value or Marriage Value

An additional element of value created by the combination of two or more interests where the value of the combined interest is worth more than the sum of the original interests. Synergistic Value can be a type of Special Value. (IVS2-6.7)

⑤Investment Value / Worth

The value of property to a particular investors, or a class of investors, for identified investment or operational objectives. This subjective concept relates specific property to a specific investor, group of investors, or entity with identifiable investment objectives and /or criteria. (IVS1-3.3)

4. Approaches to Value

Several methods are used for land valuations. Their applicability differs according to the type of value estimated and availability of data (GN1-5.9). Where there is sufficient market data to support the valuation, Market Value is derived. In other circumstances, where there is insufficient market data or special instructions have been given, the result will be a value other than Market Value (GN1 – 5.16).

(a) **Sales Comparison Approach**

This approach considers the sales of similar or substitute properties and related market data, and establishes a value estimate by processes involving comparison. In general, a property being valued is compared with sales of similar properties that have been transacted in the market. Listing and offerings may also be considered.

(b) **Income Capitalization Approach**

This approach considers income and expense data relating to the property being valued and estimates value through a capitalization process. Capitalization relates income (usually a net income figure) and defined value type by converting an income amount into a value estimate. This process may consider direct relationships (where by an overall capitalization rate is applied), a yield or discount rate or both.

(c) **Cost Approach**

陳腐化による減価を差し引いて査定する。「特殊不動産（specialized property：公共部門の施設、特殊な生産施設、教会、博物館など、資産の特質・構造・立地・その他の特殊性のために、事業の構成要素として一括して取引される以外に、市場で取引されることがほとんどない資産）」の市場での価値を示す数値として、償却後取替原価による積算価格は、財務報告での評価に利用される価値又は手法である。この価値と事業を廃止して他の用途に転用する場合の価値は大きく異なるので、これに関する記述が必要になる。詳しくは、「財務報告のための特別な積算価格の評価」（VIP No.10）を参照。

英国会計基準では、長い間、特殊不動産の価値の査定は市場資料の裏づけがないため信頼性が劣るとして、財務諸表上、評価とは別扱いされてきた。しかし、国際会計基準ではそのような区別はなく、資産の公正価値は、市場資料に基づいても、あるいは収益や積算に基づいてもいいとしている。信頼性の問題は資料手法の開示によって対応する。

③**特殊価値**（Special Value）

例えば、土地所有者が隣地不動産に市場価値をはるかに超える上乗せ価格を支払う場合のように、特定の買主のみに当てはまる価値増による特殊価値（GAVP-9.3.2、S2-6.6）。

④**シナジー価値**（Synergistic Value/Marriage Value）

複数の権利利益が併合されることで新たに生み出される価値で、特殊価値の一種（S2-6.7）。

⑤**投資価値**（Investment Value/Worth）

特定の投資家が、特定の投資物件について、当該投資家だけに当てはまる期待収益率に基づいて認める主観的な資産価値である（S2-3.3、GAVP-9.3.3）。

4．鑑定評価の方式・手順

評価に当たっては、次の一つ又は複数の方式を適用する。どの方式を適用できるかは、どのような価値を求めるのか及び市場でデータを入手できるかによる（GN1-5.9）。市場から十分なデータを収集かつ検証できる場合には、その分析によって「市場価値（Market Value）」を導くことができる。しかしながら、市場から十分なデータを収集かつ検証できなかったり、又は特別な評価の前提条件がある場合には、データの分析によって得られる価値は「市場価値以外の価値（Value Other Than Market Value）」になる（GN1-5.16）。

(a) **取引事例比較方式**（Sales Comparison Approach）

市場での取引事例を収集かつ検証した後、一つ又は複数の「比較単位（unit of comparison）」を選び、「比較要因（Element of comparison）」について分析・修正して、価値を求める。比較単位は、市場の典型的な売買当事者が意思決定の際に重視する二つの要素からなる指標である（例えば、単位面積当たりの取引価格、還元利回り、収益乗数）。比較要因として、対象となる権利・利益、ファイナンス条件、取引事情、取引直後の費用（例えば修復費用）、市場の状況、立地、物的特性、収益的特性、用途規制、不動産以外の要素があり、分析・修正の基本となる（GN1-5.22）。

(b) **収益還元方式**（Income Capitalization Approach）

直接還元法もDCF法も、還元利回りや割引率について市場データの裏づけがとれる限り、市場価値の査定に適用できる（GN1-5, 12.5）。

(c) **原価方式**（Cost Approach）

This approach considers the possibility that, as an alternative to the purchase of a given property, one could acquire a modern equivalent asset that would provide equal utility. In real estate context, this would involve the cost of acquiring equivalent land and constructing an equivalent new structure. Unless undue time, inconvenience, and risk are involved, the price that a buyer would pay for the asset being valued would not be more than the cost of the modern equivalent. Often the asset being valued will be less attractive than the cost of the modern equivalent because of age or obsolescence. A depreciation adjustment is required to the replacement cost to reflect this.

5. Valuation Reports

(a) **Minimum content of reports**
identity of the valuer and the date of the report;
identity of the client;
instructions, date of the value estimate, purpose and intended use of the valuation;
basis of the valuation, including type and definition of value;
identity, tenure, and location(s) of the interest(s) to be valued;
date and extent of inspections;
scope and extent of the work used to develop the valuation;
any assumptions and limiting conditions; and any special, unusual, or
extraordinary assumptions;
a compliance statement that the valuation has been performed in accordance with these
Standards and any required disclosures;
The professional qualification and signature of the Valuer ; and
As required in some States, specific certification by the Valuer in the prescribed form.

(b) **Verbal report**
The results of a valuation, verbally communicated to a client or presented before a court. A report communicated orally to a client must be supported by a work file and at a minimum followed up by a written summary of the valuation (IVS3.2).

6. Implementation of Valuation Standards

Valuers comply with these Standards either by choice or by requirement placed upon them by law or regulation or at the instructions of clients, intended users, and/or national societies or organizations. A valuation claiming to be prepared under IVS binds the Valuer to follow the IVSC Code of Conduct. This Code does not have any formal authority in law, neither is it intended to be other than complementary to the rules, by-laws and regulations of national societies or organization controlling or monitoring the activities of Valuers (IVS Code of Conduct 2.0).

Valuer compliance with the IVSs may be voluntary, mandated by law or regulation, or at the instruction of clients, intended users, and/or national societies or organizations. Having no enforcement power of its own, the IVSC looks to national institutes and financial professionals and authorities to enforce standards.

原価方式では、同じ効用を持つ土地及び新築建物を取得するか、既存建物を同じ用途に改造する費用を見積もって、価値を求める（GN1-5.13）。

5．鑑定評価報告書

(a) 必要的記載事項

鑑定人氏名、依頼者、評価の利用目的、価値の種類、評価の対象である権利の内容・種類・所在地、実査の日付と内容、業務の範囲、想定条件・限定条件・特別想定条件、国際評価基準の遵守と必要な開示事項に関する記述（S3-5.0）。

評価書が電子により電送される場合は、鑑定人は評価書のデータ・文章が確かに原本であることを証明するための相応の手立てをとり、電送中に誤りが生じないように万全を期する。データ・文章は「読み取り専用」とする（S3-5.2）。

(b) 口頭による報告

口頭による報告とは、評価の結果を、口頭で依頼者に伝えること又は法廷で専門家として証言あるいは宣誓証言することである。口頭で依頼者に伝達される評価の結果は、作業ファイルに裏づけられていて、評価の要約書を提出しなければならない（S3-3.2）。

6．鑑定評価基準の履行

IVS基準の遵守は任意であり、法令、依頼者、利用者、各国の政府又は団体の指示によって強制力を得る。IVS自身は基準を履行させることはできず、各国機関、財務の専門機関や政府が履行を担うことになる（CC-2.0）。

Chapter 2.Ⅵ. International Valuation Standards (IVS)

7. Availability of Data

(a) **Property-Specific Data (Primary Data)**

Property-Specific data, or data more directly relevant to the property being valued and to comparable properties are also gathered and examined. Theses include site and improvement data, cost and depreciation data, income and expense data, capitalization and yield rate data, ownership and utilization histories, and other information determined to be significant and generally considered by buyers and sellers in their negotiation and transaction.

(b) **General Data**

General Economic data are collected at the neighborhood, city, regional, and even national and international levels, depending on the property involved. Social, economic, governmental, and environmental factors that have bearing on Market Value are examined to better understand the particular property. Any other specific forces that must be considered are investigated in detail.

8. Specific Valuation Standards for Securitization Purposes

International Valuation While Paper on the valuation of real estate services as collateral for securitized instruments has been provided.

7. 鑑定評価に利用するデータ

(a) 個別データ

対象不動産や比較すべき不動産に関連するデータを収集し検証する。これには、敷地や建物に関するデータ、原価及び減価のデータ、収益や費用のデータ、還元利回りや割引率のデータ、権利の確認や利用の経過に関するデータ、売買取引において考慮に入れる情報などが含まれる（GN1-5.7.2）。

(b) 一般データ

一般経済データの収集は、対象不動産に応じて、近隣、都市、圏域、さらには全国や国際的な範囲で行う（GN1-5.71）。

8. 証券化に関する基準

証券化のための担保となる不動産の評価に関する答申（White Paper）が提出されている。

PART2

Real Estate Appraisal Act

(July 16, 1963 Law No. 152)
Final revision: March 31, 2006 Law No. 10

第2編

不動産の鑑定評価に関する法律

昭和38年7月16日法律第152号
最終改正:平成18年3月31日法律第10号

Table of Contents

CHAPTER 1. GENERAL PROVISIONS (Articles 1 and 2) ······················112

CHAPTER 2. LICENSED REAL ESTATE APPRAISERS (LREAs)··········114
    Section 1. General Provisions (Articles 3 to 7) ···114
    Section 2. LREA Examination (Omitted)··114
    Section 3. Practical Training (Omitted) ···114
    Section 4. Registration (Omitted except for Articles 15 and 16) ······················114

CHAPTER 3. REAL ESTATE APPRAISAL BUSINESS ······················118
    Section 1. Registration (Omitted except for Articles 22, 25 and 33)················118
    Section 2. Operations (Articles 35 to 39) ··120

CHAPTER 4. OVERSIGHT (Articles 40 to 46) ·····························122

CHAPTER 5. MISCELLANEOUS PROVISIONS (Articles 47 to 55) ······126

CHAPTER 6. SANCTIONS (Articles 56 to 61) ·····························128

SUPPLEMENTARY PROVISIONS ···130

目　次

第 1 章　総則（第 1 条・第 2 条） …………………………………………………………… 113

第 2 章　不動産鑑定士 ………………………………………………………………………… 115
　第 1 節　総則（第 3 条―第 7 条） ………………………………………………………… 115
　第 2 節　不動産鑑定士試験（省略） ……………………………………………………… 115
　第 3 節　実務修習（省略） ………………………………………………………………… 115
　第 4 節　登録（第15条及び第16条以外は省略） ………………………………………… 115

第 3 章　不動産鑑定業 ………………………………………………………………………… 119
　第 1 節　登録（第22条、第25条及び第33条以外は省略） ……………………………… 119
　第 2 節　業務（第35条―第39条） ………………………………………………………… 121

第 4 章　監督（第40条―第46条） …………………………………………………………… 123

第 5 章　雑則（第47条―第55条） …………………………………………………………… 127

第 6 章　罰則（第56条―第61条） …………………………………………………………… 129

附　則 …………………………………………………………………………………………… 131

CHAPTER 1. GENERAL PROVISIONS

Article 1. Purpose
The purpose of this law is to prescribe the necessary matters regarding licensed real estate appraisers (LREA) and real estate appraisal business, and thereby to contribute to the formation of suitable values for land, etc.

Article 2. Definitions
1. In this law, "real estate appraisal" means evaluating the economic value of real estate (land, buildings, and related rights other than ownership; the same applies below) and expressing the result of such evaluation as a monetary value.
2. In this law, "real estate appraisal business" means the business of providing real estate appraisal services upon the request of another person and for compensation, regardless of whether these services are provided by the business operator or by another person engaged to provide the services.
3. In this law, "real estate appraisal business operator" means a person who is registered under Article 24.

第1章 総則

（目的）
第1条 この法律は、不動産の鑑定評価に関し、不動産鑑定士及び不動産鑑定業について必要な事項を定め、もつて土地等の適正な価格の形成に資することを目的とする。

（定義）
第2条 この法律において「不動産の鑑定評価」とは、不動産（土地若しくは建物又はこれらに関する所有権以外の権利をいう。以下同じ。）の経済価値を判定し、その結果を価額に表示することをいう。
2 この法律において「不動産鑑定業」とは、自ら行うと他人を使用して行うとを問わず、他人の求めに応じ報酬を得て、不動産の鑑定評価を業として行うことをいう。
3 この法律において「不動産鑑定業者」とは、第24条の規定による登録を受けた者をいう。

CHAPTER 2. LICENSED REAL ESTATE APPRAISERS (LREAs)

Section 1. General Provisions

Article 3. LREA operations

1. An LREA performs real estate appraisals.
2. An LREA may engage in the business of investigating and analyzing the factors affecting the objective value of real estate, or of providing consultation regarding real estate utilization, transactions, and investment, using the name of "LREA." However, this shall not apply if such operations are restricted under other laws.

Article 4. LREA qualifications

A person who has passed the LREA examination, completed practical training as prescribed in Article 14-2, and obtained approval by the Minister of Land, Infrastructure and Transport as prescribed in Article 14-23 is qualified to become an LREA.

Article 5. Duties of an LREA

An LREA must conscientiously and faithfully perform the operations specified in Article 3 (hereinafter "appraisal and related operations"), and must not commit any act that would injure the reputation of LREAs.

Article 6. Confidentiality

An LREA shall not divulge any secret information learned in relation to appraisal and related operations without a justifiable reason. The same shall apply even after the person is no longer an LREA.

Article 7. Maintaining and improving knowledge and skills

An LREA must strive to maintain and improve the knowledge and skills which are needed for appraisal and related operations.

Section 2. LREA Examination (Omitted)

Section 3. Practical Training (Omitted)

Section 4. Registration (Omitted except for Articles 15 and 16)

Article 15. Registration

To become an LREA, a person who is qualified to become an LREA shall have his/her name, date of birth, address, and any other matters specified by order of the Ministry of Land, Infrastructure and Transport recorded in the LREA register maintained by the Ministry of Land, Infrastructure and Transport.

Article 16. Grounds for disqualification

A person to whom any of the following applies may not obtain LREA registration.

(a) A minor.
(b) A person who has been adjudged incompetent or quasi-incompetent.
(c) A person who has been declared bankrupt and has not been reinstated.
(d) A person who has received a sentence of imprisonment or greater severity, if less

第2章　不動産鑑定士

第1節　総則

（不動産鑑定士の業務）
第3条　不動産鑑定士は、不動産の鑑定評価を行う。
2　不動産鑑定士は、不動産鑑定士の名称を用いて、不動産の客観的価値に作用する諸要因に関して調査若しくは分析を行い、又は不動産の利用、取引若しくは投資に関する相談に応じることを業とすることができる。ただし、他の法律においてその業務を行うことが制限されている事項については、この限りでない。

（不動産鑑定士となる資格）
第4条　不動産鑑定士試験に合格した者であつて、第14条の2に規定する実務修習を修了し第14条の23の規定による国土交通大臣の確認を受けた者は、不動産鑑定士となる資格を有する。

（不動産鑑定士の責務）
第5条　不動産鑑定士は、良心に従い、誠実に第3条に規定する業務（以下「鑑定評価等業務」という。）を行うとともに、不動産鑑定士の信用を傷つけるような行為をしてはならない。

（秘密を守る義務）
第6条　不動産鑑定士は、正当な理由がなく、鑑定評価等業務に関して知り得た秘密を他に漏らしてはならない。不動産鑑定士でなくなつた後においても、同様とする。

（知識及び技能の維持向上）
第7条　不動産鑑定士は、鑑定評価等業務に必要な知識及び技能の維持向上に努めなければならない。

第2節　不動産鑑定士試験　（省略）

第3節　実務修習　（省略）

第4節　登録（第15条及び第16条以外は省略）

（登録）
第15条　不動産鑑定士となる資格を有する者が、不動産鑑定士となるには、国土交通省に備える不動産鑑定士名簿に、氏名、生年月日、住所その他国土交通省令で定める事項の登録を受けなければならない。

（欠格条項）
第16条　次の各号のいずれかに該当する者は、不動産鑑定士の登録を受けることができない。
　一　未成年者
　二　成年被後見人又は被保佐人
　三　破産者で復権を得ない者
　四　禁錮以上の刑に処せられた者で、その執行を終わり、又は執行を受けることがなくなつた日

than three years have elapsed since the completion of that sentence or exemption from the execution of sentence.
(e) A civil servant who has received a disciplinary discharge, if less than three years have elapsed since discharge.
(f) A person whose registration has been canceled under Article 20, Paragraph 1, Item (d) or Article 40, Paragraph 1 or 3, if less than three years have elapsed since cancellation.
(g) A person who has been prohibited from performing appraisal and related operations under Article 40, Paragraph 1 or 2, if that person's registration has been canceled under Article 20, Paragraph 1, Item (a) during the period of prohibition, and that period has not yet been completed.

から3年を経過しないもの
五　公務員で懲戒免職の処分を受け、その処分の日から3年を経過しない者
六　第20条第1項第4号又は第40条第1項若しくは第3項の規定による登録の消除の処分を受け、その処分の日から3年を経過しない者
七　第40条第1項又は第2項の規定による禁止の処分を受け、その禁止の期間中に第20条第1項第1号の規定に基づきその登録が消除され、まだその期間が満了しない者

CHAPTER 3. REAL ESTATE APPRAISAL BUSINESS

Section 1. Registration (Omitted except for Articles 22, 25 and 33)

Article 22. Registration of real estate appraisal business operators

1. A person wishing to operate a real estate appraisal business shall obtain registration in the register of real estate appraisal business operators maintained by the Ministry of Land, Infrastructure and Transport if he/she will establish offices in two or more prefectures, or otherwise, in the register maintained by the prefecture where his/her office is located.
2. The effective period of the registration of real estate appraisal business operators shall be five years.
3. If the person wishes to continue operating a real estate appraisal business after expiration of the effective period under the preceding paragraph, he/she shall obtain a renewal registration.
4. If application for renewal registration has been filed, but no decision on the application has been issued by the expiration of the effective period under Paragraph 2, then the former registration shall remain in effect from the expiration of that effective period until the date when a decision is issued.
5. In the case of the preceding paragraph, when renewal registration is obtained, the effective period of that registration shall begin on the day after expiration of the effective period of the former registration.

Article 25. Denial of registration

The Minister of Land, Infrastructure and Transport or the prefectural governor shall deny registration if any of the following applies to the registration applicant, or if any important matters are falsified or important facts are omitted on the registration application or documents appended to that application.

(a) A person who has been declared bankrupt and has not been reinstated.
(b) A person who has received a sentence of imprisonment or greater severity, or has been sentenced to a fine for a violation of this law or a violation regarding appraisal and related operations, if less than three years have elapsed since the completion of that sentence or exemption from the execution of sentence.
(c) A person subject to Article 16, Item (f) or (g).
(d) A person whose registration has been canceled under Article 30, Paragraph 1, Item (f) or Article 41, if less than three years have elapsed since cancellation.
(e) A person who has been ordered to suspend operations under Article 41, if Article 29, Paragraph 1, Item (a) applies during the period of suspension, and the person's registration has been canceled under Article 30, Item (a) or (b), and that period has not yet been completed.
(f) A person who has been adjudged incompetent or a minor, lacking the business capacity of an adult, if any of the preceding items applies to that person's legal representative.

第3章 不動産鑑定業

第1節 登録（第22条、第25条及び第33条以外は省略）

（不動産鑑定業者の登録）
第22条 不動産鑑定業を営もうとする者は、2以上の都道府県に事務所を設ける者にあつては国土交通省に、その他の者にあつてはその事務所の所在地の属する都道府県に備える不動産鑑定業者登録簿に登録を受けなければならない。
2　不動産鑑定業者の登録の有効期間は、5年とする。
3　前項の有効期間の満了後引き続き不動産鑑定業を営もうとする者は、更新の登録を受けなければならない。
4　更新の登録の申請があつた場合において、第2項の有効期間の満了の日までにその申請に対する処分がなされないときは、従前の登録は、同項の有効期間の満了後もその処分がなされるまでの間は、なお効力を有する。
5　前項の場合において、更新の登録がなされたときは、その登録の有効期間は、従前の登録の有効期間の満了の日の翌日から起算するものとする。

（登録の拒否）
第25条 国土交通大臣又は都道府県知事は、登録申請者が次の各号のいずれかに該当する者であるとき、又は登録申請書若しくはその添付書類に重要な事項について虚偽の記載があり、若しくは重要な事実の記載が欠けているときは、その登録を拒否しなければならない。
一　破産者で復権を得ない者
二　禁錮以上の刑に処せられ、又はこの法律の規定に違反し、若しくは鑑定評価等業務に関し罪を犯して罰金の刑に処せられ、その執行を終わり、又は執行を受けることがなくなつた日から3年を経過しない者
三　第16条第6号又は第7号に該当する者
四　第30条第6号又は第41条の規定により登録を消除され、その登録の消除の日から3年を経過しない者
五　第41条の規定による業務の停止の命令を受け、その停止の期間中に第29条第1項第1号に該当し、第30条第1号又は第2号の規定に基づきその登録が消除され、まだその期間が満了しない者
六　営業に関し成年者と同一の行為能力を有しない未成年者又は成年被後見人で、その法定代理人が前各号のいずれかに該当するもの
七　法人で、その役員のうちに第1号から第5号までのいずれかに該当する者のあるもの

(g) A corporation, if any of items (a) through (e) applies to any of the corporation's executives.

Article 33. Prohibition of unregistered operations
Parties that have not obtained registration as a real estate appraisal business operator shall not operate a real estate appraisal business.

Section 2. Operations
Article 35. LREA appointment
1. A real estate appraisal business operator who is not an LREA shall appoint at least one full-time LREA for each office of that business. The same shall apply for any office where a real estate appraisal business operator who is an LREA will not him/herself perform real estate appraisals.
2. If a real estate appraisal business operator has an office that comes into violation of the preceding paragraph, that operator must take the necessary steps within two weeks for conformity with the provisions of that paragraph.

Article 36. Prohibition of appraisal by non–LREAs
1. A person who is not an LREA shall not perform real estate appraisal in connection with the operations of a real estate appraisal business operator.
2. A real estate appraisal business operator shall not cause any person who is not an LREA, or a person who is subject to a disciplinary measure under Article 40, Paragraph 1 or who is prohibited from performing appraisal and related operations under Article 40, Paragraph 2, to perform real estate appraisal and related operations in connection with that business.

Article 37 (Omitted)

Article 38. Confidentiality
A real estate appraisal business operator shall not divulge secret information learned in relation to business operations without a justifiable reason. The same shall apply even after the operator has discontinued the real estate appraisal business.

Article 39. Appraisal document, etc.
1. A real estate appraisal business operator shall issue an appraisal document, stating the final opinion of value and other matters specified by order of the Ministry of Land, Infrastructure and Transport, to the party requesting appraisal of real estate.
2. On the appraisal document, the LREA involved in the appraisal of that real estate shall enter his/her signature and seal and indicate his/her qualifications.
3. The real estate appraisal business operator shall retain a copy of the appraisal document and other documentation as specified by order of the Ministry of Land, Infrastructure and Transport.

（無登録業務の禁止）
第33条 不動産鑑定業者の登録を受けない者は、不動産鑑定業を営んではならない。

第2節　業務

（不動産鑑定士の設置）
第35条 不動産鑑定士でない不動産鑑定業者は、その事務所ごとに専任の不動産鑑定士を1人以上置かなければならない。不動産鑑定士である不動産鑑定業者がみずから実地に不動産の鑑定評価を行なわない事務所についても、同様とする。
2　不動産鑑定業者は、前項の規定に抵触するに至つた事務所があるときは、2週間以内に、同項の規定に適合させるため必要な措置をとらなければならない。

（不動産鑑定士でない者等による鑑定評価の禁止）
第36条 不動産鑑定士でない者は、不動産鑑定業者の業務に関し、不動産の鑑定評価を行つてはならない。
2　不動産鑑定業者は、その業務に関し、不動産鑑定士でない者又は第40条第1項に不動産の鑑定評価を、第2項の規定による禁止の処分を受けた者に鑑定評価等業務を行わせてはならない。

第37条　削除

（秘密を守る義務）
第38条 不動産鑑定業者は、正当な理由がなく、その業務上取り扱つたことについて知り得た秘密を他に漏らしてはならない。不動産鑑定業者がその不動産鑑定業を廃止した後においても、同様とする。

（鑑定評価書等）
第39条 不動産鑑定業者は、不動産の鑑定評価の依頼者に、鑑定評価額その他国土交通省令で定める事項を記載した鑑定評価書を交付しなければならない。
2　鑑定評価書には、その不動産の鑑定評価に関与した不動産鑑定士がその資格を表示して署名押印しなければならない。
3　不動産鑑定業者は、国土交通省令で定めるところにより、鑑定評価書の写しその他の書類を保存しなければならない。

CHAPTER 4. OVERSIGHT

Article 40. Disciplinary measures for improper appraisals, etc.

1. If an LREA has intentionally prepared an unjust or improper appraisal or committed another unjust or improper act with regard to appraisal and related operations (hereinafter "improper appraisal, etc."), then as a disciplinary measure, the Minister of Land, Infrastructure and Transport may prohibit the LREA from performing appraisal and related operations for a period of up to one year, or may cancel the registration of that LREA. The same shall apply if the LREA has violated Article 6 or Article 33.
2. If an LREA has committed an improper appraisal, etc. because of failure to use due caution, then as a disciplinary measure, the Minister of Land, Infrastructure and Transport may issue a reprimand or prohibit the LREA from performing appraisal and related operations for a period of up to one year.
3. If an LREA violates a prohibition under the two preceding articles, the Minister of Land, Infrastructure and Transport may cancel the registration of that LREA.

Article 41. Supervisory disposition of real estate appraisal operators

If any of the following applies to a registered real estate appraisal business operator, the Minister of Land, Infrastructure and Transport or the prefectural governor may issue a reprimand, order the suspension of all or a portion of that business for a period of up to one year, or cancel the operator's registration.

(a) If the operator has violated this law or a measure taken by the Minister of Land, Infrastructure and Transport or the prefectural governor on the basis of this law.
(b) If an LREA who is engaged in operations of that real estate appraisal business operator has been subjected to a disciplinary measure under the preceding article, for reasons which were the responsibility of the real estate appraisal business operator.

Article 42. Action requirement regarding improper real estate appraisals, etc.

If there are grounds for reasonable suspicion that an LREA has committed an improper appraisal, etc., then any person may report those circumstances to the Minister of Land, Infrastructure and Transport or the governor of the prefecture in which the real estate appraisal business operator employing that LREA is registered, appending documentation; and may request that appropriate measures be taken.

Article 43. Procedures for disciplinary measures, etc.

(Omitted)

Article 44. Public notice of disciplinary measures, etc.

If the Minister of Land, Infrastructure and Transport or a prefectural governor has taken disciplinary measures under Article 40 or Article 41, then public notice to this effect shall be issued as specified by government decree.

Article 45. Reporting and inspections

1. If deemed necessary by the Minister of Land, Infrastructure and Transport or a prefectural governor in order to ensure the proper administration of real estate appraisal bus-

第4章　監　督

（不当な鑑定評価等についての懲戒処分）
第40条　国土交通大臣は、不動産鑑定士が、故意に、不当な不動産の鑑定評価その他鑑定評価等業務に関する不正又は著しく不当な行為（以下「不当な鑑定評価等」という。）を行つたときは、懲戒処分として、1年以内の期間を定めて鑑定評価等業務を行うことを禁止し、又はその不動産鑑定士の登録を消除することができる。不動産鑑定士が、第6条又は第33条の規定に違反したときも、同様とする。
2　国土交通大臣は、不動産鑑定士が、相当の注意を怠り、不当な鑑定評価等を行つたときは、懲戒処分として、戒告を与え、又は1年以内の期間を定めて鑑定評価等業務を行うことを禁止することができる。
3　国土交通大臣は、不動産鑑定士が、前2項の規定による禁止の処分に違反したときは、その不動産鑑定士の登録を消除することができる。

（不動産鑑定業者に対する監督処分）
第41条　国土交通大臣又は都道府県知事は、その登録を受けた不動産鑑定業者が次の各号のいずれかに該当するときは、その不動産鑑定業者に対し、戒告を与え、1年以内の期間を定めてその業務の全部若しくは一部の停止を命じ、又はその登録を消除することができる。
一　この法律又はこの法律に基づく国土交通大臣若しくは都道府県知事の処分に違反したとき。
二　不動産鑑定業者の業務に従事する不動産鑑定士が、前条の規定による処分を受けた場合において、その不動産鑑定業者の責めに帰すべき理由があるとき。

（不当な鑑定評価等に対する措置の要求）
第42条　不動産鑑定士が不当な鑑定評価等を行つたことを疑うに足りる事実があるときは、何人も、国土交通大臣又は当該不動産鑑定士がその業務に従事する不動産鑑定業者が登録を受けた都道府県知事に対し、資料を添えてその事実を報告し、適当な措置をとるべきことを求めることができる。

（懲戒処分等の手続）
第43条　省略

（懲戒処分等の公告）
第44条　国土交通大臣又は都道府県知事は、第40条又は第41条の規定による処分をしたときは、政令で定めるところにより、その旨を公告しなければならない。

（報告及び検査）
第45条　国土交通大臣又は都道府県知事は、不動産鑑定業の適正な運営を確保するため必要がある

iness, the Minister may demand the necessary reports from all real estate appraisal business operators, or a prefectural governor may demand the necessary reports from all real estate appraisal business operators registered in that prefecture; or the Minister or governor may order their staff members to enter the premises of the offices or other locations related to those businesses and inspect ledgers and records related to the businesses (including electromagnetic records, if those ledgers and records were prepared or stored in electromagnetic form).
2. Staff members conducting an on-site inspection under the preceding paragraph shall carry certification of their identities, and shall present such certification if requested by a related person.
3. The authority to conduct on-site inspections under Paragraph 1 shall not be construed as having been approved for criminal investigations.

Article 46. Counsel and advice

If deemed necessary by the Minister of Land, Infrastructure and Transport or a prefectural governor in order to ensure the proper administration of real estate appraisal business or to promote the sound development of such business, the Minister or governor may provide the necessary counsel or advice regarding real estate appraisal business to the real estate appraisal business operators registered with the Minister or governor.

と認めるときは、国土交通大臣にあつてはすべての不動産鑑定業者について、都道府県知事にあつてはその登録を受けた不動産鑑定業者について、その業務に関し必要な報告を求め、又はその職員にその業務に関係のある事務所その他の場所に立ち入り、その業務に関係のある帳簿書類（その作成又は保存に代えて電磁的記録の作成又は保存がされている場合における当該電磁的記録を含む。）を検査させることができる。
2　前項の規定により立入検査をしようとする職員は、その身分を示す証明書を携帯し、関係人の請求があつたときは、これを提示しなければならない。
3　第1項の規定による立入検査の権限は、犯罪捜査のために認められたものと解釈してはならない。

（助言又は勧告）
第46条　国土交通大臣又は都道府県知事は、不動産鑑定業の適正な運営の確保又はその健全な発達を図るため必要があるときは、その登録を受けた不動産鑑定業者に対し、その営む不動産鑑定業に関し必要な助言又は勧告をすることができる。

CHAPTER 5. MISCELLANEOUS PROVISIONS

Article 47. Examiners
(Omitted)

Article 48. LREA organizations, etc.
Associations and foundations whose purpose is to help maintain and enhance the position of LREAs and to advance and improve business operations related to real estate appraisal, and which have been specified by order of the Ministry of Land, Infrastructure and Transport, shall submit the information required by order of the Ministry of Land, Infrastructure and Transport to the Minister of Land, Infrastructure and Transport or the prefectural governor, as specified by order of the Ministry of Land, Infrastructure and Transport.

Article 49
Associations and foundations which have submitted information under the preceding article must provide training for LREAs as specified by government decree.

Article 50
If deemed necessary by the Minister of Land, Infrastructure and Transport or a prefectural governor in order to ensure the proper implementation of real estate appraisal or to promote the sound development of real estate appraisal business, the Minister or governor may require reports from the associations and foundations which have submitted information under Article 48, or provide them with counsel or advice.

Article 51. Prohibition of name usage
Persons who are not LREAs may not use the name of LREA.

Article 52. Exclusions regarding farmland, etc.
Acts constituting any of the following shall not be included in real estate appraisal under this law.
   (a) Evaluating the transaction price of farmland, pastureland, or forestland (not including the case of transactions in which the land will not be used for a different purpose than farmland, pastureland, or forestland).
   (b) Calculating the insurable value or indemnity amount for a building subject to property insurance.
   (c) Appraising a building as a service of a registered architect's office (not including the office of a registered wooden building architect) under the Registered Architect Law (Law No. 202 of 1950).

Article 53. Special exception for applications by methods using electronic data processing systems
(Omitted)

Article 54. Delegation of authority
(Omitted)

Article 55. Classification of clerical operations
(Omitted)

第5章 雑　則

（試験委員）
第47条　省略

（不動産鑑定士等の団体）
第48条　不動産鑑定士の品位の保持及び資質の向上を図り、あわせて不動産の鑑定評価に関する業務の進歩改善を図ることを目的とする社団又は財団で、国土交通省令で定めるものは、国土交通省令で定めるところにより、国土交通大臣又は都道府県知事に対して、国土交通省令で定める事項を届け出なければならない。

第49条　前条の規定による届出をした社団又は財団は、政令で定めるところにより、不動産鑑定士に対する研修を実施しなければならない。

第50条　国土交通大臣又は都道府県知事は、不動産の鑑定評価の適正な実施の確保又は不動産鑑定業の健全な発達を図るため必要があるときは、第48条の規定による届出をした社団又は財団に対し、報告を求め、又は助言若しくは勧告をすることができる。

（名称の使用禁止）
第51条　不動産鑑定士でない者は、不動産鑑定士の名称を用いてはならない。

（農地等に関する適用除外）
第52条　次の各号のいずれかに該当する場合においては、当該評価等の行為は、この法律にいう不動産の鑑定評価に含まれないものとする。
　一　農地、採草放牧地又は森林の取引価格（農地、採草放牧地及び森林以外のものとするための取引に係るものを除く。）を評価するとき。
　二　損害保険の目的である建物の保険価額又は損害塡補額を算定するとき。
　三　建築士法（昭和25年法律第202号）による建築士事務所（木造建築士事務所を除く。）の業務として、建物につき鑑定するとき。

（電子情報処理組織を使用する方法により行う申込み等の特例）
第53条　省略

（権限の委任）
第54条　省略

（事務の区分）
第55条　省略

CHAPTER 6. SANCTIONS

Article 56
A person to whom any of the following applies shall be sentenced to imprisonment of up to one year, a fine of up to one million yen, or both.
- (a) A person who has obtained registration as a real estate appraisal business operator by deceit or other improper means.
- (b) A person who has operated a real estate appraisal business in violation of Article 33.
- (c) A person who has operated a business in violation of an order to suspend operations under Article 41.

Article 57
A person to whom any of the following applies shall be sentenced to imprisonment of up to six months, a fine of up to five hundred thousand yen, or both.
- (a) A person who has divulged secret information in violation of Article 6, Article 14-13, Paragraph 1, or Article 38.
- (b) A person who has divulged LREA examination questions in advance or improperly scored an LREA examination.
- (c) A person who has violated an order to suspend practical training operations under Article 14-16.
- (d) A person who has obtained LREA registration by deceit or other improper means.
- (e) A person who has performed real estate appraisal in violation of Article 36, Paragraph 1.
- (f) A person who has performed real estate appraisal, or appraisal and related operations, in violation of Article 36, Paragraph 2.
- (g) A person who has performed appraisal and related operations in violation of prohibition under Article 40, Paragraph 1 or 2.

Article 58
A person to whom any of the following applies shall be sentenced to a fine of up to three hundred thousand yen.
- (a) A person who has discontinued all practical training operations without obtaining approval under Article 14-10.
- (b) A person who has failed to keep a register, failed to enter the required information in the ledger, made false entries in the ledger, or failed to retain the ledger, in violation of Article 14-17.
- (c) A person who has failed to submit a report or submitted a falsified report when asked to submit a report under Article 14-19.
- (d) A person who has refused, obstructed, or challenged an inspection under Article 14-20.
- (e) A person who has failed to submit a report under Article 14-22 or submitted a falsified report.
- (f) A person who has closed or opened an office in violation of Article 26, Paragraph 1.

第6章 罰 則

第56条 次の各号のいずれかに該当する者は、1年以下の懲役若しくは100万円以下の罰金に処し、又はこれを併科する。
　一　偽りその他不正の手段により不動産鑑定業者の登録を受けた者
　二　第33条の規定に違反して、不動産鑑定業を営んだ者
　三　第41条の規定による業務の停止の命令に違反して、業務を営んだ者

第57条 次の各号のいずれかに該当する者は、6月以下の懲役若しくは50万円以下の罰金に処し、又はこれを併科する。
　一　第6条、第14条の13第1項又は第38条の規定に違反して、秘密を漏らした者
　二　不動産鑑定士試験に関し、事前に試験問題を漏らし、又は不正の採点をした者
　三　第14条の16の規定による実務修習業務の停止の命令に違反した者
　四　偽りその他不正の手段により不動産鑑定士の登録を受けた者
　五　第36条第1項の規定に違反して、不動産の鑑定評価を行つた者
　六　第36条第2項の規定に違反して、不動産の鑑定評価又は鑑定評価等業務を行わせた者
　七　第40条第1項又は第2項の規定による禁止の処分に違反して、鑑定評価等業務を行つた者

第58条 次の各号のいずれかに該当する者は、30万円以下の罰金に処する。
　一　第14条の10の許可を受けないで、実務修習業務の全部を廃止した者
　二　第14条の17の規定に違反して帳簿を備えず、帳簿に記載せず、若しくは帳簿に虚偽の記載をし、又は帳簿を保存しなかつた者
　三　第14条の19の規定による報告を求められて、報告をせず、又は虚偽の報告をした者
　四　第14条の20の規定による検査を拒み、妨げ、又は忌避した者
　五　第14条の22の規定による報告をせず、又は虚偽の報告をした者
　六　第26条第1項の規定に違反して、事務所を廃止し、又は設けた者
　七　第27条第1項の規定に違反して、変更の登録を申請せず、又は虚偽の申請をした者
　八　第28条の規定に違反して、書類の提出を怠り、又は虚偽の記載をして書類を提出した者
　九　第45条第1項の規定による報告を求められて、その報告をせず、若しくは虚偽の報告をし、又は同項の規定による立入検査を拒み、妨げ、若しくは忌避した者
　十　第51条の規定に違反して、不動産鑑定士の名称を用いた者

(g) A person who has failed to apply for a change registration or submitted a falsified application, in violation of Article 27, Paragraph 1.
(h) A person who has failed to submit documentation or submitted documentation containing false statements, in violation of Article 28.
(i) A person who has failed to submit a report or submitted a falsified report when asked to submit a report under Article 45, Paragraph 1, or who has refused, obstructed, or challenged an on-site inspection under the same paragraph.
(j) A person who has used the name of LREA in violation of Article 51.

Article 59

If a representative of a corporation, or an agent, employee, or other individual engaged by a corporation or person, has committed an act violating Article 56, Article 57, Item (f), or Article 58, Items (f) through (i) with regard to the operations of that corporation or person, then in addition to punitive measures for the violator, the corporation or person will also be fined under the relevant article.

Article 60

An administrative fine of up to two hundred thousand yen shall be imposed on any person who has failed to retain financial statements, etc., failed to enter the necessary information, or entered falsified information in the financial statements, etc. in violation of Article 14-11, Paragraph 1, or who has refused a request under any item of Paragraph 2 of that article.

Article 61

An administrative fine of up to one hundred thousand yen shall be imposed on any person who has violated Article 19, Paragraph 1 or Article 29, Paragraph 1.

Supplementary Provisions
(Omitted)

第59条 法人の代表者又は法人若しくは人の代理人、使用人その他の従業者が、その法人又は人の業務に関し、第56条、第57条第6号又は前条第6号から第9号までの違反行為をしたときは、その行為者を罰するほか、その法人又は人に対しても、各本条の罰金刑を科する。

第60条 第14条の11第1項の規定に違反して財務諸表等を備えて置かず、財務諸表等に記載すべき事項を記載せず、若しくは虚偽の記載をし、又は正当な理由がないのに同条第2項各号の規定による請求を拒んだ者は、20万円以下の過料に処する。

第61条 第19条第1項又は第29条第1項の規定に違反した者は、10万円以下の過料に処する。

附　則　省略

PART3

Real Estate Appraisal Standards

Revised on July 3, 2002
Partly revised on April 2, 2007
Ministry of Land, Infrastructure, Transport and Tourism

第3編

不動産鑑定評価基準

平成14年7月3日全部改正
平成19年4月2日一部改正
国 土 交 通 省

Table of Contents

GENERAL STANDARDS (GS):

CHAPTER 1. FOUNDATIONS OF REAL ESTATE APPRAISAL ············138
- Section 1. Real Estate and Its Value ················138
- Section 2. Characteristics of Real Estate Value ················138
- Section 3. Appraisal of Real Estate ················142
- Section 4. Responsibility of LREAs ················142

CHAPTER 2. USE CATEGORIES AND PHYSICAL DEVELOPMENT & TITLE CATEGORIES OF REAL ESTATE ················146
- Section 1. Real Estate Use Categories ················146
- Section 2. Physical Development & Title Categories ················148

CHAPTER 3. INFLUENCES ON REAL ESTATE VALUE ················152
- Section 1. General Value Influences ················152
- Section 2. Area-Specific Value Influences ················154
- Section 3. Property-Specific Value Influences ················158

CHAPTER 4. PRINCIPLES OF REAL ESTATE VALUE ················164

CHAPTER 5. BASIC APPRAISAL PROBLEM ················168
- Section 1. Identification of the Subject Property ················168
- Section 2. Identification of the Date of the Value Opinion ················170
- Section 3. Identification of the Type of Value or Rental Value ················170

CHAPTER 6. MARKET AREA ANALYSIS AND PROPERTY ANALYSIS ················176
- Section 1. Market Area Analysis ················176
- Section 2. Property Analysis ················182

CHAPTER 7. APPRAISAL METHOD ················186
- Section 1. Appraisal Approaches for Determining Real Estate Value ················186
- Section 2. Appraisal Approaches for Determining Real Estate Rental Value ················208

CHAPTER 8. APPRAISAL PROCESS ················218
- Section 1. Identification of Basic Appraisal Problem ················218
- Section 2. Drafting of a Processing Plan ················218
- Section 3. Identification of the Subject Property ················218
- Section 4. Gathering and Organizing of Data ················220
- Section 5. Review of Data and Analysis of Value Influences ················220
- Section 6. Application of Appraisal Method ················222
- Section 7. Reconciliation of the Indicated Value or Rent ················222

目　次

総　論

第1章　不動産の鑑定評価に関する基本的考察 …………………………………139
- 第1節　不動産とその価格 …………………………………………………………139
- 第2節　不動産とその価格の特徴 …………………………………………………139
- 第3節　不動産の鑑定評価 …………………………………………………………143
- 第4節　不動産鑑定士の責務 ………………………………………………………143

第2章　不動産の種別及び類型 ……………………………………………………147
- 第1節　不動産の種別 ………………………………………………………………147
- 第2節　不動産の類型 ………………………………………………………………149

第3章　不動産の価格を形成する要因 ……………………………………………153
- 第1節　一般的要因 …………………………………………………………………153
- 第2節　地域要因 ……………………………………………………………………155
- 第3節　個別的要因 …………………………………………………………………159

第4章　不動産の価格に関する諸原則 ……………………………………………165

第5章　鑑定評価の基本的事項 ……………………………………………………169
- 第1節　対象不動産の確定 …………………………………………………………169
- 第2節　価格時点の確定 ……………………………………………………………171
- 第3節　鑑定評価によって求める価格又は賃料の種類の確定 …………………171

第6章　地域分析及び個別分析 ……………………………………………………177
- 第1節　地域分析 ……………………………………………………………………177
- 第2節　個別分析 ……………………………………………………………………183

第7章　鑑定評価の方式 ……………………………………………………………187
- 第1節　価格を求める鑑定評価の手法 ……………………………………………187
- 第2節　賃料を求める鑑定評価の手法 ……………………………………………209

第8章　鑑定評価の手順 ……………………………………………………………219
- 第1節　鑑定評価の基本的事項の確定 ……………………………………………219
- 第2節　処理計画の策定 ……………………………………………………………219
- 第3節　対象不動産の確認 …………………………………………………………219
- 第4節　資料の収集及び整理 ………………………………………………………221
- 第5節　資料の検討及び価格形成要因の分析 ……………………………………221
- 第6節　鑑定評価方式の適用 ………………………………………………………223
- 第7節　試算価格又は試算賃料の調整 ……………………………………………223

    Section 8. Determination of the Final Opinion of Value ·······························222
    Section 9. Preparation of the Appraisal Report ····································224

CHAPTER 9. APPRAISAL REPORT ···226
    Section 1. Guidelines for Preparing Appraisal Report ····························226
    Section 2. Report Contents ··226
    Section 3. Addenda to Appraisal Reports ··230

SPECIFIC STANDARDS (SS):
CHAPTER 1. APPRAISAL OF REAL ESTATE VALUE ····················232
    Section 1. Land ··232
    Section 2. Built-Up Property ··242
    Section 3. Buildings ···248

CHAPTER 2. APPRAISAL OF REAL ESTATE RENTAL VALUE ········252
    Section 1. Building Sites ···252
    Section 2. Built-Up Property ··254

CHAPTER 3. APPRAISAL OF REAL ESTATE VALUE SUBJECT TO
               SECURITIZATION ···256
    Section 1. Basic Approach to Securitization-Properties ·······················256
    Section 2. Drafting a Work Plan for the Appraisal ·····························258
    Section 3. Investigating Property-Specific Value Influences acting on the
               Securitization-Property ··260
    Section 4. Application of DCF method ··264

SUPPLEMENTARY PROVISION ···268

第8節　鑑定評価額の決定 …………………………………………………………223
　　第9節　鑑定評価報告書の作成 ……………………………………………………225

第9章　鑑定評価報告書 ………………………………………………………………227
　　第1節　鑑定評価報告書の作成指針 ………………………………………………227
　　第2節　記載事項 ……………………………………………………………………227
　　第3節　附属資料 ……………………………………………………………………231

各　論
第1章　価格に関する鑑定評価 ………………………………………………………233
　　第1節　土地 …………………………………………………………………………233
　　第2節　建物及びその敷地 …………………………………………………………243
　　第3節　建物 …………………………………………………………………………249

第2章　賃料に関する鑑定評価 ………………………………………………………253
　　第1節　宅地 …………………………………………………………………………253
　　第2節　建物及びその敷地 …………………………………………………………255

第3章　証券化対象不動産の価格に関する鑑定評価 ………………………………257
　　第1節　証券化対象不動産の鑑定評価の基本的姿勢 ……………………………257
　　第2節　処理計画の策定 ……………………………………………………………259
　　第3節　証券化対象不動産の個別的要因の調査等 ………………………………261
　　第4節　DCF法の適用等 ……………………………………………………………265

附　則 ……………………………………………………………………………………269

GENERAL STANDARDS (GS)

CHAPTER 1. FOUNDATIONS OF REAL ESTATE APPRAISAL

It is of foremost importance for the Licensed Real Estate Appraiser (LREA) to fully understand what is involved in the appraisal of real estate, why appraisals are necessary, what role appraisal fulfills in the economy, and what is required of LREAs and LREA candidates.

Section 1. Real Estate and Its Value
Real estate ordinarily refers to land and improvements upon the land. Because of its utility, land is the indispensable basis of all human activity. Real estate reflects the relationship between the various uses people make of the land and the lives and activities of people. The relationship takes concrete configuration in the manner in which real estate is composed and the manner in which it contributes to human needs.

The interaction of physical, social, economic and governmental factors helps determine the configuration of real estate, which accounts for its economic value. The economic value of real estate in turn represents the main criterion in the selection of its optimal configuration.

The value of real estate is typically indicated in terms of the economic value or monetary amount that results from the interaction of the following elements:
(1) the recognized utility of that real estate,
(2) the relative scarcity of that real estate, and
(3) the effective demand for that real estate.

The economic value of real estate is basically determined by physical, social, economic and governmental factors that influence the above three elements. The relationship between real estate value and these four factors has a dual nature, in that the value of real estate is formed under the influence of these factors while at the same time value itself exerts an influence on these factors since it also becomes a criterion in the selection of real estate.

Section 2. Characteristics of Real Estate Value
Although the degree to which real estate contributes to the lives and activities of citizens is expressed as its specific value, land has special characteristics that set it apart from other ordinary assets. Included among these characteristics are:
(1) fixity of geographical location, immovability, durability, finite nature of supply, and non- fungibility ; physically speaking, land parcels cannot be substituted for or interchanged with one another.
(2) changeable social and economic utility and status (potential uses may be competitive or complementary; uses may also be changed), and physical adaptability (land parcels can be divided or consolidated).

The social and economic utility of real estate depends on whether the characteristics of a

総　論

第1章　不動産の鑑定評価に関する基本的考察

　不動産の鑑定評価とはどのようなことであるか、それは何故に必要であるか、われわれの社会においてそれはどのような役割を果たすものであるか、そしてこの役割の具体的な担当者である不動産鑑定士及び不動産鑑定士補（以下「不動産鑑定士」という。）に対して要請されるものは何であるか、不動産鑑定士は、まず、これらについて十分に理解し、体得するところがなければならない。

第1節　不動産とその価格

　不動産は、通常、土地とその定着物をいう。土地はその持つ有用性の故にすべての国民の生活と活動とに欠くことのできない基盤である。そして、この土地を我々人間が各般の目的のためにどのように利用しているかという土地と人間との関係は、不動産のあり方、すなわち、不動産がどのように構成され、どのように貢献しているかということに具体的に現れる。

　この不動産のあり方は、自然的、社会的、経済的及び行政的な要因の相互作用によって決定されるとともに経済価値の本質を決定づけている。一方、この不動産のあり方は、その不動産の経済価値を具体的に表している価格を選択の主要な指標として決定されている。

　不動産の価格は、一般に、

(1)　その不動産に対してわれわれが認める効用
(2)　その不動産の相対的稀少性
(3)　その不動産に対する有効需要

の三者の相関結合によって生ずる不動産の経済価値を、貨幣額をもって表示したものである。そして、この不動産の経済価値は、基本的にはこれら三者を動かす自然的、社会的、経済的及び行政的な要因の相互作用によって決定される。不動産の価格とこれらの要因との関係は、不動産の価格が、これらの要因の影響の下にあると同時に選択指標としてこれらの要因に影響を与えるという二面性を持つものである。

第2節　不動産とその価格の特徴

　不動産が国民の生活と活動に組み込まれどのように貢献しているかは具体的な価格として現れるものであるが、土地は他の一般の諸財と異なって次のような特性を持っている。

(1)　自然的特性として、地理的位置の固定性、不動性（非移動性）、永続性（不変性）、不増性、個別性（非同質性、非代替性）等を有し、固定的であって硬直的である。
(2)　人文的特性として、用途の多様性（用途の競合、転換及び併存の可能性）、併合及び分割の可能性、社会的及び経済的位置の可変性等を有し、可変的であって伸縮的である。

　不動産は、この土地の持つ諸特性に照応する特定の自然的条件及び人文的条件を与件として利用され、その社会的及び経済的な有用性を発揮するものである。そして、これらの諸条件の変化に伴って、その利用形態並びにその社会的及び経済的な有用性は変化する。

　不動産は、また、その自然的条件及び人文的条件の全部又は一部を共通にすることによって、

land parcel meet the specific physical and socio- economic requirements of the intended use. The type of use and the social and economic utility of the real estate change according to changes in these requirements.

In addition, because all real estate shares common physical and socio-economic attributes, each real estate product represents a component of a regional or local market, depending upon or complementing other real estate products in that market, competing with or supporting similar real estate products in that market, and demonstrating its social and economic utility through these relationships.

Although various types of regional and local real estate markets differ according to their size, composition, and functions, all markets are identified in terms of their land use, and premised on the relationship to specific physical and socio- economic requirements in the same manner as individual real estate products. While regional and local markets have characteristics that distinguish them from other regional and local markets, they also maintain a mutual relationship with markets in other regions, and occupy a social and economic ranking through that mutual relationship.

Because of the special characteristics of real estate, real estate value can be distinguished from the value of other ordinary assets.

(1) The value of real estate represents value in exchange. But real estate value is also indicated by rent paid as compensation for the rights to occupy and use real estate. A correlation between value in exchange and rent can be observed in the relationship between capital investment and dividends.

(2) The value of real estate reflects compensation paid for the ownership interest in a fee simple. The right to use or occupy a leased fee estate can be leased for compensation in the form of rent, which represents economic profit to the lessor. In situations where two or more property rights pertain to, or lessor profits derive from, the same real estate, the value (or rental value) can be estimated for each property right and lessor profit.

(3) The regional or local market for a real estate product is not static, but rather in a state of continuous change, expanding or contracting, concentrating or dispersing, growing or declining. Judging whether or not the use of real estate is optimal requires continuous review with respect to whether or not the real estate is able to maintain optimal utility over the passage of time, even if it may currently be under optimal use. Thus, the value (or rent) of real estate normally depends on long- term considerations, extending from the past into the future. The current value (or rent) is an extension of yesterday, a reflection of tomorrow, and in a process of continuous change.

(4) The sale price of real estate is normally formed on the basis of the specific circumstances of the transaction. Moreover, the sale price is also influenced by the individual attributes of the real estate. It may be extremely difficult for ordinary persons to determine the market value of real estate from sales prices. Thus, the appraisal activities of expert LREAs are essential for determining the market value of real estate.

他の不動産とともにある地域を構成し、その地域の構成分子としてその地域との間に、依存、補完等の関係に及びその地域内の他の構成分子である不動産との間に協働、代替、競争等の関係にたち、これらの関係を通じてその社会的及び経済的な有用性を発揮するものである（不動産の地域性）。

このような地域には、その規模、構成の内容、機能等に従って各種のものが認められるが、そのいずれもが、不動産の集合という意味において、個別の不動産の場合と同様に、特定の自然的条件及び人文的条件との関係を前提とする利用のあり方の同一性を基準として理解されるものであって、他の地域と区別されるべき特性をそれぞれ有するとともに、他の地域との間に相互関係にたち、この相互関係を通じて、その社会的及び経済的位置を占めるものである（地域の特性）。

このような不動産の特徴により、不動産の価格についても、他の一般の諸財の価格と異なって、およそ次のような特徴を指摘することができる。

(1) 不動産の経済価値は、一般に、交換の対価である価格として表示されるとともに、その用益の対価である賃料として表示される。そして、この価格と賃料との間には、いわゆる元本と果実との間に認められる相関関係を認めることができる。

(2) 不動産の価格（又は賃料）は、その不動産に関する所有権、賃借権等の権利の対価又は経済的利益の対価であり、また、二つ以上の権利利益が同一の不動産の上に存する場合には、それぞれの権利利益について、その価格（又は賃料）が形成され得る。

(3) 不動産の属する地域は固定的なものではなくて、常に拡大縮小、集中拡散、発展衰退等の変化の過程にあるものであるから、不動産の利用形態が最適なものであるかどうか、仮に現在最適なものであっても、時の経過に伴ってこれを持続できるかどうか、これらは常に検討されなければならない。したがって、不動産の価格（又は賃料）は、通常、過去と将来とにわたる長期的な考慮の下に形成される。今日の価格（又は賃料）は、昨日の展開であり、明日を反映するものであって常に変化の過程にあるものである。

(4) 不動産の現実の取引価格等は、取引等の必要に応じて個別的に形成されるのが通常であり、しかもそれは個別的な事情に左右されがちのものであって、このような取引価格等から不動産の適正な価格を見出すことは一般の人には非常に困難である。したがって、不動産の適正な価格については専門家としての不動産鑑定士の鑑定評価活動が必要となるものである。

Section 3. Appraisal of Real Estate

Because the characteristics of real estate differ from those of other ordinary assets, it is necessary to rely on the activities of appraisers to determine its fair value (or market value).

Real estate appraisal involves estimation of the economic value of the subject real estate in terms of a monetary amount. This process consists of determining an indication of the level of value and/or rent that the real estate is capable of sustaining within a series of value parameters. It comprises the following steps:

(1) gaining an accurate perception of the real estate to be appraised;
(2) adequately gathering and organizing all required data;
(3) fully understanding those factors that form the value of the real estate along with those principles relating to real estate value;
(4) applying appraisal techniques while;
(5) analyzing all relevant information that has been gathered and organized, and considering the effects of physical, social, economic and governmental factors on the subject real estate; and finally
(6) reaching a final judgment regarding the economic value of the subject property in terms of a monetary amount.

How well this process is performed depends on the abilities of the person carrying out the successive stages of the appraisal as well as the extent to which those abilities have been applied. In addition, it also depends on the quality of the gathering and organization of requisite data and the degree of skill in analyzing and interpreting those data. Thus, appraisals can only be rationally and objectively performed when they are done by skilled specialists, having sophisticated knowledge, extensive experience and proven judgmental skills, and who are also able to apply these capabilities in a systematic and comprehensive manner.

The objective of real estate appraisal is to estimate a fair value, or indication of the probable market value of real estate in a market rationally operating under a given set of actual economic circumstances. When performed by skilled experts as exemplified by the professional work of LREAs, a real estate appraisal can be considered to be the judgment or opinion of an expert with respect to real estate value.

Since real estate appraisal also reflects the fair or equitable value of the subject property within a series of value parameters, its social and public significance can be considered to be extremely broad.

Section 4. Responsibility of LREAs

Land utilization and transactions involving land should be conducted in the spirit of the stipulations pertaining to land in the *Basic Land Act*. In particular, land should not become the target of speculative transactions. LREAs must conduct real estate appraisals in compliance with this stipulation.

LREAs are recognized by the *Real Estate Appraisal Act* as being persons charged with the appraisal of real estate, who have the status of capable and knowledgeable specialists, and who have been granted that status by demonstrating specific qualifications. Thus, LREAs are required to fulfill the trust and expectations of society. They must understand

第3節　不動産の鑑定評価

　このように一般の諸財と異なる不動産についてその適正な価格を求めるためには、鑑定評価の活動に依存せざるを得ないこととなる。
　不動産の鑑定評価は、その対象である不動産の経済価値を判定し、これを貨幣額をもって表示することである。それは、この社会における一連の価格秩序の中で、その不動産の価格及び賃料がどのような所に位するかを指摘することであって、
(1)　鑑定評価の対象となる不動産の的確な認識の上に、
(2)　必要とする関連資料を十分に収集して、これを整理し、
(3)　不動産の価格を形成する要因及び不動産の価格に関する諸原則についての十分な理解のもとに、
(4)　鑑定評価の手法を駆使して、その間に、
(5)　既に収集し、整理されている関連諸資料を具体的に分析して、対象不動産に及ぼす自然的、社会的、経済的及び行政的な要因の影響を判断し、
(6)　対象不動産の経済価値に関する最終判断に到達し、これを貨幣額をもって表示するものである。
　この判断の当否は、これら各段階のそれぞれについての不動産鑑定士の能力の如何及びその能力の行使の誠実さの如何に係るものであり、また、必要な関連諸資料の収集整理の適否及びこれらの諸資料の分析解釈の練達の程度に依存するものである。したがって、鑑定評価は、高度な知識と豊富な経験及び的確な判断力を持ち、さらに、これらが有機的かつ総合的に発揮できる練達堪能な専門家によってなされるとき、初めて合理的であって、客観的に論証できるものとなるのである。
　不動産の鑑定評価とは、現実の社会経済情勢の下で合理的と考えられる市場で形成されるであろう市場価値を表示する適正な価格を、不動産鑑定士が的確に把握する作業に代表されるように、練達堪能な専門家によって初めて可能な仕事であるから、このような意味において、不動産の鑑定評価とは、不動産の価格に関する専門家の判断であり、意見であるといってよいであろう。
　それはまた、この社会における一連の価格秩序のなかで、対象不動産の価格の占める適正なあり所を指摘することであるから、その社会的公共的意義は極めて大きいといわなければならない。

第4節　不動産鑑定士の責務

　土地は、土地基本法に定める土地についての基本理念に即して利用及び取引が行われるべきであり、特に投機的取引の対象とされてはならないものである。不動産鑑定士は、このような土地についての基本的な認識に立って不動産の鑑定評価を行わなければならない。
　不動産鑑定士は、不動産の鑑定評価を担当する者として、十分に能力のある専門家としての地位を不動産の鑑定評価に関する法律によって認められ、付与されるものである。したがって、不動産鑑定士は、不動産の鑑定評価の社会的公共的意義を理解し、その責務を自覚し、的確かつ誠実な鑑定評価活動の実践をもって、社会一般の信頼と期待に報いなければならない。
　そのためには、まず、不動産鑑定士は、同法に規定されているとおり、良心に従い、誠実に不

General Standards Chapter 1

the social and public significance of real estate appraisal, be aware of their own responsibility, and perform their appraisal activities in an accurate and sincere manner.

In order to accomplish this, LREAs have to conduct real estate appraisals impartially in accordance with proper moral conduct and stipulations of the law; they must not be engaged in any acts that would damage the trust society has vested in them as specialized professionals. In addition, LREAs and LREA candidates must not disclose to other persons any confidential matters ascertained during the course of fulfilling their duties without proper cause, and must strive to uphold their reputation by strictly observing the guidelines indicated below.

(1) Since accurate appraisals can only be developed through the systematic integration of sophisticated knowledge, extensive experience and proven judgmental skills, efforts must be made to improve appraisal skills through continuous study and training.

(2) Not only must appraisers be able to provide clients with easily understandable and impartial explanations of appraisal results, but practical efforts should also be taken to raise the level of trust in real estate appraisals by educating the public with respect to real estate appraisal and the practice thereof.

(3) In undertaking a real estate appraisal, the appraiser should maintain a fair and reasonable attitude regardless of his / her own self interests or any other reasons.

(4) In performing a real estate appraisal, a professional specialist must take special care to consider every detail.

(5) In the case of appraisal assignments that are thought to exceed the limits of one's own capabilities or which involve associations or special interests that might impair obtaining a fair or impartial appraisal, the appraiser should, as a matter of principle, not accept such appraisal assignments.

動産の鑑定評価を行い、専門職業家としての社会的信用を傷つけるような行為をしてはならないとともに、正当な理由がなくて、その職務上取り扱ったことについて知り得た秘密を他に漏らしてはならないことはいうまでもなく、さらに次に述べる事項を遵守して資質の向上に努めなければならない。

(1) 高度な知識と豊富な経験と的確な判断力とが有機的に統一されて、初めて的確な鑑定評価が可能となるのであるから、不断の勉強と研鑽とによってこれを体得し、鑑定評価の進歩改善に努力すること。
(2) 依頼者に対して鑑定評価の結果を分かり易く誠実に説明を行い得るようにするとともに、社会一般に対して、実践活動をもって、不動産の鑑定評価及びその制度に関する理解を深めることにより、不動産の鑑定評価に対する信頼を高めるよう努めること。
(3) 不動産の鑑定評価に当たっては、自己又は関係人の利害の有無その他いかなる理由にかかわらず、公平妥当な態度を保持すること。
(4) 不動産の鑑定評価に当たっては、専門職業家としての注意を払わなければならないこと。
(5) 自己の能力の限度を超えていると思われる不動産の鑑定評価を引き受け、又は縁故若しくは特別の利害関係を有する場合等、公平な鑑定評価を害する恐れのあるときは、原則として不動産の鑑定評価を引き受けてはならないこと。

CHAPTER 2. USE CATEGORIES AND PHYSICAL DEVELOPMENT & TITLE CATEGORIES OF REAL ESTATE

In the appraisal of real estate, it is necessary to analyze the characteristics of the market area in which the subject real estate is located. It is also important to identify the use and physical development & relevant legal title of the subject real estate based on the market area characteristics of the area.

Thus, the identification of real estate is a dual concept, comprising a use category and a physical development & title category. Since these two categories essentially determine the economic value of real estate, it is only possible to conduct an accurate appraisal of real estate after first analyzing both categories.

The *use category* of real estate refers to real estate as classified with respect to one of three broad land uses, while the *physical development & title category* of real estate refers to real estate as classified according to its physical state of development and legal title and interests (i.e., freehold, leased fee, leasehold, etc.).

Section 1. Real Estate Use Categories

I Categories Describing the General Land Use in a Area

Categories describing the general land use in a district or area are divided into *building site areas, agricultural areas* and *forestland areas*.

Building site areas refer to areas, which make up lots for buildings and structures used for living, commercial activities and industrial production. The use of building sites must qualify as the rational use of a site in terms of physical, social, economic and governmental criteria. Building site areas can be further broken down into *residential areas, commercial areas* and *industrial areas*. In turn, residential areas, commercial areas and industrial areas may be further broken down according to their size, specific characteristics and functions.

Agricultural areas refer to areas used for agricultural production, i.e., for activities involving cultivation. The use of agricultural sites must be the rational use of a site in terms of physical, social, economic and governmental criteria.

Forestland areas refer to areas used for forestry production, i.e., for activities involving the planting and growing of trees, bamboo or special forest products. The use of forestland areas must be the rational use of the land in terms of physical, social, economic and governmental criteria.

Furthermore, it should be noted that some building site areas, agricultural areas and forestland areas may be undergoing transition from one use category to another use category. Some building site areas and agricultural areas may also be undergoing transition from one use sub-category to another use sub-category within each classification.

II Land Use Categories

Land use categories are identified according to the use category of the district or area. These are divided into building sites, agricultural land, forestland, sites with interim use, and lots in a transitional area. Land use categories may be further subdivided into use

第2章　不動産の種別及び類型

　不動産の鑑定評価においては、不動産の地域性並びに有形的利用及び権利関係の態様に応じた分析を行う必要があり、その地域の特性等に基づく不動産の種類ごとに検討することが重要である。
　不動産の種類とは、不動産の種別及び類型の二面から成る複合的な不動産の概念を示すものであり、この不動産の種別及び類型が不動産の経済価値を本質的に決定づけるものであるから、この両面の分析をまって初めて精度の高い不動産の鑑定評価が可能となるものである。
　不動産の種別とは、不動産の用途に関して区分される不動産の分類をいい、不動産の類型とは、その有形的利用及び権利関係の態様に応じて区分される不動産の分類をいう。

第1節　不動産の種別

Ⅰ　地域の種別

　地域の種別は、宅地地域、農地地域、林地地域等に分けられる。
　宅地地域とは、居住、商業活動、工業生産活動等の用に供される建物、構築物等の敷地の用に供されることが、自然的、社会的、経済的及び行政的観点からみて合理的と判断される地域をいい、住宅地域、商業地域、工業地域等に細分される。さらに住宅地域、商業地域、工業地域等については、その規模、構成の内容、機能等に応じた細分化が考えられる。
　農地地域とは、農業生産活動のうち耕作の用に供されることが、自然的、社会的、経済的及び行政的観点からみて合理的と判断される地域をいう。
　林地地域とは、林業生産活動のうち木竹又は特用林産物の生育の用に供されることが、自然的、社会的、経済的及び行政観点からみて合理的と判断される地域をいう。
　なお、宅地地域、農地地域、林地地域等の相互間において、ある種別の地域から他の種別の地域へと転換しつつある地域及び宅地地域、農地地域等のうちにあって、細分されたある種別の地域から、その地域の他の細分された地域へと移行しつつある地域があることに留意すべきである。

Ⅱ　土地の種別

　土地の種別は、地域の種別に応じて分類される土地の区分であり、宅地、農地、林地、見込地、移行地等に分けられ、さらに地域の種別の細分に応じて細分される。
　宅地とは、宅地地域のうちにある土地をいい、住宅地、商業地、工業地等に細分される。こ

General Standards Chapter 2

sub-categories in each of the classifications.

Building sites refer to land located in a building site area, which may be further broken down into residential, commercial, and industrial land. Residential land refers to land located in a residential area; commercial land refers to land located in a commercial area; and industrial land refers to land located in an industrial area.

Agricultural land refers to land located in an agricultural area.

Forestland refers to land located in a forestland area (excluding standing trees and bamboo).

Sites with interim use refer to land located in an area undergoing transition from one use category to a different use category. Interim use areas are divided into building sites with an interim use, agricultural land with an interim use, forestland with an interim use and so on.

Lots in a transitional area refer to land located in a building site area or agricultural area that is undergoing transition from one use sub-category to a different use sub-category.

Section 2. Physical Development & Title Categories

The following provides examples of the classification of both building sites and built-up properties according to their physical development & title categories.

I Building Sites

Building sites are classified as 1) vacant land, 2) land portion of built-up property, 3) leasehold interests in land, 4) leased fee interests in land, and 5) sectional superficies (air/underground rights).

Vacant land refers to building sites on which no buildings or other improvements stand and which are not subject to any legal or deed restrictions. (Editor's Note: vacant land connotes freehold ownership of land with no buildings or restrictions to it.)

The land portion of built-up property refers to a building site, on which buildings stand. A freehold interest in the land portion of built-up property denotes that the building(s) and lot belong to the same owner and are used by the same owner. The land should not be subject to legal or deed restrictions.

A leasehold interest in land (*shakuchiken*) refers to the interest of the tenant or lessee who holds a ground lease. Ground leases are typically held by the owners of the buildings that occupy leased sites and are classified into two types: the right to be granted by lease contract (*chinshakuken*) which are usually not registered and the right of superficies (*chijoken*) which are usually registered. Leasehold interests are defined in the *Land Lease and Building Lease Law*. (Editor's Note: An important distinction between a regular ground lease and the right of superficies is that the tenant holding a regular ground lease needs the consent of the landlord to transfer or sublease, but a holder of the right of superficies can transfer or sublease without the landlord's consent. In Japan, there are both land and building registries. Buildings are registered, but regular ground lease are usually not. However, if the tenant holds the right of superficies, the tenant's interest is registered, and his / her position is thereby enhanced.)

A leased fee interest in land refers to the leased fee estate in a building site. The owner of the building on the site is a lessee of the land on which the building stands while the

の場合において、住宅地とは住宅地域のうちにある土地をいい、商業地とは商業地域のうちにある土地をいい、工業地とは工業地域のうちにある土地をいう。

農地とは、農地地域のうちにある土地をいう。

林地とは、林地地域のうちにある土地（立木竹を除く。）をいう。

見込地とは、宅地地域、農地地域、林地地域等の相互間において、ある種別の地域から他の種別の地域へと転換しつつある地域のうちにある土地をいい、宅地見込地、農地見込地等に分けられる。

移行地とは、宅地地域、農地地域等のうちにあって、細分されたある種別の地域から他の種別の地域へと移行しつつある地域のうちにある土地をいう。

第2節　不動産の類型

宅地並びに建物及びその敷地の類型を例示すれば、次のとおりである。

I　宅地

宅地の類型は、その有形的利用及び権利関係の態様に応じて、更地、建付地、借地権、底地、区分地上権等に分けられる。

更地とは、建物等の定着物がなく、かつ、使用収益を制約する権利の付着していない宅地をいう。

建付地とは、建物等の用に供されている敷地で建物等及びその敷地が同一の所有者に属し、かつ、当該所有者により使用され、その敷地の使用収益を制約する権利の付着していない宅地をいう。

借地権とは、借地借家法（廃止前の借地法を含む。）に基づく借地権（建物の所有を目的とする地上権又は土地の賃借権）をいう。

底地とは、宅地について借地権の付着している場合における当該宅地の所有権をいう。

区分地上権とは、工作物を所有するため、地下又は空間に上下の範囲を定めて設定された地上権をいう。

building site owner/lessor holds the leased fee interest in the land.

Air/underground rights refer to sectional superficies established in vertical space under the ground or in the air. These rights make possible the conveyance of interests in the structures occupying such space.

II Built – Up Property (Buildings and the Sites on Which They Stand)

Title to buildings and the sites on which they stand is divided into the following categories: 1) the ownership interest in an owner- occupied building and its site, 2) the ownership interest in a tenant- occupied building and its site, 3) the ownership interest in the building on leased land, and 4) the ownership interest in a condominium unit.

The ownership interest in an owner- occupied building and its site refers to the ownership interest in a building and building lot where the building owner and lot owner are the same, and the property is not subject to legal or deed restrictions.

The ownership interest in a tenant- occupied building and its site refers to a building and site where the building owner and lot owner are the same, but the building is leased, i.e., the owner of the lot and building holds a leased fee interest in the building.

The ownership interest in the building on leased land refers to a situation where the ownership right to a building is held by someone with a ground lease to the site upon which the building stands. (A landlord or lessor holds title to, and leased fee interest in, the land on which the building stands.)

The ownership interest in a condominium unit refers to: exclusively- owned area stipulated in Article 2, Paragraph 3 of the *Law for Unit Ownership, etc. of Building* (the *Law for Condominium*); co- ownership of common areas stipulated in Article 2, Paragraph 4 of said Act; and co- ownership of the underlying site stipulated in Article 2, Paragraph 6 of said Act.

Ⅱ　建物及びその敷地

　建物及びその敷地の類型は、その有形的利用及び権利関係の態様に応じて、自用の建物及びその敷地、貸家及びその敷地、借地権付建物、区分所有建物及びその敷地等に分けられる。

　自用の建物及びその敷地とは、建物所有者とその敷地の所有者とが同一人であり、その所有者による使用収益を制約する権利の付着していない場合における当該建物及びその敷地をいう。

　貸家及びその敷地とは、建物所有者とその敷地の所有者とが同一人であるが、建物が賃貸借に供されている場合における当該建物及びその敷地をいう。

　借地権付建物とは、借地権を権原とする建物が存する場合における当該建物及び借地権をいう。

　区分所有建物及びその敷地とは、建物の区分所有等に関する法律第2条第3項に規定する専有部分並びに当該専有部分に係る同条第4項に規定する共用部分の共有持分及び同条第6項に規定する敷地利用権をいう。

CHAPTER 3. INFLUENCES ON REAL ESTATE VALUE

Influences on the value of real estate (henceforth called "value influences") refer to those influences that affect the utility of real estate, its relative scarcity, and the effective demand for real estate. Although real estate value is formed as a result of the interaction of numerous value influences, those value influences themselves tend to change continuously. Thus, in the appraisal of real estate, it is necessary to accurately understand how market participants view value influences, and to evaluate the effect of these influences on the utility of, scarcity of, and effective demand for real estate by adequately analyzing market changes, industry trends and the interrelationships among value influences.

Value influences are divided into general value influences, area-specific value influences and property-specific value influences.

Section 1. General Value Influences

General value influences refer to value influences that have an effect on the real estate industry, the economy, and price levels. These are broadly classified into physical, social, economic, and governmental value influences.

The following lists provide major examples of general value influences.

I **Physical Value Influences**
 1. Geological features
 2. Soil
 3. Topography
 4. Geographical location
 5. Climate

II **Social Value Influences**
 1. Population
 2. Family size and household formation
 3. Urbanization and infrastructure development
 4. Education and social welfare
 5. Real estate transactions and practice (brokerage services, tenancy, and so forth)
 6. Architectural styles
 7. Availability and dissemination of information
 8. Lifestyles

III **Economic Value Influences**
 1. Savings, consumption, investment and foreign trade balance
 2. Fiscal and monetary conditions
 3. Commodity prices, wages, employment and corporate activity
 4. Taxation
 5. Corporate accounting system
 6. Technological innovations and industrial base

第3章　不動産の価格を形成する要因

　不動産の価格を形成する要因（以下「価格形成要因」という。）とは、不動産の効用及び相対的稀少性並びに不動産に対する有効需要の三者に影響を与える要因をいう。不動産の価格は、多数の要因の相互作用の結果として形成されるものであるが、要因それ自体も常に変動する傾向を持っている。したがって、不動産の鑑定評価を行うに当たっては、価格形成要因を市場参加者の観点から明確に把握し、かつ、その推移及び動向並びに諸要因間の相互関係を十分に分析して、前記三者に及ぼすその影響を判定することが必要である。
　価格形成要因は、一般的要因、地域要因及び個別的要因に分けられる。

第1節　一般的要因
　一般的要因とは、一般経済社会における不動産のあり方及びその価格の水準に影響を与える要因をいう。それは、自然的要因、社会的要因、経済的要因及び行政的要因に大別される。
　一般的要因の主なものを例示すれば、次のとおりである。

Ⅰ　自然的要因
1．地質、地盤等の状態
2．土壌及び土層の状態
3．地勢の状態
4．地理的位置関係
5．気象の状態

Ⅱ　社会的要因
1．人口の状態
2．家族構成及び世帯分離の状態
3．都市形成及び公共施設の整備の状態
4．教育及び社会福祉の状態
5．不動産の取引及び使用収益の慣行
6．建築様式等の状態
7．情報化の進展の状態
8．生活様式等の状態

Ⅲ　経済的要因
1．貯蓄、消費、投資及び国際収支の状態
2．財政及び金融の状態
3．物価、賃金、雇用及び企業活動の状態
4．税負担の状態
5．企業会計制度の状態
6．技術革新及び産業構造の状態

General Standards Chapter 3

    7. Transportation system
    8. Globalization
IV Governmental Value Influences
    1. Land use planning and regulation
    2. Building codes and required disaster prevention safeguards
    3. Policies relating to building sites (building setbacks, building density) and housing developments
    4. Real estate taxation
    5. Regulations applying to real estate transactions

Section 2. Area – Specific Value Influences

Area-specific value influences refer to influences that have an overall effect on the formation of the value of real estate in a specific market area. Area-specific influences include those features that give an area its character, i.e., size, land use, function, and so forth. Area-specific and general value influences may often overlap.

I Building Site Areas

1. Residential areas

The following list provides major examples of area-specific value influences in residential areas.
    (1) Climate including sunlight, temperature, humidity and wind direction
    (2) Street width and structure
    (3) Distance from the city center and availability of transportation
    (4) Location of commercial facilities
    (5) Waterworks, city gas service, garbage disposal and sewers
    (6) Development of telecommunications infrastructure
    (7) Location of public institutions and utilities
    (8) Presence of nuisances such as sewage treatment plants
    (9) Risk of flooding, landslides and other natural disasters
    (10) Noise, air pollution, and soil contamination
    (11) Lot size, layout and utilization
    (12) Residences, hedges, landscaping and street appearance
    (13) Quality of the natural environment including scenic views
    (14) Land use planning and regulation

2. Commercial Areas

The following list provides examples of major market-specific value influences in commercial areas, and supplements the area-specific value influences listed in the section on residential areas above.
    (1) Types, sizes and concentration of commercial or service facilities
    (2) Quality and size of trade and customer profile
    (3) Availability of transportation for customers and employees
    (4) Convenience in loading and unloading of merchandise
    (5) Street accessibility and additional features such as covered arcades
    (6) Business types and competition

7．交通体系の状態
8．国際化の状態
Ⅳ　行政的要因
1．土地利用に関する計画及び規制の状態
2．土地及び建築物の構造、防災等に関する規制の状態
3．宅地及び住宅に関する施策の状態
4．不動産に関する税制の状態
5．不動産の取引に関する規制の状態

第2節　地域要因

地域要因とは、一般的要因の相関結合によって規模、構成の内容、機能等にわたる各地域の特性を形成し、その地域に属する不動産の価格の形成に全般的な影響を与える要因をいう。

Ⅰ　宅地地域
1．住宅地域
住宅地域の地域要因の主なものを例示すれば、次のとおりである。
(1)　日照、温度、湿度、風向等の気象の状態
(2)　街路の幅員、構造等の状態
(3)　都心との距離及び交通施設の状態
(4)　商業施設の配置の状態
(5)　上下水道、ガス等の供給・処理施設の状態
(6)　情報通信基盤の整備の状態
(7)　公共施設、公益的施設等の配置の状態
(8)　汚水処理場等の嫌悪施設等の有無
(9)　洪水、地すべり等の災害の発生の危険性
(10)　騒音、大気の汚染、土壌汚染等の公害の発生の程度
(11)　各画地の面積、配置及び利用の状態
(12)　住宅、生垣、街路修景等の街並みの状態
(13)　眺望、景観等の自然的環境の良否
(14)　土地利用に関する計画及び規制の状態

2．商業地域
前記1．に掲げる地域要因のほか、商業地域特有の地域要因の主なものを例示すれば、次のとおりである。
(1)　商業施設又は業務施設の種類、規模、集積度等の状態
(2)　商業背後地及び顧客の質と量
(3)　顧客及び従業員の交通手段の状態
(4)　商品の搬入及び搬出の利便性
(5)　街路の回遊性、アーケード等の状態
(6)　営業の種別及び競争の状態
(7)　当該地域の経営者の創意と資力

(7) Entrepreneurship and financial resources of business owners in the subject area
(8) Volume of automobile and / or pedestrian traffic
(9) Provision of parking facilities
(10) Degree of governmental assistance and regulation

3. Industrial Areas

The following list provides examples of major area-specific value influences in industrial areas, and supplements the market-specific value influences listed in the section on residential areas above.

(1) Provision of arterial roads, railroads, harbors, airports and other transport networks
(2) Availability of a work force
(3) Location of consumer market(s) and industrial suppliers
(4) Power, water and drainage costs
(5) Location of related industries
(6) Risk of water pollution and air pollution
(7) Degree of governmental assistance and regulation

II Agricultural Areas

Major examples of area-specific value influences in agricultural areas are indicated below.

1. Climate including sunlight, temperature, humidity, wind and rain
2. Topography including rolling ground, elevated highland and flat lowland areas
3. Soil
4. Water utilization and water quality
5. Risk of flooding, landslides and other natural disasters
6. Adequacy of roads
7. Location of rural communities
8. Location of distribution center(s) and farms
9. Distance from consumer market(s) and availability of transport facilities
10. Degree of governmental assistance and regulation

III Forestland Areas

Major examples of area-specific value influences in forestland areas are indicated below.

1. Climate including sunlight, temperature, humidity, wind and rain
2. Altitude and topography
3. Soil
4. Adequacy of roads
5. Availability of a work force
6. Degree of governmental assistance and regulation

Regarding areas in rapid transition from one use category to a different use category, greater emphasis should be placed on area-specific value influences affecting the use category following the transition. In the case of a gradual transition, however, the market-specific value influences affecting the use category prior to the transition should be emphasized.

(8) 繁華性の程度及び盛衰の動向
(9) 駐車施設の整備の状態
(10) 行政上の助成及び規制の程度

3．工業地域
　前記１．に掲げる地域要因のほか、工業地域特有の地域要因の主なものを例示すれば、次のとおりである。
(1) 幹線道路、鉄道、港湾、空港等の輸送施設の整備の状況
(2) 労働力確保の難易
(3) 製品販売市場及び原材料仕入市場との位置関係
(4) 動力資源及び用排水に関する費用
(5) 関連産業との位置関係
(6) 水質の汚濁、大気の汚染等の公害の発生の危険性
(7) 行政上の助成及び規制の程度

Ⅱ　農地地域
　農地地域の地域要因の主なものを例示すれば、次のとおりである。
1．日照、温度、湿度、風雨等の気象の状態
2．起伏、高低等の地勢の状態
3．土壌及び土層の状態
4．水利及び水質の状態
5．洪水、地すべり等の災害の発生の危険性
6．道路等の整備の状態
7．集落との位置関係
8．集荷地又は産地市場との位置関係
9．消費地との距離及び輸送施設の状態
10．行政上の助成及び規制の程度

Ⅲ　林地地域
　林地地域の地域要因の主なものを例示すれば、次のとおりである。
1．日照、温度、湿度、風雨等の気象の状態
2．標高、地勢等の状態
3．土壌及び土層の状態
4．林道等の整備の状態
5．労働力確保の難易
6．行政上の助成及び規制の程度

　なお、ある種別の地域から他の種別の地域へと転換し、又は移行しつつある地域については、転換し、又は移行すると見込まれる転換後又は移行後の種別の地域の地域要因をより重視すべきであるが、転換又は移行の程度の低い場合においては、転換前又は移行前の種別の地域の地域要因をより重視すべきである。

General Standards Chapter 3

Section 3. Property – Specific Value Influences

Property-specific value influences refer to those influences that give real estate its individuality and form the value of individual properties. Property-specific value influences are broken down according to land use classification.

I **Property – Specific Value Influences on Land**
  1. **Building Sites**
    (1) **Residential Land**
    Major examples of property-specific value influences on residential land are indicated below.
    ① Topography, geology and ground soil
    ② Sunlight, wind, dryness and dampness
    ③ Lot width, depth, size and shape
    ④ Land elevation in relation to the elevation of the facing street (corner lots will face two streets)
    ⑤ Width and condition of the facing street
    ⑥ Layout and network of the facing street
    ⑦ Distance from transportation
    ⑧ Proximity to commercial facilities
    ⑨ Proximity to public institution and utilities
    ⑩ Proximity to nuisances such as sewage treatment plants
    ⑪ Condition of adjacent real estate and surroundings
    ⑫ Availability of waterworks, city gas service, garbage disposal, and sewers
    ⑬ Development of telecommunications infrastructure
    ⑭ Presence of archeological artifacts buried on the site and condition of any underground structures
    ⑮ Presence and extent of soil contamination
    ⑯ Regulations or restrictions stipulated in public laws and private deeds
    (2) **Commercial Land**
    Major examples of property-specific value influences on commercial land are indicated below.
    ① Topography, geology and ground soil
    ② Lot width, depth, size and shape
    ③ Land elevation in relation to elevation of the facing street (corner lots will face two streets)
    ④ Width and condition of the facing street
    ⑤ Layout and network of the facing street
    ⑥ Proximity to center of commercial area
    ⑦ Proximity to main means of transportation
    ⑧ Location in conformity with customer flow
    ⑨ Condition of adjacent real estate and surroundings
    ⑩ Availability of waterworks, city gas service, garbage disposal and sewers
    ⑪ Availability of telecommunications infrastructure
    ⑫ Presence of archeological artifacts buried on the site and condition of any un-

第3節　個別的要因

個別的要因とは、不動産に個別性を生じさせ、その価格を個別的に形成する要因をいう。個別的要因は、土地、建物等の区分に応じて次のように分けられる。

Ⅰ　土地に関する個別的要因
　1．宅地
　　(1) 住宅地
　　　　住宅地の個別的要因の主なものを例示すれば、次のとおりである。
　　　　① 地勢、地質、地盤等
　　　　② 日照、通風及び乾湿
　　　　③ 間口、奥行、地積、形状等
　　　　④ 高低、角地その他の接面街路との関係
　　　　⑤ 接面街路の幅員、構造等の状態
　　　　⑥ 接面街路の系統及び連続性
　　　　⑦ 交通施設との距離
　　　　⑧ 商業施設との接近の程度
　　　　⑨ 公共施設、公益的施設等との接近の程度
　　　　⑩ 汚水処理場等の嫌悪施設等との接近の程度
　　　　⑪ 隣接不動産等周囲の状態
　　　　⑫ 上下水道、ガス等の供給・処理施設の有無及びその利用の難易
　　　　⑬ 情報通信基盤の利用の難易
　　　　⑭ 埋蔵文化財及び地下埋設物の有無並びにその状態
　　　　⑮ 土壌汚染の有無及びその状態
　　　　⑯ 公法上及び私法上の規制、制約等

　　(2) 商業地
　　　　商業地の個別的要因の主なものを例示すれば、次のとおりである。
　　　　① 地勢、地質、地盤等
　　　　② 間口、奥行、地積、形状等
　　　　③ 高低、角地その他の接面街路との関係
　　　　④ 接面街路の幅員、構造等の状態
　　　　⑤ 接面街路の系統及び連続性
　　　　⑥ 商業地域の中心への接近性
　　　　⑦ 主要交通機関との接近性
　　　　⑧ 顧客の流動の状態との適合性
　　　　⑨ 隣接不動産等周囲の状態
　　　　⑩ 上下水道、ガス等の供給・処理施設の有無及びその利用の難易
　　　　⑪ 情報通信基盤の利用の難易
　　　　⑫ 埋蔵文化財及び地下埋設物の有無並びにその状態
　　　　⑬ 土壌汚染の有無及びその状態
　　　　⑭ 公法上及び私法上の規制、制約等

General Standards Chapter 3

  derground structures
 ⑬ Presence and extent of soil pollution
 ⑭ Regulations or restrictions stipulated in public laws and private deeds

(3) **Industrial Land**

Major examples of property-specific value influences on industrial land are indicated below.
 ① Topography, geology and ground soil
 ② Lot width, depth, acreage and shape
 ③ Land elevation in relation to the elevation of the facing street (corner lots will face two streets)
 ④ Width and condition of the facing street
 ⑤ Layout and network of the facing street
 ⑥ Proximity to main means of transportation used by commuting employees
 ⑦ Location of arterial roads, railroads, harbors, airports and other transport networks
 ⑧ Availability of electrical power and other motive power resources
 ⑨ Adequacy of water sources and drainage facilities (and whether these facilities show any deferred maintenance)
 ⑩ Availability of waterworks, city gas service, garbage disposal and sewers
 ⑪ Development of telecommunications infrastructure
 ⑫ Presence of archeological artifacts buried on the site and condition of any underground structures
 ⑬ Presence and extent of soil pollution
 ⑭ Regulations or restrictions stipulated in public laws and private deeds

2. **Agricultural Land**

Major examples of property-specific value influences on agricultural land are indicated below.
 (1) Sunlight, dryness, dampness and rainfall
 (2) Soil
 (3) Presence and condition of farm roads
 (4) Irrigation and drainage
 (5) Ease of cultivation
 (6) Proximity to rural communities
 (7) Proximity to shipping sites
 (8) Potential risks of natural disaster
 (9) Regulations or restrictions stipulated in public laws and private deeds

3. **Forestland**

Major examples of property-specific value influences on forestland are indicated below.
 (1) Sunlight, dryness, dampness and rainfall
 (2) Altitude above sea level and topography
 (3) Soil
 (4) Ease of carrying out and transporting the lumber
 (5) Ease of management

(3) 工業地
　　工業地の個別的要因の主なものを例示すれば、次のとおりである。
　① 地勢、地質、地盤等
　② 間口、奥行、地積、形状等
　③ 高低、角地その他の接面街路との関係
　④ 接面街路の幅員、構造等の状態
　⑤ 接面街路の系統及び連続性
　⑥ 従業員の通勤等のための主要交通機関との接近性
　⑦ 幹線道路、鉄道、港湾、空港等の輸送施設との位置関係
　⑧ 電力等の動力資源の状態及び引込の難易
　⑨ 用排水等の供給・処理施設の整備の必要性
　⑩ 上下水道、ガス等の供給・処理施設の有無及びその利用の難易
　⑪ 情報通信基盤の利用の難易
　⑫ 埋蔵文化財及び地下埋設物の有無並びにその状態
　⑬ 土壌汚染の有無及びその状態
　⑭ 公法上及び私法上の規制、制約等

2．農地
　　農地の個別的要因の主なものを例示すれば、次のとおりである。
　(1) 日照、乾湿、雨量等の状態
　(2) 土壌及び土層の状態
　(3) 農道の状態
　(4) 灌漑排水の状態
　(5) 耕うんの難易
　(6) 集落との接近の程度
　(7) 集荷地との接近の程度
　(8) 災害の危険性の程度
　(9) 公法上及び私法上の規制、制約等

3．林地
　　林地の個別的要因の主なものを例示すれば、次のとおりである。
　(1) 日照、乾湿、雨量等の状態
　(2) 標高、地勢等の状態
　(3) 土壌及び土層の状態
　(4) 木材の搬出、運搬等の難易
　(5) 管理の難易

General Standards Chapter 3

(6) Regulations or restrictions stipulated in public laws and private deeds

4. Sites with Interim Use and Lots in Transitional Area

Regarding sites with an interim use and lots in a transitional area, greater emphasis should be placed on property-specific value influences affecting the land use category following the transition. In the case of a gradual transition, however, the property-specific value influences affecting the land use category prior to the transition should be emphasized.

II Property–Specific Value Influences on Building

Major examples of property-specific value influences on building are indicated below.
1. Age of the structure (and whether it is a new structure, an extension, a reconstruction or relocation)
2. Area, height, type of construction and materials
3. Design and functionality
4. Construction quality and dimensions
5. Earthquake resistance, fire resistance and compliance with other building performance standards
6. Maintenance and management
7. Presence of harmful substances and extent of contamination
8. Degree the building conforms to its environment
9. Regulations or restrictions stipulated in public laws and private deeds

III Property-Specific Value Influences on Built-Up Property (Buildings and the Underlying Sites)

In addition to those examples indicated in I and II above, major examples of property-specific value influences on buildings and building sites include the building layout, available parking lots, ground paths, gardens on the lot, and the overall compatibility between building and site, especially in regard to the size of the building relative to the dimensions of the site.

Property-specific value influences on leased real estate include how well the property is operated. Major examples are indicated below.
1. Status of the lessee and provisions of the lease contract
2. Occupancy level of the leased property
3. Quality of planned repairs and management program as well as the extent of their implementation

(6) 公法上及び私法上の規制、制約等
4．見込地及び移行地
　　見込地及び移行地については、転換し、又は移行すると見込まれる転換後又は移行後の種別の地域内の土地の個別的要因をより重視すべきであるが、転換又は移行の程度の低い場合においては、転換前又は移行前の種別の地域内の土地の個別的要因をより重視すべきである。

Ⅱ　建物に関する個別的要因
　　建物に関する個別的要因の主なものを例示すれば、次のとおりである。
１．建築（新築、増改築又は移転）の年次
２．面積、高さ、構造、材質等
３．設計、設備等の機能性
４．施工の質と量
５．耐震性、耐火性等建物の性能
６．維持管理の状態
７．有害な物質の使用の有無及びその状態
８．建物とその環境との適合の状態
９．公法上及び私法上の規制、制約等

Ⅲ　建物及びその敷地に関する個別的要因
　　前記Ⅰ及びⅡに例示したもののほか、建物及びその敷地に関する個別的要因の主なものを例示すれば、敷地内における建物、駐車場、通路、庭等の配置、建物と敷地の規模の対応関係等建物等と敷地との適応の状態がある。
　　さらに、賃貸用不動産に関する個別的要因には、賃貸経営管理の良否があり、その主なものを例示すれば、次のとおりである。
１．借主の状況及び賃貸借契約の内容
２．貸室の稼働状況
３．修繕計画及び管理計画の良否並びにその実施の状態

CHAPTER 4. PRINCIPLES OF REAL ESTATE VALUE

The value of real estate is formed by the interaction of various factors affecting the utility of the real estate, its relative scarcity, and the effective demand for that real estate. When the process of value formation is studied, basic economic laws or principles can be observed therein. Since the essence of real estate appraisal is the analysis of the value formation process as it pertains to a specific real estate product, these basic principles serve as necessary guidelines for any appraisal. The principles underlying the formation of real estate value are discussed below. An appraiser should study the operation of these principles to reach a conclusive judgment of the value of a real estate product.

Although these principles are based on general economic laws, they are identified and discussed within the specific context of appraisal.

It should be further noted that these principles are not independent of one another, but rather are directly or indirectly related.

I   Principle of Supply and Demand

While the value of a commodity is determined by the relationship between the supply of and demand for that commodity, the value of that commodity may also have an effect on the supply of and demand for the commodity.

The value of real estate is determined by the relationship between supply and demand, but real estate also has physical characteristics and socio- economic characteristics that differ from the attributes of other commodities. The effect of these additional characteristics is reflected in the dynamics of real estate supply and demand and the formation of real estate value.

II   Principle of Change

In general, the value of a commodity varies according to changes in the factors that form its value.

The value of real estate is also formed within a continuous process of change that reflects a succession of various cause and effect relationships between value influences. The value influences themselves undergo constant change. Thus, in appraising real estate, the dynamic cause and effect relationships between factors should be understood. In particular, the process of change must be analyzed in order to determine the highest and best use of real estate (see paragraph IV below).

III   Principle of Substitution

In cases where two or more commodities are interchangeable, the value of such commodities is determined by the mutual effect they exert on one another.

The value of real estate is also formed in relation to the value of other substitute real estate products.

IV   Principle of Highest and Best Use

The value of real estate is analyzed on the premise of the potential best use of the real estate, i.e., the use under which the real estate will achieve its maximal utility (henceforth

第4章　不動産の価格に関する諸原則

　不動産の価格は、不動産の効用及び相対的稀少性並びに不動産に対する有効需要に影響を与える諸要因の相互作用によって形成されるが、その形成の過程を考察するとき、そこに基本的な法則性を認めることができる。不動産の鑑定評価は、その不動産の価格の形成過程を追究し、分析することを本質とするものであるから、不動産の経済価値に関する適切な最終判断に到達するためには、鑑定評価に必要な指針としてこれらの法則性を認識し、かつ、これらを具体的に現した以下の諸原則を活用すべきである。
　これらの原則は、一般の経済法則に基礎を置くものであるが、鑑定評価の立場からこれを認識し、表現したものである。
　なお、これらの原則は、孤立しているものではなく、直接的又は間接的に相互に関連しているものであることに留意しなければならない。

Ⅰ　需要と供給の原則

　一般に財の価格は、その財の需要と供給との相互関係によって定まるとともに、その価格は、また、その財の需要と供給とに影響を及ぼす。
　不動産の価格もまたその需要と供給との相互関係によって定まるのであるが、不動産は他の財と異なる自然的特性及び人文的特性を有するために、その需要と供給及び価格の形成には、これらの特性の反映が認められる。

Ⅱ　変動の原則

　一般に財の価格は、その価格を形成する要因の変化に伴って変動する。
　不動産の価格も多数の価格形成要因の相互因果関係の組合せの流れである変動の過程において形成されるものである。したがって、不動産の鑑定評価に当たっては、価格形成要因が常に変動の過程にあることを認識して、各要因間の相互因果関係を動的に把握すべきである。特に、不動産の最有効使用（Ⅳ参照）を判定するためには、この変動の過程を分析することが必要である。

Ⅲ　代替の原則

　代替性を有する二以上の財が存在する場合には、これらの財の価格は、相互に影響を及ぼして定まる。
　不動産の価格も代替可能な他の不動産又は財の価格と相互に関連して形成される。

Ⅳ　最有効使用の原則

　不動産の価格は、その不動産の効用が最高度に発揮される可能性に最も富む使用（以下「最有効使用」という。）を前提として把握される価格を標準として形成される。この場合の最有

called "highest and best use"). The highest and best use is an objective indicator of that use, which under actual socio-economic circumstances, is both rational and legally permissible and that is also practicable by a person possessing the common sense and ordinary capabilities to operate the property under that use.

It should be further noted that the actual use of a certain property is not necessarily the highest and best use of that real estate. A use based on irrational or personal circumstances may result in under-utilization of the real estate.

V Principle of Balance

It is necessary for the constituent elements of real estate to be in balance in order for the real estate to achieve its maximum profitability or highest amenity level. Thus, in order to estimate the highest and best use of real estate, it is necessary to analyze whether or not such a balance has been achieved.

VI Principle of Increasing or Decreasing Returns

When an investment is continuously increased by a definite amount, the gross income to the investment increases with each increment. However, although the income corresponding to each increment increases up to a certain point, it eventually reaches the point of diminishing returns where it begins to decrease.

This principle applies to additional capital investment in real estate as well.

VII Principle of Income Allocation

Gross income that is generated from the combination of land, capital, labor, and management (coordination) may be allocated to each of these elements. Therefore, that portion of gross income remaining after the other portions have been allocated to capital, labor and management (coordination) may be attributed to the land, provided the allocation has been properly carried out.

VIII Principle of Contribution

The degree to which each component of real estate contributes to income generated by the overall real estate has an effect on total real estate value.

This principle is especially useful in considering the feasibility of additional investment in the real estate when the appraiser determines the highest and best use of the real estate.

IX Principle of Conformity

It is necessary for real estate to conform to its environment in order to achieve its maximum profitability or highest amenity level. Thus, an appraiser must analyze whether or not that real estate is in conformity with its environment when the appraiser determines the highest and best use of the real estate.

X Principle of Competition

In general, excess profit stimulates competition, while excess competition reduces profit and may ultimately eliminate it. With respect to real estate, a competitive relationship is also observed both between real estate products and between real estate products and other commodities striving to realize excess profit through their utilization. Thus, the value of real estate is formed as a result of this competition.

XI Principle of Anticipation

The value of a commodity is determined in anticipation of future profitability.

The value of real estate is also influenced by anticipation on the part of market participants and whatever changes they foresee in value influences.

効使用は、現実の社会経済情勢の下で客観的にみて、良識と通常の使用能力を持つ人による合理的かつ合法的な最高最善の使用方法に基づくものである。

なお、ある不動産についての現実の使用方法は、必ずしも最有効使用に基づいているものではなく、不合理な又は個人的な事情による使用方法のために、当該不動産が十分な効用を発揮していない場合があることに留意すべきである。

Ⅴ　均衡の原則

不動産の収益性又は快適性が最高度に発揮されるためには、その構成要素の組合せが均衡を得ていることが必要である。したがって、不動産の最有効使用を判定するためには、この均衡を得ているかどうかを分析することが必要である。

Ⅵ　収益逓増及び逓減の原則

ある単位投資額を継続的に増加させると、これに伴って総収益は増加する。しかし、増加させる単位投資額に対応する収益は、ある点までは増加するが、その後は減少する。

この原則は、不動産に対する追加投資の場合についても同様である。

Ⅶ　収益配分の原則

土地、資本、労働及び経営（組織）の各要素の結合によって生ずる総収益は、これらの各要素に配分される。したがって、このような総収益のうち、資本、労働及び経営（組織）に配分される部分以外の部分は、それぞれの配分が正しく行われる限り、土地に帰属するものである。

Ⅷ　寄与の原則

不動産のある部分がその不動産全体の収益獲得に寄与する度合いは、その不動産全体の価格に影響を及ぼす。

この原則は、不動産の最有効使用の判定に当たっての不動産の追加投資の適否の判定等に有用である。

Ⅸ　適合の原則

不動産の収益性又は快適性が最高度に発揮されるためには、当該不動産がその環境に適合していることが必要である。したがって、不動産の最有効使用を判定するためには、当該不動産が環境に適合しているかどうかを分析することが必要である。

Ⅹ　競争の原則

一般に、超過利潤は競争を惹起し、競争は超過利潤を減少させ、終局的にはこれを消滅させる傾向を持つ。不動産についても、その利用による超過利潤を求めて、不動産相互間及び他の財との間において競争関係が認められ、したがって、不動産の価格は、このような競争の過程において形成される。

Ⅺ　予測の原則

財の価格は、その財の将来の収益性等についての予測を反映して定まる。

不動産の価格も、価格形成要因の変動についての市場参加者による予測によって左右される。

General Standards Chapter 5

CHAPTER 5. BASIC APPRAISAL PROBLEM

Basic to the appraisal of real estate, is an identification of 1) the subject property, 2) date of value opinion, and 3) the type of value or rent estimated.

Section 1. Identification of the Subject Property

In performing a real estate appraisal, the appraiser must identify the physical characteristics of the land and/or building to be appraised as well as the property rights to be appraised, i.e., fee simple estate, leased fee estate, leasehold estate or other property rights.

Identification of the subject real estate involves clearly distinguishing the subject of the appraisal from other real estate and specifying the location, dimensions, use, and relevant ownership rights. These features should ultimately be verified by LREAs by confirming that the description of the subject property and its actual use conform with the specifications and objectives of the appraisal assignment.

I Requirements for the Subject Identification

The items required for an identification of the subject real estate are its physical characteristics and the relevant property rights.

The subject identification must verify physical characteristics such as the location and dimensions of the subject property (to ensure that the physical features of the real estate correspond to the real estate described in the client's specifications), and the legal estate in the subject property, e.g., fee simple (freehold ownership) or leasehold interest. The four possible aspects of physical real estate with which appraisal assignments deal:

1. Where the real estate is to be appraised "as is." The real estate may constitute land alone or a combination of land and buildings. Some assignments will call for the appraisal of the real estate "as is," i.e., the appraisal of the land component or the combined real estate components.

2. In situations where the real estate is a combination of land and buildings, but only the land is the subject of the appraisal, the value of the freehold interest in the site can be estimated, assuming the buildings did not exist. The value estimated in such an appraisal is referred to as *site value as if vacant*.

3. Where the real estate to be appraised is the "residual" site or the "residual" building. In situations where the real estate is a combination of land and building(s), and only one component (either the land or the building component) of that real estate is the subject of appraisal, the value estimated is referred to as the *severance value*. (Editor's Note: Unlike site value above, the severance value of land or building components is estimated based on the fact that the other property component exists.)

4. Where the real estate to be appraised is an assemblage or subdivision of real estate. Where the subject of an appraisal is the result of a consolidation or subdivision of real estate, the appraisal will necessarily be premised on that consolidation or

第5章　鑑定評価の基本的事項

不動産の鑑定評価に当たっては、基本的事項として、対象不動産、価格時点及び価格又は賃料の種類を確定しなければならない。

第1節　対象不動産の確定

不動産の鑑定評価を行うに当たっては、まず、鑑定評価の対象となる土地又は建物等を物的に確定することのみならず、鑑定評価の対象となる所有権及び所有権以外の権利を確定する必要がある。

対象不動産の確定は、鑑定評価の対象を明確に他の不動産と区別し、特定することであり、それは不動産鑑定士が鑑定評価の依頼目的及び条件に照応する対象不動産と当該不動産の現実の利用状況とを照合して確認するという実践行為を経て最終的に確定されるべきものである。

Ⅰ　対象確定条件

対象不動産の確定に当たって必要となる鑑定評価の条件を対象確定条件という。

対象確定条件は、対象不動産（依頼内容に応じて次のような条件により定められた不動産をいう。）の所在、範囲等の物的事項及び所有権、賃借権等の対象不動産の権利の態様に関する事項を確定するために必要な条件である。

1．不動産が土地のみの場合又は土地及び建物等の結合により構成されている場合において、その状態を所与として鑑定評価の対象とすること。
2．不動産が土地及び建物等の結合により構成されている場合において、その土地のみを建物等が存しない独立のもの（更地）として鑑定評価の対象とすること（この場合の鑑定評価を独立鑑定評価という。）。
3．不動産が土地及び建物等の結合により構成されている場合において、その状態を所与として、その不動産の構成部分を鑑定評価の対象とすること（この場合の鑑定評価を部分鑑定評価という。）。
4．不動産の併合又は分割を前提として、併合後又は分割後の不動産を単独のものとして鑑定評価の対象とすること（この場合の鑑定評価を併合鑑定評価又は分割鑑定評価という。）。

subdivision, and the value estimated in the appraisal is referred to as *assemblage value* or *component value*.

II Assumptions of Area – Specific or Property – Specific Value Influences

Although there are cases where a client may request the appraiser to make certain assumptions or limiting conditions with respect to the effect of area-specific or property-specific value influences on the property identified as the subject, such assumptions and limiting conditions imposed by a client must be reasonable, realistic, and legitimate. The appraiser will proceed objectively whether or not the results of the valuation jeopardize the benefits of an involved party (i.e., the client) or third party.

In general, where the assumptions and limiting conditions imposed with respect to area-specific value influences are reasonable, they are limited primarily to matters involving official agencies with the authority to alter, revise or abolish planning projects and regulations. (Editor's Note: For example, assumptions regarding the likelihood that a district will be rezoned from residential to commercial use or that a public utility plant will be constructed are only deemed reasonable when the appraiser has a good idea of how the authority with the power to approve or deny the change will act.)

Section 2. Identification of the Date of the Value Opinion

Since value influences change with the passage of time, the value of real estate is only valid on the day to which the valuation refers. Thus, in performing a real estate appraisal, it is necessary to identify the reference date of the real estate valuation; this date is referred to as *the date of the value opinion*. An additional benchmark, *the date of the opinion on rent* is the first day of each period (Editor's Note: In Japan, mostly monthly rent) for which the rental income is to be determined.

The date of the value of opinion may be current (i.e., a current value opinion), in the past (i.e., a retrospective value opinion) or in the future (i.e., a prospective value opinion), based on the data used to perform the appraisal.

Section 3. Identification of the Type of Value or Rental Value

A real estate appraisal performed by LREAs must determine that the value definition is appropriate to the assignment and then develop an estimate of that value.

I Value (Capital Value)

The value determined by a real estate appraisal is generally *market value*. However, there are other defined values such as *assemblage* or *component market value*, *market value based on special considerations*, and *non – market value*, which may also be determined according to the purpose and conditions of the client's specifications for the appraisal. Therefore, the type of value to be estimated should always be properly assessed and clarified in line with the purpose and conditions of the client's specifications. It should be further noted that there are cases where the purpose of the appraisal requires an estimate of the market value of the real estate based on special considerations.

1. Market Value

Market value refers to the probable value that would be formed for the marketable real estate in a market that satisfies conditions associated with a rational market under actual

Ⅱ 地域要因又は個別的要因についての想定上の条件

対象確定条件により確定された対象不動産について、依頼目的に応じ対象不動産に係る価格形成要因のうち地域要因又は個別的要因について想定上の条件を付加する場合があるが、この場合には、依頼により付加する想定上の条件が実現性、合法性、関係当事者及び第三者の利益を害するおそれがないか等の観点から妥当なものでなければならない。

一般に、地域要因について想定上の条件を付加することが妥当と認められる場合は、計画及び諸規制の変更、改廃に権能を持つ公的機関の設定する事項に主として限られる。

第2節　価格時点の確定

価格形成要因は、時の経過により変動するものであるから、不動産の価格はその判定の基準となった日においてのみ妥当するものである。したがって、不動産の鑑定評価を行うに当たっては、不動産の価格の判定の基準日を確定する必要があり、この日を価格時点という。また、賃料の価格時点は、賃料の算定の期間の収益性を反映するものとしてその期間の期首となる。

価格時点は、鑑定評価を行った年月日を基準として現在の場合（現在時点）、過去の場合（過去時点）及び将来の場合（将来時点）に分けられる。

第3節　鑑定評価によって求める価格又は賃料の種類の確定

不動産鑑定士による不動産の鑑定評価は、不動産の適正な価格を求め、その適正な価格の形成に資するものでなければならない。

Ⅰ 価格

不動産の鑑定評価によって求める価格は、基本的には正常価格であるが、鑑定評価の依頼目的及び条件に応じて限定価格、特定価格又は特殊価格を求める場合があるので、依頼目的及び条件に即して価格の種類を適切に判断し、明確にすべきである。なお、評価目的に応じ、特定価格として求めなければならない場合があることに留意しなければならない。

1．正常価格

正常価格とは、市場性を有する不動産について、現実の社会経済情勢の下で合理的と考えられる条件を満たす市場で形成されるであろう市場価値を表示する適正な価格をいう。この

socio-economic circumstances. A market that satisfies the conditions associated with a rational market under actual socio-economic circumstances refers to a market that satisfies the conditions listed below.

(1) The market participants must be acting on their own free will, and be able to enter or leave the market as they wish.

Motivated by the desire to maximize their returns while exhibiting wise and prudent behavior, market participants will satisfy the requirements listed below:

① No special motivation causes them to sell off or to initiate buying.
② They have only access to ordinary knowledge and information, required to conduct transactions involving the subject property or in the subject property market.
③ They have expended the labor and costs normally considered necessary to conduct transactions.
④ They premise value on the highest and best use of the subject property.
⑤ Purchasers have ordinary access to procuring funds (financing).

(2) There must be no special curbs on transactions that restrict market participants nor any extraordinary incentives that induce participants to sell off or initiate buying.

(3) The subject property must be exposed in the market for an appropriate period of time.

2. Special Value

Special value refers to the appropriate value of the marketable real estate in a limited-market of buyers and sellers, created as a result of consolidation including land acquisition or subdivision of real estate. Thus, synergistic or component value is premised on a limited-market concept.

Examples of situations in which synergistic or component value is determined are indicated below.

(1) a sale by a landlord (lessor) or purchase by a leaseholder (lessee) of a site for the purpose of consolidating the ownership interest with the leased fee interest in land.

(2) a sale or purchase for the assemblage purpose with adjacent real estate.

(3) a sale or purchase of real estate where the manner in which the real estate is subdivided is deemed to be irrational.

3. Value for Regulated Purposes (VRP)

Value for Regulated Purposes (VRP) refers to the appropriate economic value of the marketable real estate, but does not necessarily satisfy all conditions on which market value is premised. Such valuations are performed in compliance with the requirements of laws and ordinances.

Examples of cases in which Value for Regulated Purpose Appraisal is determined are listed below.

(1) where the investment profitability value is premised on valuation for a typical investor based on a specific operation management scheme performed in accordance with the *Asset Liquidation Law* and the *Investment Trust and Investment Corporation Law*.

(2) where the value determined is premised on valuation for quick sale purposes. The

場合において、現実の社会経済情勢の下で合理的と考えられる条件を満たす市場とは、以下の条件を満たす市場をいう。
(1) 市場参加者が自由意思に基づいて市場に参加し、参入、退出が自由であること。
　　なお、ここでいう市場参加者は、自己の利益を最大化するため次のような要件を満たすとともに、慎重かつ賢明に予測し、行動するものとする。
　① 売り急ぎ、買い進み等をもたらす特別な動機のないこと。
　② 対象不動産及び対象不動産が属する市場について取引を成立させるために必要となる通常の知識や情報を得ていること。
　③ 取引を成立させるために通常必要と認められる労力、費用を費やしていること。
　④ 対象不動産の最有効使用を前提とした価値判断を行うこと。
　⑤ 買主が通常の資金調達能力を有していること。
(2) 取引形態が、市場参加者が制約されたり、売り急ぎ、買い進み等を誘引したりするような特別なものではないこと。
(3) 対象不動産が相当の期間市場に公開されていること。

2．限定価格

限定価格とは、市場性を有する不動産について、不動産と取得する他の不動産との併合又は不動産の一部を取得する際の分割等に基づき正常価格と同一の市場概念の下において形成されるであろう市場価値と乖離することにより、市場が相対的に限定される場合における取得部分の当該市場限定に基づく市場価値を適正に表示する価格をいう。

限定価格を求める場合を例示すれば、次のとおりである。
(1) 借地権者が底地の併合を目的とする売買に関連する場合
(2) 隣接不動産の併合を目的とする売買に関連する場合
(3) 経済合理性に反する不動産の分割を前提とする売買に関連する場合

3．特定価格

特定価格とは、市場性を有する不動産について、法令等による社会的要請を背景とする評価目的の下で、正常価格の前提となる諸条件を満たさない場合における不動産の経済価値を適正に表示する価格をいう。

特定価格を求める場合を例示すれば、次のとおりである。
(1) 資産の流動化に関する法律又は投資信託及び投資法人に関する法律に基づく評価目的の下で、投資家に示すための投資採算価値を表す価格を求める場合
(2) 民事再生法に基づく評価目的の下で、早期売却を前提とした価格を求める場合
(3) 会社更生法又は民事再生法に基づく評価目的の下で、事業の継続を前提とした価格を求める場合

Civil Rehabilitation Law governs such valuations.
(3) where the value determined is premised on the continuation of a business. Such valuations come under the *Corporate Reorganization Law* or the *Civil Rehabilitation Law*.

(Editor's Note: Value for Regulated Purposes (VRP) may be divided into two categories: market value and value other than market value (see Part1: chap. 2. I . Japan- 3) : the value under the Asset Liquidation Law and the Investment Corporation Law, is the market value assuming an operation management scheme which reflects the expectation of a typical investor. It refers to the investment profitability value of the subject property under the securitization regulations, but represents those of a typical investor rather than a specific investor in the market.)

4. Value of Special–Purpose Property

Value of Special- Purpose Property refers to the appropriate economic value of real estate such as cultural assets that are generally not marketable. Non- market value is premised on the continuation of the existing use of the real estate.

Examples of situations in which non- market value is determined include valuations of structures that have been designated as cultural assets, and temples and public facilities, the operation of which is expected to continue in its present state. Appraisals of such facilities are performed with an emphasis on their preservation.

II Rental Value

The rent generally determined by real estate appraisal is either *market rent* or *rent under a renewed lease*. However, since there are also situations in which *synergistic or component rent* must be determined according to the purpose and conditions specified by the client, such a rent should be properly assessed and clarified.

1. Market Rent

Market rent is the appropriate rent (market rent under new lease) reflecting the probable economic value of the real estate. Market rent is the rent that would be negotiated in a new lease agreement granting the rights to use or benefit from real estate interests; such rights may be conveyed by means of leases contract, right of superficies, or easements. Market rent is premised upon the same market concept as market value.

2. Special Rent

Special rent, like synergistic or component value, is also premised upon limited- market concept. The synergistic or component rent refers to the appropriate indication of the probable economic value of the real estate, i.e., the rent that would be negotiated in a new lease agreement.

Examples of situations in which synergistic or component rent may be determined are listed below.
(1) leases granting the right to use adjacent real estate (bringing two parcels under the same use).
(2) leases of parcels of real estate that have been subdivided in an irrational manner.

3. Rent under Renewed Lease

Rent under a renewed lease is the appropriate indication of the probable economic value of the real estate, i.e., the rent that would be negotiated between the involved parties to extend the term of a real estate lease.

4．特殊価格

特殊価格とは、文化財等の一般的に市場性を有しない不動産について、その利用現況等を前提とした不動産の経済価値を適正に表示する価格をいう。

特殊価格を求める場合を例示すれば、文化財の指定を受けた建造物、宗教建築物又は現況による管理を継続する公共公益施設の用に供されている不動産について、その保存等に主眼をおいた鑑定評価を行う場合である。

Ⅱ　賃料

不動産の鑑定評価によって求める賃料は、一般的には正常賃料又は継続賃料であるが、鑑定評価の依頼目的及び条件に応じて限定賃料を求めることができる場合があるので、依頼目的及び条件に即してこれを適切に判断し、明確にすべきである。

1．正常賃料

正常賃料とは、正常価格と同一の市場概念の下において新たな賃貸借等（賃借権若しくは地上権又は地役権に基づき、不動産を使用し、又は収益することをいう。）の契約において成立するであろう経済価値を表示する適正な賃料（新規賃料）をいう。

2．限定賃料

限定賃料とは、限定価格と同一の市場概念の下において新たな賃貸借等の契約において成立するであろう経済価値を適正に表示する賃料（新規賃料）をいう。

限定賃料を求めることができる場合を例示すれば、次のとおりである。
(1)　隣接不動産の併合使用を前提とする賃貸借等に関連する場合
(2)　経済合理性に反する不動産の分割使用を前提とする賃貸借等に関連する場合

3．継続賃料

継続賃料とは、不動産の賃貸借等の継続に係る特定の当事者間において成立するであろう経済価値を適正に表示する賃料をいう。

CHAPTER 6. MARKET AREA ANALYSIS AND PROPERTY ANALYSIS

In performing analyses of the subject market area and the subject property, the appraiser must accurately understand what specific effects general value influences exert upon the area and property.

Section 1. Market Area Analysis
I The Concept of Market Area Analysis
Market area analysis refers to the investigation and analysis of the type of area the subject property is located in, the characteristics of the area, the characteristics of the market for the subject property, and how such characteristics influence land use and the formation of real estate value in the area.

II Application of Market Area Analysis
1．Market Area Characteristics
Particularly important in market area analysis is the identification of land use in the area (henceforth called "market area category"). In the broadest sense, the market area is generally the area including the subject neighborhood and similar or comparable neighborhoods in the vicinity. The subject neighborhood and these similar or comparable neighborhoods constitute the primary market area.

The typical or standard land use of real estate in a neighborhood determines the specific neighborhood characteristics, and provides information as to the relative ranking of, and real estate values in, neighborhoods of the same land use. The typical or standard land use also serves as a strong indicator for determining the highest and best use of each piece of real estate located in that neighborhood.

No market area is static, and market-specific value influences that form area characteristics are also continuously changing. Thus, in performing a area analysis, trends indicating whether the current use will continue or change must also be analyzed and assessed once the characteristics of the market for the subject property have been determined.

(1) Market Area Category
① Subject Neighborhood

A *subject neighborhood* refers to an area where most of the real estate, including the subject property, is under a common land use classification. In other words, a neighborhood is an aggregation of real estate having a defined area within a urban or rural area and used for residency, commercial activities, industrial production, or other human activities. The characteristics of a neighborhood are capable of directly affecting the formation of the value of the subject property.

Neighborhoods undergo change in accordance with the extent of change in market-specific value influences shaping the characteristics of those neighborhoods.

② Similar or Comparable Neighborhood

第6章　地域分析及び個別分析

対象不動産の地域分析及び個別分析を行うに当たっては、まず、それらの基礎となる一般的要因がどのような具体的な影響力を持っているかを的確に把握しておくことが必要である。

第1節　地域分析

Ⅰ　地域分析の意義

地域分析とは、その対象不動産がどのような地域に存するか、その地域はどのような特性を有するか、また、対象不動産に係る市場はどのような特性を有するか、及びそれらの特性はその地域内の不動産の利用形態と価格形成について全般的にどのような影響力を持っているかを分析し、判定することをいう。

Ⅱ　地域分析の適用

1．地域及びその特性

地域分析に当たって特に重要な地域は、用途の観点から区分される地域（以下「用途的地域」という。）、すなわち近隣地域及びその類似地域と、近隣地域及びこれと相関関係にある類似地域を含むより広域的な地域、すなわち同一需給圏である。

また、近隣地域の特性は、通常、その地域に属する不動産の一般的な標準的使用に具体的に現れるが、この標準的使用は、利用形態からみた地域相互間の相対的位置関係及び価格形成を明らかにする手掛りとなるとともに、その地域に属する不動産のそれぞれについての最有効使用を判定する有力な標準となるものである。

なお、不動産の属する地域は固定的なものではなく、地域の特性を形成する地域要因も常に変動するものであることから、地域分析に当たっては、対象不動産に係る市場の特性の把握の結果を踏まえて地域要因及び標準的使用の現状と将来の動向とをあわせて分析し、標準的使用を判定しなければならない。

(1)　用途的地域

①　近隣地域

近隣地域とは、対象不動産の属する用途的地域であって、より大きな規模と内容とを持つ地域である都市あるいは農村等の内部にあって、居住、商業活動、工業生産活動等人の生活と活動とに関して、ある特定の用途に供されることを中心として地域的にまとまりを示している地域をいい、対象不動産の価格の形成に関して直接に影響を与えるような特性を持つものである。

近隣地域は、その地域の特性を形成する地域要因の推移、動向の如何によって、変化していくものである。

②　類似地域

A *similar or comparable neighborhood* refers to a neighborhood having characteristics that are similar to the characteristics of the subject neighborhood. The real estate in that neighborhood resembles the real estate in the subject neighborhood because of common use.

(2) **Market Area**

The *market area* typically refers to an area in which other properties may be substituted for the subject property and where the other real estate exerts an effect on the formation of the subject's value. This area, which may include several neighborhoods, has a broad extent and is defined by the range of neighborhoods similar to the subject neighborhood.

In general, real estate in the neighborhood and real estate in similar neighborhoods located within the market area have a substitutive or competitive relationship, based on the similarity of the market- specific value influences to which the real estate is subject regardless of whether or not these neighborhoods are adjacent to each other.

In addition, even real estate located outside the neighborhood or outside similar neighborhoods but situated within the market area may have a substitutive or competitive relationship with the subject real estate because of similarities in use, size, grade and other characteristics.

Since the extent of the market area differs according to the preferences of users as to type, size and other attributes of the real estate, it is necessary to accurately understand those user preferences in order to properly define the market area.

The following discussion covers basic matters requiring particular attention in defining the market area.

① **Building Sites**

a. **Residential Land**

The market area typically includes other neighborhoods from which it is possible to commute to the city center. However, the number of such neighborhoods tends to be constricted by preferences for specific areas.

Furthermore, it should be noted that neighborhood preferences attributable to reputation, quality and so forth may also affect the specific neighborhoods included in the market area.

b. **Commercial Land**

The market area for properties in highly commercial districts tends to include other competitive districts with respect to the income generated from broad commercial support areas. The market area for properties in highly commercial districts typically covers a broad area including properties in other highly commercial districts with similar income- producing attributes.

The market area for properties in ordinary commercial districts tends to include other competitive districts with respect to income generated from narrow commercial support areas. The market area for properties in ordinary commercial districts tends to be more confined because of preferences within individual areas.

c. **Industrial Land**

類似地域とは、近隣地域の地域の特性と類似する特性を有する地域であり、その地域に属する不動産は、特定の用途に供されることを中心として地域的にまとまりを持つものである。この地域のまとまりは、近隣地域の特性との類似性を前提として判定されるものである。

(2) 同一需給圏

同一需給圏とは、一般に対象不動産と代替関係が成立して、その価格の形成について相互に影響を及ぼすような関係にある他の不動産の存する圏域をいう。それは、近隣地域を含んでより広域的であり、近隣地域と相関関係にある類似地域等の存する範囲を規定するものである。

一般に、近隣地域と同一需給圏内に存する類似地域とは、隣接すると否とにかかわらず、その地域要因の類似性に基づいて、それぞれの地域の構成分子である不動産相互の間に代替、競争等の関係が成立し、その結果、両地域は相互に影響を及ぼすものである。

また、近隣地域の外かつ同一需給圏内の類似地域の外に存する不動産であっても、同一需給圏内に存し対象不動産とその用途、規模、品等の類似性に基づいて、これら相互の間に代替、競争等の関係が成立する場合がある。

同一需給圏は、不動産の種類、性格及び規模に応じた需要者の選好性によってその地域的範囲を異にするものであるから、その種類、性格及び規模に応じて需要者の選好性を的確に把握した上で適切に判定する必要がある。

同一需給圏の判定に当たって特に留意すべき基本的な事項は、次のとおりである。

① 宅地
ア 住宅地

同一需給圏は、一般に都心への通勤可能な地域の範囲に一致する傾向がある。ただし、地縁的選好性により地域的範囲が狭められる傾向がある。

なお、地域の名声、品位等による選好性の強さが同一需給圏の地域的範囲に特に影響を与える場合があることに留意すべきである。

イ 商業地

同一需給圏は、高度商業地については、一般に広域的な商業背後地を基礎に成り立つ商業収益に関して代替性の及ぶ地域の範囲に一致する傾向があり、したがって、その範囲は高度商業地の性格に応じて広域的に形成される傾向がある。

また、普通商業地については、一般に狭い商業背後地を基礎に成り立つ商業収益に関して代替性の及ぶ地域の範囲に一致する傾向がある。ただし、地縁的選好性により地域的範囲が狭められる傾向がある。

ウ 工業地

The market area for large-scale and infrastructure-dependent properties in industrial districts typically includes other industrial districts with similar advanced transportation facilities that allow large-volume conveyance of raw materials and products. Such big properties in industrial districts require nearby infrastructure such as harbors, ports, high-speed transportation networks and other facilities. Thus, the market area of this type of industrial district tends to be nationwide.

On the other hand, the market area for medium- and small-scale and consumer market-oriented properties in industrial areas typically includes other industrial districts with similar cost levels in terms of producing and marketing products. Such smaller properties in industrial districts require proximity to a consumer market of sufficient size.

d. Land in a Transitional Area

The market area for land in transitional areas typically coincides with the market area for the land use category to which the land in the transitional area is expected to change. However, where transition is gradual, the market area tends to be the same as the market area for the land use category prior to transition.

② Agricultural Land

The market area for a parcel of agricultural land typically includes those areas that can be used for the same kind of farming operations.

③ Forestland

The market area for forestland typically includes those areas that can be used for the same kind of timber growing operations.

④ Sites with Interim Use

The market area for sites with an interim use typically includes the market area for the land use category to which the land with an interim use is expected to change. However, where the changeover is gradual, the market area tends to be the same as the market area for the land use category prior to the change.

⑤ Built-Up Property

The market area of buildings and building sites typically includes the market area of land use corresponding to the use of the subject lot. However, there are some situations where the market area of the property may not match with that of the underlying site due to its specific use, size, grade, and other attributes of the subject lot.

2. Market Characteristics Relating to the Subject Property

To understand the characteristics of the market for the subject property in a market area analysis, it is important to know the attributes of market participants in the market area, their reasons for selecting real estate under the specific use, and how they consider the effect of value influences. It is also necessary to understand supply and demand trends

同一需給圏は、港湾、高速交通網等の利便性を指向する産業基盤指向型工業地等の大工場地については、一般に原材料、製品等の大規模な移動を可能にする高度の輸送機関に関して代替性を有する地域の範囲に一致する傾向があり、したがって、その地域的範囲は、全国的な規模となる傾向がある。

また、製品の消費地への距離、消費規模等の市場接近性を指向する消費地指向型工業地等の中小工場地については、一般に製品の生産及び販売に関する費用の経済性に関して代替性を有する地域の範囲に一致する傾向がある。

エ　移行地
　　同一需給圏は、一般に当該土地が移行すると見込まれる土地の種別の同一需給圏と一致する傾向がある。ただし、熟成度の低い場合には、移行前の土地の種別の同一需給圏と同一のものとなる傾向がある。

② 　農地
　　同一需給圏は、一般に当該農地を中心とする通常の農業生産活動の可能な地域の範囲内に立地する農業経営主体を中心とするそれぞれの農業生産活動の可能な地域の範囲に一致する傾向がある。
③ 　林地
　　同一需給圏は、一般に当該林地を中心とする通常の林業生産活動の可能な地域の範囲内に立地する林業経営主体を中心とするそれぞれの林業生産活動の可能な地域の範囲に一致する傾向がある。
④ 　見込地
　　同一需給圏は、一般に当該土地が転換すると見込まれる土地の種別の同一需給圏と一致する傾向がある。ただし、熟成度の低い場合には、転換前の土地の種別の同一需給圏と同一のものとなる傾向がある。

⑤ 　建物及びその敷地
　　同一需給圏は、一般に当該敷地の用途に応じた同一需給圏と一致する傾向があるが、当該建物及びその敷地一体としての用途、規模、品等等によっては代替関係にある不動産の存する範囲が異なるために当該敷地の用途に応じた同一需給圏の範囲と一致しない場合がある。

２．対象不動産に係る市場の特性

地域分析における対象不動産に係る市場の特性の把握に当たっては、同一需給圏における市場参加者がどのような属性を有しており、どのような観点から不動産の利用形態を選択し、価格形成要因についての判断を行っているかを的確に把握することが重要である。あわせて同一需給圏における市場の需給動向を的確に把握する必要がある。

in the market area.

Not only should specific market characteristics be reflected in an assessment of the predominant land use in the neighborhood, but they should also be considered in the application of appraisal techniques and various adjustments made to value indications or rent estimates.

Section 2. Property Analysis

I The Concept of Property Analysis

The value of real estate is determined on the premise of the highest and best use of the real estate. Therefore, in performing a real estate appraisal, it is necessary to determine the highest and best use of the subject property. Subject property analysis refers to investigating the effect of property- specific value influences on the use of the subject property and the formation of its value, and thereupon determining the highest and best use of the subject property.

II Application of Property Analysis

1. Guidelines for Analyzing Property – Specific Value Influences

Each property- specific value influence individually contributes to the formation of the market value of the subject property. Therefore, in analyzing property- specific value influences, it is important to accurately determine what types of property- specific influences typical users of the Property would focus upon when considering to purchase or lease the subject property as well as the competitiveness of the subject property and its relative inferiority or superiority in regard to comparable real estate.

The results of an analysis of property- specific value influences should also be considered in the application of appraisal techniques and in the reconciliation of value indications or rent estimates.

2. Guidelines for Determining the Highest and Best Use of Property

In determining the highest and best use of real estate, special consideration should be given to the following points.

(1) The use of the real estate is that which would probably be employed by a person possessing the common sense and ordinary capabilities to operate the property under that use.

(2) The use will allow for the continuous generation of income far into the future.

(3) The time at which utility can be adequately demonstrated is at some anticipated point in the future.

(4) The highest and best use of individual real estate is typically subject to the restrictions imposed by the characteristics of the neighborhood. In performing a subject property analysis, it is necessary to assess the relationship between the subject's use and the typical or standard use of real estate in the neighborhood. There is always the possibility that the subject's use may differ from the standard use depending on the subject's location, size, environment and so forth. In such situations, the highest and best use of the property should be determined after analyzing property- specific value influences in regard to each potential use.

(5) Value influences are in a state of constant change. Thus where it may be reason-

また、把握した市場の特性については、近隣地域における標準的使用の判定に反映させるとともに鑑定評価の手法の適用、試算価格又は試算賃料の調整等における各種の判断においても反映すべきである。

第2節　個別分析

Ⅰ　個別分析の意義

　不動産の価格は、その不動産の最有効使用を前提として把握される価格を標準として形成されるものであるから、不動産の鑑定評価に当たっては、対象不動産の最有効使用を判定する必要がある。個別分析とは、対象不動産の個別的要因が対象不動産の利用形態と価格形成についてどのような影響力を持っているかを分析してその最有効使用を判定することをいう。

Ⅱ　個別分析の適用

1．個別的要因の分析上の留意点

　個別的要因は、対象不動産の市場価値を個別的に形成しているものであるため、個別的要因の分析においては、対象不動産に係る典型的な需要者がどのような個別的要因に着目して行動し、対象不動産と代替、競争等の関係にある不動産と比べた優劣及び競争力の程度をどのように評価しているかを的確に把握することが重要である。

　また、個別的要因の分析結果は、鑑定評価の手法の適用、試算価格又は試算賃料の調整等における各種の判断においても反映すべきである。

2．最有効使用の判定上の留意点

　不動産の最有効使用の判定に当たっては、次の事項に留意すべきである。
(1)　良識と通常の使用能力を持つ人が採用するであろうと考えられる使用方法であること。
(2)　使用収益が将来相当の期間にわたって持続し得る使用方法であること。
(3)　効用を十分に発揮し得る時点が予測し得ない将来でないこと。
(4)　個々の不動産の最有効使用は、一般に近隣地域の地域の特性の制約下にあるので、個別分析に当たっては、特に近隣地域に存する不動産の標準的使用との相互関係を明らかにし判定することが必要であるが、対象不動産の位置、規模、環境等によっては、標準的使用の用途と異なる用途の可能性が考えられるので、こうした場合には、それぞれの用途に対応した個別的要因の分析を行った上で最有効使用を判定すること。
(5)　価格形成要因は常に変動の過程にあることを踏まえ、特に価格形成に影響を与える地域要因の変動が客観的に予測される場合には、当該変動に伴い対象不動産の使用方法が変化する可能性があることを勘案して最有効使用を判定すること。
　特に、建物及びその敷地の最有効使用の判定に当たっては、次の事項に留意すべきである。
(6)　現実の建物の用途等が更地としての最有効使用に一致していない場合には、更地としての最有効使用を実現するために要する費用等を勘案する必要があるため、建物及びその敷地と更地の最有効使用の内容が必ずしも一致するものではないこと。
(7)　現実の建物の用途等を継続する場合の経済価値と建物の取壊しや用途変更等を行う場合

ably anticipated that changes in market- specific value influences will affect the formation of the subject's value, the highest and best use of the subject property should be determined in view of the possibility that the use of the subject property may also change.

In determining the highest and best use of a building and building site, special consideration should be given to the following matters.

(6) Where the actual use of the building does not correspond to the highest and best use of the site as if vacant, it is necessary to consider the costs and time required to realize the highest and best use of the site as if vacant. In some of these cases, the highest and best use of improved property may not be the same as the highest and best use as if vacant.

(7) The economic value that would result from continuation of the current use of the building should be rigorously compared to the costs that would be incurred to demolish the building or alter its use.

のそれらに要する費用等を適切に勘案した経済価値を十分比較考量すること。

CHAPTER 7. APPRAISAL METHOD

There are three approaches to real estate appraisal: the cost approach, the sales comparison approach, and the income capitalization approach.

The cost approach focuses on the cost required to reproduce the real estate (called reproduction cost new) including the costs of site preparation, construction and so forth. The sales comparison approach focuses on sales data or lease data from the sale or leasing of comparable real estate. The income capitalization approach focuses on the income generated from the real estate. Each method attempts to determine the value of, or rent for, the real estate.

The approaches to real estate appraisal may be classified according to approaches used to determine real estate value, and approaches used to determine real estate rental value. The value or rent determined through the application of an appraisal approach is referred to as the *indicated value* or *indicated rent*.

Section 1. Appraisal Approaches for Determining Real Estate Value

The basic appraisal approaches for determining the value of real estate are divided into cost, sales comparison, and income capitalization approaches. There is also a fourth approach, subdivision development analysis, which utilizes concepts from the above three approaches.

I General Guidelines for Determining Value Indications

1. The Correlation between General Value Influences and the Application of the Appraisal Approaches

General value influences are value influences that affect the formation of the overall value of the real estate. Not only must general value influences be considered at each step in the application of the appraisal approaches, but they must also be kept in mind when reviewing the validity of the value estimate.

2. Gathering and Selecting Data

The data required for applying the appraisal approaches consists of construction data in the cost approach, comparable sales data in the sales comparison approach, and income data in the income capitalization approach (such data is henceforth called comparable data). Comparable data should be gathered in large volume and in an orderly manner, based on a rational plan appropriate to the application of each appraisal approach. Data should not be compiled from speculative transactions.

Comparable data should satisfy all of the requirements indicated below.

(1) Comparable Real Estate Data Pertaining to:
① *Comparable real estate.* Comparable real estate should be located in the neighborhood, a comparable neighborhood in the primary market area, or when otherwise unavoidable, an area in the vicinity of the neighborhood (these are generally known as comparable neighborhoods in the primary market

第7章　鑑定評価の方式

不動産の鑑定評価の方式には、原価方式、比較方式及び収益方式の三方式がある。
原価方式は不動産の再調達（建築、造成等による新規の調達をいう。）に要する原価に着目して、比較方式は不動産の取引事例又は賃貸借等の事例に着目して、収益方式は不動産から生み出される収益に着目して、それぞれ不動産の価格又は賃料を求めようとするものである。
不動産の鑑定評価の方式は、価格を求める手法と賃料を求める手法に分類される。それぞれの鑑定評価の手法の適用により求められた価格又は賃料を試算価格又は試算賃料という。

第1節　価格を求める鑑定評価の手法

不動産の価格を求める鑑定評価の基本的な手法は、原価法、取引事例比較法及び収益還元法に大別され、このほか三手法の考え方を活用した開発法等の手法がある。

Ⅰ　試算価格を求める場合の一般的留意事項

1．一般的要因と鑑定評価の各手法の適用との関連

価格形成要因のうち一般的要因は、不動産の価格形成全般に影響を与えるものであり、鑑定評価手法の適用における各手順において常に考慮されるべきものであり、価格判定の妥当性を検討するために活用しなければならない。

2．事例の収集及び選択

鑑定評価の各手法の適用に当たって必要とされる事例には、原価法の適用に当たって必要な建設事例、取引事例比較法の適用に当たって必要な取引事例及び収益還元法の適用に当たって必要な収益事例（以下「取引事例等」という。）がある。これらの取引事例等は、鑑定評価の各手法に即応し、適切にして合理的な計画に基づき、豊富に秩序正しく収集し、選択すべきであり、投機的取引であると認められる事例等適正さを欠くものであってはならない。
取引事例等は、次の要件の全部を備えるもののうちから選択するものとする。
(1) 次の不動産に係るものであること
　① 近隣地域又は同一需給圏内の類似地域若しくは必要やむを得ない場合には近隣地域の周辺の地域（以下「同一需給圏内の類似地域等」という。）に存する不動産
　② 対象不動産の最有効使用が標準的使用と異なる場合等における同一需給圏内に存し対象不動産と代替、競争等の関係が成立していると認められる不動産（以下「同一需給圏内の代替競争不動産」という。）

area).

② *Real estate in a substitutive or competitive relationship with subject that is located in the primary market area.* Where the highest and best use of the subject property differs from the typical or standard use in the neighborhood, comparable data may include real estate in a substitutive or competitive relationship with the subject that is located in the primary market area (henceforth called substitutive or competitive real estate in the primary market area).

(2) *Comparable data.* Comparable data should reflect transactions closed under normal circumstances or else should be amenable to adjustment so as to reflect transactions closed under normal circumstances.

(3) *Comparable data* should allow adjustment for changes in price levels and market conditions over time.

(4) *Comparable data* should allow for comparison of market- specific value influences and comparison of property- specific value influences.

3. Adjustment for Conditions of Sale

Comparable data must be suitably adjusted when the transactions, from which the comparable data were compiled, were closed under special circumstances that affected the comparable property's value.

(1) For example, comparable sales data may reflect special circumstances that hasten selling or precipitate buying. Such special circumstances are attributable to the characteristics of the real estate market, the capabilities of the involved parties to the transaction, and any special motivation those parties may be acting upon. Nevertheless, the conditions under which the comparables were transacted must be rigorously investigated.

(2) Special circumstances refer to circumstances that do not satisfy conditions characterizing a rational market operating under actual socio- economic circumstances. Market value is necessarily premised upon the existence of a rational market.

4. Time Adjustment

In situations where a change in the price level is observable between the date of a transaction from which comparable data was compiled and the date of the value opinion, the value of the comparable data must be adjusted to the price level on the date of the value opinion.

5. Comparison of Area – Specific Value Influences and Property – Specific Value Influences

The value of comparable data reflects both area- specific and property- specific influences. Therefore, it is necessary to compare area- specific and property- specific value influences on the subject property and comparable property in cases where the comparable property is located in a similar neighborhood within the same market area, or is in a substitutive or competitive relationship with the subject property and located in the same primary market area. On the other hand, if the comparable property is located in the subject neighborhood, it is necessary to compare only property- specific influences on the subject property and comparable property.

(2) 取引事例等に係る取引等の事情が正常なものと認められるものであること又は正常なものに補正することができるものであること。
(3) 時点修正をすることが可能なものであること。
(4) 地域要因の比較及び個別的要因の比較が可能なものであること。

3．事情補正
　取引事例等に係る取引等が特殊な事情を含み、これが当該取引事例等に係る価格等に影響を及ぼしているときは適切に補正しなければならない。
(1) 現実に成立した取引事例等には、不動産市場の特性、取引等における当事者双方の能力の多様性と特別の動機により売り急ぎ、買い進み等の特殊な事情が存在する場合もあるので、取引事例等がどのような条件の下で成立したものであるかを資料の分析に当たり十分に調査しなければならない。
(2) 特殊な事情とは、正常価格を求める場合には、正常価格の前提となる現実の社会経済情勢の下で合理的と考えられる諸条件を欠くに至らしめる事情のことである。

4．時点修正
　取引事例等に係る取引等の時点が価格時点と異なることにより、その間に価格水準に変動があると認められる場合には、当該取引事例等の価格等を価格時点の価格等に修正しなければならない。

5．地域要因の比較及び個別的要因の比較
　取引事例等の価格等は、その不動産の存する用途的地域に係る地域要因及び当該不動産の個別的要因を反映しているものであるから、取引事例等に係る不動産が同一需給圏内の類似地域等に存するもの又は同一需給圏内の代替競争不動産である場合においては、近隣地域と当該事例に係る不動産の存する地域との地域要因の比較及び対象不動産と当該事例に係る不動産との個別的要因の比較を、取引事例等に係る不動産が近隣地域に存するものである場合においては、対象不動産と当該事例に係る不動産の個別的要因の比較をそれぞれ行う必要がある。

General Standards Chapter 7

II Cost Approach
1. Concept

The cost approach to value first determines the reproduction cost of the subject property on the date of the value opinion. Where the improvement is not a new structure, an estimate of accrued depreciation must be deducted from the reproduction cost (a value indication determined by this approach is called the value indicated by the cost approach). Where the property combines a building and building site, an estimate of the land value is added to the estimate of depreciated reproduction cost of the building to arrive at the total property value.

The cost approach is applicable in situations where the subject property is a building or building and building site and it is possible to determine the reproduction cost and properly estimate accrued depreciation. Where the subject property is only land, the cost approach can be applied if the reproduction cost of the land can be properly determined.

If the subject is a property under construction or a proposed property that does not currently exist, the cost approach can only be applied when the appraiser is able to determine the reproduction cost on the date of the value opinion.

2. Application Method
(1) Concept of Reproduction Cost

Reproduction cost refers to the total cost required to reproduce a duplicate of the subject property as of the date of the value opinion.

In situations where it is difficult to determine the reproduction cost of the subject property because of changes in building materials, construction methods and so forth, replacement cost may be determined. *Replacement cost* is the cost, at current prices as of the date of the value opinion, to construct a building of utility equivalent to that of the subject property, using modern materials and current design and layout standards.

(2) Methodology for Determining Reproduction Cost

Reproduction cost is determined by adding the ordinary incidental expenses (such as planning fees and building permits), borne directly by the builder, to the standard construction costs paid by the builder to the contractor, assuming the contractor will deliver the finished building to the builder in a state that allows immediate use in accordance with the construction contract.

Replacement cost is the total cost of constructing another property having equivalent utility to that of the subject property. Replacement cost is determined by adding the ordinary incidental expenses, borne directly by the builder, to the standard construction costs paid by the builder to the contractor.

① The reproduction cost of land is determined by adding the standard site preparation costs of the subject land and the ordinary incidental expenses, borne directly by the builder, to the standard acquisition cost of the raw land.

When the cost approach is applied to land, infrastructure development (roads, utility lines) and site improvements transform the social and economic environment, and strongly affect the price level of the land. By comparing market-specific value influences acting upon the subject land immediately after the preparation of the building site with market-specific value influences acting

Ⅱ 原価法

1．意義

原価法は、価格時点における対象不動産の再調達原価を求め、この再調達原価について減価修正を行って対象不動産の試算価格を求める手法である（この手法による試算価格を積算価格という。）。

原価法は、対象不動産が建物又は建物及びその敷地である場合において、再調達原価の把握及び減価修正を適切に行うことができるときに有効であり、対象不動産が土地のみである場合においても、再調達原価を適切に求めることができるときはこの手法を適用することができる。

この場合において、対象不動産が現に存在するものでないときは、価格時点における再調達原価を適切に求めることができる場合に限り適用することができるものとする。

2．適用方法

(1) 再調達原価の意義

再調達原価とは、対象不動産を価格時点において再調達することを想定した場合において必要とされる適正な原価の総額をいう。

なお、建設資材、工法等の変遷により、対象不動産の再調達原価を求めることが困難な場合には、対象不動産と同等の有用性を持つものに置き換えて求めた原価（置換原価）を再調達原価とみなすものとする。

(2) 再調達原価を求める方法

再調達原価は、建設請負により、請負者が発注者に対して直ちに使用可能な状態で引き渡す通常の場合を想定し、発注者が請負者に対して支払う標準的な建設費に発注者が直接負担すべき通常の付帯費用を加算して求めるものとする。

なお、置換原価は、対象不動産と同等の有用性を持つ不動産を新たに調達することを想定した場合に必要とされる原価の総額であり、発注者が請負者に対して支払う標準的な建設費に発注者が直接負担すべき通常の付帯費用を加算して求める。

① 土地の再調達原価は、その素材となる土地の標準的な取得原価に当該土地の標準的な造成費と発注者が直接負担すべき通常の付帯費用とを加算して求めるものとする。

なお、土地についての原価法の適用において、宅地造成直後の対象地の地域要因と価格時点における対象地の地域要因とを比較し、公共施設、利便施設等の整備及び住宅等の建設等により、社会的、経済的環境の変化が価格水準に影響を与えていると認められる場合には、地域要因の変化の程度に応じた増加額を熟成度として加算することができる。

② 建物及びその敷地の再調達原価は、まず、土地の再調達原価（再調達原価が把握できない既成市街地における土地にあっては取引事例比較法及び収益還元法によって求めた更地の価格）又は借地権の価格を求め、この価格に建物の再調達原価を加算して求めるものとする。

upon the subject land as of the date of the value opinion, an appraiser can determine the increment in land value that corresponds to the change in market-specific value influences.

② The reproduction cost of a building and building site is determined by first estimating the reproduction cost of the land (if the site is located in a built-up area where the reproduction cost cannot be determined, the value of the freehold interest in the land can be determined by the sales comparison and income capitalization approaches) or by estimating the value of a leasehold interest in the land, and then adding the depreciated reproduction cost of the building to that value.

③ Direct and indirect methods are used to determine reproduction cost. Either method may be applied depending on the degree of reliability of the construction data gathered, or both methods may be used together.

    a. The direct method is a method for directly determining the reproduction cost of the subject property.

        The direct method determines the reproduction cost of the subject property by 1) investigating the category, grade and volume of materials used and the kinds and duration of the required labor; 2) estimating the direct construction costs based on the unit price on the date of the value opinion in the area where the subject property is located; 3) adding to this estimate all indirect construction costs and a general management fee that includes a reasonable profit for the contractor; and 4) finally adding the ordinary incidental expenses borne directly by the builder.

        In situations where the appraiser knows the value of the raw land, direct and indirect construction costs required to prepare the actual site for construction, general management expenses (including a reasonable profit for the contractor), incidental expenses borne directly by the builder, and building specifications (including category, grade, volume, time and unit price) for the subject property, the appraiser can determine the reproduction cost by analyzing and appropriately updating the specifications, and adjusting for changes over time as required.

    b. The indirect method is a method for determining the reproduction cost of the subject property indirectly from real estate similar to the subject property and located in the same or a similar neighborhood within the primary market area, or from other substitutive or competitive real estate in the primary market area.

        In situations where the appraiser knows the value of the raw land, the direct and indirect construction costs of the real estate, general management expenses (including a reasonable profit for the contractor), incidental expenses borne directly by the builder, and the building specifications (including category, grade, volume, time and unit price) for comparable property, the appraiser can use the indirect method to determine the reproduction cost of the subject property by analyzing and suitably updating these specifications,

③ 再調達原価を求める方法には、直接法及び間接法があるが、収集した建設事例等の資料としての信頼度に応じていずれかを適用するものとし、また、必要に応じて併用するものとする。

　ア　直接法は、対象不動産について直接的に再調達原価を求める方法である。

　　　直接法は、対象不動産について、使用資材の種別、品等及び数量並びに所要労働の種別、時間等を調査し、対象不動産の存する地域の価格時点における単価を基礎とした直接工事費を積算し、これに間接工事費及び請負者の適正な利益を含む一般管理費等を加えて標準的な建設費を求め、さらに発注者が直接負担すべき通常の付帯費用を加算して再調達原価を求めるものとする。

　　　また、対象不動産の素材となった土地（素地）の価格並びに実際の造成又は建設に要した直接工事費、間接工事費、請負者の適正な利益を含む一般管理費等及び発注者が直接負担した付帯費用の額並びにこれらの明細（種別、品等、数量、時間、単価等）が判明している場合には、これらの明細を分析して適切に補正し、かつ、必要に応じて時点修正を行って再調達原価を求めることができる。

　イ　間接法は、近隣地域若しくは同一需給圏内の類似地域等に存する対象不動産と類似の不動産又は同一需給圏内の代替競争不動産から間接的に対象不動産の再調達原価を求める方法である。

　　　間接法は、当該類似の不動産等について、素地の価格やその実際の造成又は建設に要した直接工事費、間接工事費、請負者の適正な利益を含む一般管理費等及び発注者が直接負担した付帯費用の額並びにこれらの明細（種別、品等、数量、時間、単価等）を明確に把握できる場合に、これらの明細を分析して適切に補正し、必要に応じて時点修正を行い、かつ、地域要因の比較及び個別的要因の比較を行って、対象不動産の再調達原価を求めるものとする。

adjusting for changes over time as required, and comparing both market- specific value influences and property- specific value influences.

3. Accrued Depreciation

The purpose of estimating accrued depreciation is to determine an appropriate deduction to apply to the reproduction cost of the subject property in order to arrive at the indicated value of the subject on the date of the value opinion.

The amount of accrued depreciation may be determined by an itemized and comprehensive analysis of the subject property according to the following types of depreciation.

(1) Types of Accrued Depreciation

Accrued Depreciation is broken down into physical deterioration, functional obsolescence and economic obsolescence.

It should be noted that these three types of accrued depreciation are not independent of one another, but rather are mutually related and interactive.

① **Physical Deterioration**

Examples of physical deterioration include wear and tear from the use of the real estate, deterioration occurring over the passage of time or resulting from natural causes, and incidental damage.

② **Functional Obsolescence**

Examples of functional obsolescence affecting real estate include uncompatibility between building and site, bad design, outdated form, and inadequate facilities of reduced capacity.

③ **Economic Obsolescence**

Examples of economic obosolescence include non- complementarity between the real estate and its environment resulting from neighborhood decline, non- conformity between the real estate and its surroundings, or a decline in the marketability of the real estate vis- a- vis either real estate in a substitutive or competitive relationship with the subject or other real estate in the vicinity.

(2) Methods of Estimating Accrued Depreciation

The two methods indicated below are used to determine the total depreciation in a property. Generally, these two methods are used in conjunction with one another.

① **Methods of Estimating Accrued Depreciation over a Period**

Methods of estimating accrued depreciation over a period consist of the straight- line method and the declining balance method. The decision as to which of these methods should be used is made according to the actual situation of the subject property.

When applying these methods, the appraiser should give greater weight to the remaining economic life of the property rather than its actual age.

In situations where the subject property is composed of two or more divisible components, and the respective depreciation periods or remaining economic lives of these components are different, how depreciation in each component is to be assessed and how salvage value and land value are to be estimated at the termination of the period should be decided according to the actual situation of the subject property.

3．減価修正

減価修正の目的は、減価の要因に基づき発生した減価額を対象不動産の再調達原価から控除して価格時点における対象不動産の適正な積算価格を求めることである。

減価修正を行うに当たっては、減価の要因に着目して対象不動産を部分的かつ総合的に分析検討し、減価額を求めなければならない。

(1) 減価の要因

減価の要因は、物理的要因、機能的要因及び経済的要因に分けられる。

これらの要因は、それぞれ独立しているものではなく、相互に関連し、影響を与え合いながら作用していることに留意しなければならない。

① 物理的要因

物理的要因としては、不動産を使用することによって生ずる摩滅及び破損、時の経過又は自然的作用によって生ずる老朽化並びに偶発的な損傷があげられる。

② 機能的要因

機能的要因としては、不動産の機能的陳腐化、すなわち、建物と敷地との不適応、設計の不良、型式の旧式化、設備の不足及びその能率の低下等があげられる。

③ 経済的要因

経済的要因としては、不動産の経済的不適応、すなわち、近隣地域の衰退、不動産とその付近の環境との不適合、不動産と代替、競争等の関係にある不動産又は付近の不動産との比較における市場性の減退等があげられる。

(2) 減価修正の方法

減価額を求めるには、次の二つの方法があり、原則としてこれらを併用するものとする。

① 耐用年数に基づく方法

耐用年数に基づく方法には、定額法、定率法等があるが、これらのうちいずれの方法を用いるかは、対象不動産の実情に即して決定すべきである。

この方法を用いる場合には、経過年数よりも経済的残存耐用年数に重点をおいて判断すべきである。

なお、対象不動産が二以上の分別可能な組成部分により構成されていて、それぞれの耐用年数又は経済的残存耐用年数が異なる場合に、これらをいかに判断して用いるか、また、耐用年数満了時における残材価額をいかにみるかについても、対象不動産の実情に即して決定すべきである。

② **Methods Based on Observation**
Accrued Depreciation may be estimated on the basis of direct observation. The appraiser investigates the functionality of the design, layout and facilities of the subject property; its maintenance and management; the condition of any repairs; how well the property conforms with the surrounding environment, and other possible factors contributing to accrued depreciation.

III Sales Comparison Approach
1. Concept

The sales comparison approach uses data on the sales of comparable properties to determine the subject property's value. First, the appraiser gathers a large amount of comparable sales data, from which the most appropriate data are selected. The market prices negotiated in the comparable sales are adjusted for differences in sales conditions or changes occurring over the passage of time, if required. Market- specific and property- specific value influences are then compared to get value indicated by the sales comparison approach.

The sales comparison approach is applied when there is an availability of sales data involving comparable properties in the neighborhood or a similar neighborhood within the primary market area, or sales data involving substitutive or competitive real estate in the primary market area.

2. Application Method
(1) Gathering and Selection of Data

Since the sales comparison method uses comparable sales data found in the market as the basis for estimating value, the appraiser must first gather a large amount of comparable sales data.

Comparable sales data is gathered from data on real estate located in the neighborhood or similar neighborhoods within the primary market area. In situations where the highest and best use of the subject differs from the typical or standard use in the neighborhood, the selection of comparable sales data on real estate in a substitutive or competitive relationship with the subject will be unavoidable. In any case, comparable sales data must be found within the vicinity of the neighborhood and primary market area and satisfy all of the requirements indicated below.

① the data should reflect normal circumstances under which transactions are closed or else the data should be amenable to adjustment to reflect normal circumstances.

② the data should allow adjustment for changes in price levels and market conditions over time.

③ the data should allow comparison of market- specific value influences and comparison of property- specific value influences.

(2) Sales Condition and Time Adjustments

When comparable sales data reflect special circumstances affecting the sale price, an appropriate adjustment must be made. When a period of time has lapsed since the time of a comparable sale, and a change in the price level has occurred during that period, the value of the comparable sale must be adjusted to the price level on the date

② 観察減価法

観察減価法は、対象不動産について、設計、設備等の機能性、維持管理の状態、補修の状況、付近の環境との適合の状態等各減価の要因の実態を調査することにより、減価額を直接求める方法である。

Ⅲ 取引事例比較法

1．意義

取引事例比較法は、まず多数の取引事例を収集して適切な事例の選択を行い、これらに係る取引価格に必要に応じて事情補正及び時点修正を行い、かつ、地域要因の比較及び個別的要因の比較を行って求められた価格を比較考量し、これによって対象不動産の試算価格を求める手法である（この手法による試算価格を比準価格という。）。

取引事例比較法は、近隣地域若しくは同一需給圏内の類似地域等において対象不動産と類似の不動産の取引が行われている場合又は同一需給圏内の代替競争不動産の取引が行われている場合に有効である。

2．適用方法

(1) 事例の収集及び選択

取引事例比較法は、市場において発生した取引事例を価格判定の基礎とするものであるので、多数の取引事例を収集することが必要である。

取引事例は、原則として近隣地域又は同一需給圏内の類似地域に存する不動産に係るもののうちから選択するものとし、必要やむを得ない場合には近隣地域の周辺の地域に存する不動産に係るもののうちから、対象不動産の最有効使用が標準的使用と異なる場合等には、同一需給圏内の代替競争不動産に係るもののうちから選択するものとするほか、次の要件の全部を備えなければならない。

① 取引事情が正常なものと認められるもの又は正常なものに補正することができるものであること。
② 時点修正をすることが可能なものであること。
③ 地域要因の比較及び個別的要因の比較が可能なものであること。

(2) 事情補正及び時点修正

取引事例が特殊な事情を含み、これが当該事例に係る取引価格に影響していると認められるときは、適切な補正を行い、取引事例に係る取引の時点が価格時点と異なることにより、その間に価格水準の変動があると認められるときは、当該事例の価格を価格時点の価格に修正しなければならない。

of the value opinion.

In making a time adjustment, the appraiser adjusts the sale price after determining the rate of growth in the value of land or buildings under the same land use classification as the comparable real estate in the neighborhood or a similar area, which has gone through a process of appreciation or decline in value similar to the neighborhood.

(3) **Comparison of Market – Specific Value Influences and Property – Specific Value Influences**

A sale price reflects both market- specific and property- specific value influences. Therefore, it is necessary to compare market- specific and property- specific value influences on the subject property and comparable property when the comparable real estate is located in a similar neighborhood within the same primary market area, or when it is in a substitutive or competitive relationship with the subject real estate and is located in the same primary market area. On the other hand, if the comparable property is located in the subject neighborhood, it is only necessary to compare property- specific value influences on the subject property and the comparable property.

To facilitate the comparison of market- specific value influences and property- specific value influences, the appraiser might identify a benchmark site subject to typical property- specific value influences in each area.

(4) **Allocation Method**

Situations will arise where comparable sales data is selected from real estate with two components, while the subject property has only one of two. The value of the extra component of the comparable property must be estimated first, and them must be deducted from the overall sale price to generate a comparable price for the subject property.

Alternatively, an allocation method may be used. Ratios between the values of property components as reflected by the comparable sales data can be developed on the basis of sales prices or development costs. The sale price derived from the comparable data is then multiplied by the percentage for the common component of the subject and comparable properties.

Ⅳ Income Capitalization Approach

1. Concept

The income capitalization approach estimates the total present value of the adjusted net operating income or net cash flow (NCF) that the subject property is expected to generate in a future period (a value indication derived from this approach is called the value indicated by the income approach).

The income capitalization approach is applicable for determining the value of lease- based properties and owner- occupied properties for business operation.

The formation of real estate value generally reflects the profitability of the given real estate, and income represents the essence of the economic value of real estate. Thus, the income capitalization approach cannot be applied to real estate that does not have general marketability, such as structures designated as cultural assets. However, it can be applied to owner- occupied residential properties upon the assumption that these properties are being leased.

時点修正に当たっては、事例に係る不動産の存する用途的地域又は当該地域と相似の価格変動過程を経たと認められる類似の地域における土地又は建物の価格の変動率を求め、これにより取引価格を修正すべきである。

(3) 地域要因の比較及び個別的要因の比較

取引価格は、取引事例に係る不動産の存する用途的地域の地域要因及び当該不動産の個別的要因を反映しているものであるから、取引事例に係る不動産が同一需給圏内の類似地域等に存するもの又は同一需給圏内の代替競争不動産である場合においては、近隣地域と当該事例に係る不動産の存する地域との地域要因の比較及び対象不動産と当該事例に係る不動産との個別的要因の比較を、取引事例に係る不動産が近隣地域に存するものである場合においては、対象不動産と当該事例に係る不動産との個別的要因の比較をそれぞれ行うものとする。

また、このほか地域要因及び個別的要因の比較については、それぞれの地域における個別的要因が標準的な土地を設定して行う方法がある。

(4) 配分法

取引事例が対象不動産と同類型の不動産の部分を内包して複合的に構成されている異類型の不動産に係る場合においては、当該取引事例の取引価格から対象不動産と同類型の不動産以外の部分の価格が取引価格等により判明しているときは、その価格を控除し、又は当該取引事例について各構成部分の価格の割合が取引価格、新規投資等により判明しているときは、当該事例の取引価格に対象不動産と同類型の不動産の部分に係る構成割合を乗じて、対象不動産の類型に係る事例資料を求めるものとする(この方法を配分法という。)。

Ⅳ 収益還元法

1．意義

収益還元法は、対象不動産が将来生み出すであろうと期待される純収益の現在価値の総和を求めることにより対象不動産の試算価格を求める手法である（この手法による試算価格を収益価格という。）。

収益還元法は、賃貸用不動産又は賃貸以外の事業の用に供する不動産の価格を求める場合に特に有効である。

また、不動産の価格は、一般に当該不動産の収益性を反映して形成されるものであり、収益は、不動産の経済価値の本質を形成するものである。したがって、この手法は、文化財の指定を受けた建造物等の一般的に市場性を有しない不動産以外のものにはすべて適用すべきものであり、自用の住宅地といえども賃貸を想定することにより適用されるものである。

なお、市場における土地の取引価格の上昇が著しいときは、その価格と収益価格との乖離が増大するものであるので、先走りがちな取引価格に対する有力な検証手段として、この手法が活用されるべきである。

General Standards Chapter 7

Furthermore, when there is a precipitous increase in the sale price of land, a considerable disparity between the sale price and the value indicated by the income approach may result. In such situations, the income capitalization approach should be utilized to verify sale prices, which tend to be somewhat speculative.

2. Methods for Determining Value Indicated by the Income Approach

There are two basic methods for determining value indicated by the income approach. One method, called direct capitalization, applies a capitalization rate directly to net cash flow (NCF); the other method, discounted cash flow (DCF), discounts the net cash flow (NCF) generated over the typical holding period together with the reversionary value at the end of the holding period. Each income stream is discounted to present value at the time it is generated. All the discounted income streams are then added up.

These methods are basically represented by the following formulas.

(1) **Direct Capitalization Method**

$$P = \frac{a}{R}$$

where
P : Subject property value indicated by the income approach
a : Net cash flow (NCF) for one period
R : Capitalization rate

(2) **DCF Method**

$$P = \sum_{k=1}^{n} \frac{a_k}{(1+Y)^k} + \frac{P_R}{(1+Y)^n}$$

where
P : Subject property value indicated by the income approach
a_k : Net cash flow (NCF) for each period
Y : Discount rate
n : Holding period (or analysis period in cases where resale is not assumed, as is understood hereinafter)
P_R : Reversionary value

The reversion refers to the value of the subject property at the end of the holding period, and is basically represented by the following formula.

$$P_R = \frac{a_{n+1}}{R_n}$$

where
a_{n+1}: Net cash flow (NCF) for period $n+1$
Rn : Capitalization rate at the end of the holding period (terminal capitalization rate)

3. Application Methodology

(1) **Net cash flow (NCF)**

① **Concept of Net Cash Flow (or Adjusted Net Operating Income)**

Net cash flow (NCF) refers to the reasonable income to the real estate. NCF represents the portion of gross income remaining after allocations have been made for the contributions of capital (excluding capital converted into real estate), labor

2．収益価格を求める方法

収益価格を求める方法には、一期間の純収益を還元利回りによって還元する方法（以下「直接還元法」という。）と、連続する複数の期間に発生する純収益及び復帰価格を、その発生時期に応じて現在価値に割り引き、それぞれを合計する方法（Discounted Cash Flow法（以下「ＤＣＦ法」という。））がある。

これらの方法は、基本的には次の式により表される。

(1) 直接還元法

$$P = \frac{a}{R}$$

P ：求める不動産の収益価格
a ：一期間の純収益
R ：還元利回り

(2) ＤＣＦ法

$$P = \sum_{k=1}^{n} \frac{a_k}{(1+Y)^k} + \frac{P_R}{(1+Y)^n}$$

P ：求める不動産の収益価格
a_k ：毎期の純収益
Y ：割引率
n ：保有期間（売却を想定しない場合には分析期間。以下同じ。）
P_R ：復帰価格
　　復帰価格とは、保有期間の満了時点における対象不動産の価格をいい、基本的には次の式により表される。

$$P_R = \frac{a_{n+1}}{R_n}$$

a_{n+1} ：n＋1期の純収益
R_n 　：保有期間の満了時点における還元利回り（最終還元利回り）

3．適用方法

(1) 純収益

① 純収益の意義

　純収益とは、不動産に帰属する適正な収益をいい、収益目的のために用いられている不動産とこれに関与する資本（不動産に化体されているものを除く。）、労働及び経営（組織）の諸要素の結合によって生ずる総収益から、資本（不動産に化体されているも

and management (coordination). (Editor's Note: Economic theory understands income- producing real estate as a product that combines four elements: land, capital (excluding capital converted into real estate), labor and management (coordination).)

② **Calculation of Net Cash Flow**

The net cash flow (NCF) of a subject property is typically determined by subtracting total expenses from the total income generated in one year. In addition, net cash flow (NCF) varies depending on the manner in which gross income and total costs are regarded, i.e., either as perpetual (level) NCF or non- perpetual (variable) NCF, or as NCF before depreciation allowance or NCF after depreciation. It should also be noted that the variability in NCF is closely related to selection of the method (direct capitalization or DCF) for determining value indications by the income approach and the method for determining capitalization rates or discount rates.

Furthermore, in direct capitalization, the net cash flow (NCF) used may, in some cases, be the subject property's first- year NCF and, in other cases, a stabilized NCF.

The net cash flow (NCF) of the subject property should be appropriately estimated by carefully analyzing each detailed line item in regard to past developments and future trends. The appraiser's analysis must be based on a direct understanding of the subject property's gross income and total related costs. The outlook for increased earnings and particularly the anticipated limits on earnings growth must be examined carefully.

The Discounted Cash Flow method explicitly indicates periodic or annual net cash flow (NCF), the reversion, and the times at which these income streams are generated. Thus, it is necessary to thoroughly investigate the outlook for net cash flow (NCF).

In the application of direct capitalization, the net cash flow (NCF) of the subject property may be indirectly determined on the basis of the net cash flow (NCF) of real estate similar to the subject property, located in the subject neighborhood or similar neighborhoods within the same primary market area, or the NCF of real estate in a substitutive or competitive relationship with the subject, located within the same market area. In such cases, it is necessary to compare respective area- specific value influences and property- specific value influences and appropriately adjust the net cash flow (NCF) of the comparable properties.

a. **Calculation of Gross Income and Commentary**

(a) **Lease – based property or owner – occupied property for business operation**

For lease- based property, gross income generally includes nominal rent, interest earned on refundable deposits, interest earned and amortization of non- refundable deposits, and other income such as parking revenue. For owner- occupied property for business operation, gross income is the gross earning generated by sales.

In applying the DCF method to leased- property, the appraiser must give

のを除く。)、労働及び経営(組織)の総収益に対する貢献度に応じた分配分を控除した残余の部分をいう。

② 純収益の算定

対象不動産の純収益は、一般に1年を単位として総収益から総費用を控除して求めるものとする。また、純収益は、永続的なものと非永続的なもの、償却前のものと償却後のもの等、総収益及び総費用の把握の仕方により異なるものであり、それぞれ収益価格を求める方法及び還元利回り又は割引率を求める方法とも密接な関連があることに留意する必要がある。

なお、直接還元法における純収益は、対象不動産の初年度の純収益を採用する場合と標準化された純収益を採用する場合があることに留意しなければならない。

純収益の算定に当たっては、対象不動産からの総収益及びこれに係る総費用を直接的に把握し、それぞれの項目の細部について過去の推移及び将来の動向を慎重に分析して、対象不動産の純収益を適切に求めるべきである。この場合において収益増加の見通しについては、特に予測の限界を見極めなければならない。

特にDCF法の適用に当たっては、毎期の純収益及び復帰価格並びにその発生時期が明示されることから、純収益の見通しについて十分な調査を行うことが必要である。

なお、直接還元法の適用に当たって、対象不動産の純収益を近隣地域又は同一需給圏内の類似地域等に存する対象不動産と類似の不動産若しくは同一需給圏内の代替競争不動産の純収益によって間接的に求める場合には、それぞれの地域要因の比較及び個別的要因の比較を行い、当該純収益について適切に補正することが必要である。

ア 総収益の算定及び留意点
(ア) 対象不動産が賃貸用不動産又は賃貸以外の事業の用に供する不動産である場合

総収益は、一般に、賃貸用不動産にあっては、支払賃料に預り金的性格を有する保証金等の運用益、賃料の前払的性格を有する権利金等の運用益及び償却額並びに駐車場使用料等のその他収入を加えた額とし、賃貸以外の事業の用に供する不動産にあっては、売上高とする。

なお、賃貸用不動産についてのDCF法の適用に当たっては、特に賃貸借契約の内容並びに賃料及び貸室の稼動率の毎期の変動に留意しなければならない。

special attention to the provisions of the lease agreement(s), and changes in the rents and the occupancy rates of the leased space for each period.

(b) **Highest and Best Use of vacant land is for lease – based development**

The gross income that is likely to be generated by the built- up property is appropriately estimated by assuming the leased building as the highest and best use of the subject property.

b. **Calculation of Total Expenses and Commentary**

Where the subject property is a lease- based property or where construction of a leased building represents the highest and best use of the land (see paragraph a- (b) above), the total expenses of the subject property include depreciation (excluded where net cash flow (NCF) is determined before depreciation allowance), maintenance and management fees (including maintenance costs, management fees and repair expenses), real estate taxes (property taxes, city planning tax) and insurance premiums, and other miscellaneous expenses. Where the subject real estate is an owner- occupied property for business operation, the total expenses of the property include cost of purchases and sales, general and administrative cost. In applying the DCF method, the appraiser must give special attention to the times that expenses, such as large- scale repairs, occur during the holding period.

(2) **Capitalization and Discount Rates**

① **Concept of Capitalization and Discount Rates**

The capitalization rate and discount rate both reflect the profitability of real estate, and although they are both used in the income approach to determine the indicated value, they are basically different, as is explained below.

The (overall) capitalization rate is the rate used in direct capitalization where property value is determined from the net cash flow (NCF) for a single period. In DCF analysis, the terminal capitalization rate is applied to estimate the reversion or anticipated property value at the end of the holding period. Capitalization rates incorporate a component for the uncertainty accompanying anticipated change in future income.

The discount rate is a rate used in DCF analysis to calculate the present value of income to be generated in the future. The discount rate excludes any component for uncertainty, accompanying anticipated change in the net cash flow (NCF) and reversion that are forecast over consecutive periods according to the income outlook.

② **Selecting and Supporting the Capitalization Rate and Discount Rate**

a. **Commentary on Determining Capitalization Rate and Discount Rates**

Since both the capitalization rate and discount rate are closely related to the profitability of comparable assets and investment yields in the financial market, the appraiser must investigate trends in the returns on real estate and other investments.

(イ) 対象不動産が更地であるものとして、当該土地に最有効使用の賃貸用建物等の建築を想定する場合

　　対象不動産に最有効使用の賃貸用建物等の建設を想定し、当該複合不動産が生み出すであろう総収益を適切に求めるものとする。

イ　総費用の算定及び留意点

　　対象不動産の総費用は、賃貸用不動産(アの(イ)の複合不動産を想定する場合を含む。)にあっては、減価償却費（償却前の純収益を求める場合には、計上しない。）、維持管理費（維持費、管理費、修繕費等）、公租公課（固定資産税、都市計画税等）、損害保険料等の諸経費等を、賃貸以外の事業の用に供する不動産にあっては、売上原価、販売費及び一般管理費等をそれぞれ加算して求めるものとする。なお、DCF法の適用に当たっては、特に保有期間中における大規模修繕費等の費用の発生時期に留意しなければならない。

(2) 還元利回り及び割引率

① 還元利回り及び割引率の意義

　　還元利回り及び割引率は、共に不動産の収益性を表し、収益価格を求めるために用いるものであるが、基本的には次のような違いがある。

　　還元利回りは、直接還元法の収益価格及びDCF法の復帰価格の算定において、一期間の純収益から対象不動産の価格を直接求める際に使用される率であり、将来の収益に影響を与える要因の変動予測と予測に伴う不確実性を含むものである。

　　割引率は、DCF法において、ある将来時点の収益を現在時点の価値に割り戻す際に使用される率であり、還元利回りに含まれる変動予測と予測に伴う不確実性のうち、収益見通しにおいて考慮された連続する複数の期間に発生する純収益や復帰価格の変動予測に係るものを除くものである。

② 還元利回り及び割引率の算定

ア　還元利回り及び割引率を求める際の留意点

　　還元利回り及び割引率は、共に比較可能な他の資産の収益性や金融市場における運用利回りと密接な関連があるので、その動向に留意しなければならない。

　　さらに、還元利回り及び割引率は、地方別、用途的地域別、品等別等によって異なる傾向を持つため、対象不動産に係る地域要因及び個別的要因の分析を踏まえつつ適切に求めることが必要である。

General Standards Chapter 7

Moreover, since the capitalization rate and discount rate tend to differ according to region and property type and grade, both rates must be appropriately determined by analysis of area- specific value influences and property- specific value influences acting upon the subject property.

b . **Methods for Determining Capitalization Rates**

Examples of methods used to determine capitalization rates are provided below.

(a) **Determination by Comparison with Comparable Sales Data on Similar Real Estate**

This method determines the capitalization rate by making adjustments to market- derived capitalization rates for differences occurring over the time since the transaction involving the comparable property was closed, for the special circumstances of the transaction, and for changes in market- specific value influences and property- specific value influences.

(b) **Determination by Means of Band of Investment Method based on Equity – Mortgage Ratio**

The capitalization rate may be determined by weighting and averaging the respective capitalization rates for components of a capital investment (loan and equity) required for the acquisition of the subject property.

(c) **Determination from Capitalization Rates for Land and Building Components**

Where the subject property comprises a building and building site, the capitalization rate may be determined by weighting and averaging the respective capitalization rates for physical components (land and building) according to the respective ratios between the components.

(d) **Determination from the Relationship with the Discount Rate**

The capitalization rate may be determined by considering the growth rate in the subject property's net cash flow (NCF) based on the discount rate applied.

c . **Methods for Determining Discount Rates**

Examples of methods used to determine discount rates are provided below.

(a) **Determination by Comparison with Comparable Sales Data on Similar Real Estate**

This method determines the discount rate by making adjustments to market- derived discount rates for differences occurring since the time the transaction was concluded, for the special circumstances of the transaction, and for changes in market- specific value influences and property- specific value influences. Adjustments are based on the discount rate determined from comparable sales data on the subject property and similar real estate.

(b) **Determination by Means of Discount Rates on Loans and Equity (Band of Investment Method Based on Equity – Mortgage Ratio)**

The discount rate may be determined by weighting and averaging the

イ　還元利回りを求める方法
　　還元利回りを求める方法を例示すると次のとおりである。

㈎　類似の不動産の取引事例との比較から求める方法
　　この方法は、対象不動産と類似の不動産の取引事例から求められる利回りをもとに、取引時点及び取引事情並びに地域要因及び個別的要因の違いに応じた補正を行うことにより求めるものである。

㈏　借入金と自己資金に係る還元利回りから求める方法
　　この方法は、対象不動産の取得の際の資金調達上の構成要素（借入金及び自己資金）に係る各還元利回りを各々の構成割合により加重平均して求めるものである。

㈐　土地と建物に係る還元利回りから求める方法
　　この方法は、対象不動産が建物及びその敷地である場合に、その物理的な構成要素（土地及び建物）に係る各還元利回りを各々の価格の構成割合により加重平均して求めるものである。

㈑　割引率との関係から求める方法
　　この方法は、割引率をもとに対象不動産の純収益の変動率を考慮して求めるものである。

ウ　割引率を求める方法
　　割引率を求める方法を例示すると次のとおりである。
㈎　類似の不動産の取引事例との比較から求める方法
　　この方法は、対象不動産と類似の不動産の取引事例から求められる割引率をもとに、取引時点及び取引事情並びに地域要因及び個別的要因の違いに応じた補正を行うことにより求めるものである。

㈏　借入金と自己資金に係る割引率から求める方法
　　この方法は、対象不動産の取得の際の資金調達上の構成要素（借入金及び自己資金）に係る各割引率を各々の構成割合により加重平均して求めるものである。

respective discount rates for components of a capital investment (loan and equity) required for the acquisition of the subject property.

(c) **Determination Based on the Uniqueness of the Real Estate Investment Relative to Yields on Financial Assets**
This method determines the discount rate by considering the uniqueness of the subject property as an investment in terms of risk, non- liquidity, management difficulty, and asset security relative to yields on bonds and other financial assets.

(3) **Basis for Selecting the Application of Direct Capitalization or DCF**
The appraiser must decide whether it is appropriate to apply direct capitalization or DCF analysis according to the availability of data, the title category of the subject property, and the purpose of the client's request.

Section 2. Appraisal Approaches for Determining Real Estate Rental Value

There are several appraisal approaches for determining the rent paid for real estate. Where the rent is to be established for a new lease, acceptable methods include the summation approach, the rental data comparison approach, and the income analysis approach; where the rent is to be established for a renewed lease, acceptable methods include the rental disparity analysis approach, the yield approach, the trend approach, and the rental data comparison approach.

I **General Commentary on Determining Rental Value**

In a rental appraisal, the appraiser normally estimates the real rent to be paid to the lessor of the subject property over the period of payment. However, the appraiser may estimate the nominal rent in addition to the real rent, if the client requests him/her to do so and provides him/her with: 1) the specifics of the payment period and timing; and 2) information on paid deposits, such as *kenrikin*, a non- refundable deposit on residential space; *shikikin*, a refundable security deposit on residential space; and *hoshokin*, a refundable security deposit on commercial space.

1. **Real Rent and Nominal Rent**

Real rent refers to all reasonable economic compensation payable to the lessor over the period of payment regardless of the specific form in which the rent is paid. Real rent represents gross rent, i.e., net rent plus miscellaneous expenses normally required to operate the real estate (called "operating expenses").

Nominal rent refers to rent paid at the time of each scheduled installment. It is the real rent less the interest on the deposits and the amortization of non- refundable deposits, provided the lessor has received deposits such as *kenrikin*, *shikikin*, and *hoshokin*, specified in the lease contract.

Furthermore, although it is common practice for utility expenses, cleaning and sanitation costs as well as heating and cooling costs to be paid each month in the form of so- called added rent or as common area charges for leased space, it must be noted that some portions of these payments can be equivalent to rent.

2. **Determination of Nominal Rent**

(ウ)　金融資産の利回りに不動産の個別性を加味して求める方法

　　　　この方法は、債券等の金融資産の利回りをもとに、対象不動産の投資対象としての危険性、非流動性、管理の困難性、資産としての安全性等の個別性を加味することにより求めるものである。

　(3)　直接還元法及びDCF法の適用のあり方

　　　直接還元法又はDCF法のいずれの方法を適用するかについては、収集可能な資料の範囲、対象不動産の類型及び依頼目的に即して適切に選択することが必要である。

第2節　賃料を求める鑑定評価の手法

　不動産の賃料を求める鑑定評価の手法は、新規賃料にあっては積算法、賃貸事例比較法、収益分析法等があり、継続賃料にあっては差額配分法、利回り法、スライド法、賃貸事例比較法等がある。

I　賃料を求める場合の一般的留意事項

　賃料の鑑定評価は、対象不動産について、賃料の算定の期間に対応して、実質賃料を求めることを原則とし、賃料の算定の期間及び支払いの時期に係る条件並びに権利金、敷金、保証金等の一時金の授受に関する条件が付されて支払賃料を求めることを依頼された場合には、実質賃料とともに、その一部である支払賃料を求めることができるものとする。

1．実質賃料と支払賃料

　実質賃料とは、賃料の種類の如何を問わず貸主に支払われる賃料の算定の期間に対応する適正なすべての経済的対価をいい、純賃料及び不動産の賃貸借等を継続するために通常必要とされる諸経費等（以下「必要諸経費等」という。）から成り立つものである。

　支払賃料とは、各支払時期に支払われる賃料をいい、契約に当たって、権利金、敷金、保証金等の一時金が授受される場合においては、当該一時金の運用益及び償却額と併せて実質賃料を構成するものである。

　なお、慣行上、建物及びその敷地の一部の賃貸借に当たって、水道光熱費、清掃・衛生費、冷暖房費等がいわゆる付加使用料、共益費等の名目で支払われる場合もあるが、これらのうちには実質的に賃料に相当する部分が含まれている場合があることに留意する必要がある。

2．支払賃料の求め方

When the lessee has paid deposits stipulated in the lease, the nominal rent is determined by deducting the interest earned on the deposits and the amortization of non-refundable deposits from the effective rent.

The interest earned and the amortization of non-refundable deposits should be appropriately determined based on the circumstances, including changes in the value of the subject property during the lease period.

The appraiser may determine the investment yield by comparing various investment returns, such as the expected yield on real estate, the market-derived capitalization rate, the interest on long-term deposits, the yield on government and corporate bonds, and the interest paid on loans from financial institutions, while bearing in mind differences in the kinds of deposits specified in the lease contract, the specific term and rental payments negotiated, and the type and condition of the subject property.

3. Calculation Periods for Rent

For leased building sites and leased properties comprising buildings and building lots, one-month units are generally used to calculate the rent determined by an appraisal. One-year units are used for calculating rent for other types of land.

II Appraisal Approaches for Determining the Market Rent under New Lease

1. Summation Approach

(1) **Concept**

The summation approach first determines the base value of the subject property on the date of the value opinion; the base value is then multiplied by the anticipated yield, and operating expenses are added to the resulting amount to arrive at gross rent (the rent estimated by this method is called rent indicated by the summation approach).

The summation approach is applicable where the base value of the subject property, the anticipated yield, and the operating expenses can be accurately determined.

(2) **Application**

① **Base Value**

The base value serves as the basis of the subject property's value to be used for determining the indicated rent by the summation approach; base value is determined by the cost and the sales comparison approaches.

② **Anticipated Yield**

Anticipated yield is the ratio between the anticipated net cash flow (NCF) to the capital invested in the leased real estate.

The method for determining anticipated yield is the same as the method for determining the capitalization rate in the income capitalization approach. In this particular application, special attention should be given to the characteristics of the rent.

③ **Operating Expenses**

Examples of expenses that are included in the total estimate of operating expenses for leased real estate are provided below.

    a. Depreciation
    b. Maintenance and management fees (including maintenance costs, management fees and repair expenses)

契約に当たって一時金が授受される場合における支払賃料は、実質賃料から、当該一時金について賃料の前払的性格を有する一時金の運用益及び償却額並びに預り金的性格を有する一時金の運用益を控除して求めるものとする。

　なお、賃料の前払的性格を有する一時金の運用益及び償却額については、対象不動産の賃貸借等の持続する期間の効用の変化等に着目し、実態に応じて適切に求めるものとする。

　運用利回りは、賃貸借等の契約に当たって授受される一時金の性格、賃貸借等の契約内容並びに対象不動産の種類及び性格等の相違に応じて、当該不動産の期待利回り、不動産の取引利回り、長期預金の金利、国債及び公社債利回り、金融機関の貸出金利等を比較考量して決定するものとする。

3．賃料の算定の期間

　鑑定評価によって求める賃料の算定の期間は、原則として、宅地並びに建物及びその敷地の賃料にあっては1月を単位とし、その他の土地にあっては1年を単位とするものとする。

Ⅱ　新規賃料を求める鑑定評価の手法

1．積算法

(1) 意義

　積算法は、対象不動産について、価格時点における基礎価格を求め、これに期待利回りを乗じて得た額に必要諸経費等を加算して対象不動産の試算賃料を求める手法である（この手法による試算賃料を積算賃料という。）。

　積算法は、対象不動産の基礎価格、期待利回り及び必要諸経費等の把握を的確に行い得る場合に有効である。

(2) 適用方法

① 基礎価格

　基礎価格とは、積算賃料を求めるための基礎となる価格をいい、原価法及び取引事例比較法により求めるものとする。

② 期待利回り

　期待利回りとは、賃貸借等に供する不動産を取得するために要した資本に相当する額に対して期待される純収益のその資本相当額に対する割合をいう。

　期待利回りを求める方法については、収益還元法における還元利回りを求める方法に準ずるものとする。この場合において、賃料の有する特性に留意すべきである。

③ 必要諸経費等

　不動産の賃貸借等に当たってその賃料に含まれる必要諸経費等としては、次のものがあげられる。

　ア　減価償却費
　イ　維持管理費（維持費、管理費、修繕費等）
　ウ　公租公課（固定資産税、都市計画税等）

c. Real estate taxes (including property taxes and city planning tax)
d. Insurance premiums (including premiums for fire, machinery, boiler and other insurance)
e. Allowance for collection loss
f. Vacancy allowance

2. Rental Data Comparison Approach

(1) Concept

In the rental data comparison approach, the appraiser first gathers data on a large number of new leases in order to select actual real rents (actual real rent refers to the total economic compensation to the real estate as reflected in the rent). Then, if required, the appraiser makes adjustments to the comparable rents with regard to lease condition and time factor. Finally, the appraiser compares the subject property with the comparables in terms of market- specific and property- specific value influences to arrive at the indicated rent (the rent determined by this approach is called rent indicated by the rental data comparison approach).

The rental data comparison approach is applicable where there is an availability of leasing data on comparable properties in the neighborhood or similar neighborhoods in the primary market area, or leasing data on properties in a substitutive or competitive relationship with the subject property, located in the primary market area.

(2) Application

① Gathering and Selection of Data

The process of gathering and selecting lease data is the same as in the sales comparison approach. In this particular application, the lease data should be selected from lease contracts with similar terms and rental payments.

② Comparing Lease Conditions, and Changes in Rent Levels, and Market – specific and Property – specific Value Influences

The comparative procedures (i.e., the comparisons between the subject and comparable properties for different conditions of lease and rent levels over the time since the comparable transactions took place as well as the comparisons of market- specific and property- specific value influences) are the same as in the sales comparison approach.

3. Income Analysis Approach

(1) Concept

The income analysis approach determines the indicated rent for a non- leased income- producing property on the basis of its net income after depreciation. This is the net income attributable to the subject property over a fixed period. The appraiser adds operating expenses to the net income to estimate the indicated rent (the rent determined by this approach is called rent indicated by the income analysis approach).

The income analysis approach is applicable where the net income attributable to owner- occupied property for business operation can be properly determined.

(2) Application

① Calculation of Net Income

The procedure for calculating net income is the same as that for calculating net cash

エ　損害保険料（火災、機械、ボイラー等の各種保険）
オ　貸倒れ準備費
カ　空室等による損失相当額

2．賃貸事例比較法
(1)　意義
　　賃貸事例比較法は、まず多数の新規の賃貸借等の事例を収集して適切な事例の選択を行い、これらに係る実際実質賃料（実際に支払われている不動産に係るすべての経済的対価をいう。）に必要に応じて事情補正及び時点修正を行い、かつ、地域要因の比較及び個別的要因の比較を行って求められた賃料を比較考量し、これによって対象不動産の試算賃料を求める手法である（この手法による試算賃料を比準賃料という。）。
　　賃貸事例比較法は、近隣地域又は同一需給圏内の類似地域等において対象不動産と類似の不動産の賃貸借等が行われている場合又は同一需給圏内の代替競争不動産の賃貸借等が行われている場合に有効である。

(2)　適用方法
①　事例の収集及び選択
　　賃貸借等の事例の収集及び選択については、取引事例比較法における事例の収集及び選択に準ずるものとする。この場合において、賃貸借等の契約の内容について類似性を有するものを選択すべきことに留意しなければならない。
②　事情補正及び時点修正並びに地域要因の比較及び個別的要因の比較
　　事情補正及び時点修正並びに地域要因の比較及び個別的要因の比較については、取引事例比較法の場合に準ずるものとする。

3．収益分析法
(1)　意義
　　収益分析法は、一般の企業経営に基づく総収益を分析して対象不動産が一定期間に生み出すであろうと期待される純収益（減価償却後のものとし、これを収益純賃料という。）を求め、これに必要諸経費等を加算して対象不動産の試算賃料を求める手法である（この手法による試算賃料を収益賃料という。）。
　　収益分析法は、企業の用に供されている不動産に帰属する純収益を適切に求め得る場合に有効である。

(2)　適用方法
①　収益純賃料の算定
　　収益純賃料の算定については、収益還元法における純収益の算定に準ずるものとする。

flow (NCF) in the income capitalization approach. In this particular application, special attention must be paid to the characteristics of the imputed rent.

② **Methodology for Determining an Indication of Rent by the Income Analysis Approach**

In the income analysis approach, the appraiser estimates the subject property's indicated rent by adding the net income to the expected operating expenses, assuming the property is being leased.

In some cases, the appraiser can conclude an indication of the rent (net rent plus operating expenses) by analyzing the total revenues and expenses of the subject non-leased income-producing properties.

Ⅲ Appraisal Approaches for Determining Rent under Renewed Lease

1. Rental Disparity Analysis Approach

(1) **Concept**

The rental disparity analysis approach arrives at the reasonable market rent of the subject property by adding an estimated increase to, or deducting an estimated decrease from, the actual rent. The increased or decreased amount is obtained by first determining the difference between the reasonable market rent and the actual real rent or actual nominal rent. The appraiser then estimates the portion of the difference assignable to the lessor by a thorough analysis of lease terms, contract negotiations and so forth. Finally, the assignable amount is either added to, or deducted from, the actual rent.

(2) **Application**

① The reasonable real rent based on the economic value of the subject property is the market rent assumed on the date of the value opinion. The reasonable real rent may be determined by the summation approach or the rental data comparison approach.

Where deposits have been paid to the lessor as a condition of the lease contract, the reasonable nominal rent based on the economic value of the subject property is determined by deducting the interest earned and/or the amortization of deposits, such as *kenrikin*, *shikikin*, and *hoshokin* from the effective rent.

② The economic benefit or disadvantage assignable to the lessor is determined by analyzing a wide range of factors that may account for a difference between reasonable market rent and actual rent. The appraiser analyzes general value influences and market-specific value influences, and examines the contractual matters indicated below.

　　a. The years passed and the remaining lease term
　　b. Background factors at the time the lease contract was negotiated and relations between the tenant and landlord up to the present
　　c. Degree to which the lessor or tenant contributes to the neighborhood

2. Yield Approach

(1) **Concept**

The yield approach arrives at an estimate of gross rent by adding operating expenses to base value multiplied by the rental yield rate under a renewed lease.

この場合において、賃料の有する特性に留意しなければならない。

② 収益賃料を求める手法
収益賃料は、収益純賃料の額に賃貸借等に当たって賃料に含まれる必要諸経費等を加算することによって求めるものとする。
なお、一般企業経営に基づく総収益を分析して収益純賃料及び必要諸経費等を含む賃料相当額を収益賃料として直接求めることができる場合もある。

Ⅲ 継続賃料を求める鑑定評価の手法
1．差額配分法
(1) 意義
差額配分法は、対象不動産の経済価値に即応した適正な実質賃料又は支払賃料と実際実質賃料又は実際支払賃料との間に発生している差額について、契約の内容、契約締結の経緯等を総合的に勘案して、当該差額のうち貸主に帰属する部分を適切に判定して得た額を実際実質賃料又は実際支払賃料に加減して試算賃料を求める手法である。

(2) 適用方法
① 対象不動産の経済価値に即応した適正な実質賃料は、価格時点において想定される正常賃料であり、積算法、賃貸事例比較法等により求めるものとする。
対象不動産の経済価値に即応した適正な支払賃料は、契約に当たって一時金が授受されている場合については、実質賃料から権利金、敷金、保証金等の一時金の運用益及び償却額を控除することにより求めるものとする。
② 貸主に帰属する部分については、一般的要因の分析及び地域要因の分析により差額発生の要因を広域的に分析し、さらに対象不動産について次に掲げる契約の事項等に関する分析を行うことにより適切に判断するものとする。
ア　契約上の経過期間と残存期間
イ　契約締結及びその後現在に至るまでの経緯
ウ　貸主又は借主の近隣地域の発展に対する寄与度

2．利回り法
(1) 意義
利回り法は、基礎価格に継続賃料利回りを乗じて得た額に必要諸経費等を加算して試算賃料を求める手法である。

(2) **Application**

① The methods of determining base value and operating expenses in the yield approach are the same as in the summation approach.

② The rental yield rate under a renewed lease is based on the ratio of net rent to base value at the time the current rent was negotiated. It may be determined by thoroughly comparing 1) yield rates reflected in the data, including the yield at the time the contract was signed and each time the rent was revised, 2) the growth rate in base value, and 3) yield rates reflected in comparable data on similar properties in the neighborhood or similar neighborhoods in the primary market area, or comparable rental data on real estate in a substitutive or competitive relationship with the subject, and located in the primary market area.

3. Trend Approach

(1) **Concept**

The trend approach arrives at an estimate of gross rent by adding operating expenses on the date of the value opinion to the net rent, at the time the current rent was negotiated, which is multiplied by a trend factor for the growth rate in rent.

Where it is possible to determine a trend factor for the actual real rent or actual nominal rent since the time the current rent was agreed upon, the appraiser can arrive at the indicated rent by directly multiplying the current rent by the trend factor.

(2) **Application**

① A trend factor represents the amount of change in rent corresponding to changes in economic conditions between the time the current rent was agreed upon and the date of the value opinion. It may be determined by a thorough analysis of various indicators, including changes in land and building values, changes in commodity prices and changes in income level.

② The method for determining operating expenses is the same as in the summation approach.

4. Rental Data Comparison Approach

The rental data comparison approach is applied the same way as the rental data comparison approach for determining rent under a new lease.

(2) 適用方法
① 基礎価格及び必要諸経費等の求め方については、積算法に準ずるものとする。
② 継続賃料利回りは、現行賃料を定めた時点における基礎価格に対する純賃料の割合を標準とし、契約締結時及びその後の各賃料改定時の利回り、基礎価格の変動の程度、近隣地域若しくは同一需給圏内の類似地域等における対象不動産と類似の不動産の賃貸借等の事例又は同一需給圏内の代替競争不動産の賃貸借等の事例における利回りを総合的に比較考量して求めるものとする。

3．スライド法

(1) 意義

スライド法は、現行賃料を定めた時点における純賃料に変動率を乗じて得た額に価格時点における必要諸経費等を加算して試算賃料を求める手法である。

なお、現行賃料を定めた時点における実際実質賃料又は実際支払賃料に即応する適切な変動率が求められる場合には、当該変動率を乗じて得た額を試算賃料として直接求めることができるものとする。

(2) 適用方法
① 変動率は、現行賃料を定めた時点から価格時点までの間における経済情勢等の変化に即応する変動分を表すものであり、土地及び建物価格の変動、物価変動、所得水準の変動等を示す各種指数等を総合的に勘案して求めるものとする。
② 必要諸経費等の求め方は、積算法に準ずるものとする。

4．賃貸事例比較法

賃貸事例比較法は、新規賃料に係る賃貸事例比較法に準じて試算賃料を求める手法である。

CHAPTER 8. APPRAISAL PROCESS

Real estate appraisal requires a planned, orderly process based on realistic understanding and reasonable judgment. This process typically includes 1) identifying basic appraisal problem, 2) drafting a processing plan, 3) identifying of the subject property, 4) gathering and organizing data, 5) reviewing data and analyzing value influences, 6) applying appraisal methodologies, 7) reconciling the indicated values or indicated rents, 8) determining the final value opinion, and 9) preparing the appraisal report. The appraiser carries out these steps in an orderly manner.

Section 1. Identification of Basic Appraisal Problem
Basic appraisal matters include clear confirmation of the intentions of the client with respect to the purpose of the appraisal and any limiting conditions.

Section 2. Drafting of Processing Plan
A processing plan must be drafted in an orderly manner in respect to the appraisal matters identified above (i.e., with respect to verifying the description of the subject property, gathering and organizing data, reviewing data and analyzing value influences, applying appraisal methodologies, adjusting the indicated values and indicated rents, and determining the final value opinion) according to the quality and quantity of work to be done and processing abilities required.

Section 3. Identification of the Subject Property
To identify the subject property, the elements of the subject property's identification, as confirmed in the first step above, must be checked. These include the subject property's physical characteristics and ownership and interests. This step is carried out by means of sufficient investigation, including a property inspection, interviews, confirmation of public data, and so forth.

Ⅰ **Identification of the Physical Characteristics of the Subject Property**
To identify the physical characteristics of the subject property, the subject property and property components must be compared with identification data (see Section 4-Ⅰ below) and checked by site inspection to confirm the location, lot number, area and so forth; in addition to the above items, the appraiser must confirm the house number, structure and use of buildings.

　　The appraiser also has to ascertain whether the components of the subject property registered in the real property registry book differ in any way from the actual circumstances.

Ⅱ **Identification of Ownership and Interests**
To identify ownership and interests, the appraiser must check the title to the subject property, as physically described above in paragraph Ⅰ, against identification data. All titles to or interests in the subject property must be confirmed.

第8章　鑑定評価の手順

　鑑定評価を行うためには、合理的かつ現実的な認識と判断に基づいた一定の秩序的な手順を必要とする。この手順は、一般に鑑定評価の基本的事項の確定、処理計画の策定、対象不動産の確認、資料の収集及び整理、資料の検討及び価格形成要因の分析、鑑定評価方式の適用、試算価格又は試算賃料の調整、鑑定評価額の決定並びに鑑定評価報告書の作成の作業から成っており、不動産の鑑定評価に当たっては、これらを秩序的に実施すべきである。

第1節　鑑定評価の基本的事項の確定
　鑑定評価に当たっては、まず、鑑定評価の基本的事項を確定しなければならない。このため、鑑定評価の依頼目的及び条件について依頼者の意思を明瞭に確認するものとする。

第2節　処理計画の策定
　処理計画の策定に当たっては、前記第1節により確定された鑑定評価の基本的事項に基づき、実施すべき作業の性質及び量、処理能力等に即応して、対象不動産の確認、資料の収集及び整理、資料の検討及び価格形成要因の分析、鑑定評価方式の適用、試算価格又は試算賃料の調整、鑑定評価額の決定等鑑定評価の作業に係る処理計画を秩序的に策定しなければならない。

第3節　対象不動産の確認
　対象不動産の確認に当たっては、前記第1節により確定された対象不動産についてその内容を明瞭にしなければならない。対象不動産の確認は、対象不動産の物的確認及び権利の態様の確認に分けられ、実地調査、聴聞、公的資料の確認等により、的確に行う必要がある。

Ⅰ　対象不動産の物的確認
　対象不動産の物的確認に当たっては、土地についてはその所在、地番、数量等を、建物についてはこれらのほか家屋番号、建物の構造、用途等を、それぞれ実地に確認することを通じて、前記第1節により確定された対象不動産の存否及びその内容を、確認資料（第4節のⅠ参照）を用いて照合しなければならない。
　また、物的確認を行うに当たっては、対象不動産について登記簿等において登記又は登録されている内容とその実態との異同について把握する必要がある。

Ⅱ　権利の態様の確認
　権利の態様の確認に当たっては、前記Ⅰによって物的に確認された対象不動産について、当該不動産に係るすべての権利関係を明瞭に確認することにより、前記第1節により確定された鑑定評価の対象となる権利の存否及びその内容を、確認資料を用いて照合しなければならない。

General Standards Chapter 8

Section 4. Gathering and Organizing of Data
Since the results of an appraisal depend on the data that is used, the gathering and selection of data must be performed in a dependable manner through site inspection, interviews and confirmation of public data. This step of the appraisal process should be based on a rational plan appropriate to the appraisal assignment, and should produce objective and valid data.

Data required for appraisals can generally be categorized as indicated below.

I Property Identification Data
Property identification data refers to the data required to identify the physical characteristics of, and title encumbrances on, the real estate. Examples of identification data include the land registry book, drawings of the land or building, photographs, and maps showing the location of the real estate.

II Data on Value Influences
This category of data refers to data that reflects a variety of value influences. Data on value influences may be divided into data pertaining to general value influences, data pertaining to market- specific value influences, and data pertaining to property- specific value influences.

General and market- specific data should be routinely gathered in an organized manner for a broad range of value influences. Property- specific data should be appropriately gathered on different types of properties and property characteristics.

III Comparable Data
Comparable data refers to data relating to actual transaction prices or rents required to apply the appraisal approaches. Examples of comparable data include construction data, comparable sales data, income data and leasing data.

There are also cases in which the appraiser can refer to the previous appraisal values and asking prices of comparable properties.

Section 5. Review of Data and Analysis of Value Influences
The data gathered must be examined to determine whether it satisfies the needs of the appraisal assignment, and whether or not it is sufficiently reliable. In particular, the data should be reviewed to determine whether or not it describes properties similar to the subject property, suits the purpose of the assignment, and allows for proper analysis of value influences.

In analyzing value influences, the appraiser examines all the data that has been collected. After investigating general value influences, the appraiser studies market- specific and property- specific value influences to determine the highest and best use of the subject property.

In cases where the effect of influences on the value of the subject property cannot be clearly determined despite the appraiser's having undertaken all the required research, it may be necessary to rely on the results of the investigation of another professional. Sometimes, because of restrictions resulting from the client's request, the appraiser will only be able to perform the appraisal by imposing additional assumptions or limiting conditions with the consent of the client. In other cases, the appraiser will have to determine the effect of

第4節　資料の収集及び整理

　鑑定評価の成果は、採用した資料によって左右されるものであるから、資料の収集及び整理は、鑑定評価の作業に活用し得るように適切かつ合理的な計画に基づき、実地調査、聴聞、公的資料の確認等により的確に行うものとし、公正妥当を欠くようなことがあってはならない。
　鑑定評価に必要な資料は、おおむね次のように分けられる。

I　確認資料

　確認資料とは、不動産の物的確認及び権利の態様の確認に必要な資料をいう。確認資料としては、登記簿謄本、土地又は建物等の図面、写真、不動産の所在地に関する地図等があげられる。

II　要因資料

　要因資料とは、価格形成要因に照応する資料をいう。要因資料は、一般的要因に係る一般資料、地域要因に係る地域資料及び個別的要因に係る個別資料に分けられる。一般資料及び地域資料は、平素からできるだけ広くかつ組織的に収集しておくべきである。個別資料は、対象不動産の種類、対象確定条件等案件の相違に応じて適切に収集すべきである。

III　事例資料

　事例資料とは、鑑定評価の手法の適用に必要とされる現実の取引価格、賃料等に関する資料をいう。事例資料としては、建設事例、取引事例、収益事例、賃貸借等の事例等があげられる。
　なお、鑑定評価先例価格は鑑定評価に当たって参考資料とし得る場合があり、売買希望価格等についても同様である。

第5節　資料の検討及び価格形成要因の分析

　資料の検討に当たっては、収集された資料についてそれが鑑定評価の作業に活用するために必要にして十分な資料であるか否か、資料が信頼するに足りるものであるか否かについて考察しなければならない。この場合においては、価格形成要因を分析するために、その資料が対象不動産の種類並びに鑑定評価の依頼目的及び条件に即応しているか否かについて検討すべきである。
　価格形成要因の分析に当たっては、収集された資料に基づき、一般的要因を分析するとともに、地域分析及び個別分析を通じて対象不動産についてその最有効使用を判定しなければならない。
　さらに、価格形成要因について、専門職業家としての注意を尽くしてもなお対象不動産の価格形成に重大な影響を与える要因が明らかでない場合には、原則として他の専門家が行った調査結果等を活用することが必要である。ただし、依頼目的や依頼条件による制約がある場合には、依頼者の同意を得て、想定上の条件を付加して鑑定評価を行うこと又は自己の調査分析能力の範囲内で当該要因に係る価格形成上の影響の程度を推定して鑑定評価を行うことができる。この場合、想定上の条件を付加するためには条件設定に係る一定の要件を満たすことが必要であり、また、推定を行うためには客観的な推定ができると認められることが必要である。

General Standards Chapter 8

value influences on the subject property based on his / her own investigative and analytical capabilities. In such situations, it is necessary to report all additional assumptions imposed to perform the appraisal assignment and to arrive at the value estimate.

Section 6. Application of Appraisal Method

The appraisal method applied should be appropriate to the subject of the appraisal. As a general rule, all three methodologies, i. e., the cost approach, sales comparison approach, and income capitalization approach, should be employed. Where the type of subject property or circumstances involving the property's location or reliability of the data make it difficult to apply each of the three approaches, every possible effort should be made to incorporate concepts from all approaches.

Section 7. Reconciliation of the Indicated Value or Rent

Reconciliation of the indicated values or indicated rents refers to the task of reconsidering the value or rent indicated by each appraisal approach, and judging the persuasiveness of each indicated value or indicated rent. Upon completing this step, the appraiser can determine the opinion of value that serves as the final judgment of the appraisal.

In reconciling the indicated values or indicated rents, it is important for the appraiser to be able to explain value influences acting on the subject property in both a logical and empirical manner. Consequently, reconciliation is performed by objectively and critically reconsidering each stage of the appraisal process and judging the weight to be placed on each indicated value or indicated rent. Attention must be given to the matters listed below.

I In reconsidering each indicated value or indicated rent, the following should be addressed:
1. the suitability of the data selected and reviewed
2. the appropriateness of the data used in view of the principles of value applied in valuing the subject real estate
3. the suitability of the analysis of general value influences as well as the analyses of the neighborhood and subject property
4. the appropriateness of judgments pertaining to various adjustments made in applying each method
5. the consistency of judgment applied to value influences commonly dealt with in each method
6. the suitability of the correlation between unit price and total value

II In forming judgments about the weight to be placed on each indicated value or indicated rent, the following should be addressed:
1. the consistency between the results obtained and each technique applied in the analyses of the neighborhood and subject property
2. the relative reliability of the indicated value or indicated rent, based on the characteristics and/or limitations of the data used in applying each method

Section 8. Determination of the Final Opinion of Value

After having performed the procedures described above, the appraiser is able to determine

第6節　鑑定評価方式の適用

　鑑定評価方式の適用に当たっては、鑑定評価方式を当該案件に即して適切に適用すべきである。この場合、原則として、原価方式、比較方式及び収益方式の三方式を併用すべきであり、対象不動産の種類、所在地の実情、資料の信頼性等により三方式の併用が困難な場合においても、その考え方をできるだけ参酌するように努めるべきである。

第7節　試算価格又は試算賃料の調整

　試算価格又は試算賃料の調整とは、鑑定評価の複数の手法により求められた各試算価格又は試算賃料の再吟味及び各試算価格又は試算賃料が有する説得力に係る判断を行い、鑑定評価における最終判断である鑑定評価額の決定に導く作業をいう。

　試算価格又は試算賃料の調整に当たっては、対象不動産の価格形成を論理的かつ実証的に説明できるようにすることが重要である。このため、鑑定評価の手順の各段階について、客観的、批判的に再吟味し、その結果を踏まえた各試算価格又は各試算賃料が有する説得力の違いを適切に反映することによりこれを行うものとする。この場合において、特に次の事項に留意すべきである。

Ⅰ　各試算価格又は試算賃料の再吟味
　1．資料の選択、検討及び活用の適否
　2．不動産の価格に関する諸原則の当該案件に即応した活用の適否
　3．一般的要因の分析並びに地域分析及び個別分析の適否
　4．各手法の適用において行った各種補正、修正等に係る判断の適否
　5．各手法に共通する価格形成要因に係る判断の整合性
　6．単価と総額との関連の適否

Ⅱ　各試算価格又は試算賃料が有する説得力に係る判断
　1．対象不動産に係る地域分析及び個別分析の結果と各手法との適合性
　2．各手法の適用において採用した資料の特性及び限界からくる相対的信頼性

第8節　鑑定評価額の決定

　以上に述べた手順を十分に尽した後、専門職業家としての良心に従い適正と判断される鑑定評

a final opinion of value, considered to be reasonable and conscionable.

In compliance with Article 2, Paragraph 1 of the *Land Price Publication Act*, the published land price must be used as a standard for determining the market value of land in published land areas.

Section 9. Preparation of the Appraisal Report
The appraisal report is prepared after the final opinion of value has been determined.

価額を決定すべきである。
　この場合において、地価公示法第2条第1項の公示区域において土地の正常価格を求めるときは、公示価格を規準としなければならない。

第9節　鑑定評価報告書の作成
　鑑定評価額が決定されたときは、鑑定評価報告書を作成するものとする。

General Standards Chapter 9

CHAPTER 9. APPRAISAL REPORT

The appraisal report is a document containing the results of a real estate appraisal. Its purpose is to clearly present the judgment and opinion of the LREA, based on his or her specialized knowledge and experience, and to clarify the scope of the appraiser's liability.

Section 1. Guidelines for Preparing Appraisal Report

The primary objective of the appraisal report is to communicate the basis of the appraisal and the final value opinion, to explain the rationale for the final value opinion, and to indicate the extent of the liability of the LREA involved in the real estate appraisal. Thus, the appraiser should prepare the report by first organizing all data used in the appraisal process, and then clarifying matters relating to judgment of value influences, judgment in applying appraisal methodology, and so forth.

The contents of the appraisal report are the substance of the appraisal document presented to the client by the LREA's firm. (Editor's Note: The standards distinguish an appraisal report from an appraisal document although the contents of the two documents are identical. The report is presented to the client with the signature of the appraiser through the appraisal firms) The appraisal report has an effect on not only the client but also on third parties, and serves as a basis for an orderly real estate value formation. Thus, offering clarification to ensure there is no room for misunderstanding, every effort must be made in preparing the report to adequately explain to the client and third party readers the rationale for the final value opinion.

Section 2. Report Contents

The appraisal report must contain, as a minimum, the following items (I through IX), and address the other matters indicated below.

I **Final Opinion of Value and Type of Value or Rental Value**

In accordance with the function and conditions of the valuation as requested by the client, the appraiser may estimate special value, value for regulated purposes (VRP) or special rent in an assignment that might be to arrive at market value or market rent. When the appraiser chooses to do so, the appraiser must report the market value or market rent in parentheses after the appraised value or rent. When asked to estimate nominal rent, as defined in CHAPTER 7, Section 2- I- 1, the appraiser must also indicate the type of rent beside the appraisal figure. If the nominal rent differs from the real rent, the appraiser also includes the real rent in parentheses after the nominal rent.

II **Assumptions and Limiting Conditions of the Appraisal**

Where deemed necessary, the report will not only clarify the rationale for imposing assumptions and limiting conditions regarding market- specific and property- specific value influences (and explain their validity in terms of the function of the appraisal and the client's request) but also indicate what the value would be if such assumptions had not been made.

第9章　鑑定評価報告書

　鑑定評価報告書は、不動産の鑑定評価の成果を記載した文書であり、不動産鑑定士が自己の専門的学識と経験に基づいた判断と意見を表明し、その責任を明らかにすることを目的とするものである。

第1節　鑑定評価報告書の作成指針

　鑑定評価報告書は、鑑定評価の基本的事項及び鑑定評価額を表し、鑑定評価額を決定した理由を説明し、その不動産の鑑定評価に関与した不動産鑑定士の責任の所在を示すことを主旨とするものであるから、鑑定評価報告書の作成に当たっては、まずその鑑定評価の過程において採用したすべての資料を整理し、価格形成要因に関する判断、鑑定評価方式の適用に係る判断等に関する事項を明確にして、これに基づいて作成すべきである。

　鑑定評価報告書の内容は、不動産鑑定業者が依頼者に交付する鑑定評価書の実質的な内容となるものである。したがって、鑑定評価報告書は、鑑定評価書を通じて依頼者のみならず第三者に対しても影響を及ぼすものであり、さらには不動産の適正な価格の形成の基礎となるものであるから、その作成に当たっては、誤解の生ずる余地を与えないよう留意するとともに、特に鑑定評価額の決定の理由については、依頼者その他第三者に対して十分に説明し得るものとするように努めなければならない。

第2節　記載事項

　鑑定評価報告書には、少なくともⅠ～Ⅸの事項について、次に記する点に留意して記載しなければならない。

Ⅰ　鑑定評価額及び価格又は賃料の種類

　正常価格又は正常賃料を求めることができる不動産について、依頼目的及び条件により限定価格、特定価格又は限定賃料を求めた場合は、かっこ書きで正常価格又は正常賃料である旨を付記してそれらの額を併記しなければならない。また、総論第7章、第2節、Ⅰの1．に定める支払賃料の鑑定評価を依頼された場合における鑑定評価額の記載は、支払賃料である旨を付記して支払賃料の額を表示するとともに、当該支払賃料が実質賃料と異なる場合においては、かっこ書きで実質賃料である旨を付記して実質賃料の額を併記するものとする。

Ⅱ　鑑定評価の条件

　対象確定条件又は依頼目的に応じ付加された地域要因若しくは個別的要因についての想定上の条件についてそれらが妥当なものであると判断した根拠を明らかにするとともに、必要があると認められるときは、当該条件が付加されない場合の価格等の参考事項を記載すべきである。

III Location of the subject property, lot number, category of land, house number, structure, use, area and the types of title encumbrances pertaining to the subject property

IV Correspondence between the Function and Conditions of the Appraisal and the Type of Value or Rent Estimated

The report must state the rationale for determining the type of value estimated according to the function and conditions of the appraisal. In particular, where the type of value is value for regulated purposes (VRP), the report must clearly indicate the relevant laws and ordinances, which call for the special considerations. Where the type of value is value of special-purpose property, the report must indicate the facts such as the property's designation as a cultural asset.

V Date of the Value Opinion and Date of the Appraisal Report

Together with the date of the opinion of value and the date when the appraisal is completed, the report must indicate the date of the property inspection. This is important because questions about the actual state of the property may arise at a later date.

VI The Principal Reasons for the Final Opinion of Value

The principal reasons for selecting the final value opinion are discussed under the topics listed below.

1. **Analyses of the Neighborhood of value and Subject Property**

   The appraisal report must include discussion of the following items: the location and character of the primary market area and neighborhood, the value influences acting on the subject property, market trends in the primary market area and the behavior of typical market participants in the primary market area, the superiority or inferiority of the subject property in relation to substitutive or competitive real estate, and the relative competitiveness of the subject property.

2. **The Highest and Best Use of the Subject Property**

   The highest and best use of the subject property and how it was determined must be clearly described. Furthermore, where the highest and best use of a building and the building site are to be determined, the report must identify the highest and best use of the building site as though vacant.

3. **The Application of the Appraisal Approaches**

   Where all three appraisal approaches cannot be applied, the reason for not doing so must be explained.

4. **The Indicated Value or Indicated Rent**

   The report must explain the appraiser's reconciliation of the indicated values or indicated rents and the reason that the appraiser judged it to be persuasive.

5. **Compliance with the Requirement to Report the Published Price of Land**

6. **Other Matters**

   Where the purpose of the appraisal is to determine nominal rent as discussed in CHAPTER 7, Section 2-I-1 of these Standards, the report must describe the relationship between that nominal rent and the effective rent.

VII Handling of Ambiguous Appraisal Matters and the Scope of the Investi-

Ⅲ 対象不動産の所在、地番、地目、家屋番号、構造、用途、数量等及び対象不動産に係る権利の種類

Ⅳ 鑑定評価の依頼目的及び条件と価格又は賃料の種類との関連
　鑑定評価の依頼目的及び条件に応じ、当該価格を求めるべきと判断した理由を記載しなければならない。特に、特定価格を求めた場合には法令等による社会的要請の根拠、また、特殊価格を求めた場合には文化財の指定の事実等を明らかにしなければならない。

Ⅴ 価格時点及び鑑定評価を行った年月日
　後日対象不動産の現況把握に疑義が生ずる場合があることを考慮して、実際に現地に赴き対象不動産の現況を確認した年月日（実査日）をあわせて記載しなければならない。

Ⅵ 鑑定評価額の決定の理由の要旨
　鑑定評価額の決定の理由の要旨は、下記に掲げる内容について記載するものとする。

　1．地域分析及び個別分析に係る事項
　　同一需給圏及び近隣地域の範囲及び状況、対象不動産に係る価格形成要因についての状況、同一需給圏の市場動向及び同一需給圏における典型的な市場参加者の行動、代替、競争等の関係にある不動産と比べた対象不動産の優劣及び競争力の程度等について記載しなければならない。

　2．最有効使用の判定に関する事項
　　最有効使用及びその判定の理由を明確に記載する。なお、建物及びその敷地に係る鑑定評価における最有効使用の判定の記載は、建物及びその敷地の最有効使用のほか、その敷地の更地としての最有効使用についても記載しなければならない。

　3．鑑定評価方式の適用に関する事項
　　鑑定評価の三方式を併用することが困難な場合にはその理由を記載するものとする。

　4．試算価格又は試算賃料の調整に関する事項
　　試算価格又は試算賃料の再吟味及び説得力に係る判断の結果を記載しなければならない。

　5．公示価格との規準に関する事項

　6．その他
　　総論第7章、第2節、Ⅰの1．に定める支払賃料を求めた場合には、その支払賃料と実質賃料との関連を記載しなければならない。

Ⅶ 鑑定評価上の不明事項に係る取扱い及び調査の範囲

General Standards Chapter 9

gation

The report must clearly indicate how matters were handled that could not be clarified because of limitations on, or insufficiency of, data at any stage of the appraisal process (e.g., in identifying the subject property, reviewing the data compiled, or analyzing value influences). LREAs must describe the scope and content of the investigations they themselves conducted, and when they made use of investigations conducted by other professionals, the scope and content of those investigations must be clearly indicated.

Ⅷ **Interests in the Subject Property Held by the LREA Involved in the Real Estate Appraisal, or Any Relationships to Persons with Interests in the Subject Property That May Give Rise to Conflicts of Interest**

Ⅸ **Name of the LREA involved in the appraisal of the real estate**

Section 3. Addenda to Appraisal Reports

Maps clearly showing the location of the subject property, drawings of the land and/or buildings, photographs and other identification data as well as comparable data may be attached to the appraisal report when appropriate.

Data acquired from the reports of investigations conducted by other professionals may also be attached to the appraisal report. However, such data may only be attached to the appraisal report when the consent of the professional, who complied it, has been obtained.

対象不動産の確認、資料の検討及び価格形成要因の分析等、鑑定評価の手順の各段階において、鑑定評価における資料収集の限界、資料の不備等によって明らかにすることができない事項が存する場合の評価上の取扱いを明示する必要がある。その際、不動産鑑定士が自ら行った調査の範囲及び内容を明確にするとともに、他の専門家が行った調査結果等を活用した場合においては、当該専門家が調査した範囲及び内容を明確にしなければならない。

Ⅷ　その不動産の鑑定評価に関与した不動産鑑定士の対象不動産に関する利害関係又は対象不動産に関し利害関係を有する者との縁故若しくは特別の利害関係の有無及びその内容

Ⅸ　その不動産の鑑定評価に関与した不動産鑑定士の氏名

第3節　附属資料

　対象不動産等の所在を明示した地図、土地又は建物等の図面、写真等の確認資料、事例資料等は、必要に応じて鑑定評価報告書に添付するものとする。

　なお、他の専門家が行った調査結果等を活用するために入手した調査報告書等の資料についても、必要に応じて、附属資料として添付するものとする。ただし、当該他の専門家の同意が得られないときは、この限りでない。

SPECIFIC STANDARDS (SS)

LREAs perform appraisals of individual properties on the basis of their own specialized knowledge, professional capabilities, and in accordance with General Standards. To ensure competent appraisals of specific property types, practitioners should employ techniques corresponding to those associated with the use and title categories of real estate discussed below.

CHAPTER 1. APPRAISAL OF REAL ESTATE VALUE

Section 1. Land
Ⅰ **Building Sites**
  1. **Vacant Land**
  The final opinion of the value of vacant land is determined by reconciling the value indicated by the sales comparison approach (based on comparable sales data on both vacant land and land with owner-occupied improvements) and the value indicated by the income capitalization approach (when the appraiser can estimate the value of the improvements, using methods other than the income capitalization approach, and is also able to determine the expected building and land capitalization rates, the value of the land is developed by the land residual technique, which allocates the net operating income [NOI] to the property between the building and the land, and capitalizes NOI to the land.).

  Where reproduction cost can be estimated, the final value opinion should be formed by reconciling value indications from the sales comparison, income capitalization, and cost approaches. In cases where the area of the subject land is larger than the area of the standard plot size for the neighborhood, the final value opinion should be determined by comparing the values that would result from the following alternative valuation methods (subdivision development analysis):

  (1) When a condominium or townhouse building is recognized as being the rational use, the value of the vacant land may be obtained by deducting the normal building construction costs and incidental expenses (to be borne directly by the builder) from the total sales price, assuming the construction of the building, which represents the highest and best use of the site as of the date of the value opinion.

  (2) When subdivision is recognized as being the rational use, the value of the vacant land may be obtained by deducting the normal site preparation costs and incidental expenses (to be borne directly by the builder) from the total sales price, assuming the subdivision of the vacant land and creation of standard sized building sites as of the date of the value opinion (this approach is referred to as the subdivision development approach).

  When applying allocation and land residual techniques, the appraiser should use comparable sales data and income data that reflect the prices paid for, or income

各 論

　不動産鑑定士は、総論において記述したところに従い自己の専門的学識と応用能力に基づき、個々の案件に応じて不動産の鑑定評価を行うべきであるが、具体的な案件に臨んで的確な鑑定評価を期するためには、基本的に以下に掲げる不動産の種類別に応じた鑑定評価の手法等を活用する必要がある。

第1章　価格に関する鑑定評価

第1節　土地

Ⅰ　宅地

1．更地

　更地の鑑定評価額は、更地並びに自用の建物及びその敷地の取引事例に基づく比準価格並びに土地残余法（建物等の価格を収益還元法以外の手法によって求めることができる場合に、敷地と建物等からなる不動産について敷地に帰属する純収益から敷地の収益価格を求める方法）による収益価格を関連づけて決定するものとする。再調達原価が把握できる場合には、積算価格をも関連づけて決定すべきである。当該更地の面積が近隣地域の標準的な土地の面積に比べて大きい場合等においては、さらに次に掲げる価格を比較考量して決定するものとする（この手法を開発法という。）。

(1)　一体利用をすることが合理的と認められるときは、価格時点において、当該更地に最有効使用の建物が建築されることを想定し、販売総額から通常の建物建築費相当額及び発注者が直接負担すべき通常の付帯費用を控除して得た価格

(2)　分割利用をすることが合理的と認められるときは、価格時点において、当該更地を区画割りして、標準的な宅地とすることを想定し、販売総額から通常の造成費相当額及び発注者が直接負担すべき通常の付帯費用を控除して得た価格

　なお、配分法及び土地残余法を適用する場合における取引事例及び収益事例は、敷地が最有効使用の状態にあるものを採用すべきである。

generated by, the lot under its highest and best use.

2. Land Portion of Built-Up Property

The land portion of a built-up property refers to a building site on which an improvement stands. The utility of land in this category is recognized as being closely associated with the building. Thus, the land portion of built-up property is appraised on the basis of its severance value when the current use is deemed reasonable.

As a general rule, the upper limit on the value of the land portion of built-up property is set by the value of the land as though vacant. The appraised value of the land portion of built-up property is determined by reconciling the value indicated by the sales comparison approach (developed by the allocation method) with the value indicated by the income capitalization approach (developed by the land residual technique).

The appraiser should consider 1) whether there is any difference between the highest and best use of the property as improved and the site as though vacant, 2) the degree of difficulty in demolishing the improvements, and 3) how well the building suits the site.

3. Leasehold Interests in Land and Leased Fee Interests in Land

Since the value of the leasehold interest in land and the value of the leased fee interest in land are closely related, the appraiser should compare the two values. In particular, the appraiser should consider the matters indicated below.

① Leasing practices involving building sites, and the characteristics of the sales market of leasehold and leased fee interests may differ depending on the city, and even within the same city, depending on the area.

② The existence of a leasehold interest in land does not necessarily mean that the leasehold interest in the land has value. Furthermore, there are some cities or areas where the conveyance of leasehold interests in land is negotiated independently. While in other cities or areas, the conveyance of leasehold interests in land is negotiated in conjunction with building transactions.

③ The appraiser should consider the area where the leasehold interest in land is being conveyed, i.e.,
   a. Whether or not it is an area where leasehold interests bear value when they are originally contracted or transferred
   b. Whether or not it is an area where leasehold interests in land are conveyed by transactions that typically involve persons other than owners
   c. Whether or not it is an area where many leasehold interests in land are held by the owners of steel and concrete frame (solid) buildings
   d. Whether or not it is an area where tenants have a strong awareness of leasehold interests in land
   e. Whether or not it is an area where receipt of deposits is a common practice
   f. Whether or not it is an area where the seller or the buyer of a leasehold in land usually pays a transfer agreement fee

④ The appraiser should consider the forms of the leasehold interest in land, i.e.,
   a. Originally contracted or transferred,
   b. Whether a superficies or a regular ground lease
   c. Whether or not a sublease

2．建付地

建付地は、建物等と結合して有機的にその効用を発揮しているため、建物等と密接な関連を持つものであり、したがって、建付地の鑑定評価は、建物等と一体として継続使用することが合理的である場合において、その敷地について部分鑑定評価をするものである。

建付地の鑑定評価額は、原則として更地としての鑑定評価額を限度とし、配分法に基づく比準価格及び土地残余法による収益価格を関連づけて決定するものとする。

この場合において、当該建付地の更地としての最有効使用との格差、更地化の難易の程度等敷地と建物等との関連性を考慮すべきである。

3．借地権及び底地

借地権及び底地の鑑定評価に当たっては、借地権の価格と底地の価格とは密接に関連し合っているので、以下に述べる諸点を十分に考慮して相互に比較検討すべきである。

① 宅地の賃貸借等及び借地権取引の慣行の有無とその成熟の程度は、都市によって異なり、同一都市内においても地域によって異なることもあること。
② 借地権の存在は、必ずしも借地権の価格の存在を意味するものではなく、また、借地権取引の慣行について、借地権が単独で取引の対象となっている都市又は地域と、単独で取引の対象となることはないが建物の取引に随伴して取引の対象となっている都市又は地域とがあること。

③ 借地権取引の態様
　ア　借地権が一般に有償で創設され、又は継承される地域であるか否か。
　イ　借地権の取引が一般に所有者以外の者を対象として行われる地域であるか否か。
　ウ　堅固建物の所有を目的とする借地権の多い地域であるか否か。
　エ　借地権に対する権利意識について借地人側が強い地域であるか否か。
　オ　一時金の授受が慣行化している地域であるか否か。
　カ　借地権の譲渡に当たって名義書替料を一般に譲受人又は譲渡人のいずれが負担する地域であるか。

④ 借地権の態様
　ア　創設されたものか継承されたものか。
　イ　地上権か賃借権か。
　ウ　転借か否か。

Specific Standards Chapter 1

d. Whether the purpose is to own a steel and concrete frame (solid) building or a wooden frame (non- solid) building
e. Whether it is primarily a building for residency or for commercial use
f. The presence or absence of a stipulated lease term
g. The presence or absence of special provisions
h. Whether the contract is written or oral
i. The presence or absence of title registration
J. Periodic leasehold interests in land (periodic leasehold interests in land as stipulated in Section 2, Paragraph 4 of the *Land Lease and Building Lease Law*) (Editor's Note: A periodic lease on land is a land lease for a fixed term.)

(1) **Leasehold Interests in Land**
① **Value of Leasehold Interests in Land**
The value of a leasehold interest in land reflects the monetary value of the economic advantage, including the amortized amount of non- refundable deposits, attributable to the tenant, who leases the land based on the *Land Lease and Building Lease Law* (including the former *Ground Lease Law*).

The economic advantage attributable to the tenant includes a wide variety of benefits generated by use of the land. This advantage primarily consists of:
a. Stability from being able to occupy the land for a long period of time and to enjoy the benefit from its exclusive use.
b. The marketability of a leasehold interest in land supported by the present value of the difference between market rent and contract rent. The present value is calculated on the basis of the period during which that difference lasts. The market rent here reflects the market value of the site, in which the leasehold interest exists.

② **Appraisal of Leasehold Interests in Land**
The approach used for appraising leasehold interests in land differs according to the maturity of the leasing market.

a. **Areas where a mature leasing market exists**
The final opinion of the value of a leasehold interest in land is based on reconciling the value indications from four possible methods. These include: (i) the sales comparison approach (based on either comparable leasehold interests in land or comparable properties on leased land); (ii) the land residual technique (applied here to arrive at the value of the leasehold interest in land); (iii) the income capitalization approach (based on capitalizing the difference between the market rent and contract rent); and (iv) the leasehold ratio method (the ratio of a typical leasehold value to fee simple value in an area). The appraiser should place more weight on the first two methods in reconciling indicated values.

The following matters should all be considered.
(a) The potential for future revision of the rent and the amount of this revision
(b) The forms of the leasehold interest in land (see above 3.-④-(a) through (j)) and the remaining economic life of the building

エ　堅固の建物の所有を目的とするか、非堅固の建物の所有を目的とするか。
オ　主として居住用建物のためのものか、主として営業用建物のためのものか。
カ　契約期間の定めの有無
キ　特約条項の有無
ク　契約は書面か口頭か
ケ　登記の有無
コ　定期借地権等（借地借家法第二章第四節に規定する定期借地権等）

(1)　借地権
　①　借地権の価格
　　借地権の価格は、借地借家法（廃止前の借地法を含む。）に基づき土地を使用収益することにより借地人に帰属する経済的利益（一時金の授受に基づくものを含む。）を貨幣額で表示したものである。
　　借地人に帰属する経済的利益とは、土地を使用収益することによる広範な諸利益を基礎とするものであるが、特に次に掲げるものが中心となる。
　ア　土地を長期間占有し、独占的に使用収益し得る借地人の安定的利益
　イ　借地権の付着している宅地の経済価値に即応した適正な賃料と実際支払賃料との乖離（以下「賃料差額」という。）及びその乖離の持続する期間を基礎にして成り立つ経済的利益の現在価値のうち、慣行的に取引の対象となっている部分

　②　借地権の鑑定評価
　　借地権の鑑定評価は、借地権の取引慣行の有無及びその成熟の程度によってその手法を異にするものである。
　ア　借地権の取引慣行の成熟の程度の高い地域
　　借地権の鑑定評価額は、借地権及び借地権を含む複合不動産の取引事例に基づく比準価格並びに土地残余法による収益価格を関連づけて得た価格を標準とし、当該借地権の設定契約に基づく賃料差額のうち取引の対象となっている部分を還元して得た価格及び借地権取引が慣行として成熟している場合における当該地域の借地権割合により求めた価格を比較考量して決定するものとする。
　　この場合においては、次に掲げる事項を総合的に勘案するものとする。
　　(ｱ)　将来における賃料の改定の実現性とその程度
　　(ｲ)　借地権の態様及び建物の残存耐用年数
　　(ｳ)　契約締結の経緯並びに経過した借地期間及び残存期間
　　(ｴ)　契約に当たって授受された一時金の額及びこれに関する契約条件
　　(ｵ)　将来見込まれる一時金の額及びこれに関する契約条件
　　(ｶ)　借地権の取引慣行及び底地の取引利回り
　　(ｷ)　当該借地権の存する土地に係る更地としての価格又は建付地としての価格

(c) The background to the contract negotiations (i.e., relations between the renter and the landlord), the lease period that has already elapsed, and the remaining period of the lease
(d) The amount of the deposit received in closing the contract and any related contract terms
(e) The expected amounts of future deposits and related contract terms
(f) The typical transaction pattern of leasehold interests in land (leasehold interests in the land alone or in land with improvements) and market- derived capitalization rates of ground leases
(g) The value of the site being leased (vacant land or the land portion of built- up property)

b. Areas where a mature leasing market does not exist

The final opinion of the value of the leasehold interest in land is mainly based on the value indicated by the land residual technique. The appraiser also considers 1) the value obtained by capitalizing the difference between the market and contract rent (based on the conditions set in the leasehold contract); and 2) the value obtained by deducting the value of the leased fee interest in the land from the value of the site being leased (vacant land or the land portion of built- up property).

In these situations, items (a) through (g) above should all be considered.

(2) Leased Fee Interests in Land

The value of a leased fee interest in land reflects the economic benefit to the lessor. The benefit is closely related to the value of the leasehold interest in land.

The economic benefit to the lessor refers to the present value of the net operating income generated over the lease period, i.e., the amount remaining after deducting operating expenses from the actual nominal rent paid for the building site, plus the present value of the reversion upon the termination of the ground lease.

The final opinion of the value of a leased fee interest in land is determined by reconciling the value indicated by the income capitalization approach (the total present value of net operating income (NOI) based on the actual nominal rent and the reversion), and the value indicated by the sales comparison approach. In these situations, items (1)- ②- a- (a) through (g) above should all be considered.

In addition, it should be noted that if the tenant acquires the leased fee interest in the land, the economic value of the land may increase. This is attributable to the building site's greater marketability, resulting from the fact that the building and building site now belong to the same owner.

4. Sectional Superficies

The value of sectional superficies is typically based upon the value of the land, on which the sectional superficies are established. The specific economic benefits that derive from the creation of such superficies help determine their value. The value of sectional superficies is a monetary amount, reflecting two components: the economic value of the superficies, i.e., the rights to air or subsurface space ("two- or three- dimensional division of space"); and the economic value of the surrounding space whose utilization is restrict-

イ　借地権の取引慣行の成熟の程度の低い地域
　　　　　借地権の鑑定評価額は、土地残余法による収益価格を標準とし、当該借地権の設定契約に基づく賃料差額のうち取引の対象となっている部分を還元して得た価格及び当該借地権の存する土地に係る更地又は建付地としての価格から底地価格を控除して得た価格を比較考量して決定するものとする。
　　　　　この場合においては、前記アの㈦から㈹までに掲げる事項を総合的に勘案するものとする。

(2)　底地
　底地の価格は、借地権の付着している宅地について、借地権の価格との相互関連において賃貸人に帰属する経済的利益を貨幣額で表示したものである。
　賃貸人に帰属する経済的利益とは、当該宅地の実際支払賃料から諸経費等を控除した部分の賃貸借等の期間に対応する経済的利益及びその期間の満了等によって復帰する経済的利益の現在価値をいう。
　底地の鑑定評価額は、実際支払賃料に基づく純収益等の現在価値の総和を求めることにより得た収益価格及び比準価格を関連づけて決定するものとする。この場合においては、前記(1)、②、アの㈦から㈹までに掲げる事項を総合的に勘案するものとする。
　また、底地を当該借地人が買い取る場合における底地の鑑定評価に当たっては、当該宅地又は建物及びその敷地が同一所有者に帰属することによる市場性の回復等に即応する経済価値の増分が生ずる場合があることに留意すべきである。

4．区分地上権
　区分地上権の価格は、一般に区分地上権の設定に係る土地（以下「区分地上権設定地」という。）の経済価値を基礎として、権利の設定範囲における権利利益の内容により定まり、区分地上権設定地全体の経済価値のうち、平面的・立体的空間の分割による当該権利の設定部分の経済価値及び設定部分の効用を保持するため他の空間部分の利用を制限することに相応する経済価値を貨幣額で表示したものである。
　この場合の区分地上権の鑑定評価額は、設定事例等に基づく比準価格、土地残余法に準じ

ed by structures in the superficies space.

The final opinion of the value of sectional superficies is obtained by reconciling 1) the value indicated by the sales comparison approach based on analysis of contract data, 2) the value indicated by the income capitalization approach using a residual technique, and 3) the value developed by applying a vertical allotment ratio for sectional superficies, which is derived from comparable properties.

II Agricultural Land

Appraisals of agricultural land may be requested for transactions where the objective is to convert the agricultural land to another land use, e.g., the acquisition of land to be used for public works.

In such situations, the final opinion of the value of agricultural land is based on the values indicated by the sales comparison and income capitalization approaches. Where reproduction cost can be estimated, the final value opinion should be formed by reconciling the above value indications with the value indicated by the cost approach.

It should be noted that in acquisitions of agricultural land for public works, agricultural compensation is sometimes provided separately as compensation for the losses normally incurred in the land acquisition.

III Forestland

Appraisals of forestland may be requested for transactions where the objective is to convert the forestland to another land use, e.g., the acquisition of land to be used for public works.

In such situations, the final opinion of the value of forestland is based on the values indicated by the sales comparison and income approaches. Where reproduction cost can be estimated, the final value opinion should be formed by reconciling the above value indications with the value indicated by the cost approach.

It should be noted that in acquisitions of forestland for public works, there are cases in which forestation compensation is sometimes provided separately as compensation for the losses normally incurred in the land acquisition.

IV Building Sites with Interim Uses

The final opinion of the value of a building site with an interim use is determined by reconciling the value indicated by the sales comparison approach and the value indicated by the steps in the following method: (a) estimating the value of the subject site assuming all the site services are provided on the date of the value opinion; (b) deducting normal site preparation costs and normal incidental expenses (to be borne directly by the builder) from the estimated land value in (a); and (c) forecasting the time required to realize the land use conversion and adjusting the value derived in (b) accordingly. In particular, the appraiser should consider the effect of urban growth on the neighborhood as well as the following matters.

1. Government measures and/or regulations that facilitate or hinder conversion of the interim use building site to a building site ready to accommodate its next use
2. Current and anticipated construction of public and institutional facilities in the vicinity
3. Current and anticipated construction of housing, commercial facilities, and factories in the vicinity

て求めた収益価格及び区分地上権の立体利用率により求めた価格を関連づけて得た価格を標準とし、区分地上権の設定事例等に基づく区分地上権割合により求めた価格を比較考量して決定するものとする。

Ⅱ 農地

公共事業の用に供する土地の取得等農地を農地以外のものとするための取引に当たって、当該取引に係る農地の鑑定評価を求められる場合がある。

この場合における農地の鑑定評価額は、比準価格を標準とし、収益価格を参考として決定するものとする。再調達原価が把握できる場合には、積算価格をも関連づけて決定すべきである。

なお、公共事業の用に供する土地の取得に当たっては、土地の取得により通常生ずる損失の補償として農業補償が別途行われる場合があることに留意すべきである。

Ⅲ 林地

公共事業の用に供する土地の取得等林地を林地以外のものとするための取引に当たって、当該取引に係る林地の鑑定評価を求められる場合がある。

この場合における林地の鑑定評価額は、比準価格を標準とし、収益価格を参考として決定するものとする。再調達原価が把握できる場合には、積算価格をも関連づけて決定すべきである。

なお、公共事業の用に供する土地の取得に当たっては、土地の取得により通常生ずる損失の補償として立木補償等が別途行われる場合があることに留意すべきである。

Ⅳ 宅地見込地

宅地見込地の鑑定評価額は、比準価格及び当該宅地見込地について、価格時点において、転換後・造成後の更地を想定し、その価格から通常の造成費相当額及び発注者が直接負担すべき通常の付帯費用を控除し、その額を当該宅地見込地の熟成度に応じて適切に修正して得た価格を関連づけて決定するものとする。この場合においては、特に都市の外延的発展を促進する要因の近隣地域に及ぼす影響度及び次に掲げる事項を総合的に勘案するものとする。

1．当該宅地見込地の宅地化を助長し、又は阻害している行政上の措置又は規制
2．付近における公共施設及び公益的施設の整備の動向
3．付近における住宅、店舗、工場等の建設の動向
4．造成の難易及びその必要の程度
5．造成後における宅地としての有効利用度

また、熟成度の低い宅地見込地を鑑定評価する場合には、比準価格を標準とし、転換前の土地の種別に基づく価格に宅地となる期待性を加味して得た価格を比較考量して決定するものとする。

Specific Standards Chapter 1

4. How difficult the task of site preparation will be and how extensive the required site preparation will be
5. How effectively the site will be used as a building site following site preparation

When the interim use of a building site is anticipated to have a long duration, the final opinion of value is determined by placing the most emphasis on the sales comparison approach. The appraiser also looks at the value based on the original land use, considering the expected appreciation in value.

Section 2. Built-Up Property
I Owner – Occupied Building and Its Site

The final opinion of the value of an owner- occupied building and its site is determined by reconciling the values indicated by the cost, sales comparison and income capitalization approaches.

Where converting the use of the building or remodeling the building for another use is the highest and best use of an owner- occupied building and its site, the appraiser determines the value of the subject property after taking into account both the increase in economic value resulting from the change in use and the required remodeling costs.

Where demolition of the building is the highest and best use of an owner- occupied building and its site, the final opinion of value is determined by first deducting an estimate of the required expenses of demolition and removal of debris from the salvage value of the materials remaining after demolition of the building. The difference is added to the value of the lot under its highest and best use.

II Tenant – Occupied Buildings and Its Sites

In arriving at the final opinion of the value of a tenant- occupied building and its site, the appraiser places the most emphasis on the value indicated by the income capitalization approach (estimated as the total present value of both net operating income [NOI] generated from the actual effective rent and reversion). (In transactions where the seller does not pass on to the buyer part of the deposits that the seller received, the interest on and amortization of such portion of deposits are not included in the estimated NOI.) Then the appraiser compares this value with the values indicated by the cost and sales comparison approaches. All of the following matters should be considered.

1. The potential for future revision of rent and the amount of this revision
2. The amount of the deposit received in closing the contract and any related contract terms
3. The expected amounts of future deposits and related contract terms
4. Background to the contract negotiations (i.e., relations between the renter and the landlord), the lease period that has already elapsed, the remaining period of the lease, and the remaining economic life of the building
5. The typical transaction pattern of tenant- occupied buildings and its sites and the market- derived capitalization rates
6. Whether the tenancy in the leased building is residential or commercial, the form of the contract, whether or not the title is registered, whether or not there is a sublease, and whether or not it is a periodic building lease as stipulated in Article 38 of the

第2節　建物及びその敷地

I　自用の建物及びその敷地

　　自用の建物及びその敷地の鑑定評価額は、積算価格、比準価格及び収益価格を関連づけて決定するものとする。

　　なお、建物の用途を転換し、又は建物の構造等を改造して使用することが最有効使用と認められる場合における自用の建物及びその敷地の鑑定評価額は、用途変更後の経済価値の上昇の程度、必要とされる改造費等を考慮して決定するものとする。

　　また、建物を取り壊すことが最有効使用と認められる場合における自用の建物及びその敷地の鑑定評価額は、建物の解体による発生材料の価格から取壊し、除去、運搬等に必要な経費を控除した額を、当該敷地の最有効使用に基づく価格に加減して決定するものとする。

II　貸家及びその敷地

　　貸家及びその敷地の鑑定評価額は、実際実質賃料（売主が既に受領した一時金のうち売買等に当たって買主に承継されない部分がある場合には、当該部分の運用益及び償却額を含まないものとする。）に基づく純収益等の現在価値の総和を求めることにより得た収益価格を標準とし、積算価格及び比準価格を比較考量して決定するものとする。この場合において、次に掲げる事項を総合的に勘案するものとする。

1．将来における賃料の改定の実現性とその程度
2．契約に当たって授受された一時金の額及びこれに関する契約条件
3．将来見込まれる一時金の額及びこれに関する契約条件
4．契約締結の経緯、経過した借家期間及び残存期間並びに建物の残存耐用年数
5．貸家及びその敷地の取引慣行並びに取引利回り
6．借家の目的、契約の形式、登記の有無、転借か否かの別及び定期建物賃貸借（借地借家法第38条に規定する定期建物賃貸借をいう。）か否かの別
7．借家権価格

　　また、貸家及びその敷地を当該借家人が買い取る場合における貸家及びその敷地の鑑定評価に当たっては、当該貸家及びその敷地が自用の建物及びその敷地となることによる市場性の回復等に即応する経済価値の増分が生ずる場合があることに留意すべきである。

Specific Standards Chapter 1

Land Lease and Building Lease Law (Editor's Note: A periodic lease on a building is a building lease for a fixed term.)

7. The value of the tenant's rights (leasehold interest in building only)

It should be noted that if the tenant acquires the leased building and building site, the economic value of the site may increase. This is attributable to the greater marketability of the building and building site, resulting from the fact that the building and building site now belong to the same owner.

III Buildings on Leased Land

1. Owner – Occupied Buildings on Leased Land

The final opinion of the value of a building on land held in leasehold, where the leaseholder owns the building, is determined by reconciling the values indicated by the cost, sales comparison and income capitalization approaches. All the items indicated above in (1)- ②- a- (a) through (g) (the section on the Appraisal of Leasehold Interests in Land) should be considered.

2. Tenant – Occupied Buildings on Leased Land

In arriving at the final opinion of the value of a leased building on land held in leasehold, where the leaseholder to the land rents out the building, the appraiser places the most emphasis on the value indicated by the income capitalization approach (estimated as the total present value of both net operating income (NOI) generated from the actual effective rent and reversion). (In transactions where the seller does not pass on to the buyer part of the deposits that the seller received, the interest on and amortization of such portion of deposits are not included in estimated NOI). Then, the appraiser compares this value with the values indicated by the cost and sales comparison approaches.

The appraiser should consider all of the above indicated items (1)- ②- a- (a) through (g) (Leasehold Interests in Land) and 1 through 7 in II Tenant- Occupied Buildings and Building Sites.

IV Condominium Units

1. Value Influences on Condominium Units

The following list identifies typical property- specific value influences on condominium units.

(1) **Property – Specific Value Influences on the Building and Building Site where the Condominium Project is Located**

① **Influences on the Building**

a. The age of the structure (whether a new structure, an expansion/reconstruction, or relocation)

b. Building area, height, structure and materials

c. Design and functionality

d. Construction quality and volume

e. Type of entryway, availability of conference rooms and other facilities

f. The number of floors in the building

g. Intended usage and actual use of the building

h. Quality of the maintenance and management

i. Status of residents and mix of shops

Ⅲ　借地権付建物
　1．建物が自用の場合
　　　借地権付建物で、当該建物を借地権者が使用しているものについての鑑定評価額は、積算価格、比準価格及び収益価格を関連づけて決定するものとする。この場合において、前記借地権②、アの㋐から㋖までに掲げる事項を総合的に勘案するものとする。

　2．建物が賃貸されている場合
　　　借地権付建物で、当該建物が賃貸されているものについての鑑定評価額は、実際実質賃料（売主が既に受領した一時金のうち売買等に当たって買主に承継されない部分がある場合には、当該部分の運用益及び償却額を含まないものとする。）に基づく純収益等の現在価値の総和を求めることにより得た収益価格を標準とし、積算価格及び比準価格を比較考量して決定するものとする。
　　　この場合において、前記借地権②、アの㋐から㋖まで及び前記Ⅱの1．から7．までに掲げる事項を総合的に勘案するものとする。

Ⅳ　区分所有建物及びその敷地
　1．区分所有建物及びその敷地の価格形成要因
　　　区分所有建物及びその敷地における固有の個別的要因を例示すれば次のとおりである。

　　⑴　区分所有建物が存する一棟の建物及びその敷地に係る個別的要因

　　　　①　建物に係る要因
　　　　　ア　建築（新築、増改築又は移転）の年次
　　　　　イ　面積、高さ、構造、材質等
　　　　　ウ　設計、設備等の機能性
　　　　　エ　施工の質と量
　　　　　オ　玄関、集会室等の施設の状態
　　　　　カ　建物の階数
　　　　　キ　建物の用途及び利用の状態
　　　　　ク　維持管理の状態
　　　　　ケ　居住者、店舗等の構成の状態
　　　　　コ　耐震性、耐火性等建物の性能

Specific Standards Chapter 1

  j. Earthquake resistance, fire resistance and compliance with other building codes
  k. Whether any harmful substance was used in the construction, how it was used and whether it has been removed
 ② **Influences on the Site**
  a. The shape of the site and dimensions of any open space
  b. Facilities on the site
  c. The size of the site
  d. Ownership and interests in the site
 ③ **Influences on the Building and Building Site**
  a. Layout of the building and ancillary facilities on the site
  b. Relationship between the building and site size
  c. Any long-term repair project(s), the sufficiency thereof, and the amount of funds reserved for the repair project(s)
(2) **Property – Specific Value Influences on the Exclusively Owned Area**
 ① Floor level and location
 ② Sunlight, view and scenery
 ③ Interior finish and quality of maintenance and management
 ④ Area of the condominium unit, its floor plan and room layout
 ⑤ Whether adjacent real estate is in use and the nature of that use
 ⑥ Convenience of elevators and other common facilities
 ⑦ Unit entitlement to the fee simple/leasehold interest in the site
 ⑧ Amount of unpaid management and other fees by condominium owners

2. The Appraisal of Condominium Units

(1) **Owner – Occupied Units**

The final opinion of the value of an owner-occupied condominium unit, the exclusively owned portion of which is held in freehold by the condominium owner, is determined by reconciling the values indicated by the cost, sales comparison and income capitalization approaches.

The value indicated by the cost approach is developed on the basis of the depreciated cost of the building and the site value where the condominium unit is located. This figure is then multiplied by the distribution factor for the subject unit, determined from the utility ratio for each floor of the building and for each location on each floor.

(2) **Tenant – Occupied Units**

In arriving at the final opinion of value of a tenant-occupied condominium unit, the appraiser places the most emphasis on the value indicated by the income capitalization approach (estimated from the total present value of both the net operating income (NOI) generated from the actual real rent and reversion). (In transactions where the seller does not pass on to the buyer part of the deposits that the seller received, the interest on and amortization of such portion of deposits are not included in estimated NOI.) Then, the appraiser compares this value with the values indicated by the cost and sales comparison approaches.

The appraiser should consider all of the items 1 through 7 in II Tenant-Occupied

サ　有害な物質の使用の有無及びその状態

　②　敷地に係る要因
　　　ア　敷地の形状及び空地部分の広狭の程度
　　　イ　敷地内施設の状態
　　　ウ　敷地の規模
　　　エ　敷地に関する権利の態様
　③　建物及びその敷地に係る要因
　　　ア　敷地内における建物及び附属施設の配置の状態
　　　イ　建物と敷地の規模の対応関係
　　　ウ　長期修繕計画の有無及びその良否並びに修繕積立金の額

(2)　専有部分に係る個別的要因
　①　階層及び位置
　②　日照、眺望及び景観の良否
　③　室内の仕上げ及び維持管理の状態
　④　専有面積及び間取りの状態
　⑤　隣接不動産等の利用の状態
　⑥　エレベーター等の共用施設の利便性の状態
　⑦　敷地に関する権利の態様及び持分
　⑧　区分所有者の管理費等の滞納の有無

2．区分所有建物及びその敷地の鑑定評価
(1)　専有部分が自用の場合
　　区分所有建物及びその敷地で、専有部分を区分所有者が使用しているものについての鑑定評価額は、積算価格、比準価格及び収益価格を関連づけて決定するものとする。
　　積算価格は、区分所有建物の対象となっている一棟の建物及びその敷地の積算価格を求め、当該積算価格に当該一棟の建物の各階層別及び同一階層内の位置別の効用比により求めた配分率を乗ずることにより求めるものとする。

(2)　専有部分が賃貸されている場合
　　区分所有建物及びその敷地で、専有部分が賃貸されているものについての鑑定評価額は、実際実質賃料（売主が既に受領した一時金のうち売買等に当たって買主に承継されない部分がある場合には、当該部分の運用益及び償却額を含まないものとする。）に基づく純収益等の現在価値の総和を求めることにより得た収益価格を標準とし、積算価格及び比準価格を比較考量して決定するものとする。
　　この場合において、前記Ⅱの1．から7．までに掲げる事項を総合的に勘案するものとする。

Buildings and Building Sites.

Section 3. Buildings

The utility of a building is closely related to the utility of the building site. It is common practice to appraise a building and building site as a single unit. Depending on the purpose and conditions of specific assignments, however, the building may be appraised separately for both marketable and non-marketable properties.

I Appraising Buildings for Marketable Properties

A building may be appraised alone by estimating its severance value, i.e., by breaking down the final opinion of value of the total property, in which the building and building site are integrated into a single unit.

The final opinion of the value of the building is determined by reconciling the values indicated by the cost approach, sales comparison approach based on the allocation method, and income capitalization approach using the building residual technique. (In order to employ the building residual technique, the appraiser estimates the value of the site using any methods other than the income capitalization approach. The expected land and building capitalization rates are determined. Then, after allocating the net operating income [NOI] attributable to the property between the building and the site, the appraiser capitalizes the NOI to the building.)

II Appraising Buildings for Non–Marketable Properties

In appraising buildings for non-marketable properties, the appraiser typically estimates value of special-purpose property. Non-marketable properties include cultural heritage buildings, religious buildings, and utilities and institutional properties. The primary premise of such appraisals is to assume continuation of the current usage. The final opinion of the value of such buildings is determined by the value indicated by the cost approach.

III Tenant's Rights

Tenant's rights involve those rights associated with leasehold estates in buildings, to which the *Land Lease and Building Lease Law,* including the former *Building Lease Law*, applies. (Editor's note: It should be kept in mind that where the tenant is paying less than market rent, the leasehold is able to realize its value.)

Only a few types of tenant's rights can be traded in the market. When estimating the value of such transferable tenant's rights, the appraiser places the most weight on the value indicated by the sales comparison approach. In the process of using the sales comparison approach, the appraiser must take into consideration the specific features of the subject and comparable tenant's right contracts. The value of a tenant's right may also be calculated by the following steps: (1) estimating the value of the subject property both as if owner-occupied and as is; (2) deducting the value as is from the value as if owner-occupied; and (3) determining, out of the difference, an appropriate amount as the tenant's right. Furthermore, where the value of the tenant's rights may be determined on a percentage basis, this value should also be accounted for. In any event, the appraiser should consider all of the items indicated above as 1 through 7 in II Tenant-Occupied Buildings and Building Sites.

On the other hand, even a non-tradable tenant's right can give rise to value in one kind

第3節　建物

建物は、その敷地と結合して有機的に効用を発揮するものであり、建物とその敷地とは密接に関連しており、両者は一体として鑑定評価の対象とされるのが通例であるが、鑑定評価の依頼目的及び条件により、建物及びその敷地が一体として市場性を有する場合における建物のみの鑑定評価又は建物及びその敷地が一体として市場性を有しない場合における建物のみの鑑定評価がある。

Ⅰ　建物及びその敷地が一体として市場性を有する場合における建物のみの鑑定評価

この場合の建物の鑑定評価は、その敷地と一体化している状態を前提として、その全体の鑑定評価額の内訳として建物について部分鑑定評価を行うものである。

この場合における建物の鑑定評価額は、積算価格、配分法に基づく比準価格及び建物残余法（敷地の価格を収益還元法以外の手法によって求めることができる場合に、敷地と建物等からなる不動産について建物等に帰属する純収益から建物等の収益価格を求める方法）による収益価格を関連づけて決定するものとする。

Ⅱ　建物及びその敷地が一体として市場性を有しない場合における建物のみの鑑定評価

この場合の建物の鑑定評価は、一般に特殊価格を求める場合に該当するものであり、文化財の指定を受けた建造物、宗教建築物又は現況による管理を継続する公共公益施設の用に供されている不動産のうち建物について、その保存等に主眼をおいて行うものであるが、この場合における建物の鑑定評価額は、積算価格を標準として決定するものとする。

Ⅲ　借家権

借家権とは、借地借家法（廃止前の借家法を含む。）が適用される建物の賃借権をいう。

借家権の取引慣行がある場合における借家権の鑑定評価額は、当事者間の個別的な事情を考慮して求めた比準価格を標準とし、自用の建物及びその敷地の価格から貸家及びその敷地の価格を控除し、所要の調整を行って得た価格を比較考量して決定するものとする。借家権割合が求められる場合は、借家権割合により求めた価格をも比較考量するものとする。この場合において、前記貸家及びその敷地の1．から7．までに掲げる事項を総合的に勘案するものとする。

さらに、借家権の価格といわれているものには、賃貸人から建物の明渡しの要求を受け、借家人が不随意の立退きに伴い事実上喪失することとなる経済的利益等、賃貸人との関係において個別的な形をとって具体に現れるものがある。この場合における借家権の鑑定評価額は、当該建物及びその敷地と同程度の代替建物等の賃借の際に必要とされる新規の実際支払賃料と現在の実際支払賃料との差額の一定期間に相当する額に賃料の前払的性格を有する一時金の額等を加えた額並びに自用の建物及びその敷地の価格から貸家及びその敷地の価格を控除し、所要の調整を行って得た価格を関連づけて決定するものとする。この場合において当事者間の個別的事情を考慮するものとするほか、前記貸家及びその敷地の1．から7．までに掲げる事項を総合的に勘案するものとする。

Specific Standards Chapter 1

of situation involving the tenant and the landlord. When the landlord requests the tenant to vacate the building, the landlord usually pays the tenant's moving costs and compensates the tenant for disruption of the tenant's business. Therefore, in this kind of situation, the tenant's right is deemed to be equivalent to the tenant's de facto loss because the tenant was forced to move out of the premises. In this case, the appraiser determines the value of the tenant's rights by reconciling the value indications derived from the following two methods. In the first method, the appraiser: (1) estimates the difference between the actual market rent under a new lease (i.e., the market rent required to lease a unit in a substitutive or competitive building) and the current actual nominal rent; (2) calculates the present value of that difference for each year of the duration the difference is expected to last; and (3) adds both the amount of deposits, which are considered to be prepaid rents and other appropriate items, to the present value calculated in (2). In the second method, the appraiser: (1) estimates the value of the subject property both as if owner-occupied and as is; (2) deducts the value as is from the value as if owner-occupied; and (3) determines, out of the difference, an appropriate amount as the tenant's right. In addition to the individual circumstances of the involved parties, the appraiser should consider all the items indicated as 1 through 7 in II Tenant-Occupied Buildings and Building Sites.

各論・第1章

Specific Standards Chapter 2

CHAPTER 2. APPRAISAL OF REAL ESTATE RENTAL VALUE

Section 1. Building Sites

I Determining Market Rent Under New Lease

To determine the market rent of a building site, an estimate of the reasonable rent must be in line with the economic value of the building site, based on its use and the conditions of the lease contract.

The final opinion of the market rent of the building site is determined by reconciling the rent indicated by the summation approach, the rent indicated by the rental data comparison approach, and the rent indicated by the allocation method of the rental data comparison approach. When the net income can be properly estimated, the appraiser also considers the rent indicated by the income analysis approach.

The final opinion of rent may be required under circumstances where the building site is to be combined with another site or is to be subdivided. The synergistic or component rent is determined by reconciling the rent indicated by the summation approach (where the base value represents the assemblage value of the building site combined with an adjacent building site, or the component value of the building site resulting from subdivision), and the rent indicated by the rental data comparison approach (rental data that pertains to building sites that were combined with adjacent building sites or have been subdivided). The appraiser considers the following matters in this type of assemblage or subdivision.

1. Ownership and interests in the adjacent building sites
2. Conditions in the lease contracts from which the data is gathered

II Determining Rent Under Renewed Lease

1. Revising Actual Nominal Rent upon an Existing Ground Lease Contract

The appraiser arrives at the final opinion of the rental value at which to renew the actual nominal rent in an existing ground lease contract by reconciling rental estimates derived from the rental disparity analysis approach, the yield approach, the trend approach, and rental data comparison approach. The appraiser should consider all of the following items in this type of rental valuation.

(1) Contract conditions and background of the contract negotiations
(2) Elapsed term and remaining life of the contract
(3) Previous rent revisions
(4) Whether a renewal charge is required
(5) Rent paid for comparable building sites in the neighborhood or similar neighborhoods within the primary market area, or rent paid for substitutive or competitive building sites in the primary market area, and the amount by which these rents have been revised
(6) Market trends in net rent as a proportion of gross rent
(7) Market trends in yields on ground leases

第2章 賃料に関する鑑定評価

第1節 宅地

Ⅰ 新規賃料を求める場合

宅地の正常賃料を求める場合の鑑定評価に当たっては、賃貸借等の契約内容による使用方法に基づく宅地の経済価値に即応する適正な賃料を求めるものとする。

宅地の正常賃料の鑑定評価額は、積算賃料、比準賃料及び配分法に準ずる方法に基づく比準賃料を関連づけて決定するものとする。この場合において、純収益を適切に求めることができるときは収益賃料を比較考量して決定するものとする。

宅地の限定賃料の鑑定評価額は、隣接宅地の併合使用又は宅地の一部の分割使用をする当該宅地の限定価格を基礎価格として求めた積算賃料及び隣接宅地の併合使用又は宅地の一部の分割使用を前提とする賃貸借等の事例に基づく比準賃料を関連づけて決定するものとする。この場合においては、次に掲げる事項を総合的に勘案するものとする。

1. 隣接宅地の権利の態様
2. 当該事例に係る賃貸借等の契約の内容

Ⅱ 継続賃料を求める場合

1. 継続中の宅地の賃貸借等の契約に基づく実際支払賃料を改定する場合

継続中の宅地の賃貸借等の契約に基づく実際支払賃料を改定する場合の鑑定評価額は、差額配分法による賃料、利回り法による賃料、スライド法による賃料及び比準賃料を関連づけて決定するものとする。この場合においては、次に掲げる事項を総合的に勘案して決定するものとする。

(1) 契約の内容及び契約締結の経緯
(2) 契約上の経過期間及び残存期間
(3) 賃料改定の経緯
(4) 更新料の必要性
(5) 近隣地域若しくは同一需給圏内の類似地域等における宅地の賃料又は同一需給圏内の代替競争不動産の賃料、その改定の程度及びそれらの推移、動向
(6) 賃料に占める純賃料の推移、動向
(7) 底地に対する利回りの推移、動向
(8) 公租公課の推移、動向

なお、賃料の改定が契約期間の満了に伴う更新又は借地権の第三者への譲渡を契機とする場合において、更新料又は名義書替料が支払われるときは、これらの額を総合的に勘案して求めるものとする。

(8) Trends in real estate taxes

There are several reasons for revising rent. These include renewal of the lease upon conclusion of the lease or contract term, transfer of the leasehold interest in the land to a third party, and periodic rental renewals during a lease term. In the first two cases, a lump sum payment, called either `renewal fee´ or `transfer fee´, is often paid to the landlord. The appraiser must take into account such a lump sum payment in determining the final opinion of rental value.

2. Revising Rent upon a Change in the Contract Terms

When a ground lease contract is amended (e.g., through the elimination of restrictions on building renovations/additions, or on the type of building structures), a higher rent can be charged by the landlord. When asked to perform a rental renewal appraisal in this situation, the appraiser first estimates the new rent based on the approaches explained in the section above (1. Revising Actual Nominal Rent Based on an Existing Ground Lease Contract) assuming there was no amendment. Then, the appraiser analyzes the expected increase in the value of the subject land and improvements resulting from the amendment. Finally, the appraiser estimates the growth in rental value associated with the increase in property value over the rent first estimated without assuming the amendment.

In addition to the items indicated above in 1, the appraiser should consider all of the following matters.
(1) Characteristics of the lease
(2) Details of changes in the contract terms
(3) Amounts paid for consent to change the lease terms

Section 2. Built-Up Property

I Determining Market Rent Under New Lease

To determine the market rent of a building and building site, the rental estimate must be in line with the economic value of the building and building site, based on its use and the conditions of the lease contract.

The appraiser arrives at a final opinion of the market rent of a building and building site by reconciling the rents indicated by the summation approach and the rental data comparison approach. When the net income from the property can be properly estimated, the appraiser also considers the rent indicated by the income analysis approach.

Where a portion of the building and building site is being leased, the appraiser arrives at a final value opinion of the market rent by considering the size and other attributes of the leased portion in relation to those of the entire building and building site.

II Determining Rent Under Renewed Lease

Estimates of the revision of actual nominal rent in existing lease contracts to buildings and building sites are done the same way as appraisals to determine rent under renewed leases to building sites.

2．契約上の条件又は使用目的が変更されることに伴い賃料を改定する場合

契約上の条件又は使用目的が変更されることに伴い賃料を改定する場合の鑑定評価に当たっては、契約上の条件又は使用目的の変更に伴う宅地及び地上建物の経済価値の増分のうち適切な部分に即応する賃料を前記１．を想定した場合における賃料に加算して決定するものとする。

この場合においては、前記１．に掲げる事項のほか、特に次に掲げる事項を総合的に勘案するものとする。
(1) 賃貸借等の態様
(2) 契約上の条件又は使用目的の変更内容
(3) 条件変更承諾料又は増改築承諾料が支払われるときはこれらの額

第2節　建物及びその敷地

I　新規賃料を求める場合

建物及びその敷地の正常賃料を求める場合の鑑定評価に当たっては、賃貸借の契約内容による使用方法に基づく建物及びその敷地の経済価値に即応する賃料を求めるものとする。

建物及びその敷地の正常賃料の鑑定評価額は、積算賃料及び比準賃料を関連づけて決定するものとする。この場合において、純収益を適切に求めることができるときは収益賃料を比較考量して決定するものとする。

なお、建物及びその敷地の一部を対象とする場合の正常賃料の鑑定評価額は、当該建物及びその敷地の全体と当該部分との関連について総合的に比較考量して求めるものとする。

II　継続賃料を求める場合

継続中の建物及びその敷地の賃貸借の契約に基づく実際支払賃料を改定する場合の鑑定評価は、宅地の継続賃料を求める場合の鑑定評価に準ずるものとする。

Specific Standards Chapter 3

CHAPTER 3. APPRAISAL OF REAL ESTATE VALUE SUBJECT TO SECURITIZATION

Section 1. Basic Approach to Securitization-Properties
I Definition of Securitization-Properties
In this chapter, the term "securitization- properties" refers to properties (including those held under trust beneficiary rights), which are subject to or likely to become subject to a real estate transaction of any of the following types.
  (1) Assets undergoing liquidation as specified in the *Asset Liquidation Law (Shisan Ryudoka Ho)*; real estate transactions involving investment trusts as specified in the *Investment Trust and Investment Corporation Law (Toshin Ho or Kaisei SPC Ho)*; or real estate transactions undertaken by investment corporations as defined in that law.
  (2) Real estate transactions related to contracts involving real estate syndication as defined in the Real Estate Syndication Act (Fudosan Kyodo Jigyo Ho).
  (3) Real estate transactions generating income or profit, and undertaken for the main purpose of fulfilling obligations on securities as specified in the *Financial Instruments Trading Law (Kinsho Ho)*, Article 2, Paragraph 1, No. 5, No. 9 (which deals only with stock corporations established for the sole purpose of real estate trading, including limited companies (yugen kaisha), which survive as stock corporations under Article 2, Paragraph 1 of the *Law Concerning the Coordination, Etc. of Relevant Laws Relating to the Enforcement of the Corporation Act*), No. 14, or No. 16, or property rights considered to be securities under Paragraph 2, No. 1, 3, or 5 of that article.

The appraisal of securitization properties must be conducted as is prescribed in this chapter. A statement to this effect must be included in the appraisal report.

Even when appraising properties other than securitization properties, it is important that the appraiser endeavor to conduct the appraisal as is prescribed in this chapter for appraisals of a large-scale rental property held for investment purposes, and whenever it is considered necessary to protect the investor, purchaser, or other interested party.

II Responsibility of LREAs
  (1) LREAs must always conduct appraisals in a manner giving full consideration to the proper procedures for the appraisal of securitization properties, while recognizing that they (LREAs) exert a significant influence on the decision making, not only of the persons requesting the appraisal of securitization properties (hereinafter referred to as "clients") but also of a wide range of investors and others, and also keeping in mind that they (LREAs) bear the important responsibility of upholding the public reputation of the real estate appraisal profession.
  (2) When appraising a property for securitization purposes, the LREA should seek to facilitate the securitization, etc., of the property by providing the client with explanations of the data, procedures, and other matters related to the appraisal, thereby enhancing the client's understanding, and obtaining his cooperation. The LREA must also take care as to the way information is presented in the appraisal report in order

第3章　証券化対象不動産の価格に関する鑑定評価

第1節　証券化対象不動産の鑑定評価の基本的姿勢
Ⅰ　証券化対象不動産の範囲
　この章において「証券化対象不動産」とは、次のいずれかに該当する不動産取引の目的である不動産又は不動産取引の目的となる見込みのある不動産（信託受益権に係るものを含む。）をいう。
(1)　資産の流動化に関する法律に規定する資産の流動化並びに投資信託及び投資法人に関する法律に規定する投資信託に係る不動産取引並びに同法に規定する投資法人が行う不動産取引
(2)　不動産特定共同事業法に規定する不動産特定共同事業契約に係る不動産取引
(3)　金融商品取引法第2条第1項第5号、第9号（専ら不動産取引を行うことを目的として設置された株式会社（会社法の施行に伴う関係法律の整備等に関する法律第2条第1項の規定により株式会社として存続する有限会社を含む。）に係るものに限る。）、第14号及び第16号に規定する有価証券並びに同条第2項第1号、第3号及び第5号の規定により有価証券とみなされる権利の債務の履行等を主たる目的として収益又は利益を生ずる不動産取引
　証券化対象不動産の鑑定評価は、この章の定めるところに従って行わなければならない。この場合において、鑑定評価報告書にその旨を記載しなければならない。
　証券化対象不動産以外の不動産の鑑定評価を行う場合にあっても、投資用の賃貸大型不動産の鑑定評価を行う場合その他の投資家及び購入者等の保護の観点から必要と認められる場合には、この章の定めに準じて、鑑定評価を行うよう努めなければならない。

Ⅱ　不動産鑑定士の責務
(1)　不動産鑑定士は、証券化対象不動産の鑑定評価の依頼者（以下単に「依頼者」という。）のみならず広範な投資家等に重大な影響を及ぼすことを考慮するとともに、不動産鑑定評価制度に対する社会的信頼性の確保等について重要な責任を有していることを認識し、証券化対象不動産の鑑定評価の手順について常に最大限の配慮を行いつつ、鑑定評価を行わなければならない。
(2)　不動産鑑定士は、証券化対象不動産の鑑定評価を行う場合にあっては、証券化対象不動産の証券化等が円滑に行なわれるよう配慮しつつ、鑑定評価に係る資料及び手順等を依頼者に説明し、理解を深め、かつ、協力を得るものとする。また、証券化対象不動産の鑑定評価書については、依頼者及び証券化対象不動産に係る利害関係者その他の者がその内容を容易に把握・比較することができるようにするため、鑑定評価報告書の記載方法等を工夫し、及び鑑定評価に活用した資料等を明示することができるようにするなど説明責任が十分に果たされるものとしなければならない。

Specific Standards Chapter 3

to make the content of the appraisal report on the securitization property easier for the client, persons holding interests in the securitization property, and others to understand and use in comparisons with reports on other properties. The LREA must be fully accountable, ensuring that the data and other informational materials used in the appraisal are available for disclosure.

(3) Whenever several LREAs are working jointly on the appraisal of a securitization-property, the roles of each LREA must be clearly defined, and all of the LREAs must work as a team to complete the appraisal assignment, sharing information on the overall appraisal and maintaining close and thorough collaboration.

Section 2. Drafting a Work Plan for the Appraisal

I **Verifying the data needed to develop the work plan**

When drafting a work plan for the appraisal, the LREA should verify with the client in advance matters related to the appraisal of a securitization property, in order to develop an appropriate and reasonable work plan that allows competent and reliable implementation of the appraisal. The verified information should be reflected in the work plan for the appraisal, and the plan should be changed whenever any change occurs in the information specified. Matters that should be verified include:

(1) Purpose of the request for the appraisal and background as to why the request was made.

(2) Classification of the subject property transaction under (1), (2), or (3) of Section 1, I above.

(3) Main subjects covered in the engineering report (an investigative report on the condition of the securitization property, conducted by a person having specialized knowledge of buildings, mechanical and electrical [M&E] systems, environmental matters, etc.; the same applies in Section 3 below), data needed to apply DCF analysis, and other relevant documents; and the time when these documents will be available.

(4) Whether there are explanatory comments from the preparer of the engineering report.

(5) Scope of the field surveys, including visual inspection of the interior of the subject property.

(6) Other matters needed to develop the work plan for the appraisal.

II **Records of verified information**

After verifying the matters listed in (1) through (6) of Section 2, I (1) above, records must be prepared for each of these items, and these records must be attached to the appraisal report as appendices. Included among these records are:

(1) Date verified

(2) Name of the LREA who verified the information

(3) Name and occupation of the person who provided the verification

(4) Content of the information confirmed, and whether it has been reflected in the work plan for the appraisal

(5) Details of any changes in the appraisal procedures or changes in the content of the

(3) 証券化対象不動産の鑑定評価を複数の不動産鑑定士が共同して行う場合にあっては、それぞれの不動産鑑定士の役割を明確にした上で、常に鑑定評価業務全体の情報を共有するなど密接かつ十分な連携の下、すべての不動産鑑定士が一体となって鑑定評価の業務を遂行しなければならない。

第2節　処理計画の策定
Ⅰ　処理計画の策定に当たっての確認事項
　処理計画の策定に当たっては、あらかじめ、依頼者に対し、証券化対象不動産の鑑定評価に関する次の事項を確認し、鑑定評価の作業の円滑かつ確実な実施を行うことができるよう適切かつ合理的な処理計画を策定するものとする。この場合において、確認された事項については、処理計画に反映するとともに、当該事項に変更があった場合にあっては、処理計画を変更するものとする。
(1) 鑑定評価の依頼目的及び依頼が必要となった背景
(2) 対象不動産が第1節Ⅰ(1)、(2)又は(3)のいずれに係るものであるかの別
(3) エンジニアリング・レポート（建築物、設備等及び環境に関する専門的知識を有する者が行った証券化対象不動産の状況に関する調査報告書をいう。以下同じ。）、ＤＣＦ法等を適用するために必要となる資料その他の資料の主な項目及びその入手時期
(4) エンジニアリング・レポートを作成した者からの説明の有無
(5) 対象不動産の内覧の実施を含めた実地調査の範囲
(6) その他処理計画の策定のために必要な事項

Ⅱ　確認事項の記録
　第2節Ⅰ(1)から(6)までの事項の確認を行った場合には、それぞれ次の事項に関する記録を作成し、及び鑑定評価報告書の附属資料として添付しなければならない。
(1) 確認を行った年月日
(2) 確認を行った不動産鑑定士の氏名
(3) 確認の相手方の氏名及び職業
(4) 確認の内容及び当該内容の処理計画への反映状況
(5) 確認の内容の変更により鑑定評価の作業、内容等の変更をする場合にあっては、その内容

report, etc., which were made as a result of changes in the verified information

III Purpose of the request for the appraisal, and the relationship between the client and the parties involved in the securitization of the property

In many cases, a wide variety of parties are involved and hold complex interests in a securitization- property. The appraisal report must state the purpose of the request for the appraisal of the securitization property, the background as to why the request was made, and the following items concerning the interests of the client with regard to the securitization property.

(1) Whether the client holds interests in the securitization of the property (parties such as an originator, arranger, asset manager, lender, equity investor, special purpose company [SPC], corporate investor, or funding agency [referred to below as "parties involved in the securitization"] should be identified).

(2) Whether the client has capital ties or business connections to any of the parties involved in the securitization; and if so, the details of those relationships.

(3) The details of any other special interests between the client and any of the parties involved in the securitization.

Section 3. Investigating Property-Specific Value Influences acting on the Securitization-Property

I Investigation of property-specific value influences acting on the subject property

In the investigation of property-specific value influences acting on a securitization property, there must be a reliable and detailed confirmation of information about the physical and legal characteristics of the securitization property. The field survey for the requested appraisal of the securitization property, including the visual inspection of the interior of the subject property, must be conducted in the presence of the client (or persons designated by the client); and the data needed for the appraisal, including the identification of associated rights and interests, restrictions under public statute, the presence of toxic substances such as asbestos, determination of earthquake resistance, and the history of remodeling, expansion, etc., must be verified by means such as interviews with the manager, etc., of the subject property.

II Property inspection

The LREA must include the following matters relating to the field survey in the appraisal report.

(1) Date of the field survey.
(2) Name of the LREA who performed the field survey.
(3) Names and occupations of witnesses to the survey and managers of the subject property.
(4) Scope of the field survey (including whether or not the interior was visually inspected) and matters verified in the field survey.
(5) If it was not possible to perform any part of the field survey, the reasons must be stated.

Ⅲ 鑑定評価の依頼目的及び依頼者の証券化関係者との関係
　証券化対象不動産については、関係者が多岐にわたり利害関係が複雑であることも多く、証券化対象不動産の鑑定評価の依頼目的及び依頼が必要となった背景等並びに依頼者と証券化対象不動産との利害関係に関する次の事項を鑑定評価報告書に記載しなければならない。
(1) 依頼者が証券化対象不動産の証券化に係る利害関係者(オリジネーター、アレンジャー、アセットマネジャー、レンダー、エクイティ投資家又は特別目的会社・投資法人・ファンド等をいい、以下「証券化関係者」という。)のいずれであるかの別
(2) 依頼者と証券化関係者との資本関係又は取引関係の有無及びこれらの関係を有する場合にあっては、その内容
(3) その他依頼者と証券化関係者との特別な利害関係を有する場合にあっては、その内容

第3節　証券化対象不動産の個別的要因の調査等

Ⅰ　対象不動産の個別的要因の調査等
　証券化対象不動産の個別的要因の調査等に当たっては、証券化対象不動産の物的・法的確認を確実かつ詳細に行うため、依頼された証券化対象不動産の鑑定評価のための実地調査について、依頼者(依頼者が指定した者を含む。)の立会いの下、対象不動産の内覧の実施を含めた実地調査を行うとともに、対象不動産の管理者からの聴聞等により権利関係、公法上の規制、アスベスト等の有害物質、耐震性及び増改築等の履歴等に関し鑑定評価に必要な事項を確認しなければならない。

Ⅱ　実地調査
　不動産鑑定士は、実地調査に関し、次の事項を鑑定評価報告書に記載しなければならない。
(1) 実地調査を行った年月日
(2) 実地調査を行った不動産鑑定士の氏名
(3) 立会人及び対象不動産の管理者の氏名及び職業
(4) 実地調査を行った範囲(内覧の有無を含む。)及び実地調査により確認した内容
(5) 実地調査の一部を実施することができなかった場合にあっては、その理由

Specific Standards Chapter 3

III Handling of the engineering report, and the property investigation by the LREA

(1) In the appraisal of a securitization property, the LREA must ask the client to submit the engineering report required for the appraisal, and after analyzing and evaluating its content, the LREA must incorporate its conclusions in the appraisal. However, if no engineering report is submitted, or if its content is considered to be inadequate for use in the appraisal, the LREA must then take action such as conducting an independent investigation to substitute for the engineering report and thereby fulfill the requirements of the assignment; and the appraisal report must describe the results of that investigation as well as the reasons why it is considered to be appropriate.

(2) For example, the engineering report could be lacking or inadequate for use in reappraising a securitization property, which has previously been appraised, or the securitization property may be an empty lot (or one on which the buildings are to be demolished).

(3) The appraisal report must include a statement of what decision was made as to whether or not to use the content of the engineering report in the appraisal, along with the reasons for that decision. For all the items listed in the following table, the information specified must be included in the appraisal report. Appendix 1 provides a sample format for an appraisal report. The same applies in the case of the second statement at III(1) above (beginning with "however").

Item	Content
Basic information about the engineering report	· Name, etc., of the preparer of the engineering report · Date of the investigation undertaken for the engineering report, and date when the engineering report was prepared
How the engineering report was obtained, and how it was handled in the appraisal	· Party providing the engineering report (name, occupation, etc.) · Date obtained · Whether explanatory comments were obtained from the preparer of the engineering report · How the engineering report was handled in the appraisal
Method of investigation of property-specific influences , which is required for the appraisal	Statement as to whether the engineering report was used for the investigation of property-specific influences, or whether the LREA investigated these influences himself (the investigation may have also been done by another expert,at the request of the LREA): Property-specific influences to be investigated include: · Regulations and restrictions under public and private statutes (including the state of compliance with the law) · Renovation plan · Replacement cost · Building environment with regard to toxic substances, including asbestos · Soil pollution

Ⅲ　エンジニアリング・レポートの取扱いと不動産鑑定士が行う調査
(1)　証券化対象不動産の鑑定評価に当たっては、不動産鑑定士は、依頼者に対し当該鑑定評価に際し必要なエンジニアリング・レポートの提出を求め、その内容を分析・判断した上で、鑑定評価に活用しなければならない。ただし、エンジニアリング・レポートの提出がない場合又はその記載された内容が鑑定評価に活用する資料として不十分であると認められる場合には、エンジニアリング・レポートに代わるものとして不動産鑑定士が調査を行うなど鑑定評価を適切に行うため対応するものとし、対応した内容及びそれが適切であると判断した理由について、鑑定評価報告書に記載しなければならない。
(2)　エンジニアリング・レポートの提出がない場合又はその記載されている内容が不十分である場合として想定される場合を例示すれば、既に鑑定評価が行われたことがある証券化対象不動産の再評価をする場合、証券化対象不動産が更地である場合（建物を取り壊す予定である場合を含む。）等がある。
(3)　エンジニアリング・レポートの内容を鑑定評価に活用するか否かの検討に当たっては、その判断及び根拠について、鑑定評価報告書に記載しなければならない。この場合においては、少なくとも次の表の項目ごとに、それぞれ同表に掲げる内容を鑑定評価報告書に記載しなければならない。この場合における鑑定評価報告書の様式の例は、別表1のとおりとする。なお、(1)ただし書きの場合においても、同様とする。

項　目	内　容
エンジニアリング・レポートの基本的属性	・エンジニアリング・レポートの作成者の名称等 ・エンジニアリング・レポートの調査が行われた日及び作成された日
エンジニアリング・レポートの入手経緯、対応方針等	・入手先（氏名及び職業等） ・入手した日 ・エンジニアリング・レポートの作成者からの説明の有無等 ・入手したエンジニアリング・レポートについて鑑定評価を行う上での対応方針等
鑑定評価に必要となる専門性の高い個別的要因に関する調査	次に掲げる専門性の高い個別的要因に関する調査について、エンジニアリング・レポートを活用するか又は不動産鑑定士の調査を実施（不動産鑑定士が他の専門家へ調査を依頼する場合を含む。）するかの別 ・公法上及び私法上の規制、制約等（法令遵守状況調査を含む。） ・修繕計画 ・再調達価格 ・有害な物質（アスベスト等）に係る建物環境 ・土壌汚染 ・地震リスク ・耐震性 ・地下埋設物

Specific Standards Chapter 3

	· Earthquake risk · Earthquake resistance · Buried structures or objects
LREA's conclusions about the method of investigation of property-specific influences, which is required for the appraisal	Decisions on whether to use the content of the engineering report or an investigation by the LREA of property-specific influences, along with the reasons for that decision, etc.

(4) Because the engineering report may need to be revised or supplemented owing to changes in the market environment for real estate securitization, the LREA must maintain close contact with the preparer of the engineering report, and must also endeavor to improve his own knowledge and understanding of engineering reports.

Section 4. Application of DCF method
When appraising the value of a securitization property by the income approach, DCF method must be applied. In addition, it is also appropriate to apply direct capitalization method for verification.

I **Clarifying the procedure for applying DCF method**
   (1) The appraisal report must include statements regarding the suitability of the data used to determine the property's value by the income approach. Along with the reasons for the conclusion, these statements must indicate the following:
   ① Whether the data that was obtained from the client for the subject property, such as the income and expense amounts, has been used without modification.
   ② Whether the data that was obtained from the client for the subject property, such as the income and expense amounts, has been adjusted or modified.
   ③ Whether the LREA himself has obtained data for the subject property, such as the income and expense amounts.
   (2) When DCF method is used to determine the value by the income approach, in addition to explaining the selection of the terminal capitalization rate, discount rate, forecasts of future income and expenses, and other individual items that have been assessed, the appraisal report must lay out the procedure by which that data was used to determine the value by the income approach and the reasons for using that procedure, clearly indicating such factors as the possibility of change in the economic situation, the specific comparables which were examined, and the logical consistency. When several LREAs work jointly to appraise a group of securitization properties, they must endeavor to ensure logical consistency among all of the subject properties with regard to the selection of terminal capitalization rates, discount rates, forecasts of future income and expenses, and other data used in applying DCF method.

鑑定評価に必要となる専門性の高い個別的要因に関する調査についての不動産鑑定士の判断	専門性の高い個別的要因に関する調査に関する対応について、エンジニアリング・レポートの記載内容を活用した場合、不動産鑑定士の調査で対応した場合等の内容、根拠等

(4) エンジニアリング・レポートについては、不動産証券化市場の環境の変化に対応してその内容の改善・充実が図られていくことにかんがみ、エンジニアリング・レポートを作成する者との密接な連携を図りつつ、常に自らのエンジニアリング・レポートに関する知識・理解を深めるための研鑽に努めなければならない。

第4節 ＤＣＦ法の適用等

証券化対象不動産の鑑定評価における収益価格を求めるに当たっては、ＤＣＦ法を適用しなければならない。この場合において、併せて直接還元法を適用することにより検証を行うことが適切である。

Ⅰ ＤＣＦ法の適用過程等の明確化

(1) ＤＣＦ法の適用に当たっては、ＤＣＦ法による収益価格を求める際に活用する資料を次に定める区分に応じて、その妥当性や判断の根拠等を鑑定評価報告書に記載しなければならない。

① 依頼者から入手した対象不動産に係る収益又は費用の額その他の資料をそのまま活用する場合

② 依頼者から入手した対象不動産に係る収益又は費用の額その他の資料に修正等を加える場合

③ 自らが入手した対象不動産に係る収益又は費用の額その他の資料を活用する場合

(2) ＤＣＦ法による収益価格を求める場合に当たっては、最終還元利回り、割引率、収益及び費用の将来予測等査定した個々の項目等に関する説明に加え、それらを採用して収益価格を求める過程及びその理由について、経済事情の変動の可能性、具体的に検証した事例及び論理的な整合性等を明確にしつつ、鑑定評価報告書に記載しなければならない。また、複数の不動産鑑定士が共同して複数の証券化対象不動産の鑑定評価を行う場合にあっては、ＤＣＦ法の適用において活用する最終還元利回り、割引率、収益及び費用の将来予測等について対象不動産相互間の論理的な整合性を図らなければならない。

(3) 鑑定評価報告書には、ＤＣＦ法で査定した収益価格（直接還元法による検証を含む。）と原価法及び取引事例比較法等で求めた試算価格との関連について明確にしつつ、鑑定評価額を決定した理由について記載しなければならない。

(4) ＤＣＦ法の適用については、今後、さらなる精緻化に向けて自己研鑽に努めることにより、説明責任の向上を図る必要がある。

Specific Standards Chapter 3

(3) The appraisal report must contain a clear statement of the relationship between the value indicated by the income approach, using DCF method (including verification by direct capitalization), and the indicated value using the cost approach, and sales comparison approach; and the appraisal report must also state the reasons for concluding the final opinion of value.

(4) The LREA must strive for greater accountability, endeavoring to improve his own knowledge and understanding in order to achieve further proficiency in the application of DCF method.

Ⅱ **Uniformity in income and expense items in DCF method**

(1) When using DCF method to determine the value by the income approach, the income and expense amounts for the securitization property (hereinafter referred to as "income and expense items") must be entered in the appraisal report for each of several continuous time periods, classified according to the items shown in the following table. Each of the income and expense items should be accompanied by a breakdown of how the figures were calculated. When entering this data in the appraisal report, each item in the "Item" column of the following table should be defined as specified in the table.

	Item	Definition
Effective gross income	Potential gross income	When all or a portion of the subject property is rented or operated by a contractor, the recurring income (assuming full occupancy).
	Income from common area charges	Income collected under contracts with tenants for that portion of the recurring expenses in the maintenance, management, and operation of the subject property (including expenses for electricity, water, gas, regional heating and air conditioning, etc.), which apply to the common areas.
	Utility fee income	Income collected under contracts with tenants for that portion of the recurring expenses for electricity, water, gas, regional heating and air conditioning, etc., in the operation of the subject property, which apply to leased areas (assuming full occupancy).
	Parking fee income	Income from leasing the subject property's parking spaces to tenants, or from renting parking spaces by the hour.
	Other income	Other income from facility installation fees for signs, antennas, vending machines, etc., and income from lump-sum payments, which are not refundable, such as key money and renewal fees.
	Vacancy allowance	Decrease in each income item, based on predicted vacancies, periods it will take to replace tenants, etc.
	Collection losses allowance	Decrease in each income item, based on predicted debt collection losses.
Operating expenses	Maintenance and management expenses	Recurring expenses for the maintenance and management of the subject property, including building and mechanical and electrical (M&E) system management, security, and cleaning.
	Utility expenses	Expenses for electricity, water, gas, regional heating and air conditioning, etc., incurred in the operation of the subject property.
	Repair expenses	That portion of the expenditures for building and M&E system repair, renovation, etc., of the subject property, which is a recurring expense

Ⅱ　DCF法の収益費用項目の統一等
(1)　DCF法の適用により収益価格を求めるに当たっては、証券化対象不動産に係る収益又は費用の額につき、連続する複数の期間ごとに、次の表の項目（以下「収益費用項目」という。）に区分して鑑定評価報告書に記載しなければならない（収益費用項目ごとに、記載した数値の積算内訳等を付記するものとする）。この場合において、同表の項目の欄に掲げる項目の定義は、それぞれ同表の定義の欄に掲げる定義のとおりとする。

	項　　目	定　　義
運営収益	貸室賃料収入	対象不動産の全部又は貸室部分について賃貸又は運営委託をすることにより経常的に得られる収入（満室想定）
	共益費収入	対象不動産の維持管理・運営において経常的に要する費用（電気・水道・ガス・地域冷暖房熱源等に要する費用を含む）のうち、共用部分に係るものとして賃借人との契約により徴収する収入（満室想定）
	水道光熱費収入	対象不動産の運営において電気・水道・ガス・地域冷暖房熱源等に要する費用のうち、貸室部分に係るものとして賃借人との契約により徴収する収入（満室想定）
	駐車場収入	対象不動産に附属する駐車場をテナント等に賃貸することによって得られる収入及び駐車場を時間貸しすることによって得られる収入
	その他収入	その他看板、アンテナ、自動販売機等の施設設置料、礼金・更新料等の返還を要しない一時金等の収入
	空室等損失	各収入について空室や入替期間等の発生予測に基づく減少分
	貸倒れ損失	各収入について貸倒れの発生予測に基づく減少分
運営費用	維持管理費	建物・設備管理、保安警備、清掃等対象不動産の維持・管理のために経常的に要する費用
	水道光熱費	対象不動産の運営において電気・水道・ガス・地域冷暖房熱源等に要する費用
	修繕費	対象不動産に係る建物、設備等の修理、改良等のために支出した金額のうち当該建物、設備等の通常の維持管理のため、又は一部がき損した建物、設備等につきその原状を回復するために経常的に要する費用
	プロパティマネジメントフィー	対象不動産の管理業務に係る経費
	テナント募集費用等	新規テナントの募集に際して行われる仲介業務や広告宣伝等に要する費用及びテナントの賃貸借契約の更新や再契約業務に要する費用等

Specific Standards Chapter 3

		for ordinary building and M&E system maintenance and management, etc., or is expended to restore damaged building and M&E system portions to their original condition.
	Property management fees	Expenses for management services in the subject property.
	Tenant recruitment expenses, etc.	Expenses for rental agency services, advertising, etc., to recruit new tenants; and expenses for lease renewal or repeat leasing contracts with existing tenants.
	Real estate taxes	Property taxes (on land, buildings, and depreciable assets) and city planning taxes (on land and buildings).
	Casualty insurance premiums	Premiums for fire insurance on the subject property and accessory equipment; liability insurance for losses by third parties, etc., due to subject property defects or management failures, etc.
	Other expenses	Other expenses for ground rent, road occupancy and utilization, etc.
Net Operating Income		Operating income minus operating expenses.
Operating profit on lump-sum payments		Operating profit on security deposits and other lump-sum payments, which are f refundable deposits.
Capital expenditures		That portion of expenditures for building and M&E system repair, renovation, etc., which is recognized as increasing the value of the building, M&E system, etc., or strengthening its durability.
Net Cash Flow (Adjusted NOI)		Net operating income, plus operating profit on lump-sum payments, minus capital expenditures.

(2) When using DCF analysis to determine the value by the income approach, the LREA must identify and explain the income and expense items and their definitions to the client before obtaining the requisite data, and must check that each income and expense item corresponds to its specified definition.

(3) Appendix 2 is a sample format for an appraisal report when DCF analysis is applied. This format may be revised as is necessary to conform to the specific appraisal situation, based on factors such as the purpose and the category of the securitization property.

Supplementary provision (Revised, July 3, 2002)

The Real Estate Appraisal Standards become effective on January 1, 2003.

Supplementary provisions (Partly revised, April 2, 2007)

1. These standards become effective on July 1, 2007.
2. In the revised standards, LREA candidates are included under the designation, Licensed Real Estate Appraiser (LREA).
3. Approximately once per year, the Ministry of Land, Infrastructure, Transport and Tourism will study the situation of current practice basis of the Real Estate Appraisal Standards as revised by this notification, and will take steps such as revising these standards if necessary, on the basis of the results of that study.

	公租公課	固定資産税（土地・建物・償却資産）、都市計画税（土地・建物）
	損害保険料	対象不動産及び附属設備に係る火災保険、対象不動産の欠陥や管理上の事故による第三者等の損害を担保する賠償責任保険等の料金
	その他費用	その他支払地代、道路占用使用料等の費用
運営純収益		運営収益から運営費用を控除して得た額
一時金の運用益		預り金的性格を有する保証金等の運用益
資本的支出		対象不動産に係る建物、設備等の修理、改良等のために支出した金額のうち当該建物、設備等の価値を高め、又はその耐久性を増すこととなると認められる部分に対応する支出
純収益		運営純収益に一時金の運用益を加算し資本的支出を控除した額

(2) DCF法の適用により収益価格を求めるに当たっては、収益費用項目及びその定義について依頼者に提示・説明した上で必要な資料を入手するとともに、収益費用項目ごとに定められた定義に該当していることを確認しなければならない。

(3) DCF法を適用する際の鑑定評価報告書の様式の例は、別表2のとおりとする。証券化対象不動産の用途、類型等に応じて、実務面での適合を工夫する場合は、同表2に必要な修正を加えるものとする。

附　則（平成14年7月3日全部改正）
　この不動産鑑定評価基準は、平成15年1月1日から施行する。
附　則（平成19年4月2日一部改正）
　1．この基準は、平成19年7月1日から施行する。
　2．不動産鑑定士補は、改正後の基準の適用については、不動産鑑定士とみなす。
　3．国土交通省は、毎年一回程度、この通知による改正後の不動産鑑定評価基準に基づく実務の状況について検討を加え必要があると認めるときには、その結果に基づいてこの基準の改訂など所要の措置を講ずるものとする。

Specific Standards Chapter 3

Appendix 1

LREA		Affiliation	

Basic information about the engineering report and its acquisition

Basic information about the engineering report and its acquisition		Preparer	Client
	A		
	B		
	C		
	D		

How the submitted engineering report was handled in the appraisal; whether an additional investigation by the LREA was needed; results of the investigation by LREA, etc.	

Results of the investigation and preparer comments (Enter A, B, C, or D in the "Preparer" column)	Explanatory comments from the preparer	Item	Was the engineering report used, or did LREA conduct an investigation?
1. Building condition survey		Location overview	
		Building overview	
		M&E system overview	
		Structural overview	
		Regulations and restrictions under public and private statutes (state of compliance with the law)	
		Renovation/renewal history and plans	
		Emergency repair/renewal expenses	
		Short-term repair/renewal expenses	
		Long-term repair/renewal expenses	
		Replacement cost	
2. Building environment survey		Asbestos (Phase 1)	
		PCBs	
		Other	
3. Soil pollution risk assessment		Soil survey (Phase 1)	
4. Earthquake risk assessment		Simple analysis	
		Detailed analysis	

Buried structures or objects			
Building environment survey		Asbestos (Phase 2)	
Soil pollution risk assessment		Soil survey (Phase 2)	
		Environmental assessment, etc.	
Earthquake resistance survey		Earthquake resistance determination by architects, etc.	

Note: "Phase 1" indicates investigating the possible presence of toxic substances or pollutants by performing field surveys, collecting and analyzing data, and conducting interviews; "Phase 2" indicates confirming the presence or absence of toxic substances or pollutants by taking samples and conducting chemical analyses. "Simple analysis" indicates analysis by means of statistical methods, while "detailed analysis" indicates the use of analytical techniques.

Date of form completion		Name of property		Location of property	

Date investigated	Date prepared	Obtained from	Date obtained

Items used in appraisal, and reasons for doing so

Specific Standards Chapter 3

別表１

	不動産鑑定士		所属	

エンジニアリング・レポートの基本的属性・入手経緯			
エンジニアリング・レポートの基本的属性・入手経緯		作成者	委託者
	A		
	B		
	C		
	D		

提出されたエンジニアリング・レポートについて、鑑定評価を行う上での対応方針、不動産鑑定士の調査の必要性・内容等	

調査内容及び作成者 (※作成者欄には上記A、B、C又はDを記載)	作成者からの説明	項目	エンジニアリング・レポートの活用又は不動産鑑定士の調査の別
1 建物状況調査		立地概要調査	
		建物概要調査	
		設備概要調査	
		構造概要調査	
		公法上及び私法上の規制、制約等（法令遵守状況調査を含む。）	
		更新・改修履歴とその計画の調査	
		緊急修繕更新費	
		短期修繕更新費	
		長期修繕更新費	
		再調達価格	
2 建物環境調査		アスベスト（フェーズⅠ）	
		PCB	
		その他の項目	
3 土壌汚染リスク評価		土壌調査（フェーズⅠ）	
4 地震リスク評価		簡易分析	
		詳細分析	

地下埋設物			
建物環境調査		アスベスト（フェーズⅡ）	
土壌汚染リスク評価		土壌調査（フェーズⅡ）	
		環境アセスメント等	
耐震性調査		建築士等による耐震診断	

（注）「フェーズⅠ」とは現地調査・資料収集分析・ヒアリングによる有害又は汚染物質の可能性の調査、「フェーズⅡ」とは試料採取と化学的分析による有害又は汚染物質の有無の確認を行う調査。「簡易分析」とは統計的な手法による分析、「詳細分析」とは解析的な手法による分析。

各論・第3章

記入日		物件名称		物件所在地	

調査年月日	作成年月日	入手先	入手年月日

鑑定評価において活用した事項とその根拠

Specific Standards Chapter 3

Appendix 2

Identification of the subject property

	Location and block number	Land category	Lot area			
Land						
Building	Location	House number	Structure	Purpose	Floor area	Date co...

			1	2	·	·	·	·	·	·	·
(a)	Effective gross income	Potential gross income									
(b)		Income from common area charges									
(c)		Rental income, including income from common area charges [(a)+(b)]									
(d)		Utility fee income									
(e)		Parking fee income									
(f)		Other income									
①		(c) + (d) + (e) + (f)									
		Vacancy allowance for (c) and (d)									
		Vacancy allowance for (e) and (f)									
(g)		Total vacancy allowance									
(h)		Collection losses allowance									
②	Effective gross income [①−(g)−(h)]										
(i)	Operating expenses	Maintenance and management expenses									
(j)		Utility expenses									
(k)		Repair expenses									
(l)		Property management fees									
(m)		Tenant recruitment expenses, etc.									
(n)		Real estate taxes — Land									
		Real estate taxes — Buildings									
		Real estate taxes — Depreciable assets									
(o)		Casualty insurance premiums									
(p)		Other expenses									
③		Operating expenses [(i)+(j)+(k)+(l)+(m)+(n)+(o)+(p)]									
④	Net operating income [②−③]										
(q)		Operating profit on lump-sum payments									
(r)		Capital expenditures									
⑤	Net cash flow [④+(q)−(r)]										
		(Reference)									
		Operating efficiency ratio (OER)									
		Balance of lump-sum payments (refundable deposits)									
		Compound present value rate									
(s)		Present value									
(t)		Total for (s) column									

Value indicated by the income approach ((t)+(x)) *	

(u) Sale value — ⑤ for n+1 years / z
(v) Sale expenses
(w) Reversionary value (u)-(v)
(x) Current reversionary value
(y) Discount rate
(z) Terminal capitalization rate

各論・第3章

mpleted

n	Year after expiration of the preservation period (n+1)	Grounds for assessment			Additional comments
		Assessment method			
		If data obtained from the client or other informational materials were used, were any modifications made, or did the LREA use data which he had obtained himself? State the grounds for those decisions.	Anticipated changes		

		Reasons for conclusion	Additional comments
	%		
	%		

275

Specific Standards Chapter 3

別表2

対象不動産の表示

	所在及び地番	地目	地目		
土地					
建物	所在	家屋番号	構造	用途	床面積	新築

				1	2	・	・	・	・	・	・
(a)	運営収益 ①		貸室賃料収入								
(b)			共益費収入								
(c)			(共益費込み貸室賃料収入) [(a)＋(b)]								
(d)			水道光熱費収入								
(e)			駐車場収入								
(f)			その他収入（　　　）								
			(c)＋(d)＋(e)＋(f)								
			(c)(d)空室等損失								
			(e)(f)空室等損失								
(g)			空室等損失合計								
(h)			貸倒損失								
②	運営収益　[①−(g)−(h)]										
(i)	運営費用 ③		維持管理費								
(j)			水道光熱費								
(k)			修繕費								
(l)			プロパティマネジメントフィー								
(m)			テナント募集費用等								
(n)		公租公課	土地								
			建物								
			償却資産								
(o)			損害保険料								
(p)			その他費用								
③			運営費用 [(i)＋(j)＋(k)＋(l)＋(m)＋(n)＋(o)＋(p)]								
④	運営純収益　[②−③]										
(q)			一時金の運用益								
(r)			資本的支出								
⑤	純収益 [④＋(q)−(r)]										
			(参考)								
			OEM（運用費用／運営収益）								
			預り一時金（敷金・保証金等）残高								
			複利現価率								
(s)			現在価値								
(t)			(S)欄合計								

収益価格((t)＋(x))　※　_____

(u)	売却価額（(n+1)年度の⑤÷(z)）
(v)	売却費用
(w)	復帰価格(u)−(v)
(x)	復帰価格現在価値
(y)	割引率
(z)	最終還元利回り

各論・第3章

年月日				

n	保有期間満了時点翌年(n+1)	査定根拠		
		査定方法	変動予測	補足
		依頼者から入手した資料又はその他の史料を採用する場合、修正を加える場合、自らが入手した資料を採用する場合の別及びその根拠		

	査定根拠	補足
%		
%		

277

PART4

Guidance Notes on the Real Estate Appraisal Standards

Revised on July 3, 2002
Partly revised on April 2, 2007
Ministry of Land, Infrastructure, Transport and Tourism

第4編

不動産鑑定評価基準運用上の留意事項

平成14年7月3日全部改正
平成19年4月2日一部改正
国 土 交 通 省

Table of Contents

GUIDANCE NOTES ON GENERAL STANDARDS (GS):

Guidance Note I on GS. Chap. 2 :
USE CATEGORIES AND PHYSICAL DEVELOPMENT
& TITLE CATEGORIES OF REAL ESTATE ············282

Guidance Note II on GS. Chap. 3 :
INFLUENCES ON REAL ESTATE VALUE ············286
1. Property-Specific Value Influences on Land ············286
2. Property-Specific Value Influences on Buildings ············288
3. Property-Specific Value Influences on Built-Up Property ············288

Guidance Note III on GS. Chap. 5 :
BASIC APPRAISAL PROBLEM ············290
1. Identification of the Subject Property ············290
2. Identification of the Date of the Value Opinion ············292
3. Identification of the Type of Value to be Determined by the Appraisal ············292

Guidance Note IV on GS. Chap. 6 :
MARKET AREA ANALYSIS AND PROPERTY ANALYSIS ············298
1. Performing the Market Area Analysis ············298
2. Performing the Property Analysis ············302

Guidance Note V on GS. Chap. 7 :
APPRAISAL METHOD ············304
1. Appraisal Approaches for Determining Real Estate Value ············304
2. Appraisal Approaches for Determining Rent ············326

Guidance Note VI on GS. Chap. 8 :
APPRAISAL PROCESS ············328

GUIDANCE NOTES ON SPECIFIC STANDARDS (SS):

Guidance Note VII on SS. Chap. 1 :
APPRAISAL OF REAL ESTATE VALUE ············330
1. Building Sites ············330
2. Built-Up Property ············338

Guidance Note VIII on SS. Chap. 2 :
APPRAISAL OF REAL ESTATE RENTAL VALUE ············340
1. Building Sites ············340
2. Built-Up Property ············340

Guidance Note IX on SS. Chap. 3 :
APPRAISAL OF REAL ESTATE VALUE SUBJECT TO SECURITIZATION ············342

SUPPLEMENTARY PROVISION ············344

目　次

総論　留意事項
Ⅰ 「総論第2章　不動産の種別及び類型」について …………………………………283
Ⅱ 「総論第3章　不動産の価格を形成する要因」について ……………………………287
　1．土地に関する個別的要因について …………………………………287
　2．建物に関する個別的要因について …………………………………289
　3．建物及びその敷地に関する個別的要因について …………………………………289
Ⅲ 「総論第5章　鑑定評価の基本的事項」について …………………………………291
　1．対象不動産の確定について …………………………………291
　2．価格時点の確定について …………………………………293
　3．鑑定評価によって求める価格の確定について …………………………………293
Ⅳ 「総論第6章　地域分析及び個別分析」について …………………………………299
　1．地域分析の適用について …………………………………299
　2．個別分析の適用について …………………………………303
Ⅴ 「総論第7章　鑑定評価の方式」について …………………………………305
　1．価格を求める鑑定評価の手法について …………………………………305
　2．賃料を求める鑑定評価の手法について …………………………………327
Ⅵ 「総論第8章　鑑定評価の手順」について …………………………………329

各論　留意事項
Ⅶ 「各論第1章　価格に関する鑑定評価」について …………………………………331
　1．宅地について …………………………………331
　2．建物及びその敷地について …………………………………339

Ⅷ 「各論第2章　賃料に関する鑑定評価」について …………………………………341
　1．宅地について …………………………………341
　2．建物及びその敷地について …………………………………341

Ⅸ 「各論第3章　証券化対象不動産の価格に関する鑑定評価」について …………………………………343

附　則 …………………………………345

Guidance Notes on the General Standards (GS) and the Specific Standards (SS) of the Real Estate Appraisal Standards are provided below.

> ## Guidance Note I on GS. Chap. 2 :
> ## USE CATEGORIES AND PHYSICAL DEVELOPMENT & TITLE CATEGORIES OF REAL ESTATE

Classification of real estate by use category is an important step carried out through various procedures in the appraisal process, such as market area analysis, property analysis and the application of the appraisal approaches. Exact classification further enhances the accuracy of the appraisal. The following detailed categories should be considered in analyzing residential and commercial neighborhoods.

(1) **Residential Areas**
① Residential areas with an established reputation, characterized by large lots, blocks and plots in an orderly arrangement; abundant green space, and scenic views; rows of buildings of high- quality construction; and a remarkably pleasant residential environment.
② Residential areas in a pleasant residential environment, created primarily by residences of standard- quality construction on standard- sized lots.
③ Residential areas made up of concentrations of comparatively small single- family residences and low- rise apartment houses, or residential areas consisting primarily of residences but also containing a mix of shops, offices and small factories.
④ Rural community areas and residential areas that have not become a part of built- up urban areas; primarily consisting of conventional farmhouses (such rural communities may be located within commuting distance of urban areas).

(2) **Commercial Areas**
① **Prime Commercial Areas**
Prime commercial areas are located in the centers or nodes of large cities (such as Tokyo and other major cities with the ward system) that draw clientele from over a large trade area. Prime commercial areas are characterized by a high concentration of comparatively large- scale, medium- or high- rise shops and offices. These areas may be further broken down into the following subcategories according to the specific features of the prime commercial area.
  a. **Prime Retail Areas**
  Areas with a high concentration of high- end shops with large sales volume.
  b. **Prime Office Areas**
  Areas with a high concentration of office buildings, occupied by government agencies, corporations and financial institutions.
  c. **Prime Areas of Retail/Office Mix**
  Areas with a high concentration of shops and offices.
② **Central Commercial Areas**
Following prime commercial areas in order of magnitude, central commercial areas draw clientele from over a broad trade area, and are characterized by rows of shops

不動産鑑定評価基準総論（以下「総論」という。）及び同基準各論（以下「各論」という。）運用上の留意事項は以下のとおり。

I 「総論第2章　不動産の種別及び類型」について

不動産の種別の分類は、不動産の鑑定評価における地域分析、個別分析、鑑定評価手法の適用等の各手順を通じて重要な事項となっており、これらを的確に分類、整理することは鑑定評価の精密さを一段と高めることとなるものである。鑑定評価において代表的な宅地地域である住宅地域及び商業地域について、さらに細分化すると次のような分類が考えられる。

(1) 住宅地域
① 敷地が広く、街区及び画地が整然とし、植生と眺望、景観等が優れ、建築の施工の質の高い建物が連たんし、良好な近隣環境を形成する等居住環境の極めて良好な地域であり、従来から名声の高い住宅地域
② 敷地の規模及び建築の施工の質が標準的な住宅を中心として形成される居住環境の良好な住宅地域
③ 比較的狭小な戸建住宅及び共同住宅が密集する住宅地域又は住宅を主として店舗、事務所、小工場等が混在する住宅地域
④ 都市の通勤圏の内外にかかわらず、在来の農家住宅等を主とする集落地域及び市街地的形態を形成するに至らない住宅地域

(2) 商業地域
① 高度商業地域
　高度商業地域は、例えば、大都市（東京23区、政令指定都市等）の都心又は副都心にあって、広域的商圏を有し、比較的大規模な中高層の店舗、事務所等が高密度に集積している地域であり、高度商業地域の性格に応じて、さらに、次のような細分類が考えられる。
　ア　一般高度商業地域
　　主として繁華性、収益性等が極めて高い店舗が高度に集積している地域
　イ　業務高度商業地域
　　主として行政機関、企業、金融機関等の事務所が高度に集積している地域
　ウ　複合高度商業地域
　　店舗と事務所が複合して高度に集積している地域

② 準高度商業地域
　高度商業地域に次ぐ商業地域であって、広域的な商圏を有し、店舗、事務所等が連たんし、商業地としての集積の程度が高い地域

Guidance Note I

and offices, and high commercial concentration.

③ **Second – tier Commercial Areas**

Second- tier commercial areas refer to commercial areas other than prime commercial areas, central commercial areas, neighborhood commercial areas (see below) or suburban roadside commercial areas (see below); these commercial areas are located in the city center or an urban node and consist of rows of shops, offices, and buildings with other uses.

④ **Neighborhood Commercial Areas**

Areas consisting of rows of shops that sell articles of daily consumption, primarily for neighborhood residents.

⑤ **Suburban Roadside Commercial Areas**

Areas consisting of rows of shops and businesses located along arterial roads (national highways, prefecture highways) outside cities.

③ 普通商業地域
　　高度商業地域、準高度商業地域、近隣商業地域及び郊外路線商業地域以外の商業地域であって、都市の中心商業地域及びこれに準ずる商業地域で、店舗、事務所等が連たんし、多様な用途に供されている地域

④ 近隣商業地域
　　主として近隣の居住者に対する日用品等の販売を行う店舗等が連たんしている地域

⑤ 郊外路線商業地域
　　都市の郊外の幹線道路（国道、都道府県道等）沿いにおいて、店舗、営業所等が連たんしている地域

Guidance Note II on GS. Chap. 3 : INFLUENCES ON REAL ESTATE VALUE

Particular attention should be given to the following items with respect to property- specific value influences relating to land, buildings, and buildings and building sites, discussed in Chapter 3 of the General Topics (Influences on the Value of Real Estate).

1. Guidance on Property – Specific Value Influences on Land

(1) The Presence of Buried Cultural Assets

There are situations where the presence of buried cultural assets, as defined in the *Cultural Properties Protection Law,* may have a considerable effect on the value of a site. This may be the result of excavation surveys required under the above law, the cessation and prohibition of activities that would alter the condition of buried cultural assets, the costs of changing building plans, or possible restrictions on land use.

Particular attention must be paid to the following matters regarding both the likelihood of cultural assets being buried on the subject property and their condition. In so doing, the appraiser must consider procedures mandated under the *Cultural Properties Protection Law* as well as the characteristics of the subject property.

① Whether or not the subject property is included in an area containing known buried cultural assets, as defined in the *Cultural Properties Protection Law*

② Whether or not measures such as registered excavation surveys or test drilling surveys have indicated the presence of buried cultural assets

③ Whether or not it has already been determined that buried cultural assets exist on the site (if an excavation survey had been conducted in the past, what were the findings and what measures were taken?)

④ Whether civil engineering work should be halted or the building design changed to protect important remains discovered in the course of a survey

(2) The Presence and Current Status of Soil Contamination

Soil contamination may have a considerable effect on the value of a site as a result of the cost incurred to remove the contaminants and possible restrictions on land use.

Particular attention must be paid to the following matters regarding the presence of contaminants on the subject property and their condition. In so doing, the appraiser must consider procedures mandated under the *Soil Contamination Measures Law* as well as the characteristics of the subject property.

① Whether or not the subject property includes a factory or business facility that uses harmful substances and falls under the category of a polluted site stipulated in Article 3 of the *Soil Contamination Measures Law*, and whether or not a factory or business facility that falls under the category stipulated in Article 3 of the above Act existed on the subject site before the law came into effect.

② Whether or not an investigation into the status of soil pollution on the subject site is required after operation of the factory or business facility that used harmful sub-

Ⅱ 「総論第3章　不動産の価格を形成する要因」について

「総論第3章　不動産の価格を形成する要因」で例示された土地、建物並びに建物及びその敷地に係る個別的要因に関しては、特に次のような観点に留意すべきである。

1．土地に関する個別的要因について
(1) 埋蔵文化財の有無及びその状態について

文化財保護法で規定された埋蔵文化財については、同法に基づく発掘調査、現状を変更することとなるような行為の停止又は禁止、設計変更に伴う費用負担、土地利用上の制約等により、価格形成に重大な影響を与える場合がある。

埋蔵文化財の有無及びその状態に関しては、対象不動産の状況と文化財保護法に基づく手続きに応じて次に掲げる事項に特に留意する必要がある。

① 対象不動産が文化財保護法に規定する周知の埋蔵文化財包蔵地に含まれるか否か。
② 埋蔵文化財の記録作成のための発掘調査、試掘調査等の措置が指示されているか否か。
③ 埋蔵文化財が現に存することが既に判明しているか否か（過去に発掘調査等が行われている場合にはその履歴及び措置の状況）。
④ 重要な遺跡が発見され、保護のための調査が行われる場合には、土木工事等の停止又は禁止の期間、設計変更の要否等。

(2) 土壌汚染の有無及びその状態について

土壌汚染が存する場合には、汚染物質に係る除去等の費用の発生や土地利用上の制約により、価格形成に重大な影響を与える場合がある。

土壌汚染対策法で規定された土壌汚染の有無及びその状態に関しては、対象不動産の状況と土壌汚染対策法に基づく手続きに応じて次に掲げる事項に特に留意する必要がある。

① 対象不動産が、土壌汚染対策法第3条に規定する有害物質使用特定施設に係る工場又は事業場の敷地を含むか否か、又は同法の施行の前に有害物質使用特定施設に相当する工場又は事業場の敷地であった履歴を有する土地を含むか否か。
② 対象不動産について有害物質使用特定施設の使用の廃止に伴い、土壌汚染対策法第3条に規定する土壌の汚染の状況についての調査義務が発生しているか否か、又は同法第4条の規定により都道府県知事から土壌の汚染の状況についての調査を実施することを命ぜられているか否か。
③ 対象不動産について土壌汚染対策法第5条に規定する指定区域の指定がなされているか否か、又は過去において指定区域指定の解除がなされた履歴があるか否か。

stances has ceased, in accordance with Article 3 of the *Soil Contamination Measures Law*, and whether or not a local governor has ordered a survey of the status of soil pollution under the provisions of Article 4 of the same Act.

③　Whether or not the subject property has been included in a designated area under Article 5 of the *Soil Contamination Measures Law*, and whether or not that designation was later repealed.

④　Whether or not a local governor, under the provisions of Article 7 of the *Soil Contamination Measures Law*, has ordered that measures be deployed to clean up pollution on the subject property.

2. Guidance on Property – Specific Value Influences on Buildings

(1) Design, Facilities and Functionality

Particular attention must be given to typical floorplate size, ceiling height, floor loads, telecommunications facilities, air-conditioning facilities and electrical capacity.

(2) Building Performance

The appraiser must ascertain whether the earthquake resistance of a building complies with earthquake resistance standards based on the *Building Standards Act*. In addition, for residential valuations, the appraiser should investigate the following items based on guidelines of the *Japan Home Performance Standards*, which were established under the *Housing Quality Assurance Law*: stability of the building structure, fire safety and the curing of deterioration, the level of maintenance and management, climate control and heating, air quality, lighting and visual environment, noise abatement, and special considerations for the elderly and handicapped.

(3) Level of Maintenance and Management

Particular attention must be paid to the upkeep of depreciable items, among which are included the roof, exterior walls, floors, interior finish, electrical wiring, water and drainage facilities and sanitary facilities.

(4) Presence of Harmful Substances and Current Status

The appraiser must check on the presence of asbestos insulation, the implementation of measures to prevent its dissipation, and the presence of polychloride biphenyls (PCBs) and the condition of their storage.

3. Guidance on Property-Specific Value Influences on Built-Up Property

(1) Tenant Status and Lease Contract Provisions

Particular attention must be given to any history of arrears in rent or breaches of contract. Tenant attributes (e. g., industry type, company size), and the ratio of the rental area occupied by the anchor tenant relative to the total rentable area should also be investigated.

(2) Quality of Repair Projects, Management Plans and Implementation

The appraiser must investigate any large-scale repair projects, the history of building repair projects, management bylaws, the property manager, and management services provided.

④ 対象不動産について土壌汚染対策法第7条の規定により都道府県知事から汚染の除去等の措置を講ずべきことを命ぜられているか否か。

2．建物に関する個別的要因について
(1) 設計、設備等の機能性
　　基準階面積、階高、床荷重、情報通信対応設備の状況、空調設備の状況、電気容量等に特に留意する必要がある。
(2) 建物の性能
　　建物の耐震性については、建築基準法に基づく耐震基準との関係について特に留意する必要がある。また、建物の構造の安定、火災時の安全、劣化の軽減、維持管理への配慮、温熱環境、空気環境、光・視環境、音環境、高齢者等への配慮に関する事項については、住宅の場合、住宅の品質確保の促進等に関する法律に基づく日本住宅性能表示基準による性能表示を踏まえることに留意する必要がある。

(3) 維持管理の状態
　　屋根、外壁、床、内装、電気設備、給排水設備、衛生設備等に関する破損・老朽化等の状況及び保全の状態について特に留意する必要がある。

(4) 有害な物質の使用の有無及びその状態
　　建設資材としてのアスベストの使用の有無及び飛散防止等の措置の実施状況並びにポリ塩化ビフェニル（PCB）の使用状況及び保管状況に特に留意する必要がある。

3．建物及びその敷地に関する個別的要因について
(1) 借主の状況及び賃貸借契約の内容
　　賃料の滞納の有無及びその他契約内容の履行状況、借主の属性（業種、企業規模等）、総賃貸可能床面積に占める主たる借主の賃貸面積の割合に特に留意する必要がある。

(2) 修繕計画及び管理計画の良否並びにその実施の状態
　　大規模修繕に係る修繕計画の有無及び修繕履歴の内容、管理規約の有無、管理委託先、管理サービスの内容等に特に留意する必要がある。

Guidance Note III on GS. Chap. 5 : BASIC APPRAISAL PROBLEM

1. Guidance on Identification of the Subject Property
(1) Setting Assumptions and Limiting Conditions for the Appraisal

The value of real estate sometimes cannot simply be determined on the basis of the actual use of the subject, ownership and interests in the property and value influences acting on the area or property. In order to reflect the attributes of various real estate transactions and to meet other requirements, the appraiser must make special assumptions and limiting conditions in certain appraisal assignments.

Setting assumptions and limiting conditions for the appraisal helps ensure that the identification of the subject property fits the specifications and the purpose of the client's request and that any additional conditions regarding specific value influences acting on the area or property are clear. Thus, setting assumptions and limiting conditions for the appraisal defines the scope of the appraisal as well as the scope of liability of the LREA, who performs the appraisal.

(2) Procedures for Setting Assumptions and Limiting Conditions for the Appraisal

Since the assumptions and limiting conditions for the appraisal are set by the specifications in the client's request, they are confirmed indirectly by the LREA when the real estate appraisal firm accepts the assignment. However, since the final value opinion may differ depending on the subject property identification and any conditions assumed with respect to value influences acting on the area and property, the LREA should directly confirm the specifications in the client's request.

① **Requirement for the Subject Identification**

The appraiser must consider how valid the specifications and purpose of the client's request are after identifying the subject property and confirming the attributes of the subject. Under ordinary circumstances, the appraiser may value the subject site as though vacant and free of encumbrances even if improvements occupy the site or restrictive covenants run with the site. However, when the appraisal is expected to significantly affect the benefits to involved parties or interested third parties, the appraiser should value the property as is (i.e., the appraiser should consider all the existing improvements and encumbrances on the property.) Examples of such situations include appraisals for mortgage origination and the issuing of securities based on mortgages.

② **Setting Additional Assumptions and Limiting Conditions Regarding Value Influences Acting on the Market Area or Subject Property**

Where assumptions are added:

    a. Additional conditions imposed must be agreed upon in the appraisal contract with the client, and there must be a reasonable certainty of said conditions being realized in view of the ability of involved parties to bring them about. Where additional assumptions are made with respect to market- specific value

Ⅲ 「総論第5章 鑑定評価の基本的事項」について

1．対象不動産の確定について

(1) 鑑定評価の条件設定の意義

　　鑑定評価に際しては、現実の用途及び権利の態様並びに地域要因及び個別的要因を所与として不動産の価格を求めることのみでは多様な不動産取引の実態に即応することができず、社会的な需要に応ずることができない場合があるので、条件設定の必要性が生じてくる。

　　条件の設定は、依頼目的に応じて対象不動産の内容を確定し（対象確定条件）、又は付加する地域要因若しくは個別的要因についての想定上の条件を明確にするものである。したがって、条件設定は、鑑定評価の妥当する範囲及び鑑定評価を行った不動産鑑定士の責任の範囲を示すという意義を持つものである。

(2) 鑑定評価の条件設定の手順

　　鑑定評価の条件は、依頼内容に応じて設定するもので、不動産鑑定士は不動産鑑定業者の受付という行為を通じてこれを間接的に確認することとなる。しかし、同一不動産であっても設定された対象確定条件の如何又は付加する地域要因若しくは個別的要因についての想定上の条件の如何によっては鑑定評価額に差異が生ずるものであるから、不動産鑑定士は直接、依頼内容の確認を行うべきである。

① 対象確定条件について

　　対象確定条件については、対象不動産に係る諸事項についての調査、確認を行った上で、依頼目的に照らしてその条件の妥当性を検討しなければならない。特に、対象不動産が土地及び建物の結合により構成される場合又はその使用収益を制約する権利が付着している場合において、例えば抵当権の設定のための鑑定評価、設定された抵当権をもとに証券を発行するための鑑定評価等関係当事者及び第三者の利益に当該鑑定評価が重大な影響を及ぼす可能性のあるときは、独立鑑定評価を行うべきでなく、その状態を所与として鑑定評価を行うべきである。

② 地域要因又は個別的要因についての想定上の条件の付加について

　　想定上の条件を付加する場合において、

　ア　実現性とは、依頼者との間で条件付加に係る鑑定評価依頼契約上の合意があり、当該条件を実現するための行為を行う者の事業遂行能力等を勘案した上で当該条件が実現する確実性が認められることをいう。なお、地域要因についての想定上の条件を付加する場合には、その実現に係る権能を持つ公的機関の担当部局から当該条件が実現する確実性について直接確認すべきことに留意すべきである。

Guidance Note III

influences, the certainty of said conditions being realized should be confirmed directly with the responsible section of the authority involved in their realization.

b. "Legally permissible" means that additional assumptions and limiting conditions must comply with the stipulations of relevant laws and covenants.

c. Many parties rely on appraisals performed by LREAs. Involved parties and interested third parties include the client, persons with a close interest in the results of the appraisal, purchasers of securities issued on the basis of revenue generated by the real estate (the law mandates that such real estate must be appraised by an LREA) and purchasers of securities issued on mortgages approved on the basis of the conclusions of an appraisal.

Where it is recognized that additional assumptions or limiting conditions lack validity, such assumptions and limiting conditions must be revised and the client informed.

2. Guidance on Identification of the Date of the Value Opinion

A retrospective value opinion can only be performed when it is possible to confirm the attributes of the subject property at that point in time, and to gather data on value influences and comparable data required for the valuation. With the passage of time between the date of the value opinion and the date of the appraisal report, change will likely have occurred in the subject property and neighborhood. Thus, confirmation of the attributes of the subject property on the date of the value opinion (in cases where the property has undergone change during the interim) should be based on as much identification data as can be gathered for a point in time near the date of the value opinion.

A prospective value opinion assumes it is possible to identify the future attributes of the subject real estate, to forecast future value influences, and to determine the property's future highest and best use. Since all information gathered is necessarily limited to circumstances up to the date of the appraisal report, the results of a prospective appraisal can only be tentative, and as a general rule, prospective appraisals should not be performed. However, some situations will require a value opinion at some future date. Prospective appraisals can only be performed when sound appraisal procedures are assured.

3. Guidance on Identification of the Type of Value to be Determined by the Appraisal

(1) Market Value

Reasonable conditions under actual socio-economic circumstances are described below.

① Ordinary Ability of a Buyer to Procure Funds

The ordinary ability of a buyer to procure funds is understood within the context of normal or typical borrowing conditions (in terms of the loan-to-value ratio, the interest rate on the loan, and the amortization period of the loan) for the market in which the subject property is being acquired.

② Appropriate Market Exposure Time for the Subject Property

An appropriate exposure time on the market refers to the period of time required for in-

イ　合法性とは、公法上及び私法上の諸規制に反しないことをいう。
　　ウ　関係当事者及び第三者とは、依頼者及び鑑定評価の結果について依頼者と密接な利害関係を有する者のほか、法律に義務づけられた不動産鑑定士による鑑定評価を踏まえ不動産の生み出す収益を原資として発行される証券の購入者、鑑定評価を踏まえ設定された抵当権をもとに発行される証券の購入者等をいう。
　　想定上の条件が妥当性を欠くと認められる場合には依頼者に説明の上、妥当な条件へ改定することが必要である。

2．価格時点の確定について

　過去時点の鑑定評価は、対象不動産の確認等が可能であり、かつ、鑑定評価に必要な要因資料及び事例資料の収集が可能な場合に限り行うことができる。また、時の経過により対象不動産及びその近隣地域等が価格時点から鑑定評価を行う時点までの間に変化している場合もあるので、このような事情変更のある場合の価格時点における対象不動産の確認等については、価格時点に近い時点の確認資料等をできる限り収集し、それを基礎に判断すべきである。
　将来時点の鑑定評価は、対象不動産の確定、価格形成要因の把握、分析及び最有効使用の判定についてすべて想定し、又は予測することとなり、また、収集する資料についても鑑定評価を行う時点までのものに限られ、不確実にならざるを得ないので、原則として、このような鑑定評価は行うべきではない。ただし、特に必要がある場合において、鑑定評価上妥当性を欠くことがないと認められるときは将来の価格時点を設定することができるものとする。

3．鑑定評価によって求める価格の確定について
(1)　正常価格について

　現実の社会経済情勢の下で合理的と考えられる条件について

① 買主が通常の資金調達能力を有していることについて
　通常の資金調達能力とは、買主が対象不動産の取得に当たって、市場における標準的な借入条件（借入比率、金利、借入期間等）の下での借り入れと自己資金とによって資金調達を行うことができる能力をいう。

② 対象不動産が相当の期間市場に公開されていることについて
　相当の期間とは、対象不動産の取得に際し必要となる情報が公開され、需要者層に十分浸透するまでの期間をいう。なお、相当の期間とは、価格時点における不動産市場の需給動向、

Guidance Note III

formation to disseminate among potential buyers prior to the acquisition of the subject property. The appropriate period of time differs according to supply and demand trends in the real estate market on the date of the value opinion as well as the type and nature of the subject property.

In addition, exposure implies that the subject property was placed on the market before the date of the value opinion. In other words, an exposure period does not mean the time between the date of the value opinion and the consummation of a sale.

(2) **Value for Regulated Purposes (VRP)**
① **In Compliance with Specific Laws and Ordinances**
The term "laws and ordinances" is a broad category, which includes government laws and ordinances, cabinet ordinances, ministerial ordinances, other regulations, proclamations, directives and notifications of government agencies, as well as supreme court rulings, the ordinances and regulations of local public entities, and corporate accounting and auditing standards. (see Part1 Chap.2. I .Japan- 3)
② **Examples of Situations Requiring Value for Regulated Purposes (VRP)**
The rationale for requiring VRP is discussed below. Basic appraisal procedure is also illustrated in the three examples that follow.

a. **Where the purpose of the appraisal is to arrive at an indication of investment profitability value for investors as required under the** *Asset Liquidation Law* **or the** *Investment Trust and Investment Corporation Law.*

In this case, the determination of investment profitability value is based on the value indicated by the income capitalization approach, which reflects the earning ability of the subject property. The purpose of such appraisals is to protect investors by disclosing the value of the real estate assets of investment corporations, investment trusts or special purpose corporation (collectively referred to as investment corporations) either at the time of the acquisition of the real estate assets or during the holding period.

When appraising a real property for investors corporation either at the time of acquisition or during the holding period, the appraiser must estimate its value based on an operation management scheme, which is disclosed to the investors. Therefore, the value does not necessarily satisfy all conditions for the highest and best use on which market value is premised. Thus, the VRP must be determined. It should also be noted that the value in appraisals, requested by investors for the disposal of real estate, is determined on the basis of market value.

The primary appraisal method used is Discounted Cash Flow Analysis (a method in the income capitalization approach). The final value opinion is determined by verifying the DCF indication against the value indicated by direct capitalization, and reconciling this figure with the values indi cated by the sales comparison approach and the cost approach.

b. **Where appraisals are required for a quick sale under the** *Civil Rehabilitation Law*

The determination of VRP is also required in the disposition of assets under the

対象不動産の種類、性格等によって異なることに留意すべきである。
　また、公開されていることとは、価格時点において既に市場で公開されていた状況を想定することをいう（価格時点以降売買成立時まで公開されることではないことに留意すべきである。）。

(2) 特定価格について
① 法令等について
　法令等とは、法律、政令、内閣府令、省令、その他国の行政機関の規則、告示、訓令、通達等のほか、最高裁判所規則、条例、地方公共団体の規則、企業会計の基準、監査基準をいう。

② 特定価格を求める場合の例について
　特定価格として求める場合の例として掲げられているものについての特定価格として求める理由及び鑑定評価の基本的な手法等は次のとおりである。

ア　資産の流動化に関する法律又は投資信託及び投資法人に関する法律に基づく鑑定評価目的の下で、投資家に示すための投資採算価値を表す価格を求める場合
　この場合は、投資法人、投資信託又は特定目的会社（以下「投資法人等」という。）に係る特定資産としての不動産の取得時又は保有期間中の価格として投資家に開示されることを目的に、投資家保護の観点から対象不動産の収益力を適切に反映する収益価格に基づいた投資採算価値を求める必要がある。
　特定資産の取得時又は保有期間中の価格としての鑑定評価に際しては、資産流動化計画等により投資家に開示される対象不動産の運用方法を所与とする必要があることから、必ずしも対象不動産の最有効使用を前提とするものではないため、特定価格として求めなければならない。なお、投資法人等が特定資産を譲渡するときに依頼される鑑定評価で求める価格は正常価格として求めることに留意する必要がある。
　鑑定評価の方法は、基本的に収益還元法のうちＤＣＦ法により求めた試算価格を標準とし、直接還元法による検証を行って求めた収益価格に基づき、比準価格及び積算価格による検証を行い鑑定評価額を決定する。

イ　民事再生法に基づく鑑定評価目的の下で、早期売却を前提とした価格を求める場合
　この場合は、民事再生法に基づく鑑定評価目的の下で、財産を処分するものとしての価格を求めるものであり、対象不動産の種類、性格、所在地域の実情に応じ、早期の処分可

Guidance Note III

Civil Rehabilitation Law. An appraiser must estimate a reasonable disposition value, considering the possibility of a quick sale of the subject property as well as the property type, its attributes, and the characteristics of the market.

Since the appraisal is premised on a quick sale, the value to be determined is VRP.

The final value opinion is determined by reconciling the values indicated by the sales comparison approach and income capitalization approach, premised upon the assumption of a quick sale. This figure is then verified against the value indicated by the cost approach. In situations where there is little comparable data, the final value opinion may be determined by adjusting the market value of the subject property (obtained by ordinary methods) downward to reflect the circumstance of the quick sale.

c. Where the purpose of the appraisal is to determine the value, premised on continuation of an enterprise, as required under the *Corporate Reorganization Law* and the *Civil Rehabilitation Law*

The *Corporate Reorganization Law* and the *Civil Rehabilitation Law* require an appraisal, which is based on the premise that the particular property is estimated as a part of the entity's continuing business.

Since the appraisal is premised upon the existing use of the subject property, which may not always represent the highest and best use, the value to be determined is VRP.

The final value opinion is generally determined from the value indicated by the income capitalization approach (based on the net cash flow (NCF) attributable to the real estate, as a portion of net cash flow (NCF) to the enterprise) compared with the value indicated by the sales comparison approach and verified against the value indicated by the cost approach.

能性を考慮した適正な処分価格として求める必要がある。

鑑定評価に際しては、通常の市場公開期間より短い期間で売却されることを前提とするものであるため特定価格として求めなければならない。

鑑定評価の方法は、この前提を所与とした上で、原則として、比準価格と収益価格を関連づけ、積算価格による検証を行って鑑定評価額を決定する。なお、比較可能な事例資料が少ない場合は、通常の方法で正常価格を求めた上で、早期売却に伴う減価を行って鑑定評価額を求めることもできる。

ウ　会社更生法又は民事再生法に基づく鑑定評価目的の下で、事業の継続を前提とした価格を求める場合

この場合は、会社更生法又は民事再生法に基づく鑑定評価目的の下で、現状の事業が継続されるものとして当該事業の拘束下にあることを前提とする価格を求めるものである。

鑑定評価に際しては、対象不動産の利用現況を所与とするため、必ずしも対象不動産の最有効使用を前提とするものではないことから特定価格として求めなければならない。

鑑定評価の方法は、原則として事業経営に基づく純収益のうち不動産に帰属する純収益に基づく収益価格を標準とし、比準価格を比較考量の上、積算価格による検証を行って鑑定評価額を決定する。

Guidance Note IV

> **Guidance Note IV on GS. Chap. 6 :**
> **MARKET AREA ANALYSIS AND PROPERTY ANALYSIS**

1. Guidance on Performing the Market Area Analysis
(1) Area Analysis of Subject Neighborhood

① Area analysis consists of investigating the neighborhood where the subject property is located, and ascertaining the characteristics of that neighborhood.

In analyzing the characteristics of the subject's market, the appraiser scrutinizes market-specific value influences, and identifies similarities and differences in influences affecting areas that surround the subject.

This process requires the analysis of an extensive area, including the subject's immediate neighborhood and other neighborhoods in the vicinity, to identify those areas in which the real estate is subject to common value influences.

② To ascertain the relative position of the subject neighborhood, the characteristics of the subject's market are first identified. Then, differences in area-specific value influences are assessed by comparing the area-specific value influences acting on similar neighborhoods in the subject's primary market area with market-specific value influences acting on the subject neighborhood. It is also useful to compare area-specific value influences acting on the subject neighborhood with market-specific value influences acting on other types of neighborhoods within the market.

③ Although the neighborhood analysis involves an investigation of data on value influences affecting the neighborhood where the subject property is located, the characteristics of the subject's market and specific value influences acting on the broader district that includes the neighborhood must be investigated prior to the neighborhood analysis. To accomplish this, data on value influences affecting a broad area must be routinely gathered and analyzed.

④ In analyzing area-specific value influences and trends or changes in market-specific value influences over the course of time, the appraiser must also identify trends in area-specific value influences affecting other areas surrounding the neighborhood as well as the degree to which those trends affect the neighborhood. The effects of such trends on the characteristics of the subject's market, and the use and value of land in the neighborhood should be understood.

With respect to interim use sites and lots in transitional areas, trends and changes in value influences affecting the surrounding areas serve as particularly useful indications of trends and changes in land use.

(2) Defining the Boundaries of the Neighborhood

To define the boundaries of the neighborhood, the appraiser should consider the following items, which influence basic land use and development readiness.

① **Natural Factors**
　a. **Rivers**
　　Wide rivers may affect street grid patterns, the placement of buildings, and the

Ⅳ 「総論第6章 地域分析及び個別分析」について

1．地域分析の適用について
(1) 近隣地域の地域分析について
① 近隣地域の地域分析は、まず対象不動産の存する近隣地域を明確化し、次いでその近隣地域がどのような特性を有するかを把握することである。

この対象不動産の存する近隣地域の明確化及びその近隣地域の特性の把握に当たっては、対象不動産を中心に外延的に広がる地域について、対象不動産に係る市場の特性を踏まえて地域要因をくり返し調査分析し、その異同を明らかにしなければならない。

これはまた、地域の構成分子である不動産について、最終的に地域要因を共通にする地域を抽出することとなるため、近隣地域となる地域及びその周辺の他の地域を併せて広域的に分析することが必要である。

② 近隣地域の相対的位置の把握に当たっては、対象不動産に係る市場の特性を踏まえて同一需給圏内の類似地域の地域要因と近隣地域の地域要因を比較して相対的な地域要因の格差の判定を行うものとする。さらに、近隣地域の地域要因とその周辺の他の地域の地域要因との比較検討も有用である。

③ 近隣地域の地域分析においては、対象不動産の存する近隣地域に係る要因資料についての分析を行うこととなるが、この分析の前提として、対象不動産に係る市場の特性や近隣地域を含むより広域的な地域に係る地域要因を把握し、分析しなければならない。このためには、日常から広域的な地域に係る要因資料の収集、分析に努めなければならない。

④ 近隣地域の地域分析における地域要因の分析に当たっては、近隣地域の地域要因についてその変化の過程における推移、動向を時系列的に分析するとともに、近隣地域の周辺の他の地域の地域要因の推移、動向及びそれらの近隣地域への波及の程度等について分析することが必要である。この場合において、対象不動産に係る市場の特性が近隣地域内の土地の利用形態及び価格形成に与える影響の程度を的確に把握することが必要である。

なお、見込地及び移行地については、特に周辺地域の地域要因の変化の推移、動向がそれらの土地の変化の動向予測に当たって有効な資料となるものである。

(2) 近隣地域の範囲の判定について
近隣地域の範囲の判定に当たっては、基本的な土地利用形態や土地利用上の利便性等に影響を及ぼす次に掲げるような事項に留意することが必要である。
① **自然的状態に係るもの**
ア　河川
川幅が広い河川等は、土地、建物等の連たん性及び地域の一体性を分断する場合がある

boundaries of contiguous areas.
- b. **Mountains and Hills**
  Mountains and hills not only affect street grid, building placement, and area unity; they can also have an effect on an area's sunlight, wind, dryness and dampness.
- c. Topography, Geology and Soil
  In addition to their effect on an area's sunlight, wind, dryness and dampness, the topography, geology and soil also have an effect on residential and commercial land use.

② **Socio – Economic Factors**
- a. **Political Boundaries**
  Political boundaries influence development readiness, and account for differences in the level of construction of streets, utilities, schools and other public facilities as well as in the real estate taxes levied.
- b. **Land Use Regulations**
  Land use regulations based on the *City Planning Act* and other laws affect land use.
- c. **Railways and Parks**
  Railway lines and parks may also influence the street grid, building placement, and area unity.
- d. **Roads**
  Similarly, wide roads may also affect the street grid, building placement, and area unity.

(3) **Characteristics of the Market for the Subject Property**
① **Market Definition**
- a. **The Attributes and Behavior of Market Participants in the Market Area**
  The appraiser should pay particular attention to the following matters in determining the attributes and behavior of market participants in the market area.
  - (a) In the case of commercial and industrial real estate, the attributes of market participants include the specific industries and businesses that make up the major demand and supply groups, and the form of legal entity (corporate or private individual). The extent of the area in which potential buyers are found must also be considered.

    In the case of residential real estate, the attributes of market participants include the age, family composition and income level of the major demand and supply groups and the area in which potential buyers are found.
  - (b) The appraiser should also identify specific value influences that will be considered by market participants, whose attributes were explained in the above paragraph, when they make decisions involving property transactions, including price levels and other criteria.
- b. **Supply and Demand Trends in the Market Area**
  The appraiser should give special consideration to the following matters in determining supply and demand trends in the market area.

イ　山岳及び丘陵

山岳及び丘陵は、河川と同様、土地、建物等の連たん性及び地域の一体性を分断するほか、日照、通風、乾湿等に影響を及ぼす場合があること。

ウ　地勢、地質、地盤等

地勢、地質、地盤等は、日照、通風、乾湿等に影響を及ぼすとともに、居住、商業活動等の土地利用形態に影響を及ぼすこと。

② 人文的状態に係るもの
ア　行政区域

行政区域の違いによる道路、水道その他の公共施設及び学校その他の公益的施設の整備水準並びに公租公課等の負担の差異が土地利用上の利便性等に影響を及ぼすこと。

イ　公法上の規制等

都市計画法等による土地利用の規制内容が土地利用形態に影響を及ぼすこと。

ウ　鉄道、公園等

鉄道、公園等は、土地、建物等の連たん性及び地域の一体性を分断する場合があること。

エ　道路

広幅員の道路等は、土地、建物等の連たん性及び地域の一体性を分断する場合があること。

(3)　対象不動産に係る市場の特性について
① 把握の観点
ア　同一需給圏における市場参加者の属性及び行動

同一需給圏における市場参加者の属性及び行動を把握するに当たっては、特に次の事項に留意すべきである。

(ア)　市場参加者の属性については、業務用不動産の場合、主たる需要者層及び供給者層の業種、業態、法人か個人かの別並びに需要者の存する地域的な範囲。

また、居住用不動産の場合、主たる需要者層及び供給者層の年齢、家族構成、所得水準並びに需要者の存する地域的な範囲

(イ)　(ア)で把握した属性を持つ市場参加者が取引の可否、取引価格、取引条件等について意思決定する際に重視する価格形成要因の内容

イ　同一需給圏における市場の需給動向

同一需給圏における市場の需給動向を把握するに当たっては、特に次に掲げる事項に留意すべきである。

Guidance Note IV

(a) Trends characterizing the supply of, and demand for, real estate similar to the subject property in terms of use, size and grade, and which is currently available in the market area.
(b) The effect of trends in the supply and demand situation (identified above) on the value of the subject property and how significant the effect of such trends is.

② **References and Publications Used**
To identify the characteristics of the subject's market, the appraiser must gather information on transactions (including the volume of transactions, sales prices, asking prices and offering prices) by routinely interviewing real estate firms, construction companies and financial institutions. It is also important to consult a wide range of publications relating to the local economy and transitions and trends in the real estate market, issued by public agencies, real estate firms, financial institutions and trade groups.

2. Guidance on Performing the Property Analysis
(1) Commentary on Analyzing Property – Specific Value Influences
The appraiser should address the following to determine the superiority or inferiority of the subject compared to real estate in a substitutive or competitive relationship, and the subject's competitiveness.
① The most popular price range for the same type of properties, and the attributes of the principal potential buyers
② Preferences of potential buyers as to property location, size, functions and surrounding environment
③ Number of inquiries about the subject property

(2) Commentary on Determining the Highest and Best Use
① **Important Pointers for Determining the Highest and Best Use: Premised on Changes Anticipated in Market – Specific Value Influences**
A high probability of the anticipated changes being realized within a specific timeframe must be supported by reliable data gathered at the time the appraisal is performed.

② **Important Pointers for Determining the Highest and Best Use of Building and Building Site:**
When demolition of the subject building or alteration of its use is assumed to be the highest and best use, the appraiser should compare the property's economic value after demolition or alteration against the required costs of demolition or alteration. The appraiser should also compare the property's economic value based on the assumption that the current use of the building were to continue unchanged.

a. The likelihood of demolition of the building or alteration of its use must be considered from the perspectives of physical possibility and legal permissibility.
b. Both the uncertainty of anticipated changes in income to the subject property, based on its increased competitiveness following demolition of the building or alteration of its use, and the expected amount of income lost during the alteration of use must be considered.

(ｱ) 同一需給圏内に存し、用途、規模、品等等が対象不動産と類似する不動産に係る需給の推移及び動向
　　(ｲ) (ｱ)で把握した需給の推移及び動向が対象不動産の価格形成に与える影響の内容及びその程度

② 把握のための資料
　対象不動産に係る市場の特性の把握に当たっては、平素から、不動産業者、建設業者及び金融機関等からの聴聞等によって取引等の情報（取引件数、取引価格、売り希望価格、買い希望価格等）を収集しておく必要がある。あわせて公的機関、不動産業者、金融機関、商工団体等による地域経済や不動産市場の推移及び動向に関する公表資料を幅広く収集し、分析することが重要である。

2．個別分析の適用について

(1) 個別的要因の分析上の留意点について
　対象不動産と代替、競争等の関係にある不動産と比べた優劣及び競争力の程度を把握するに当たっては、次の点に留意すべきである。
① 同一用途の不動産の需要の中心となっている価格帯及び主たる需要者の属性
② 対象不動産の立地、規模、機能、周辺環境等に係る需要者の選好
③ 対象不動産に係る引き合いの多寡

(2) 最有効使用の判定上の留意点について
① 地域要因が変動する予測を前提とした最有効使用の判定に当たっての留意点
　地域要因の変動の予測に当たっては、予測の限界を踏まえ、鑑定評価を行う時点で一般的に収集可能かつ信頼できる情報に基づき、当該変動の時期及び具体的内容についての実現の蓋然性が高いことが認められなければならない。

② 建物及びその敷地の最有効使用の判定に当たっての留意点
　最有効使用の観点から現実の建物の取壊しや用途変更等を想定する場合において、それらに要する費用等を勘案した経済価値と当該建物の用途等を継続する場合の経済価値とを比較考量するに当たっては、特に下記の内容に留意すべきである。
ア　物理的、法的にみた当該建物の取壊し、用途変更等の実現可能性
イ　建物の取壊し、用途変更後における対象不動産の競争力の程度等を踏まえた収益の変動予測の不確実性及び取壊し、用途変更に要する期間中の逸失利益の程度

Guidance Note V

Guidance Note V on GS. Chap. 7 : APPRAISAL METHOD

1. **Guidance on Appraisal Approaches for Determining Real Estate Value**
   (1) **General Guidance on Determining Value Indications**
       ① **Selection of Comparables**
           a. **In Situations Where the Appraiser Must Choose Comparables from Outside the Subject Neighborhood and Similar Neighborhoods**
           Such situations arise when most of the comparable sales data gathered in the subject neighborhood or similar neighborhoods nearby is significantly affected by special circumstances, and the appraisal cannot be performed without recourse to comparables in other areas.
           b. **Selection of Comparables from Substitutive or Competitive Real Estate in the Market Area for a Subject Property with a Highest and Best Use That Differs from the Standard Property Use in the Market Area**
           The highest and best use of the subject property often differs from the standard property use in its neighborhood because the subject property is fairly unique and its use is rarely subject to the market-specific value influences of its neighborhood, as shown in the following examples.
           (a) Large-scale plots in a predominantly single-family residential district that are especially suitable for multi-family buildings due to the area's excellent location and development potential; in a nearby residential district large-scale multi-family buildings have already been developed.
           (b) Hotels drawing a broad clientele and conveniently accessible but located in districts of medium- and high-rise office building use.
           (c) Regional shopping centers along arterial roads, drawing patrons from over a broad trade area but located in residential areas.
           (d) Large-scale, highly competitive office buildings developed on tracts assembled from smaller lots in small- and medium-size office building districts.
           c. **Commentary for Assessing a Substitutive or Competitive Relationship**
           Comparables selected from substitutive or competitive real estate in the primary market area (see the section (1)-①-b above) must satisfy the requirements indicated below.
           (a) Similarity to the subject property in terms of use, size and grade must be clearly observable.
           (b) The direct influence of the comparable property on the value of the subject property must be demonstrable.
       ② **Comparison of Market–Specific and Property–Specific Value Influences**
       In selecting data on substitutive or competitive real estate in the primary market area, the appraiser should not only compare property-specific value influences, but

V 「総論第7章 鑑定評価の方式」について

1．価格を求める鑑定評価の手法について
(1) 試算価格を求める場合の一般的留意事項について
① 取引事例等の選択について
ア 必要やむを得ない場合に近隣地域の周辺地域に存する不動産に係るものを選択する場合について

　この場合における必要やむを得ない場合とは、近隣地域又は同一需給圏内の類似地域に存する不動産について収集した取引事例等の大部分が特殊な事情による影響を著しく受けていることその他の特別な事情により当該取引事例等のみによっては鑑定評価を適切に行うことができないと認められる場合をいう。

イ 対象不動産の最有効使用が標準的使用と異なる場合等において同一需給圏内の代替競争不動産に係るものを選択する場合について

　この場合における対象不動産の最有効使用が標準的使用と異なる場合等とは、次のような場合として例示される対象不動産の個別性のために近隣地域の制約の程度が著しく小さいと認められるものをいう。

　(ｱ) 戸建住宅地域において、近辺で大規模なマンションの開発がみられるとともに、立地に優れ高度利用が可能なことから、マンション適地と認められる大規模な画地が存する場合

　(ｲ) 中高層事務所として用途が純化された地域において、交通利便性に優れ広域的な集客力を有するホテルが存する場合

　(ｳ) 住宅地域において、幹線道路に近接して、広域的な商圏を持つ郊外型の大規模小売店舗が存する場合

　(ｴ) 中小規模の事務所ビルが集積する地域において、敷地の集約化により完成した卓越した競争力を有する大規模事務所ビルが存する場合

ウ 代替、競争等の関係を判定する際の留意点について

　イの場合において選択する同一需給圏内の代替競争不動産に係る取引事例等は、次に掲げる要件に該当するものでなければならない。

　(ｱ) 対象不動産との間に用途、規模、品等等からみた類似性が明確に認められること。

　(ｲ) 対象不動産の価格形成に関して直接に影響を与えていることが明確に認められること。

② 地域要因の比較及び個別的要因の比較について
　取引事例等として同一需給圏内の代替競争不動産に係るものを選択する場合において、価格形成要因に係る対象不動産との比較を行う際には、個別的要因の比較だけでなく市場の特性に影響を与えている地域要因の比較もあわせて行うべきことに留意すべきである。

also the effect of market-specific influences on market characteristics.

(2) Guidance on Sales Comparison Approach

In applying the sales comparison approach, a large amount of comparable sales data must be gathered, and data must be selected that serves as a reliable indicator of value. To ensure the usefulness of that data, the appraiser should gather a wide range of information, including asking prices, offering prices and expert opinions in addition to comparable sales data.

Such information can be readily used for determining the price levels in the neighborhood as well as trends in land values.

① Gathering Data

Analysis of a large amount of comparable sales data is indispensable to identifying the special circumstances of individual transactions, determining the time adjustment, and deciding the effect of value influences on the value of the subject property. The comparable sales data selected provides the basis for the value indicated by the sales comparison approach while the reliability of the comparable sales data gathered determines the accuracy of that value indication.

The price of each sales comparable is affected by the use of the real estate, the appeal of the real estate, and the motives of the seller and buyer shaping the circumstances of the transaction. Thus, the appraiser must carefully analyze the circumstances of each transaction in the comparable sales data, the attributes of the involved parties (which are the same as the attributes of market participants described in Chapter IV of Guidance Notes to the Standards, "Chapter 6 of the General Topics: Neighborhood Analysis and Subject Property Analysis"), and trends in sales price levels.

② Adjustment for Conditions of Sale

To determine the need for, and magnitude of an adjustment for conditions of sale, a large amount of comparable sales data should be reviewed and analyzed. If it is determined that a conditions of sale adjustment is required, the appropriate adjustment will be based on the objective price level of the market in which the transactions took place.

Examples of special circumstances requiring adjustment for the conditions of sale are indicated below.

a. Special Circumstances Requiring a Downward Adjustment

(a) When transactions involve real estate, which has certain locational and/or operational advantages

(b) When transactions take place in markets characterized by atypical conditions, such as an extreme supply shortage or an overly optimistic outlook for the future

(c) When transactions occur between businesses or affiliated firms for the purpose of making profits on resale

(d) When transactions result in excessively high prices because buyers clearly lack information about, and knowledge of, the real estate

(e) When transactions include amounts other than compensation for the real es-

(2) 取引事例比較法について

　この手法の適用に当たっては、多数の取引事例を収集し、価格の指標となり得る事例の選択を行わなければならないが、その有効性を高めるため、取引事例はもとより、売り希望価格、買い希望価格、精通者意見等の資料を幅広く収集するよう努めるものとする。
　なお、これらの資料は、近隣地域等の価格水準及び地価の動向を知る上で十分活用し得るものである。

① 事例の収集について

　豊富に収集された取引事例の分析検討は、個別の取引に内在する特殊な事情を排除し、時点修正率を把握し、及び価格形成要因の対象不動産の価格への影響の程度を知る上で欠くことのできないものである。特に、選択された取引事例は、取引事例比較法を適用して比準価格を求める場合の基礎資料となるものであり、収集された取引事例の信頼度は比準価格の精度を左右するものである。
　取引事例は、不動産の利用目的、不動産に関する価値観の多様性、取引の動機による売主及び買主の取引事情等により各々の取引について考慮されるべき視点が異なってくる。したがって、取引事例に係る取引事情を始め取引当事者の属性（本留意事項の「Ⅳ「総論第6章　地域分析及び個別分析」について」に掲げる市場参加者の属性に同じ。）及び取引価格の水準の変動の推移を慎重に分析しなければならない。

② 事情補正について

　事情補正の必要性の有無及び程度の判定に当たっては、多数の取引事例等を総合的に比較対照の上、検討されるべきものであり、事情補正を要すると判定したときは、取引が行われた市場における客観的な価格水準等を考慮して適切に補正を行わなければならない。
　事情補正を要する特殊な事情を例示すれば、次のとおりである。

ア　補正に当たり減額すべき特殊な事情
　㈠　営業上の場所的限定等特殊な使用方法を前提として取引が行われたとき。
　㈡　極端な供給不足、先行きに対する過度に楽観的な見通し等特異な市場条件の下に取引が行われたとき。
　㈢　業者又は系列会社間における中間利益の取得を目的として取引が行われたとき。
　㈣　買手が不動産に関し明らかに知識や情報が不足している状態において過大な額で取引が行われたとき。
　㈤　取引価格に売買代金の割賦払いによる金利相当額、立退料、離作料等の土地の対価以外のものが含まれて取引が行われたとき。

Guidance Note V

tate, i.e., amounts equivalent to interest earned on the installment payments of the negotiated purchasing price, the costs of tenant removal (Editor's Note : e.g., when a landlord needs to demolish the existing building and rebuild the site), or compensation for early termination of agricultural production.

b. Special Circumstances Requiring an Upward Adjustment
(a) When transactions result in excessively low prices because sellers clearly lack information about, and knowledge of, the real estate
(b) When transactions take place under circumstances in which the property must be sold quickly, e.g., an inheritance or an employee transfer

c. Special Circumstances Requiring a Downward or Upward Adjustment
(a) When transactions, though conducted in a spirit of good will, take place between corporations under financial pressure or faced with bankruptcy; or when transactions are conducted between friends or relatives
(b) When transactions involve a property for which unreasonable site preparation costs or repair expenses are anticipated
(c) When the price has been established through arbitration, liquidation, auction sale or compulsory sale

③ **Time Adjustment Factor**

a. The time adjustment is determined by means of time-series analysis of a large quantity of data on comparable sales transacted prior to the date of the value opinion. The appraiser also takes into account trends in general value influences when estimating the time adjustment factor. General value influences to be examined include both socio-economic factors (such as growth in GDP, fiscal/monetary policies, public investment, building starts, and real estate sales) and governmental factors (such as land use regulations and tax policies).

b. The time adjustment should be determined as described in a. above, and references such as surveys of land values published by the central and prefectural governments should be consulted. However, in cases where suitable comparable sales data is lacking, the appraiser can also use other miscellaneous information such as trends in asking prices and offering prices, and market supply and demand.

(3) Guidance on Income Capitalization Approach
① **Application of Direct Capitalization Method**

a. Calculation of Net Cash Flow (NCF) for a Single Year

In direct capitalization, the net cash flow (NCF) for a single year and the capitalization rate applied to it must be determined in a consistent manner.

Namely, where an estimate of the net cash flow (NCF) for a single year reflects stabilized income over a certain period of time, a capitalization rate used must be developed on the same basis. In developing an estimate of net cash flow (NCF) to real estate that includes a building or other depreciable property component (to be referred to as buildings), the appraiser may calculate net cash flow (NCF) before depreciation (i.e., NCF from which depreciation has not been deducted). The appraiser should capitalize this estimated NCF by applying a capitalization rate appropriate to the NCF estimate.

イ　補正に当たり増額すべき特殊な事情
(ア)　売主が不動産に関し明らかに知識や情報が不足している状態において、過少な額で取引が行われたとき。
(イ)　相続、転勤等により売り急いで取引が行われたとき。

ウ　補正に当たり減額又は増額すべき特殊な事情
(ア)　金融逼迫、倒産時における法人間の恩恵的な取引又は知人、親族間等人間関係による恩恵的な取引が行われたとき。
(イ)　不相応な造成費、修繕費等を考慮して取引が行われたとき。
(ウ)　調停、清算、競売、公売等において価格が成立したとき。

③　時点修正について
ア　時点修正率は、価格時点以前に発生した多数の取引事例について時系列的な分析を行い、さらに国民所得の動向、財政事情及び金融情勢、公共投資の動向、建築着工の動向、不動産取引の推移等の社会的及び経済的要因の変化、土地利用の規制、税制等の行政的要因の変化等の一般的要因の動向を総合的に勘案して求めるべきである。
イ　時点修正率は原則として前記アにより求めるが、地価公示、都道府県地価調査等の資料を活用するとともに、適切な取引事例が乏しい場合には、売り希望価格、買い希望価格等の動向及び市場の需給の動向等に関する諸資料を参考として用いることができるものとする。

(3)　収益還元法について
①　直接還元法の適用について
ア　一期間の純収益の算定について
　　直接還元法の適用において還元対象となる一期間の純収益と、それに対応して採用される還元利回りは、その把握の仕方において整合がとれたものでなければならない。
　　すなわち、還元対象となる一期間の純収益として、ある一定期間の標準化されたものを採用する場合には、還元利回りもそれに対応したものを採用することが必要である。また、建物その他の償却資産（以下「建物等」という。）を含む不動産の純収益の算定においては、基本的に減価償却費を控除しない償却前の純収益を用いるべきであり、それに対応した還元利回りで還元する必要がある。

Guidance Note V

$$P = \frac{a}{R}$$

where
P is the property value indicated by the income capitalization approach
a is the net cash flow (NCF) to the property before depreciation
R is the capitalization rate corresponding to net cash flow (NCF) prior to depreciation

On the other hand, where an estimate of the net cash flow (NCF) after depreciation (i.e., NCF from which depreciation has been deducted) is calculated, a capitalization rate appropriate to net cash flow (NCF) after depreciation must be used.

The straight-line method or sinking fund factor method is usually used to calculate the depreciation, but another method should be applied where the circumstances are appropriate.

$$P = \frac{a'}{R'}$$

where
P is the property value indicated by the income capitalization approach
a' is the net cash flow (NCF) to the property after depreciation
R' is the capitalization rate corresponding to net cash flow (NCF) after depreciation

The following formula is used to determine the capitalization rate corresponding to net cash flow (NCF) after depreciation, when the depreciation and the capitalization rate for net cash flow (NCF) before depreciation can be calculated.

$$R' = \frac{a'}{(a'+d)} \times R$$

where
R' is the capitalization rate corresponding to net cash flow (NCF) after depreciation
R is the capitalization rate corresponding to net cash flow (NCF) prior to depreciation
a' is the net cash flow (NCF) after depreciation
d is the depreciation

b. Land Residual Technique or Building Residual Technique

Where real estate includes land and building components, and the value of either the land or building may be determined by an approach other than the income capitalization approach, a residual technique (the land residual technique or building residual technique) is applied. This technique capitalizes the net cash flow (NCF) remaining after deduction of the net cash flow (NCF) attributable to the building or the land from the net cash flow (NCF) to the property.

Residual techniques are effective in cases where the net cash flow (NCF) gener-

$$P = \frac{a}{R}$$

P：建物等の収益価格
a：建物等の償却前の純収益
R：償却前の純収益に対応する還元利回り

　一方、減価償却費を控除した償却後の純収益を用いる場合には、還元利回りも償却後の純収益に対応するものを用いなければならない。
　減価償却費の算定方法には定額法、償還基金率を用いる方法等があり、適切に用いることが必要である。

$$P = \frac{a'}{R'}$$

P ：建物等の収益価格
a'：建物等の償却後の純収益
R'：償却後の純収益に対応する還元利回り

　なお、減価償却費と償却前の純収益に対応する還元利回りを用いて償却後の純収益に対応する還元利回りを求める式は以下のとおりである。

$$R' = \frac{a'}{(a' + d)} \times R$$

R' ：償却後の純収益に対応する還元利回り
R ：償却前の純収益に対応する還元利回り
a'：償却後の純収益
d ：減価償却費

イ　土地残余法又は建物残余法
　不動産が敷地と建物等との結合によって構成されている場合において、収益還元法以外の手法によって敷地と建物等のいずれか一方の価格を求めることができるときは、当該不動産に基づく純収益から建物等又は敷地に帰属する純収益を控除した残余の純収益を還元利回りで還元する手法（土地残余法又は建物残余法という。）を適用することができる。
　これらの方法は、土地と建物等から構成される複合不動産が生み出す純収益を土地又は建物等に適正に配分することができる場合に有効である。
　土地残余法を適用するに当たっては、建物等が古い場合には複合不動産の生み出す純収

Guidance Note V

ated by a building and building site (land) can be rationally allocated between the land and building.

The land residual technique should only be applied in situations where the buildings are of recent construction because the older the building, the more difficult it becomes to break out the net cash flow (NCF) attributable to the land from the net cash flow (NCF) to the overall property (building and building site). Even when the subject property is a freehold interest in land, this technique can be applied by assuming the construction of a leased building is the highest and best use of the land.

(a) **Land Residual Technique**

The formula below demonstrates how land value is determined by the land residual technique.

$$P_L = \frac{a - B \times R_B}{R_L}$$

where
- P_L is the land value indicated by the land residual technique
- a is the net cash flow (NCF) to the building and building site before depreciation
- B is the building value
- R_B is the building capitalization rate
- R_L is the capitalization rate corresponding to that share of net cash flow (NCF) allocated to land (the allocation of NCF between land and building is based on NCF before depreciation)

(b) **Building Residual Technique**

The formula below demonstrates how building value is determined by the building residual technique.

$$P_B = \frac{a - L \times R_L}{R_B}$$

where
- P_B is the building value indicated by the building residual approach
- a is the net cash flow (NCF) to the building and building site before depreciation
- L is the land value
- R_L is the land capitalization rate
- R_B is the capitalization rate corresponding to that share of net cash flow (NCF) allocated to the building (the allocation of NCF between land and building is based on NCF before depreciation)

c. **Capitalization over a Definite Term**

Where the real estate includes land and building components, its value may be determined by multiplying an ordinary level annuity factor, developed on the basis of both an appropriate discount rate and the expected period of the income streams, by the net cash flow (NCF) before depreciation, based on the rental income to leased real estate or the income to business operations making use of real estate for

益から土地に帰属する純収益が的確に求められないことが多いので、建物等は新築か築後間もないものでなければならない。なお、対象不動産が更地である場合においても、当該土地に最有効使用の賃貸用建物等の建築を想定することによりこの方法を適用することができる。

(ア) 土地残余法

土地残余法を適用して土地の収益価格を求める場合は、基本的に次の式により表される。

$$P_L = \frac{a - B \times R_B}{R_L}$$

P_L ： 土地の収益価格
a ： 建物等及びその敷地の償却前の純収益
B ： 建物等の価格
R_B ： 建物等の還元利回り
R_L ： 償却前の純収益に対応する土地の還元利回り

(イ) 建物残余法

建物残余法を適用して建物等の収益価格を求める場合は、基本的に次の式により表される。

$$P_B = \frac{a - L \times R_L}{R_B}$$

P_B ： 建物等の収益価格
a ： 建物等及びその敷地の償却前の純収益
L ： 土地の価格
R_L ： 土地の還元利回り
R_B ： 償却前の純収益に対応する建物等の還元利回り

ウ　有期還元法

不動産が敷地と建物等との結合により構成されている場合において、その収益価格を、不動産賃貸又は賃貸以外の事業の用に供する不動産経営に基づく償却前の純収益に割引率と有限の収益期間とを基礎とした複利年金現価率を乗じて求める方法があり、基本的に次の式により表される。

Guidance Note V

purposes other than leasing. The formulas below demonstrate how value is determined by this method.

$$P = a \times \frac{(1+Y)^N - 1}{Y(1+Y)^N}$$

where
P is the value of the building and building site indicated by the income capitalization approach
a is the net cash flow (NCF) to the building and building site before depreciation
Y is the discount rate
N is the expected period of the income streams (i.e., the period during which income is anticipated, corresponding to the economic life of the building)
$\frac{(1+Y)^N - 1}{Y(1+Y)^N}$ is the ordinary level annuity factor

The present value of the building (assuming that the economic life of the building is longer than the income period), the present value of the land, and the present value of the costs to demolish the building less salvage value are added to, or subtracted from, the value of the property, derived by ordinary level annuity capitalization. This calculation is generally referred to as the Inwood Method.

The formulas below demonstrate the use of a discount rate based on this concept.

$$P = a \times \frac{(1+Y)^n - 1}{Y(1+Y)^n} + \frac{P_{Ln} + P_{Bn}}{(1+Y)^n} \quad \text{or}$$

$$P = a \times \frac{(1+Y)^N - 1}{Y(1+Y)^N} + \frac{P_{LN} - E}{(1+Y)^N}$$

where
P is the value of the building and building site indicated by the income capitalization approach
a is the net cash flow (NCF) to the building and building site before depreciation
Y is the discount rate
N or n is the expected period of the income streams (period during which income is anticipated; N is the period coinciding with the economic life of the building while n indicates situations in which the period is shorter than the economic life)
P_{Ln} is the land value after n years
P_{Bn} is the building value after n years
P_{Ln} is the land value after N years
E is the building demolition costs

Under the Hoskold method, on the other hand, a discount rate and a sinking fund factor, which is based on the safe rate, are used instead of ordinary level annuity

$$P = a \times \frac{(1+Y)^N - 1}{Y(1+Y)^N}$$

P : 建物等及びその敷地の収益価格
a : 建物等及びその敷地の償却前の純収益
Y : 割引率
N : 収益期間（収益が得られると予測する期間であり、ここでは建物等の経済的残存耐用年数と一致する場合を指す。）

$\dfrac{(1+Y)^N - 1}{Y(1+Y)^N}$ ： 複利年金現価率

なお、複利年金現価率を用い、収益期間満了時における土地又は建物等の残存価格並びに建物等の撤去費が予想されるときには、それらの額を現在価値に換算した額を加減する方法（インウッド式）がある。この方法の考え方に基づき、割引率を用いた式を示すと次のようになる。

$$P = a \times \frac{(1+Y)^n - 1}{Y(1+Y)^n} + \frac{P_{Ln} + P_{Bn}}{(1+Y)^n} \quad \text{又は}$$

$$P = a \times \frac{(1+Y)^N - 1}{Y(1+Y)^N} + \frac{P_{LN} - E}{(1+Y)^N}$$

P : 建物等及びその敷地の収益価格
a : 建物等及びその敷地の償却前の純収益
Y : 割引率
N, n : 収益期間（収益が得られると予測する期間であり、ここでは建物等の経済的残存耐用年数と一致する場合にはN、建物等の経済的残存耐用年数より短い期間である場合はnとする。）
P_{Ln} : n年後の土地価格
P_{Bn} : n年後の建物等の価格
P_{LN} : N年後の土地価格
E : 建物等の撤去費

また、上記複利年金現価率の代わりに蓄積利回り等を基礎とした償還基金率と割引率とを用いる方法（ホスコルド式）がある。

capitalization shown above.

The formulas below demonstrate the use of a discount rate based on this concept.

$$P = a \times \frac{1}{Y + \frac{i}{(1+i)^n - 1}} + \frac{P_{Ln} + P_{Bn}}{(1+Y)^n} \quad \text{or}$$

$$P = a \times \frac{1}{Y + \frac{i}{(1+i)^N - 1}} + \frac{P_{Ln} - E}{(1+Y)^N}$$

where

P is the value of the building and building site indicated by the income capitalization approach

a is the net cash flow (NCF) to the building and building site before depreciantion

Y is the discount rate

i is the safe rate

N or n is the expected period of the income streams (period during which income is anticipated; N is the period coinciding with the economic life of the building while n indicates situations in which the period is shorter than the economic life)

$\frac{i}{(1+i)^n - 1}$ is the sinking fund factor

P_{Ln} is the land value after n years
P_{Bn} is the building value after n years
P_{Ln} is the land value after N years
E is the building demolition costs

d. Selecting and Supporting Capitalization Rates

The capitalization rate should be consistent with the anticipated return in the market. Since the capitalization rate includes expected change in the net operating income (NOI) to the subject property, the anticipated change must be accurately ascertained and reflected in the capitalization rate. The following methods are used for determining the capitalization rate. In some situations, only one of the following methods is employed while in others a combination of multiple methods may be employed. Sources such as the opinions of investors and well-established property indices should also be consulted, as required.

(a) **Determination from Comparable Sales Data on Similar Real Estate**

The gathering and selection of comparable sales data should comply with the procedure for applying the sales comparison approach as discussed in Chapter 7 of the General Topics, "Appraisal Methodology."

The appraiser must exercise caution as to whether the capitalization rate obtained from comparable sales data (to be referred to as the market-derived capitalization rate) corresponds to the net operating income (NOI) before or after

この方法の考え方に基づき、割引率を用いた式を示すと次のようになる。

$$P = a \times \cfrac{1}{Y + \cfrac{i}{(1+i)^n - 1}} + \cfrac{P_{Ln} + P_{Bn}}{(1+Y)^n}$$ 又は

$$P = a \times \cfrac{1}{Y + \cfrac{i}{(1+i)^N - 1}} + \cfrac{P_{LN} - E}{(1+Y)^N}$$

P ： 建物等及びその敷地の収益価格
a ： 建物等及びその敷地の償却前の純収益
Y ： 割引率
i ： 蓄積利回り
N, n ： 収益期間（収益が得られると予測する期間であり、ここでは建物等の経済的残存耐用年数と一致する場合にはN、建物等の経済的残存耐用年数より短い期間である場合はnとする。）

$\cfrac{i}{(1+i)^n - 1}$ ： 償還基金率

P_{Ln} ： n年後の土地価格
P_{Bn} ： n年後の建物等の価格
P_{LN} ： N年後の土地価格
E ： 建物等の撤去費

エ　還元利回りの求め方

還元利回りは、市場の実勢を反映した利回りとして求める必要があり、還元対象となる純収益の変動予測を含むものであることから、それらの予測を的確に行い、還元利回りに反映させる必要がある。還元利回りを求める方法を例示すれば次のとおりであるが、適用に当たっては、次の方法から一つの方法を採用する場合又は複数の方法を組み合わせて採用する場合がある。また、必要に応じ、投資家等の意見や整備された不動産インデックス等を参考として活用する。

(ア) 類似の不動産の取引事例との比較から求める方法

取引事例の収集及び選択については、「総論第7章　鑑定評価の方式」に規定する取引事例比較法の適用方法に準ずる。

取引事例から得られる利回り（以下「取引利回り」という。）については、償却前後のいずれの純収益に対応するものであるかに留意する必要がある。あわせて純収益について特殊な要因（新築、建替え直後で稼働率が不安定である等）があり、適切に補正ができない取引事例は採用すべきでないことに留意する必要がある。

この方法は、対象不動産と類似性の高い取引事例に係る取引利回りが豊富に収集可能

Guidance Note V

depreciation. There are special factors that should also be noted with respect to net operating income (NOI) such as whether the property operation has not been stabilized immediately after new construction or remodeling. Comparable sales data, which cannot be reasonably adjusted, should not be used.

This method is particularly useful when it is possible to develop the capitalization rate from a large quantity of sales data on comparable sales that are highly similar to the subject property.

(b) **Determination by Means of the Band of Investment Method Based on Equity – Mortgage Ratio**

This method focuses on the procurement of funds by potential buyers with an ordinary capability for procuring funds to acquire real estate. As a method, it is superior at reflecting the return on real estate investments and trends in the financial markets during the process of fund procurement.

The following formula demonstrates the above method for determining the capitalization rate.

$R = R_M \times W_M + R_E \times W_E$

where
R is the capitalization rate
R_M is the mortgage capitalization rate
W_M is the ratio of the loan to total property value
R_E is the equity capitalization rate
W_E is the ratio of equity to total property value

(c) **Determination from Capitalization Rates for Land and Buildings**

This method is applied to properties that include land and building components. As a method, it is superior at reflecting return trends in a market where the yields on land and buildings are considered to be different.

The following formula demonstrates the above method for determining the capitalization rate.

$R = R_L \times W_L + R_B \times W_B$

where
R is the capitalization rate
R_L is the land capitalization rate
W_L is the ratio of land value to total property value
R_B is the building capitalization rate
W_B is the ratio of building value to total property value

(d) **Determination from the Relationship of the Capitalization Rate to the Discount Rate**

This method is effective where net cash flow (NCF) can be assumed to continue in perpetuity, and it can be assumed that net cash flow (NCF) will grow at a fixed rate.

The formula representing the relationship between the capitalization rate and

(イ) 借入金と自己資金に係る還元利回りから求める方法

　　この方法は、不動産の取得に際し標準的な資金調達能力を有する需要者の資金調達の要素に着目した方法であり、不動産投資に係る利回り及び資金調達に際する金融市場の動向を反映させることに優れている。

　　上記による求め方は基本的に次の式により表される。

$R = R_M \times W_M + R_E \times W_E$

R ：還元利回り
R_M：借入金還元利回り
W_M：借入金割合
R_E：自己資金還元利回り
W_E：自己資金割合

(ウ) 土地と建物等に係る還元利回りから求める方法

　　この方法は、対象不動産が土地及び建物等により構成されている場合に、土地及び建物等に係る利回りが異なるものとして把握される市場においてそれらの動向を反映させることに優れている。

　　上記による求め方は基本的に次の式により表される。

$R = R_L \times W_L + R_B \times W_B$

R ：還元利回り
R_L：土地の還元利回り
W_L：土地の価格割合
R_B：建物等の還元利回り
W_B：建物等の価格割合

(エ) 割引率との関係から求める方法

　　この方法は、純収益が永続的に得られる場合で、かつ純収益が一定の趨勢を有すると想定される場合に有効である。

　　還元利回りと割引率との関係を表す式の例は、次のように表される。

$R = Y - g$

R：還元利回り

discount rate appears below.

$R = Y - g$

where
R is the capitalization rate
Y is the discount rate
g is the growth rate in the net cash flow (NCF)

(e) **Utilization of Debt Service Coverage Ratio**

This method determines the capitalization rate by using the debt service coverage ratio (the value obtained by dividing the net cash flow (NCF) for a certain period by the amount of the principal repayment plus the interest paid in the same period), based on the mortgage capitalization rate and ratio of the loan to total property value. It considers the safety of debt service from the perspective of net cash flow (NCF) to the subject property.

It must be noted that the debt service coverage ratio used should be based on the average net cash flow (NCF) for the loan period. This method focuses on the procurement of funds by the purchaser of the real estate, and is effective where repayment of the loan is based only on income to the subject property.

The following formula demonstrates the above method for determining the capitalization rate.

$R = R_M \times W_M \times DSCR$

where
R is the capitalization rate
R_M is the mortgage capitalization rate
W_M is the ratio of the loan to total property value
DSCR is the debt service coverage ratio; the DSCR is normally required to be 1.0 or more

② **Guidance on Application of Discounted Cash Flow Method**

DCF anticipates and clearly specifies net cash flow (NCF) generated during multiple, consecutive periods as well as the reversionary value. As a method, it is superior at explaining the process of determining value indications by the income capitalization approach.

a. **Calculation of Net Cash Flow (NCF) for Each Period**

When the net cash flow (NCF) to buildings is calculated, net cash flow (NCF) before depreciation (i.e., the depreciation is not deducted from NCF) is used. The allowance for building depreciation is considered in the reversionary value.

(a) **Calculation of Gross Income**

Two methods may be used with respect to the treatment of refundable deposits received. One method assumes the total amount is entrusted to a repayment reserve, and the investment income is recorded as it is generated. Under the other method, the entire amount is recorded as revenue or expenditure at the time of receipt or refund.

Y：割引率
g：純収益の変動率

(オ)　借入金償還余裕率の活用による方法
　　この方法は、借入金還元利回りと借入金割合をもとに、借入金償還余裕率（ある期間の純収益を同期間の借入金元利返済額で除した値をいう。）を用いて対象不動産に係る純収益からみた借入金償還の安全性を加味して還元利回りを求めるものである。
　　この場合において用いられる借入金償還余裕率は、借入期間の平均純収益をもとに算定すべきことに留意する必要がある。この方法は、不動産の購入者の資金調達に着目し、対象不動産から得られる収益のみを借入金の返済原資とする場合に有効である。
　　上記による求め方は基本的に次の式により表される。
　　$R = R_M \times W_M \times DSCR$
　　R：還元利回り
　　R_M：借入金還元利回り
　　W_M：借入金割合
　　DSCR：借入金償還余裕率（通常は1.0以上であることが必要。）

②　ＤＣＦ法の適用について
　ＤＣＦ法は、連続する複数の期間に発生する純収益及び復帰価格を予測しそれらを明示することから、収益価格を求める過程について説明性に優れたものである。

ア　毎期の純収益の算定について
　　建物等の純収益の算定においては、基本的には減価償却費を控除しない償却前の純収益を用いるものとし、建物等の償却については復帰価格において考慮される。

(ア)　総収益の算定
　　一時金のうち預り金的性格を有する保証金等については、全額を返還準備金として預託することを想定しその運用益を発生時に計上する方法と全額を受渡時の収入又は支出として計上する方法とがある。

(b) Calculation of Total Expenses

Two methods may be used to estimate costs such as large-scale repair expenses. Under one method, costs are recorded as a reserve for each period. Under the other method, costs are recorded when they are expected to be actually paid. The appraiser should forecast the timing of the expected expenditures by taking into account the attributes of the subject property.

b. Determination of the Discount Rate

The discount rate should reflect the yield in the market. Typically it is determined for one-year intervals. It should also be noted that the discount rate differs according to the degree of uncertainty over anticipated earnings.

The following methods are used for determining the discount rate. In some situations only one of the following methods is used while in others a combination of multiple methods may be used. Sources such as the opinions of investors and well-established property indices should also consulted, as required.

(a) Determination from Data on Comparable Sales

The gathering and selection of comparable sales data should comply with the procedure for applying the sales comparison approach discussed in Chapter 7 of the General Topics, "Appraisal Methodology."

The discount rate developed from comparable sales data is the internal rate of return (IRR) calculated on the basis of the sales price and income streams (IRR is the discount rate, at which the present value of future income and initial capital investment are equal). The appraiser should be able to forecast the net cash flow (NCF) of each period for the comparable property.

This method is particularly effective where a large amount of yield data can be gathered from comparable sales similar to the subject property.

(b) Determination from Mortgage and Equity Discount Rates

This method focuses on the cost of procuring funds by purchasers of real estate, and best reflects the yield on the real estate investment as well as trends in the financial markets during the process of fund procurement. The method should be based on ratios for the mortgage and equity to total property value, assumed by typical real estate investors.

The following formula demonstrates the above method for determining the discount rate.

$$Y = Y_M \times W_M + Y_E \times W_E$$

where
- Y is the discount rate
- Y_M is the mortgage discount rate
- W_M is the ratio of the loan to total property value
- Y_E is the equity discount rate
- W_E is the ratio of equity to total property value

(c) Determination by a Built-Up Rate (Adding Risk Components Associated with the Individual Real Estate to the Assured Yield on Assets Such as

(イ)　総費用の算定

　　大規模修繕費等の費用については、当該費用を毎期の積み立てとして計上する方法と、実際に支出される時期に計上する方法がある。実際に支出される時期の予測は、対象不動産の実態に応じて適切に行う必要がある。

イ　割引率の求め方について

　割引率は、市場の実勢を反映した利回りとして求める必要があり、一般に1年を単位として求める。また、割引率は収益見通しにおいて考慮されなかった収益予測の不確実性の程度に応じて異なることに留意する。

　割引率を求める方法を例示すれば次のとおりであるが、適用に当たっては、下記の方法から一つの方法を採用する場合又は複数の方法を組み合わせて採用する場合がある。また、必要に応じ、投資家等の意見や整備された不動産インデックス等を参考として活用する。

(ア)　類似の不動産の取引事例との比較から求める方法

　　取引事例の収集及び選択については、「総論第7章　鑑定評価の方式」に規定する取引事例比較法に係る適用方法に準ずる。

　　取引事例に係る割引率は、基本的に取引利回りをもとに算定される内部収益率（Internal Rate of Return（IRR）。将来収益の現在価値と当初投資元本とを等しくする割引率をいう。）として求める。適用に当たっては、取引事例について毎期の純収益が予測可能であることが必要である。

　　この方法は、対象不動産と類似性を有する取引事例に係る利回りが豊富に収集可能な場合には特に有効である。

(イ)　借入金と自己資金に係る割引率から求める方法

　　この方法は、不動産購入者の資金調達コストに着目したものであり、不動産投資に係る利回り及び資金調達に際する金融市場の動向を反映させることに優れている。適用に当たっては、不動産投資において典型的な投資家が想定する借入金割合及び自己資金割合を基本とすることが必要である。

　　上記による求め方は基本的に次の式により表される。

　　$Y = Y_M \times W_M + Y_E \times W_E$

　　Y　：割引率
　　Y_M：借入金割引率
　　W_M：借入金割合
　　Y_E：自己資金割引率
　　W_E：自己資金割合

(ウ)　金融資産の利回りに不動産の個別性を加味して求める方法

　　比較の対象となる金融資産の利回りとしては、一般に10年物国債の利回りが用いられ

Bonds)
The yield on ten-year government bonds is typically used as a bench mark. The yield rates on corporate stocks and corporate bonds may also be used for comparative purposes.

Additional risk components associated with the individual real estate include the uncertainty related to the real estate investment, the non-liquidity of the investment, potential problems in the management of the real estate, and the security of the asset. The value of a real estate investment may change as the result of a natural disaster, modification in land use planning or regulation, inability to find a buyer at the desired time, or lack of requisite knowledge and experience with respect to leasing. Risks are also associated with the amount of revenue obtained, which may differ according to the quality of management. On the other hand, the indestructive nature of land provides a positive aspect.

This method is useful when the uncertainty associated with the anticipated income to the subject property can be ascertained and can be compared against the uncertainty of other financial assets.

c. Holding period

The assumed holding period should allow for accurate anticipation of the net operating income (NOI) of each period and the reversionary value. The length should be based on the period for which typical investors would retain a real estate investment and should not extend beyond the period that would generally be assumed for typical investors.

d. Determination of the Reversionary Value

At the termination of the holding period, the sales expenses required must be deducted from the reversionary value.

The reversionary value is determined by capitalizing the net operating income (NOI) for the $(n+1)$ period at the terminal capitalization rate. Anticipated change in net operating income (NOI) beyond the $(n+1)$ period as well as the uncertainty accompanying that anticipation must be accurately reflected both in the net operating income (NOI) of the $(n+1)$ period as well as in the terminal capitalization rate.

Where demolition of the building or a change in its use is planned after the end of the holding period, or where the building is so deteriorated that demolition is expected, the reversionary value must be determined in consideration of those required costs.

e. Determination of Terminal Capitalization Rates

Terminal capitalization rates must reflect market trends at the end of the holding period, anticipated change in income after that time, and the degree of uncertainty in that anticipation based on the capitalization rate for the property on the date of the value opinion.

る。また、株式や社債の利回り等が比較対象として用いられることもある。

不動産の個別性として加味されるものには、投資対象としての危険性、非流動性、管理の困難性、資産としての安全性があり、それらは自然災害等の発生や土地利用に関する計画及び規制の変更によってその価値が変動する可能性が高いこと、希望する時期に必ずしも適切な買い手が見つかるとは限らないこと、賃貸経営管理について専門的な知識と経験を必要とするものであり管理の良否によっては得られる収益が異なること、特に土地については一般に滅失することがないことなどをいう。

この方法は、対象不動産から生ずる収益予測の不確実性が金融資産との比較において把握可能な場合に有効である。

ウ　保有期間（売却を想定しない場合には分析期間）について

保有期間は、毎期の純収益及び復帰価格について精度の高い予測が可能な期間として決定する必要があり、不動産投資における典型的な投資家が保有する期間を標準とし、典型的な投資家が一般に想定しないような長期にわたる期間を設定してはならない。

エ　復帰価格の求め方について

保有期間満了時点において売却を想定する場合には、売却に要する費用を控除することが必要である。

復帰価格を求める際に、n＋1期の純収益を最終還元利回りで還元して求める場合においては、n＋1期以降の純収益の変動予測及び予測に伴う不確実性をn＋1期の純収益及び最終還元利回りに的確に反映させることが必要である。

なお、保有期間満了時点以降において、建物の取壊しや用途変更が既に計画されている場合又は建物が老朽化していること等により取壊し等が見込まれる場合においては、それらに要する費用を考慮して復帰価格を求めることが必要である。

オ　最終還元利回りの求め方について

最終還元利回りは、価格時点の還元利回りをもとに、保有期間満了時点における市場動向並びにそれ以降の収益の変動予測及び予測に伴う不確実性を反映させて求めることが必要である。

Guidance Note V

2. Guidance on Appraisal Approaches for Determining Rent
(1) Summation Approach
The following matters should be considered in determining the base value of a property.
① Determination of Rent for a Building Site (Ground Rent)
   a. Where the lessee can use the site in line with the highest and best use as though vacant, the base value corresponds to the economic value of the freehold interest in the land.
   b. Where the highest and best use as though vacant cannot be anticipated from the provisions of the contract, the base value corresponds to the economic value of the site based on the provisions in the contract.
② Determination of Rent for a Building and Building Site (Building Rent)
The base value corresponds to the economic value of the building and building site, based on the premise that the present use of the building and building site will continue.

(2) Rental Data Comparison Approach
① Selection of Data
   a. Lease and other data should be selected from comparable properties that are as similar to the subject property as possible. The rent level typically differs according to whether the rent is paid under a new lease or under a renewed lease, and according to the use of the building.
   b. The appraiser should consider the following matters when assessing the similarity of contract provisions.
      (a) Form of the lease
      (b) Rental area
      (c) Lease term, period of the lease already elapsed and remaining period of the lease
      (d) Rental payments adjusted for deposits received
      (e) Period for which rent is calculated and method of payment
      (f) Matters pertaining to repairs and alterations
      (g) Portion of space leased and the use thereof (Editor's Note: e.g., Flex space in an industrial building may be used for office or industrial purposes; the appraiser should ascertain whether the lease includes both office and industrial space or only office space)
② Comparison of Area–specific and Property–Specific Value Influences
Comparison of market-specific value influences is useful in determining rent. However, there are some specific influences applicable only to rental values. Therefore, the boundaries and attributes of the market for the subject property may differ between rental value and property value assignments.

In comparing property-specific value influences for the determination of rent, the appraiser should pay special attention to the contract provisions as well as property-specific value influences acting on the land and building.

2. 賃料を求める鑑定評価の手法について
(1) 積算法について
基礎価格を求めるに当たっては、次に掲げる事項に留意する必要がある。
① 宅地の賃料（いわゆる地代）を求める場合
ア　最有効使用が可能な場合は、更地の経済価値に即応した価格である。
イ　建物の所有を目的とする賃貸借等の場合で契約により敷地の最有効使用が見込めないときは、当該契約条件を前提とする建付地としての経済価値に即応した価格である。

② 建物及びその敷地の賃料（いわゆる家賃）を求める場合
建物及びその敷地の現状に基づく利用を前提として成り立つ当該建物及びその敷地の経済価値に即応した価格である。

(2) 賃貸事例比較法について
① 事例の選択について
ア　賃貸借等の事例の選択に当たっては、新規賃料、継続賃料の別又は建物の用途の別により賃料水準が異なるのが一般的であることに留意して、できる限り対象不動産に類似した事例を選択すべきである。
イ　契約内容の類似性を判断する際の留意事項を例示すれば、次のとおりである。
　(ア)　賃貸形式
　(イ)　賃貸面積
　(ウ)　契約期間並びに経過期間及び残存期間
　(エ)　一時金の授受に基づく賃料内容
　(オ)　賃料の算定の期間及びその支払方法
　(カ)　修理及び現状変更に関する事項
　(キ)　賃貸借等に供される範囲及びその使用方法

② 地域要因の比較及び個別的要因の比較について
賃料を求める場合の地域要因の比較に当たっては、賃料固有の価格形成要因が存すること等により、価格を求める場合の地域と賃料を求める場合の地域とでは、それぞれの地域の範囲及び地域の格差を異にすることに留意することが必要である。
賃料を求める場合の個別的要因の比較に当たっては、契約内容、土地及び建物に関する個別的要因等に留意することが必要である。

Guidance Note VI on GS. Chap. 8 : APPRAISAL PROCESS

Review of Data and Analysis of Value Influences

(1) **The appraiser is able form an opinion regarding uncertain value influences based on the appraiser's own investigative and analytical capabilities:**

(a) if comparable data exists to analyze those value influences; and (b) if it is possible to quantify the effect of those value influences based on the data, and the degree of value decrease can be reflected in the appraised value.

(2) **The appraiser can perform an appraisal assignment without consideration of uncertain value influences:**

either (a) if the appraiser is not able to ascertain evidence of any cause and effect relationship involved in those value influences by means of common sense and general scientific knowledge, or (b) if the appraiser is not able to confirm even a clue of their existence through ordinary investigation; and if the appraiser judges those uncertain value influences not to have any significant effect on the value of the subject property.

Ⅵ 「総論第8章 鑑定評価の手順」について

資料の検討及び価格形成要因の分析について

(1) **不動産鑑定士の調査分析能力の範囲内で合理的な推定を行うことができる場合について**

　　不動産鑑定士の調査分析能力の範囲内で合理的な推定を行うことができる場合とは、ある要因について対象不動産と比較可能な類似の事例が存在し、かつ当該要因が存することによる減価の程度等を客観的に予測することにより鑑定評価額への反映が可能であると認められる場合をいう。

(2) **価格形成要因から除外して鑑定評価を行うことが可能な場合について**

　　価格形成に影響があるであろうといわれている事項について、一般的な社会通念や科学的知見に照らし原因や因果関係が明確でない場合又は不動産鑑定士の通常の調査において当該事項の存否の端緒すら確認できない場合において、当該事項が対象不動産の価格形成に大きな影響を与えることがないと判断されるときには、価格形成要因から除外して鑑定評価を行うことができるものとする。

Guidance Note VII

Guidance Note VII on SS. Chap. 1 : APPRAISAL OF REAL ESTATE VALUE

1. Guidance on Building Sites

(1) Vacant Land

The subdivision development analysis determines the value of vacant land by deducting respectively the building construction costs and incidental expenses (to be borne directly by the builder), and/or the land site preparation costs and incidental expenses (to be borne directly by the builder) at the date of the value opinion from the present value of the total sales revenue of the condominium building or subdivision development site. Since the land value of the condominium project typically differs according to the floor area ratio allowed in the zoning ordinance, the appraiser must prepare the design, layout and development schedule of the hypothetical condominium building by taking into account the land shape, frontage, and the *Building Standards Act* among other factors.

The formula below demonstrates the subdivision development approach.

$$P = \frac{S}{(1+r)^{n_1}} - \frac{B}{(1+r)^{n_2}} - \frac{M}{(1+r)^{n_3}}$$

where

- P is the land value indicated by the subdivision development analysis
- S is the total sales price
- B is building construction cost or land site preparation cost
- M is incidental expenses
- r is the discount rate
- n_1 is the period between the date of the value opinion and the time of the sale
- n_2 is the period between the date of the value opinion and the time of the payment of the construction fees
- n_3 is the period between the date of the value opinion and the time of the payment of incidental expenses

(2) Leasehold Interests in Land

The deposits paid by the tenant to the lessor with respect to the lease contract to a building site are typically classified into:

①refundable deposits, normally called *hoshokin*;

②non-refundable prepayments of rent, set as compensation for the leasehold interest in the land, normally called *kenrikin*; and

③other deposits paid to obtain consent from the landowner, e.g., for transfer of the leasehold interest in the land.

The appraiser must individually assess whether or not each of these deposits constitutes a component in the value of a leasehold interest in land by considering the nature of the deposit and actual leasing practices regardless of what they may be called.

(3) Sectional Superficies

Ⅶ 「各論第1章 価格に関する鑑定評価」について

1. 宅地について
   (1) 更地について
   　　開発法によって求める価格は、マンション等又は細区分した宅地の販売総額を価格時点に割り戻した額から建物の建築費及び発注者が直接負担すべき通常の付帯費用又は土地の造成費及び発注者が直接負担すべき通常の付帯費用を価格時点に割り戻した額をそれぞれ控除して求めるものとする。この場合において、マンション等の敷地は一般に法令上許容される容積の如何によって土地価格が異なるので、敷地の形状、道路との位置関係等の条件、建築基準法等に適合した建物の概略設計、配棟等に関する開発計画を想定し、これに応じた事業実施計画を策定することが必要である。
   　　開発法の基本式を示すと次のようになる。

   $$P = \frac{S}{(1+r)^{n_1}} - \frac{B}{(1+r)^{n_2}} - \frac{M}{(1+r)^{n_3}}$$

   　　P ：開発法による試算価格
   　　S ：販売総額
   　　B ：建物の建築費又は土地の造成費
   　　M ：付帯費用
   　　r ：投下資本収益率
   　　n_1：価格時点から販売時点までの期間
   　　n_2：価格時点から建築代金の支払い時点までの期間
   　　n_3：価格時点から付帯費用の支払い時点までの期間

   (2) 借地権について
   　　宅地の賃貸借契約等に関連して、借地人から賃貸人へ支払われる一時金には、一般に、①預り金的性格を有し、通常、保証金と呼ばれているもの、②賃料の前払的性格を有し、又は借地権の設定の対価とみなされ、通常、権利金と呼ばれているもの、③その他借地権の譲渡等の承諾を得るための一時金に分類することができる。
   　　これらの一時金が借地権価格を構成するか否かはその名称の如何を問わず、一時金の性格、社会的慣行等を考察して個別に判定することが必要である。

   (3) 区分地上権について

Guidance Note VII

The following discussion covers important considerations in the appraisal of sectional superficies.

① **Economic Value Based on the Characteristics of Sectional Superficies**

In appraising sectional superficies, the appraiser must pay particular attention to economic value, based on the characteristics of sectional superficies described below.

- a. The economic value of the land, above or below which sectional superficies have been created, reflects the total utility above and below ground, generated by each of the buildable improvements based on the highest and best use. Thus, the economic value of sectional superficies may be ascertained by the ratio of the value of those sectional superficies to the economic value of the land, upon or under which those rights are created. The functional relationship of the sectional superficies to the total utility of the land becomes the focus of the appraisal.
- b. Sectional superficies are rights created to accommodate a structure or building in a portion of the space above or below land that belongs to another person. Their economic value is determined according to the specific structure, use, purpose of that use, and duration of the rights pertaining to the superficies.

② **Value Indicated by the Sales Comparison Approach Using Data on Sectional Superficies**

The sales comparison approach determines the value of sectional super ficies by comparing data gathered on sectional superficies, created in a manner similar to the subject, and located in the same neighborhood or similar neighborhood of the primary market area. After selecting appropriate data, the appraiser makes sales condition and time adjustments as required, comparing market- specific and property- specific value influences.

The appraiser must pay particular attention to the following matters when applying this approach.

- a. There are many situations where the economic value of the land, above or below which sectional superficies are created, is affected by spatial restrictions on land use imposed to preserve adjacent structures or buildings. Since the effect of these encumbrances is factored into the economic value of the sectional superficies created above or below that land, the data gathered on the creation of comparable rights, including restrictive encumbrances and the periods for which these rights are created, should be verified.
- b. The appraiser can estimate the growth rate for the time adjustment through an analysis of land value trends in the neighborhood of a comparable property or in a similar area considered to have undergone a change in land value close to that of the comparable neighborhood.
- c. In comparing market- specific value influences and property- specific value influences, the appraiser must pay particular attention to influences that are unique to sectional superficies, as indicated below.
  - (a) With respect to market- specific value influences, the appraiser should consider market- specific influences acting on the neighborhood and on similar

区分地上権の鑑定評価に当たって留意すべき事項は次のとおりである。

① 区分地上権の特性に基づく経済価値
　区分地上権の鑑定評価においては、特に次に掲げる区分地上権の特性に基づく経済価値に留意することが必要である。
ア　区分地上権設定地の経済価値は、当該設定地の最有効使用に係る階層等に基づいて生ずる上下空間の効用の集積である。したがって、区分地上権の経済価値は、その設定地全体の効用との関数関係に着目して、その設定地全体の経済価値に占める割合として把握される。
イ　区分地上権は、他人の土地の地下又は空間の一部に工作物を設置することを目的として設定する権利であり、その工作物の構造、用途、使用目的、権利の設定期間等により、その経済価値が特定される。

② 区分地上権の設定事例等に基づく比準価格
　区分地上権の設定事例等に基づく比準価格は、近隣地域及び同一需給圏内の類似地域等において設定形態が類似している区分地上権の設定事例等を収集して、適切な事例を選択し、必要に応じ事情補正及び時点修正を行い、かつ、地域要因及び個別的要因の比較を行って求めた価格を比較考量して決定するものとする。
　この手法の適用に当たっては、特に次に掲げる事項に留意しなければならない。
ア　区分地上権設定地に係る区分地上権の経済価値には、当該区分地上権に係る工作物の保全のため必要な他の空間の使用制限に係る経済価値を含むことが多いので、区分地上権の態様、設定期間等設定事例等の内容を的確に把握すべきである。
イ　時点修正において採用する変動率は、事例に係る不動産の存する用途的地域又は当該地域と相似の価格変動過程を経たと認められる類似の地域における土地の変動率を援用することができるものとする。
ウ　地域要因及び個別的要因の比較においては、次に掲げる区分地上権に特有な諸要因について留意する必要がある。
　　(ｱ)　地域要因については、近隣地域の地域要因にとどまらず、一般に当該区分地上権の効用に寄与する他の不動産（例えば、地下鉄の区分地上権の設定事例の場合における連たんする一団の土地のように、一般に広域にわたって存在することが多い。）の存する類似地域等との均衡を考慮する必要がある。
　　(ｲ)　個別的要因については、区分地上権に係る地下又は空間の部分についての立体的及び平面的位置、規模、形状等が特に重要であり、区分地上権設定地全体との関連において平面的及び立体的分割の状態を判断しその影響の程度を考慮する必要がある。

neighborhoods where other real estate may contribute to the utility of the sectional superficies; for example, parcels of land linked in a row such as the sectional superficies where subway tracks are laid.

(b) With respect to property- specific value influences acting upon sectional superficies, particularly important are the two- dimensional and three- dimensional locations, sizes, and shapes of above- and below- ground areas subject to the sectional superficies. The appraiser should consider the effect of spatial dimensions on value by assessing the two- dimensional and three- dimensional division of space in relation to the entire land, above or below which the sectional superficies have been created.

③ **Value Determined from a Sectional Superficies/Vacant Land Value Ratio**

The value of sectional superficies may be determined by gathering data on sectional superficies, which have been created in a manner similar to the subject property and which are located in the subject neighborhood or similar neighborhoods in the primary market area. After selecting appropriate data, the appraiser determines the ratio of the value of the sectional superficies (either at the time these rights were created or at the time they were transferred) to the value of the freehold interest in the land, above or below which the sectional superficies have been created, for each of the selected data.

The reasonable ratio for the subject property is chosen by analyzing the ratios of the comparable data. The value of the freehold interest in the land, above or below which the subject sectional superficies have been created, is then multiplied by the ratio to determine the value of the sectional superficies on the date of the value opinion.

In applying this approach, the appraiser should pay particular attention to the matters described in part c. of ② above.

④ **Value Indicated by the Income Capitalization Approach Using the Quasi – Land Residual Technique**

The quasi- land residual technique may also be used to determine the value of sectional superficies. In this technique, the appraiser first estimates the net operating income (NOI) attributable to the land, above or below which the sectional superficies have been created, using two different assumptions. Under the first assumption, the appraiser employs the highest and best use of the land as though vacant without considering the sectional superficies. Under the second assumption, the appraiser assumes the highest and best use of the land taking into account the sectional superficies, the difference between the two NOIs attributable to the land is then capitalized at an appropriate capitalization rate.

⑤ **Value Determined from the Vertical Allotment Ratio for the Land above or below Which Sectional Superficies Have Been Created**

An appraiser can estimate the value of sectional superficies by multiplying the value of the underlying site, as if vacant and free of any encumbrances, by the vertical allotment ratio, based on the contract for the sectional superficies. The appraiser further adjusts this estimated value according to the specific contract provisions to arrive at a

③ 区分地上権の設定事例等に基づく区分地上権割合により求める価格

　近隣地域及び同一需給圏内の類似地域等において設定形態が類似している区分地上権の設定事例等を収集して、適切な事例を選択し、これらに係る設定時又は譲渡時における区分地上権の価格が区分地上権設定地の更地としての価格に占める割合をそれぞれ求め、これらを総合的に比較考量の上適正な割合を判定し、価格時点における当該区分地上権設定地の更地としての価格にその割合を乗じて求めるものとする。

　なお、この手法の適用に当たっては、特に、前記②のウに掲げる事項に留意する必要がある。

④ 土地残余法に準じて求める収益価格

　土地残余法に準じて求める収益価格は、区分地上権設定地について、当該区分地上権の設定がないものとして、最有効使用を想定して求めた当該設定地全体に帰属する純収益から、当該区分地上権設定後の状態を所与として最有効使用を想定して求めた当該設定地に帰属する純収益を控除して得た差額純収益を還元利回りで還元して得た額について、さらに当該区分地上権の契約内容等による修正を行って求めるものとする。

⑤ 区分地上権の立体利用率により求める価格

　区分地上権の立体利用率により求める価格は、区分地上権設定地の更地としての価格に、最有効使用を想定して求めた当該区分地上権設定地全体の立体利用率を基準として求めた当該区分地上権に係る立体利用率（当該区分地上権設定地の最有効使用を前提とした経済価値に対する区分地上権の設定部分の経済価値及び当該設定部分の効用を保持するため他の空間部分の利用を制限することに相応する経済価値の合計の割合をいう。）を乗じて得た額につ

Guidance Note VII

final value estimate. The vertical allotment ratio refers to the ratio between: a) the value of the space in which the sectional superficies are created plus the value of the adjacent space, the development of which is restricted because of structures in the superficies' space (e.g., high- voltage power lines or subway tracts); and b) the value of the underlying site based on its highest and best use. In calculating the vertical allotment ratio for sectional superficies, the appraiser determines what economic share the space in question represents of the total value of buildable area, considered as the base value.

In applying this technique, the appraiser should pay particular attention to the matters indicated in part c. of section ② above.

(4) **Appraisal in Situations Where Soil Pollution on the Subject Site Has Been Verified or Where the Soil May Be Polluted**

The appraisal of real estate on which the presence of soil pollution has been verified must make use of investigations performed by environmental specialists to ascertain how widespread the pollution is and the costs required for its removal. However, when the requirements mentioned in Basic Appraisal Matters (Chapter 5 of the General Topics and section III of the Guidance Notes, which discusses Chapter 5 of the General Topics) are satisfied, the appraisal would be performed after the client's consent has been obtained, with the additional condition that assumes removal of the pollution. Furthermore, in situations where it is possible to objectively determine the degree of value influences discussed in Appraisal Procedure (Chapter 8 of the General Topics and section VI of the Guidance Notes on Chapter 8 of the General Topics), the appraiser may perform the valuation by estimating the effect of the presence of the soil pollution on the value of the subject property.

The following discussion explains how to perform an appraisal that complies with procedures such as investigation, zone designation and clean- up, stipulated in the *Soil Contamination Measures Law*.

① When an investigation to determine the presence of soil pollution on the subject site is mandatory in accordance with the provisions of Article 3 of the *Soil Contamination Measures Law,* or an investigation of the subject site for potential soil pollution has been ordered in accordance with the provisions of Article 4, if the investigation proved there was soil contamination, the appraisal must be performed on the premise that soil pollution is present.

② Where the subject property is located in a designated zone as stipulated in Article 5 of the *Soil Contamination Measures Law,* the appraisal must be performed on the premise of the presence of soil pollution.

③ Where measures for the removal of soil pollution on the subject property have been ordered by the governor of the prefecture in accordance with the provisions of Article 7 of the *Soil Contamination Measures Law*, the appraisal must be performed on the premise of the presence of soil pollution even after those measures have been implemented, provided the subject property's designation as a contaminated site has not been lifted.

④ In the following three cases, the appraisal may be performed on the premise that

いて、さらに当該区分地上権の契約内容等による修正を行って求めるものとする。
　なお、この手法の適用に当たっては、特に、前記②のウに掲げる事項に留意する必要がある。

(4)　対象不動産について土壌汚染が存することが判明している場合又は土壌汚染が存する可能性のある場合の鑑定評価について
　土壌汚染が存することが判明した不動産については、原則として汚染の分布状況、除去等に要する費用等を他の専門家が行った調査結果等を活用して把握し鑑定評価を行うものとする。なお、この場合でも、「総論第5章　鑑定評価の基本的事項」及び本留意事項の「Ⅲ「総論第5章　鑑定評価の基本的事項」について」に規定する条件設定に係る一定の要件を満たす場合には、依頼者の同意を得て汚染の除去等の措置がなされるものとしてという条件を付加して鑑定評価を行うことができる。また、「総論第8章　鑑定評価の手順」及び本留意事項の「Ⅵ「総論第8章　鑑定評価の手順」について」に規定する客観的な推定ができると認められる場合には、土壌汚染が存することによる価格形成上の影響の程度を推定して鑑定評価を行うことができる。
　土壌汚染対策法に規定する調査、区域指定、措置等の各手続きに対応した鑑定評価上の対応を示すと次のようになる。
① 　対象不動産について土壌汚染対策法第3条の規定により土壌の汚染の状況についての調査義務が発生したとき又は対象不動産について同法第4条の規定により土壌の汚染の状況についての調査を命ぜられたときには、当該調査の結果を踏まえ、汚染が存することが判明すればそれを前提に鑑定評価を行うものとする。
② 　対象不動産について土壌汚染対策法第5条に規定する指定区域の指定がなされている場合には、汚染が存することを前提に鑑定評価を行うものとする。
③ 　対象不動産について土壌汚染対策法第7条の規定により都道府県知事から汚染の除去等の措置を講ずべきことを命ぜられた場合において、何らかの措置が行われた後であっても指定区域の指定が解除されない限りは汚染が存することを前提に鑑定評価を行うものとする。
④ 　①の法定調査の結果土壌汚染の存在が判明しなかった場合、②の指定区域の指定が解除され指定区域台帳から削除された場合及び使用の廃止を伴わない有害物質使用特定施設であって、都道府県知事から当該土地の汚染の状況についての調査や汚染の除去等の措置が命ぜられていない場合には、土壌汚染が存しないとして鑑定評価を行うことができるものとする。
　なお、汚染の除去等の措置が行われた後でも、心理的嫌悪感等による価格形成への影響を考慮しなければならない場合があることに留意する。

Guidance Note Ⅶ

soil contamination is nonexistent: (a) where the presence of soil contamination was not verified by the legal investigation (described in ① above); (b) where the status of the subject property as a designated zone (see ② above) has been lifted and the subject property has been removed from the list of designated zones; and (c) where the governor of the prefecture has not ordered an operating specified facility dealing with harmful substances to investigate potential soil contamination or to undertake measures for the removal of polluted soil.

It should be further noted, however, that even after the implementation of measures for the removal of soil pollution, the appraiser may still have to consider the stigma on the value of the subject property.

2. Guidance on Built-Up Property
(1) Tenant-Occupied Building and Its Site
Where the value of a tenant-occupied building and its site is to be determined by the income capitalization approach and the economic value of the deposit is relatively insignificant because of changes in the value of the land and building over the passage of time following the receipt of that deposit, the value is determined by capitalizing the net operating income (NOI), based on actual nominal rent, rather than actual effective rent.

(2) Condominium Units
An appraiser may confirm the physical characteristics of, and ownership and interests in, a condominium unit from land registry books, building drawing (or building documents when more detailed drawings are required), management bylaws, assessment rolls and survey drawings.

Some matters requiring special attention in the confirmation process are listed below.

① **Exclusively Owned Areas**
  a. Location, shape, size, structure and use of the condominium building
  b. Location, shape, size and use of the exclusively owned areas of the building
  c. Details of building appurtenances that go with the exclusively owned areas

② **Common Areas**
  a. Extent of common areas and co-ownership
  b. Common areas belonging to only some condominium unit owners

③ **Building Site**
  a. Location, shape and size of the site
  b. Title encumbrances upon the site
  c. Dimensions of the site assigned to the building where the subject condominium project is located
  d. Co-ownership of the site

④ **Management Fees**
  Amounts of the management fees and repair reserves.

2．建物及びその敷地について
(1) 貸家及びその敷地について
　　貸家及びその敷地の収益価格を求める場合において、一時金の授受後における期間の経過に伴う土地、建物等の価格の変動により、一時金としての経済価値的意義が薄れているときは、その実際実質賃料に代えて実際支払賃料に基づく純収益を求め、当該純収益を還元して収益価格を求めることができる。

(2) 区分所有建物及びその敷地について
　　区分所有建物及びその敷地の確認に当たっては、登記簿謄本、建物図面（さらに詳細な図面が必要な場合は、設計図書等）、管理規約、課税台帳、実測図等に基づき物的確認と権利の態様の確認を行う。
　　また、確認に当たって留意すべき主な事項は、次のとおりである。

① 専有部分
　ア　建物全体の位置、形状、規模、構造及び用途
　イ　専有部分の一棟の建物における位置、形状、規模及び用途
　ウ　専有部分に係る建物の附属物の範囲

② 共用部分
　ア　共用部分の範囲及び共有持分
　イ　一部の区分所有者のみに属する共用部分

③ 建物の敷地
　ア　敷地の位置、形状及び規模
　イ　敷地に関する権利の態様
　ウ　対象不動産が存する一棟の建物に係る規約敷地の範囲
　エ　敷地の共有持分

④ 管理費等
　　管理費及び修繕積立金の額

Guidance Note VIII

> **Guidance Note VIII on SS. Chap. 2 :**
> **APPRAISAL OF REAL ESTATE RENTAL VALUE**

1. Guidance on Building Sites

In determining the market rent under new lease to a building site, the appraiser should pay special attention to the following matters.

(1) Where the highest and best use of the building site cannot be realized because of restrictions on use imposed by the lessor in the lease contract, the base value that is used for determining rent in the summation approach must consider the resulting decrease in economic value.

In assessing the anticipated yield, the appraiser must consider both the lagging nature of rent growth compared with the change in the land value and the degree of interdependence between rent and land value.

(2) The comparable rental data analyzed must include data on leases newly closed on a date near the date of the value opinion. The location of the comparable rental properties and other influences on the rent negotiated must be similar.

(3) Analysis of comparable rental data from similar lease contracts for the built-up property may provide an indication of the rent for building sites. The appraiser arrives at the indication of rent by deducting an amount equivalent to the actual real rent paid for portions other than the building site from the actual real rent paid for the total leased area of the building, including the building site. In selecting comparable data to determine the market rent for a building site, the appraiser should especially consider the similarity in contract provisions as well as in the highest and best use of the sites.

2. Guidance on Built-Up Property

Where a building is occupied by retail shops, only the core of the building and a portion of the building facilities may be constructed by the lessor (in such cases, leases to the tenants are called "skeleton leases"). The interior finish, exterior and a portion of the building facilities are often constructed by the tenant. The appraiser must keep this circumstance in mind when estimating the base value used to determine rent in the summation approach and selecting data used to determine rent in the comparable rental data approach.

Ⅷ 「各論第2章 賃料に関する鑑定評価」について

1．宅地について
宅地の新規賃料を求める場合において留意すべき事項は、次のとおりである。
(1) 積算賃料を求めるに当たっての基礎価格は、賃貸借等の契約において、貸主側の事情によって使用方法が制約されている場合等で最有効使用の状態を確保できない場合には、最有効使用が制約されている程度に応じた経済価値の減分を考慮して求めるものとする。
　また、期待利回りの判定に当たっては、地価水準の変動に対する賃料の遅行性及び地価との相関関係の程度を考慮する必要がある。
(2) 比準賃料は、価格時点に近い時点に新規に締結された賃貸借等の事例から比準する必要があり、立地条件その他の賃料の価格形成要因が類似するものでなければならない。
(3) 配分法に準ずる方法に基づく比準賃料は、宅地を含む複合不動産の賃貸借等の契約内容が類似している賃貸借等の事例に係る実際実質賃料から宅地以外の部分に対応する実際実質賃料相当額を控除する等により求めた比準賃料をいうものであるが、宅地の正常賃料を求める場合における事例資料の選択に当たっては、賃貸借等の契約内容の類似性及び敷地の最有効使用の程度に留意すべきである。

2．建物及びその敷地について
店舗用ビルの場合には、貸主は躯体及び一部の建物設備を施工するのみで賃貸し（スケルトン貸し）、内装、外装及び建物設備の一部は借主が施工することがあるので、積算賃料を求めるときの基礎価格の判定及び比準賃料を求めるときの事例の選択に当たっては、これに留意すべきである。

Guidance Note IX

Guidance Note IX on SS. Chap. 3 : APPRAISAL OF REAL ESTATE VALUE SUBJECT TO SECURITIZATION

1. **Guidance on Basic approach regarding securitization properties**
   (1) A securitization property as defined in the Specific Standards, Chapter 3, Section 1, I must be appraised in accordance with Chapter 3 of the Specific Standards, even if this means reevaluating a property that has been previously appraised.
2. **Guidance on Drafting a processing plan**
   (1) In some cases, the person verifying the data needed to draft the processing plan may be a different person than the LREA who is in charge of appraisal of the subject property. However, the LREA bears responsibility for this as part of the appraisal.
   (2) If negotiations are conducted with the client when verifying the data needed to draft the processing plan, such as asking the client to submit information to facilitate a suitable appraisal, then the course of such negotiations must be included in the records of verified data. The records of verified data are appended to the appraisal report as supplementary information. It is not necessary to append these records to the appraisal document; however, they must be retained as data specified in Article 38, Paragraph 2 of the Real Estate Appraisal Act Enforcement Rules.
   (3) If engineering reports, data needed for application of the DCF method, or other documents have been obtained multiple times, or if multiple field surveys of the subject property have been performed, then the matters confirmed at every stage and records from every stage are needed.
   (4) The relationships between the client and the parties involved in securitization must be described, as stated in the Specific Standards, Chapter 3, Section 2, III. It is also necessary to state whether the LREA holds interests in the subject property and whether the LREA has relationships to any persons holding interests with regard to the subject property, in accordance with Chapter 9, Section 2 of the General Standards.
3. **Guidance on Investigating property – specific influences on the securitization property**
   The following must be addressed in the investigation of property- specific influences on the securitization property.
   (1) The LREA makes an independent decision as to whether to use the engineering report or not. When judging the appropriateness and accuracy of the engineering report, if necessary, the LREA must seek verification based on the views of architects or other experts. In some cases, an existing engineering report can be used; but in other cases, even if the engineering report formally states the required items, it may be inadequate for appraisal purposes, and investigation by an LREA may be required.
   (2) The matters listed in the table in Specific Standards, Chapter 3, Section 3, III, (3) and the matters listed in Appendix 1 are only the necessary minimum of physical, legal, and other matters regarding the subject property which must be confirmed

IX 「各論第3章　証券化対象不動産の価格に関する鑑定評価」について

1．証券化対象不動産の基本姿勢について
(1) 各論第3章第1節Ⅰに定める証券化対象不動産については、従前に鑑定評価が行われたものを再評価する場合にあっても、各論第3章に従って鑑定評価を行わなければならないものであることに留意する必要がある。

2．処理計画の策定について
(1) 処理計画の策定に当たっての確認については、対象不動産の鑑定評価を担当する不動産鑑定士以外の者が行う場合もあり得るが、当該不動産鑑定士が鑑定評価の一環として責任を有するものであることに留意しなければならない。
(2) 処理計画の策定に当たっての確認において、依頼者から鑑定評価を適切に行うための資料の提出等について依頼者と交渉を行った場合には、その経緯を確認事項として記録しなければならない。また、確認事項の記録を鑑定評価報告書の附属資料として添付することとしているが、鑑定評価書への添付までを求めるものではないが、同記録は不動産の鑑定評価に関する法律施行規則第38条第2項に定める資料として保管されなければならないことに留意する必要がある。
(3) エンジニアリング・レポート及びDCF法等を適用するために必要となる資料等の入手が複数回行われる場合並びに対象不動産の実地調査が複数回行われる場合にあっては、各段階ごとの確認及び記録が必要であることに留意しなければならない。
(4) 各論第3章第2節Ⅲに、依頼者の証券化関係者との関係について記載する旨定めているが、不動産鑑定士の対象不動産に関する利害関係又は対象不動産に関し利害関係を有する者との縁故若しくは特別の利害関係の有無及び内容については、総論第9章第2節により記載する必要があることに留意しなければならない。

3．証券化対象不動産の個別的要因の調査について
証券化対象不動産の個別的要因の調査に当たっては、次に掲げる事項に留意する必要がある。
(1) エンジニアリング・レポートの活用に当たっては、不動産鑑定士が主体的に責任を持ってその活用の有無について判断を行うものであることに留意する必要がある。また、エンジニアリング・レポートの内容の適切さや正確さ等の判断に当たっては、必要に応じて、建築士等他の専門家の意見も踏まえつつ検証するよう努めなければならないことに留意する必要がある。
既存のエンジニアリング・レポートの活用で対応できる場合がある一方、エンジニアリング・レポートが形式的に項目を満たしていても、鑑定評価にとって不十分で不動産鑑定士の調査が必要となる場合もある。
(2) 鑑定評価に必要な対象不動産の物的確認、法的確認等に当たっては、各論第3章第3節Ⅲ(3)の表に掲げる内容や別表1の項目に掲げる内容が必要最小限度のものを定めたものであり、必要に応じて項目・内容を追加し、確認しなければならないことに留意する必要がある。
(3) できる限り依頼者からエンジニアリング・レポートの全部の提供を受けるとともに、エンジ

Guidance Note IX

for appraisal. It may be necessary to confirm additional items and details.
(3) The LREA should obtain the full engineering report from the client and obtain an explanation directly from the preparer of the engineering report, to the extent this is possible.
(4) The preparation of an engineering report is often a contracted service. In this case, the engineering report preparer should indicate the contract provider of survey services. When identifying the engineering report preparer in the appraisal report, the name of the contract provider of survey services must also be stated.

4. **Guidance on Application of the DCF method**
The following must be addressed in the application of the DCF method.
(1) When explaining the income and expense items and their definitions to the client, in order to improve the accuracy of the data that the client provides to the LREA, it is necessary to provide guidance such as indicating the correspondences between income/expense items and data concerning the management of real estate receipts and disbursements, including a detailed breakdown of how to calculate each item.
(2) The income and expense items should not include securitization-related expenses such as trust fees, business expenses of SPCs, investment corporations, funds, etc., or asset management fees (except for expenses related to specific properties). Since net cash flow is calculated prior to depreciation, no depreciation allowances are entered. Also, the breakdown of net operating income as defined in the table in the Specific Standards, Chapter 3, Section 4, II (1) may differ from that of NOI (net operating income) as the term is used in general disclosure documents related to securitization properties.
(3) Regarding the calculation of operating profit on lump-sum payments and capital expenditures, which account for the difference between net operating income and net cash flow, two of the income and expense items in the table in the Specific Standards, Chapter 3, Section 4, II (1), it is necessary to append a note concerning the approach for the yield of operating profit on lump-sum payments, and to ensure that the categories of capital expenditures and repair expenses conform to their handling under tax procedures.
(4) When the direct capitalization method is used for verification purposes in cases when the DCF method has been applied, the income and expense items must be used in the same way.

Supplementary provision(Totally revised, July 3, 2002)
These Guidance Notes to the Japanese Real Estate Appraisal Standards become effective on January 1, 2003.

Supplementary provisions (Partly revised, April 2, 2007)
1. These Guidance Notes become effective on July 1, 2007.
2. In the revised Guidance Notes, LREA candidates are included under the term Licensed Real Estate Appraiser (LREA).

ニアリング・レポートの作成者からの説明を直接受ける機会を求めることが必要である。
(4) なお、エンジニアリング・レポートの作成は委託される場合が多いが、この場合には、エンジニアリング・レポートの作成者は調査の受託者を指すことに留意しなければならない。また、この場合においては、エンジニアリング・レポートの作成者を鑑定評価報告書に記載する際、調査の委託者の名称も記載する必要がある。

4．DCF法の適用等について

DCF法の適用等に当たっては、次に掲げる事項に留意する必要がある。
(1) 収益費用項目及びその定義を依頼者に説明するに当たって、各項目ごとの具体的な積算内訳など不動産の出納管理に関するデータ等と収益費用項目の対応関係を示すなどの工夫により、依頼者が不動産鑑定士に提供する資料の正確性の向上に十分配慮しなければならない。
(2) 収益費用項目においては、信託報酬、特別目的会社・投資法人・ファンド等に係る事務費用、アセットマネジメントフィー（個別の不動産に関する費用は除く）等の証券化関連費用は含まないこと。「純収益」は償却前のものとして求めることとしていることから減価償却費は計上しないことに留意する必要がある。また、各論第3章第4節Ⅱ(1)の表に定める「運営純収益」と証券化対象不動産に係る一般の開示書類等で見られるいわゆる「NOI（ネット・オペレーティング・インカム）」はその内訳が異なる場合があることに留意する必要がある。
(3) 各論第3章第4節Ⅱ(1)の表の収益費用項目のうち「運営純収益」と「純収益」の差額を構成する「一時金の運用益」と「資本的支出」の算出について、「一時金の運用益」の利回りの考え方を付記するとともに、「資本的支出」と「修繕費」の区分については、税務上の整理等との整合性に十分配慮する必要があることに留意しなければならない。
(4) 収益費用項目については、DCF法を適用した場合の検証として適用する直接還元法においても、同様に用いる必要がある。

附　則（平成14年7月3日全部改正）
　この不動産鑑定評価基準運用上の留意事項は、平成15年1月1日から施行する。

附　則（平成19年4月2日一部改正）
1．この留意事項は、平成19年7月1日から施行する。
2．不動産鑑定士補は、改正後の留意事項の適用については、不動産鑑定士とみなす。

PART5

Guidelines for the Appraisal of Overseas Investment Properties

Notified and enforced on January 25, 2008
Ministry of Land, Infrastructure, Transport and Tourism

第5編

海外投資不動産鑑定評価ガイドライン

平成20年1月25日通知
国 土 交 通 省

Table of Contents

Purpose of the Guidelines ··352
I   Basic Procedures for carrying out appraisals of overseas investment properties ···354
II Confirming the basic procedures for carrying out the appraisal of overseas investment properties ···············356
III Selection of a local appraiser ································356
IV Property inspection and investigation of market trends, legislation, etc. ·······································358
V   Collaboration with the local appraiser ··················362
VI Content of the contract on collaboration with the local appraiser ···364
VII Verification of the information collected or the appraisal report submitted by the local appraiser, and any additional or supplemental investigation ·············370
VIII Determining the appraised value ·························372
IX Preparation of the appraisal report, etc. ················376
X   Items included in the appraisal report, etc. ············376
XI Other important matters ·····································380
XII Relationship between the guidelines and the Real Estate Appraisal Standards ·······································382

目　次

ガイドラインの目的 …………………………………………………………………353
Ⅰ　海外不動産の鑑定評価の基本的な実施方法 ……………………………………355
Ⅱ　海外不動産の鑑定評価の基本的な実施方法の確認 ……………………………357
Ⅲ　現地鑑定人の選任 …………………………………………………………………357
Ⅳ　実地調査、市場動向、法令等の調査 ……………………………………………359
Ⅴ　現地鑑定人との連携・共同作業 …………………………………………………363
Ⅵ　現地鑑定人との連携・共同作業のための契約内容 ……………………………365
Ⅶ　現地基礎資料等又は現地鑑定報告書の検証及び追加・補完調査 ……………371

Ⅷ　鑑定評価額の決定等 ………………………………………………………………373
Ⅸ　鑑定評価報告書等の作成等 ………………………………………………………377
Ⅹ　鑑定評価報告書等の記載事項等 …………………………………………………377
Ⅺ　その他留意事項 ……………………………………………………………………381
Ⅻ　本ガイドラインの位置づけ ………………………………………………………383

January 25, 2008
Koku To Chi No. 267
Vice-Minister of Land, Infrastructure, Transport and Tourism

Notification: Guidelines for the Appraisal of Overseas Investment Properties

As the globalization of real estate markets advances, there is a growing trend toward investment in domestic real estate from abroad, as well as for investment in overseas real estate by domestic businesses and individuals. Real estate investment trust (REIT) markets are developing in many countries, and international competition in the field of real estate is becoming increasingly intense. REITs in other countries are actively incorporating foreign investment properties into their portfolios.

In July 2006, the Real Estate Investment Market Study Group of the Planning Committee of the National Land Development Council's Land Policy Board recommended the preparation of guidelines for the appraisal of overseas investment properties, with an eye to including overseas properties in J-REITs. On May 8, 2007, the same recommendation was made in the first report of the Globalization Reform Research Committee of the Council on Economic and Fiscal Policy. In response, the Ministry of Land, Infrastructure, Transport and Tourism established an expert working group to study guidelines for the appraisal of overseas investment properties. This working group submitted its report to the Real Estate Appraisal Committee of the National Land Development Council's Land Policy Board on December 14, 2007. The appended Guidelines for the Appraisal of Overseas Investment Properties were developed on the basis of a draft of that report.

The purpose for developing these guidelines was to set down standard methods for the appraisal of overseas properties by Licensed Real Estate Appraisers LREAs, including appraisal techniques and approaches to be used in collaborative work with local appraisers overseas, and to ensure the suitable and accurate appraisal of overseas investment properties, thereby promoting reliable appraisals by LREAs working on overseas assignments and with the intention of protecting investors. It is anticipated that these guidelines will be used in the sharing of information regarding overseas investment property appraisals, in the active promotion of appraiser training activities, and by LREAs in their own ongoing professional development, thereby improving the reliability of the real estate appraisal system.

Real estate in Japan and abroad will together form a single real estate market if Japanese private funds begin to include overseas properties in their investment portfolios, and if it becomes possible for J-REITs to invest in overseas properties in the future. Because of this eventuality and also the requirement that J-REIT properties be appraised by an LREA, guidance and supervision under the Real Estate Appraisal Act (Law No. 152 of 1963) is needed regarding the appraisal of such overseas properties by LREAs. Therefore, it should be noted that the content of these guidelines will apply to such appraisals in the same way as do the Japanese Real Estate Appraisal Standards; and any incompetent appraisal due to non-compliance with these guidelines will be subject to guidance and supervision under the Law on Real Estate Appraisal.

These guidelines will take effect as of the notification date. I encourage you to inform all of your member LREAs concerning these guidelines so that they can obtain an accurate understanding of the content of the guidelines and develop the necessary capabilities to further promote competent real estate appraisal practice.

通知

平成20年1月25日
国土地第267号
国土交通事務次官

海外投資不動産鑑定評価ガイドラインについて（通知）

　不動産市場のグローバル化が進行する中、海外からの国内不動産への投資や国内企業や投資家による海外不動産への投資が活発化するとともに、各国不動産投資信託（リート）市場の開設が相次ぎ、不動産分野における国際間競争力が厳しくなってきている。海外リートにおいては、運用対象資産に海外不動産を組み入れることに積極的である中、平成18年7月国土審議会土地政策分科会企画部会不動産投資市場検討小委員会においてＪリートの海外不動産導入に向けて、海外投資不動産鑑定評価ガイドラインづくりの必要性が提言された。さらに、平成19年5月8日経済財政諮問会議グローバル化改革専門調査会第一次報告において同様の提言がなされた。これらを受け、国土交通省は、海外投資不動産鑑定評価ガイドラインを検討するための有識者からなるワーキンググループを設置して検討を行い、同年12月14日に国土審議会土地政策分科会不動産鑑定評価部会に報告した。今般、当該報告案を踏まえ、別添のとおり海外投資不動産鑑定評価ガイドラインを策定したので、通知する。

　本ガイドラインの策定は、海外不動産への投資を行う際に不動産鑑定士が鑑定評価を行う場合について、投資家保護及び鑑定評価の信頼性の向上の観点から適正な鑑定評価が行われるよう、現地鑑定人との連携・共同のあり方、鑑定評価の手法等、海外投資不動産についての不動産鑑定士による鑑定評価の標準的手法について示すとともに、海外投資不動産の鑑定評価実務の適正かつ的確な遂行を図ることを目的とするものである。また、本ガイドラインを活用して、海外投資不動産の鑑定評価に関する情報の共有、研修等の積極的な推進、不動産鑑定士各自の不断の研鑽を行い、不動産鑑定評価制度の信頼性の向上が図られることを期待するものである。

　一方、日本のプライベートファンドが海外不動産を組み入れる場合や、今後、Ｊリートによる海外不動産の組み入れが可能となった場合には、海外不動産と本邦不動産とで一つの不動産市場が形成されること、Ｊリートについては不動産鑑定士による鑑定評価が義務づけられていること等にかんがみ、不動産鑑定士が行うこれらの海外不動産の鑑定評価については、不動産の鑑定評価に関する法律（昭和38年法律第152号）に基づく指導監督を行うこととする。したがって、これらの場合の鑑定評価については、本ガイドラインの内容は不動産鑑定評価基準と同等の位置づけとして取り扱うこととし、本ガイドラインを逸脱することにより不当な鑑定評価が行われた場合には、同法に基づく指導監督が行われることに留意されたい。

　なお、策定された本ガイドラインは、通知の日から施行されるものであり、所属の不動産鑑定士が内容を正確に理解し、必要な能力の研鑽に努め、適正な不動産の鑑定評価の推進に一層努めるよう、本ガイドラインの周知徹底を図られたい。

> **Purpose of the Guidelines**
>
> These guidelines specify standard procedures for the appraisal of overseas investment properties by Licensed Real Estate Appraisers (LREA).
>
> As real estate markets become increasingly global in nature, there is a growing trend for investors from overseas to purchase domestic real estate, as well as for domestic businesses and individuals to invest in overseas real estate. REIT markets are developing in many countries around the world. International competition in the field of real estate is becoming more and more intense.
>
> As regards Japan's real estate securitization market, although the laws of Japan do not prohibit the inclusion of overseas properties among the assets that J-REITs can invest in, investment in overseas real estate is prevented by the listing rules of the Japanese securities exchanges. One reason given for this situation has been the lack of standard appraisal procedures for valuing overseas properties.
>
> Domestic real estate firms are actively investing in overseas properties to disperse the risk of excessive concentration of investment in Japanese real estate; and we anticipate that the promotion of credible appraisals for overseas investment properties will contribute to sound growth in overseas property investment.
>
> In view of the above, the purpose of these guidelines is to specify appraisal procedures and principles to be followed by LREAs working in collaboration with local appraisers abroad and thereby to ensure the preparation of credible appraisals of overseas investment properties that investors can rely on.

Real estate investment trusts (REITs) were first established in the United States in 1960. In subsequent years, REITs spread to the Netherlands, Australia, and Asian nations, and they are now available in 18 countries.* Of the 18 countries where REIT markets have been set up, the inclusion of foreign real estate among the investment assets of REITs is prohibited in Japan, South Korea, Thailand, and Bulgaria. The remaining 14 countries permit investments in foreign real estate.

While there are no legal regulations in Japan forbidding the inclusion of foreign real estate in the investment assets of J–REITs, the Tokyo Stock Exchange prohibits the listing of investment trusts that do so. Should it become possible for J–REITs to invest in foreign real estate, this development can be expected to increase the attractiveness of the J–REIT market, as it makes it possible to diversify risk through exposure to foreign real estate markets that reflect greater diversity in market trends. This will result in restraining the flow of funds out of the J–REIT market into foreign REIT markets, inviting the influx of funds from foreign investors into the J–REIT market, and strengthening the international competitiveness of Japan's real estate market.

With the view of contributing to the development of an environment where foreign real estate is included among the investment assets of J–REITs, these guidelines specify standard appraisal procedures to be used by Japanese real estate appraisers in appraising foreign real estate to be acquired by private funds or domestic businesses or as other foreign property investments..

*the United States, Israel, the United Kingdom, the Netherlands, Australia, Canada, Singapore, Thailand, Taiwan, South Korea, Turkey, Germany, Japan, France, Bulgaria, Belgium, Hong Kong, and Malaysia.

〔ガイドラインの目的〕

　本ガイドラインは、海外投資不動産についての不動産鑑定士による鑑定評価の標準的手法について示すものである。

　不動産市場のグローバル化が進む中、海外からの国内不動産への投資や国内企業や投資家による海外不動産への投資も活発化するとともに、各国でリート市場の開設が相次ぎ、不動産分野における国際間競争が厳しくなってきている。

　一方、我が国の不動産証券化市場においては、日本版不動産投資信託（Jリート）の運用対象資産に海外不動産を組み入れることを禁止する法令上の規定は存在しないが、東京証券取引所の上場規程はこれを禁止している。これについては、海外不動産について、これまで標準的な鑑定評価手法が確立していないこと等がその要因となっているとの声もある。

　また、国内不動産事業者は、不動産投資の国内集中に伴うリスクを分散させる観点から、海外不動産への投資に積極的になっており、その際に必要となる適正な鑑定評価の確保により、不動産市場の一層の健全な成長が期待できる。

　本ガイドラインは、以上を踏まえ、海外不動産への投資を行う際に不動産鑑定士が鑑定評価を行う場合において、投資家保護及び鑑定評価の信頼性の向上の観点から適正な鑑定評価が行われるよう、海外現地の不動産鑑定人との連携・共同作業のあり方、鑑定評価の手法等を示すものである。

　不動産投資信託（リート）は、1960年に米国で誕生し、その後、オランダ、オーストラリアをはじめ、アジア諸国まで制度化が進み、現在では18の国又は地域（※）まで広がっている。各国リートの運用対象資産への海外不動産の組み入れの可否を見ると、現在リート市場が開設されている日本以外の17の国又は地域のうち、禁止している国は韓国、タイ、ブルガリアの3カ国となっており、これら以外の14の国又は地域では海外不動産への投資が可能となっている。

　我が国においては、Jリートの運用対象資産に海外不動産を組み入れることを禁止する法令上の規定は存在しないが、東京証券取引所の上場規程はこれを禁止している。Jリートの海外不動産への投資が可能となれば、各国不動産市場動向の多様性の確保によるリスク分散が可能となることを通じてJリート市場そのものの魅力向上が期待でき、結果としてJリート市場から海外リート市場への資金流出の抑制、海外投資家からのJリート市場への資金流入に寄与し、日本の不動産市場の国際競争力を強化することにもつながる。

　本ガイドラインは、Jリートの運用対象資産に海外不動産を導入するための環境整備の一助となることも念頭に置きつつ、プライベートファンドや国内企業による海外不動産の取得その他海外不動産への投資を行う場合において、海外不動産を鑑定評価する際の不動産鑑定士による鑑定評価の標準的手法について示すものである。

※アメリカ合衆国、イスラエル、英国、オランダ、オーストラリア、カナダ、シンガポール、タイ、台湾、大韓民国、トルコ、ドイツ、日本、フランス、ブルガリア、ベルギー、香港、マレーシア

Guideline I

> **I. Basic procedures for carrying out appraisals of overseas investment properties**
>
> (1) When an appraisal of an overseas property is requested, it is conceivable that an LREA may either travel to the location abroad to conduct the appraisal (unless the laws of that country specify that only local appraisers may do appraisal work) or the LREA may engage a local appraiser as an assistant or coworker in performing the appraisal.
> It is usually more reasonable and realistic to engage a local appraiser as an assistant or coworker when performing the appraisal, since local appraisers have expert knowledge of the market trends, social and economic conditions, and other factors affecting the specific overseas market.
>
> (2) The basic approach to an appraisal in this situation is for the LREA to conduct an appraisal according to the approved or officially authorized real estate appraisal standards of the specific overseas country in collaboration with an approved or officially authorized professional real estate appraiser of that overseas country.
>
> (3) The LREA must have an adequate understanding of the overseas country, which is essential to appraising the overseas property. This includes an understanding of real estate market trends in the overseas country, the legal and fiscal systems that apply to real estate, the national appraisal standards, and the qualifications of local appraisers. In addition, the LREA must confirm that the work of the local appraiser has been performed in a credible and reasonable manner, and must verify that the results of that work are appropriate.

In appraising real estate, the Japanese real estate appraiser or local real estate appraiser overseas must first collect and classify market data, and then arrive at an expert conclusion based on rational analysis and judgment. When real estate appraisers perform appraisals of foreign real estate, they need to understand trends in the local market overseas as well as the social and economic conditions. It is rare, however, for real estate appraisers to be fully versed in all matters needed to appraise foreign real estate, and in many cases it will be reasonable to appraise foreign real estate through collaborative work with overseas real estate appraisers. Moreover, there may be practical problems, such as local laws that impose restrictions on appraisals being performed by persons other than local real estate appraisers. It should also be noted that it may often be more realistic to carry out appraisals through collaborative work with local real estate appraisers in terms of smoothly executing the appraisal work.

When performing collaborative work with real estate appraisers overseas, Japanese real estate appraisers must have a good understanding of the foreign locality, which is essential to apprasiing foreign real estate. This entails information about local real estate market trends, legal and fiscal systems, appraisal standards as they apply to the real estate, and the system under which real estate appraisers gain their qualifications. Such an understanding is needed so that the real estate appraiser can understand the nature of the work and content of the report of the local real estate appraiser, can appropriately collaborate with the local appraiser on the appraisal, and can take responsibility for the results of the appraisal.

I 海外不動産の鑑定評価の基本的な実施方法

(1) 海外不動産の鑑定評価を依頼された場合には、
 ・不動産鑑定士が海外現地(海外不動産の存する地域をいう。以下同じ。)に赴き鑑定評価を行う
 ・海外現地の不動産鑑定人を補助員・共同作業員として鑑定評価を行う
ことが考えられるが、海外現地の市場動向、社会経済情勢等に精通している不動産鑑定人を補助員・共同作業員として鑑定評価を行うことが合理的かつ現実的である。

(2) この際の鑑定評価は、不動産鑑定士が、
 ・海外現地において専門職業家として認定又は公認された不動産鑑定人との連携・共同作業により、
 ・海外現地において認定又は公認された不動産の鑑定評価基準に基づき、
鑑定評価を行うことが原則である。

(3) 不動産鑑定士は、海外現地における不動産市場の動向、不動産に関連する法制・税制・鑑定評価基準、不動産鑑定人の資格制度等海外不動産の鑑定評価を行うために必要となる基礎的知識について十分に理解するとともに、海外現地の不動産鑑定人の作業が適切かつ合理的に行われていることを確認し、及びその作業成果が適正であることを検証しなければならない。

　不動産の鑑定評価は、不動産鑑定士又は不動産鑑定人が市場データを収集及び整理し、合理的な分析及び判断に基づく専門的判定により行われるべきである。
　不動産鑑定士が海外不動産の鑑定評価を行う場合においても、海外現地の市場動向や社会経済情勢等を理解していることが必要である。ただし、不動産鑑定士が独力で海外不動産の鑑定評価を行い得るほどこれらの諸事情に十分精通していることは希であり、海外現地の不動産鑑定人と連携・共同作業により鑑定評価を行うことが合理的な場合が多いと考えられる。また、その国の法令等により海外現地の不動産鑑定人以外の者による鑑定業が制限されるなど実務上の問題が生じることも考えられ、海外現地の不動産鑑定人との連携・共同作業により鑑定評価を行う方が、業務の円滑な遂行を確保する上では現実的な場合もあることに留意すべきである。
　海外現地の不動産鑑定人と連携・共同作業を行う場合においても、不動産鑑定士は、海外現地における不動産市場の動向、不動産に関連する法制・税制・鑑定評価基準、不動産鑑定人の資格制度等海外不動産の鑑定評価を行うために必要となる海外現地の基礎的知識について十分に理解していることが必要である。これは、海外現地の不動産鑑定人の作業内容、報告内容等について不動産鑑定士が理解し、連携・共同して適正な鑑定評価を行い、鑑定評価の結果に責任を負うためである。

II. Confirming the basic procedures for carrying out the appraisal of overseas investment properties

The LREA should explain to the client the following matters, which are the basic procedures for carrying out the appraisal of an overseas investment property, and should obtain written confirmation from the client prior to their implementation.

① Selection of a local appraiser as specified in Section III below.
② Work to be done in collaboration with the local appraiser and the division of labor.
③ Property inspection and other procedures for confirming the description of the subject property.
④ Unit of currency in which the appraised value will be reported.
⑤ Whether assessments have been done on the environment and the condition of the buildings, facilities, etc., of the subject property; and if so, the method by which the assessment reports can be obtained.

Compared to the appraisal of domestic real estate, the appraisal of foreign real estate involves the need for collaborative work with a local real estate appraiser overseas and considerable travel–related and other expenses. It is important, therefore, to discuss basic appraisal procedures with the client beforehand and to obtain the client's approval. This approval should be received in writing to prevent disputes later.

In this process, it will be necessary to explain to the client such matters as the selection of the local real estate appraiser overseas, the nature of the collaborative work with the local appraiser, the allocation of responsibilities between the Japanese appraiser and local appraiser, and the property inspection. After gaining the understanding of the client, an appraisal plan can be developed.

Should the appraisal client provide an engineering report or a ground pollution or other environmental assessment, it will be necessary to verify with the client whether another specialist was retained to prepare such a report or assessment. Should such assessments be performed, relevant reports must be obtained, analyzed, and evaluated, and they must be used as required in the appraisal.

III. Selection of a local appraiser

(1) The real estate appraisal firm should understand how appraisal work is conducted in the overseas country, the social and economic conditions affecting the subject real estate, and local real estate practice including professional real estate appraiser organizations. The firm should select an approved or officially authorized professional real estate appraiser of the overseas country as an assistant or coworker to collaborate on the work of the appraisal ("hereinafter referred to as the " local appraiser") after having that appraiser confirm all of the following items.

① Qualifications and licensure as a real estate appraiser and his professional designation.
② Resume and past experience as a real estate appraiser.

Ⅱ 海外不動産の鑑定評価の基本的な実施方法の確認

海外不動産の鑑定評価に当たっては、依頼者に対し、鑑定評価の基本的な実施方法として次の事項について説明し、書面による確認を得なければならない。
① Ⅲに定める海外現地の不動産鑑定人の選任
② 海外現地の不動産鑑定人との連携・共同作業の内容及び役割分担
③ 実地調査その他対象不動産の確認の方法
④ 鑑定評価額の通貨の単位
⑤ 対象不動産に係る建築物、設備等の状況及び環境に関する調査の有無並びに当該調査が行われる場合にあってはその報告書の入手方法

海外不動産の鑑定評価に当たっては、海外現地の不動産鑑定人との連携・共同作業が必要となることや、現地までの旅費等の費用が国内不動産の鑑定評価を行うときに比して多額となることから、依頼者との間で、鑑定評価の基本的な実施方法について事前の打ち合わせを行い、依頼者の確認を得ておくことが重要である。当該確認は、事後のトラブル防止の観点から、書面で行う必要があるものとする。

その際、海外現地の不動産鑑定人の選任、海外現地の不動産鑑定人との連携・共同作業の内容・役割分担、実地調査等につき、依頼者に対して説明し、理解を得た上で鑑定評価の処理計画を策定することが必要である。

また、依頼者がいわゆるエンジニアリング・レポートを作成する場合や土壌汚染等の環境調査を行う場合には、他の専門家へこれらを依頼しているかどうかにつき、鑑定評価の依頼者に確認することが必要である。これらの調査が行われている場合には、当該調査に係る報告書を入手し、これらを分析及び判断した上で、必要に応じて鑑定評価に活用しなければならない。

Ⅲ 現地鑑定人の選任

(1) 不動産鑑定業者は、海外現地の鑑定評価制度、不動産鑑定人団体（不動産鑑定人の資格・称号を付与する団体をいう。以下同じ。）等不動産の鑑定評価を巡る社会経済情勢について理解し、海外現地において専門職業家として認定又は公認された不動産鑑定人の中から、不動産鑑定士に少なくとも次の事項を確認させた上で、鑑定評価の連携・共同作業の補助員又は共同作業員を選任するものとする。
① 不動産鑑定人としての資格及び所属する不動産鑑定人団体
② 不動産鑑定人としての略歴及び実績
③ 依頼された鑑定評価に係る不動産取引の利害関係者以外の者であること

③ Independence as an appraiser, who cannot be an interested party in the real estate transaction in question.

(2) The local appraiser does not necessarily need to be someone residing in the overseas country but must be someone, who is recognized as being capable of performing an appraisal in the overseas country. The local appraiser should have an understanding of the economic conditions and trends affecting real estate appraisal, including the appraisal practices of the overseas country, as well as experience performing appraisals in that overseas country.

(3) In retaining the services of a local appraiser for a collaborative effort, it is desirable that the local appraiser be selected by the real estate appraisal firm. Even if the client has recommended a local appraiser, the real estate appraisal firm should only engage that appraiser after checking the appraiser's resume, past experience, qualifications, and so on, and determining that the appraiser is a suitable person to collaborate with.

The local appraiser selected must be authorized or officially recognized as a specialist in the foreign country. The local system for licensing and designating real estate appraisers must be supervised by a national organization of the foreign country. The organization must grant licenses and designations based on expertise and experience, and be empowered to suspend or revoke licenses of real estate appraisers who are involved in fraudulent or incompetent appraisals.

It would be appropriate to select a person with skills similar to persons licensed under Japan's real estate appraiser system, such as those licensed under US, UK and Australian systems, or to select a person with a license and designation granted under a system with a recognized legal or social standing.

Moreover, the selection of a local appraiser should not be decided merely based on affiliation with a certain real estate appraiser organization or a real estate appraisal firm. Rather, such matters as the candidate's resume, appraisal experience, license, and reputation should be examined; and the person determined to be best able to carry out collaborative appraisal work should be selected.

Information on the Appraisal Profession around the world is provided in a separate appendix at the end.

Ⅳ. Property inspection and investigation of market trends, legislation, etc.

(1) **Inspection of the subject property**
Data for the subject property must be confirmed by an inspection, including the interior of the property and the surrounding neighborhood.
However, for revaluing a property that has already been appraised, such confirmation may be based on a report of an inspection performed by a local appraiser, provided the inspection was personally performed by that person, and it is known that no changes have occurred that would affect the factors that determine the pricing for the subject property and the neighborhood.

(2) **Investigation of market trends, legislation, etc., in the overseas country**

> (2) (1)により選任される不動産鑑定人(以下「現地鑑定人」という。)は必ずしも海外現地の国に居住する者であることを要しないが、当該海外現地の鑑定評価制度、不動産鑑定人団体等不動産の鑑定評価を巡る社会経済情勢について理解し、海外現地において鑑定評価を行った実績があるなど海外現地における鑑定評価を行うことができると認められる者でなければならない。
>
> (3) 現地鑑定人の選任は、鑑定評価の連携・共同作業を円滑に行う上で不動産鑑定業者が行うことが必要である。依頼者が現地鑑定人の候補者を推薦した場合であっても、その者の不動産鑑定人としての略歴、実績、資格等を確認し、連携・共同作業を行う者として適切であると認められる場合に限り、不動産鑑定業者が選任するものとする。

現地鑑定人については、海外現地において専門職業家として認定又は公認された不動産鑑定人を選任する必要がある。現地の不動産鑑定人の資格・称号の制度は、海外現地の全国的組織により管理され、知識及び経験に応じて資格・称号が付与される制度であるとともに、不正又は不当な鑑定評価を行った不動産鑑定人に対する資格の停止、剥奪等の措置が執られる制度であることが必要である。

例えば、アメリカ合衆国、英国、オーストラリア等の資格・称号制度のように、日本の不動産鑑定士制度に類似する資格者の技能や法的又は社会的位置づけがある制度の下で付与された資格・称号を有する者から選任することが妥当である。

また、選任に当たって、一定の不動産鑑定人団体又は鑑定業者に所属していることのみをもって判断するのではなく、候補者の略歴、鑑定評価実績、資格、評判等を調査し、鑑定評価の連携・共同作業を行う能力があると判断される者から選任すべきである。

なお、不動産鑑定士制度を有する国又は地域を例示すると別表のとおりである。

> ## Ⅳ 実地調査、市場動向、法令等の調査
>
> (1) 対象不動産の実地調査
> 　対象不動産の内覧の実施を含めた実地調査等により対象不動産の確認を行わなければならない。
> 　ただし、既に鑑定評価が行われたことがある不動産の再評価をする場合において、自ら実地調査を行ったことがあり、当該不動産や周辺地域において価格形成要因に影響を与えるような変化がないと認められるときは、現地鑑定人等による実地調査の報告により確認を行うこととしても差し支えない。
>
> (2) 海外現地における不動産の市場動向、不動産に関連する法令等の調査
> 　海外現地における不動産市場の動向、不動産に関連する法制・税制・鑑定評

> Prior to the property inspection, the LREA needs to gain adequate understanding of real estate market trends, the legal and fiscal systems, the national appraisal standards, and other information about the overseas country. It is necessary for the LREA to personally investigate such matters, including reports prepared by local appraisers and market information on factors that determine prices.
>
> As regards the investigation of market trends, legal system, etc., the LREA must collect and analyze sufficient information for the appraisal, keeping in mind that the appraisal report will be read by investors. Among the matters to be investigated are macroeconomic analyses of the market in the overseas country; social, economic, fiscal, and administrative factors affecting prices: and contract formats and customary practices in real estate transactions. The LREA must also address these matters in the appraisal report.
>
> (3) **Other Investigations of the subject property**
> If an engineering report on the condition of the subject property's buildings, facilities and environmental factors (e.g., soil contamination) has been prepared, or if a separate soil contamination assessment or the like has been performed, then such reports should be obtained and used in the appraisal as required.

To confirm whether a subject property corresponds to the description in the reports, an inspection of the property including the interior is undertaken as the basis of any appraisal. This equally applies to an appraisal of an overseas property. Even when retaining the services of a local appraiser in a collaborative effort, as a general rule, the LREA is responsible for verifying the local appraiser's reports and preparing the appraisal report. The LREA must travel to the site and confirm the accuracy of the description of the subject property through an inspection, and interviews with the local appraiser, and property and leasing agents.

When appraising an overseas investment property, the LREA must collect, analyze, and explain a sufficiently broad scope of information that is especially important to investors, keeping in mind that the appraisal report will be read by investors. This information includes real estate market conditions in the overseas country, the fundamentals of the specific real estate market, and macroeconomic analyses. Such information is even more important for the appraisal of an overseas property than for the appraisal of a domestic property.

Therefore, in retaining the services of and working with a real estate appraiser in the overseas country, the LREA should ask his colleague or another party in the overseas country to collect the requisite information in advance.

Because of differences in the market practices of overseas countries, the engineering report may or may not be needed. If this investigation is generally performed in the overseas country (for instance, when this investigation is performed more than half of transactions for investment purposes or when this investigation is performed more than half of foreign investments even though it is rare for domestic transactions in the overseas country), the report should then be obtained, studied, and used in the appraisal.

> 価基準等については、実地調査に先立って又は海外現地において、現地鑑定人による報告及び価格形成要因に関連する資料の収集など自らの調査により十分に把握する必要がある。
>   これらの市場動向、法令等の調査については、鑑定評価書が投資家向けに開示されることも念頭に置き、海外現地における市場のマクロ的な経済分析、不動産取引の契約形態や慣行等の社会的・経済的・行政的な価格形成要因を含めて、十分な情報を収集・分析して鑑定評価報告書又は鑑定評価検証報告書に記載することが必要である。
>
> (3) 対象不動産に関する他の調査
>   対象不動産に係る建築物、設備等の状況及び環境に関する調査（いわゆるエンジニアリング・レポートが作成される場合の調査）、土壌汚染の調査等が行われる場合には、当該調査に係る報告書を入手し、必要に応じて鑑定評価に活用しなければならない。

　対象不動産が報告された内容のとおり存在しているかどうかの確認のため、内覧の実施を含めた実地調査等を行うことが鑑定評価の基本であることは、海外不動産の鑑定評価を行う場合でも同様である。現地鑑定人と連携・共同作業を行う場合であっても、鑑定評価を行う不動産鑑定士は、原則として、現地へ赴き、対象不動産について実地調査、聴聞、公的資料の確認等により、対象不動産の確認を的確に行う必要がある。

　海外投資不動産の鑑定評価に当たっては、鑑定評価書が投資家向けに開示されることも念頭に置き、海外現地における不動産市場の動向に加えて、経済成長率、物価上昇率、人口動態等のマクロ的な経済分析も含め、投資家にとっても重要と考えられる情報を十分に収集・分析して記載していくことが必要であり、かつ、その重要性は、国内不動産の鑑定評価の場合に比して高いと考えられる。

　このため、不動産鑑定士は、現地鑑定人との連携・共同作業を進めていく上で、あらかじめ、これらの必要となる資料の収集等を現地鑑定人等に依頼することが望ましい。

　いわゆるエンジニアリング・レポートが作成される場合の調査、土壌汚染の調査等については、海外現地の市場慣行に応じて、その必要性が異なると考えられる。海外現地において一般的に当該調査が行われていると認められる場合（投資用不動産の取引の過半で当該調査が行われている場合や海外現地の国内取引においては希であるものの、海外からの投資に当たっては過半で当該調査が行われている場合等が該当する。）には、調査報告書を入手し、検討した上で鑑定評価に活用する必要がある。

V. Collaboration with the local appraiser

(1) **Approaches to collaboration with the local appraiser**
The LREA collaborates with the local appraiser through close cooperation and an appropriate division of labor. In general, there are two possible approaches to this collaborative effort.

① The local appraiser may be asked to collect basic information needed for the appraisal, and to assist the LREA in the appraisal work. The LREA performs the appraisal. (Hereinafter, this approach is called an "appraisal performed with a local assistant".)

② The local appraiser may be asked to prepare an appraisal report. The LREA confirms the appraisal by reviewing and verifying the appraisal work performed by the local appraiser, adding supplemental analyses as required. (Hereinafter, this approach is called "verification of an appraisal performed by a local appraiser".)

(2) **Procedure for effective collaboration with the local appraiser**
The LREA should promote effective collaboration on the appraisal, by directly exchanging views and information with the local appraiser in meetings and via telephone and Internet communications, and by keeping informed of the appraisal work performed by the local appraiser and the results produced at each step. The real estate appraisal firm should enter into a written contract with the local appraisal firm on retaining the services of the local appraiser.

The LREA assures completion of the appraisal assignment through an appropriate division of labor with the local appraiser. In general, there are two possible approaches to this process.

① **Appraisals performed with a local assistant**
The local appraiser provides the LREA with the basic information needed for the appraisal, such as local sales data and information on market trends. The LREA performs the appraisal through analysis of this basic information, determining the appropriateness of the data and market information used in the appraisal; and the LREA also obtains the assistance of the local appraiser in undertaking the appraisal work.

② **Verification of an appraisal performed by a local appraiser**
Based on his understanding and analysis of the appraisal methods, applied by the local appraiser, and of the requisite basic information, such as local sales data and market trends considered in the appraisal work, the LREA verifies the appropriateness of the conclusions in the appraisal report and the appropriateness of the appraised value.

No matter which of these two approaches is taken, the real estate appraisal firm needs to conclude a written contract with the local appraisal firm in advance in order to assure an effective collaborative effort and satisfactory completion of the appraisal assignment. Regarding the local appraisal firm as a party to that contract, it should also be noted that in some countries, the local appraiser may be incorporated, being identical to the local appraisal firm.

The table below summarizes the division of labor between the real estate appraisal firm and the LREA with regard to the client. In both cases, the contract needs to include a provision to the effect that the local appraiser is responsible for the basic information cited in the appraisal or appraisal report, which may be used not only by the LREA, but also by the client and third parties.

> **V 現地鑑定人との連携・共同作業**
>
> (1) 現地鑑定人との連携・共同作業の方式
> 　不動産鑑定士は、現地鑑定人と適切な役割分担及び密接な連携の下、連携・共同作業を行うものとする。連携・共同作業の方式としては、主に、次の方式が考えられる。
>
> ① 現地鑑定人に、鑑定評価を行うために必要となる基礎資料等の収集・提供その他の不動産鑑定士が行う鑑定評価の補助作業(以下「現地鑑定補助作業」という。)を依頼し、不動産鑑定士が現地鑑定補助作業に係る役務の提供を受けて鑑定評価を行う方式(現地鑑定補助方式)
>
> ② 現地鑑定人に、鑑定評価の報告を依頼し、現地鑑定人が行った鑑定評価を不動産鑑定士が検証することにより鑑定評価を行う方式(現地鑑定検証方式)
>
> (2) 現地鑑定人との連携・共同作業の推進方法
> 　不動産鑑定士は、現地鑑定人が行う鑑定評価の作業の内容及び各段階における成果等について、会議の開催、電話・インターネット通信等により、現地鑑定人と直接に意見交換等を行いながら、鑑定評価の連携・共同作業を円滑かつ確実に推進するものとする。このため、不動産鑑定業者は、書面により、現地鑑定人との連携・共同作業の実施に関する契約を現地鑑定人が所属する鑑定業者(以下「現地鑑定業者」という。)と締結するものとする。

　不動産鑑定士は、現地鑑定人と適切な役割分担及び密接な連携の下、連携・共同作業により、鑑定評価を行うこととなるが、その方式は、次の二つの方式が考えられる。

① 現地鑑定補助方式
　不動産鑑定士は、現地鑑定人から海外現地の取引事例、市場動向等鑑定評価を行うために必要となる基礎資料等(以下「現地基礎資料等」という。)の提供を受けるとともに、これらの現地基礎資料等の理解・分析をし、鑑定評価の作業に関する現地鑑定人の助言、便宜の供与その他の支援を受けながら、鑑定評価を行うものとする。

② 現地鑑定検証方式
　不動産鑑定士は、現地鑑定人の行う鑑定評価の手法、鑑定評価の作業に活用される海外現地の取引事例、市場動向等鑑定評価を行うために必要となる現地基礎資料等を理解・分析し、不動産鑑定士として、現地鑑定人による鑑定評価に係る報告書(以下「現地鑑定報告書」という。)における判断の妥当性及び鑑定評価額の適正性を検証することにより、鑑定評価を行うものとする。
　これらいずれの方式を採用する場合にあっても、現地鑑定人との連携・共同作業を円滑に推進するためには、不動産鑑定業者は、あらかじめ、現地鑑定業者との間で、書面による契約を締結する必要がある。なお、契約の相手方としての現地鑑定業者は、国又は地域によっては、現地鑑定人と現地鑑定業者が同一である場合もあることに留意すべきである。
　また、これらの方式を採用した場合、依頼者に対する不動産鑑定業者、不動産鑑定士及び現地鑑定人の責任分担は、以下のとおり整理される。この場合の契約事項には、現地基礎資料等又は現地鑑定報告書の利用者の範囲は、不動産鑑定士のみならず、依頼者が含まれる旨の定めを盛り込む必要がある。これは、現地鑑定人による鑑定評価に係る業務に関する民事的な責任の範囲を契約上明確にする趣旨である(Ⅵ参照)。

	An appraisal performed with a local assistant	Verification of an appraisal performed by a local appraiser
The real estate appraisal firm is responsible for:	①Selection of local appraiser ②One set of appraisal documents (quality control)	①Selection of local appraiser ②Overall appraisal report (quality control)
The LREA is responsible for:	①Verification of basic information submitted by the local appraiser ②Appraisal document in its entirety	①Verification of the local appraiser's report ②Preparation of supplemental analyses as needed ③A Japanese language translation of the local appraisal report
The local appraiser is responsible for:	①Provision of the basic information for the appraisal	①Appraisal report

Ⅵ. Content of the contract on collaboration with the local appraiser

(1) **An appraisal performed with a local assistant**

The contract specifies the qualifications and designation of the person, who will collect the basic information needed for the appraisal and who will assist the LREA in the appraisal work (hereinafter referred to as the "local appraisal assistant's work"). The contract specifies the method of communicating at each stage of the work (through the exchange of views at meetings or via telephone and Internet), the preparation guidelines and submission deadlines for the basic information, and the compensation. The following are examples of the main provisions of such a contract.

① **Scope of the contracted services, including**
  · What work is to be performed by the local appraisal assistant;
  · That the work is to be carried out based on the exchange of views in meetings and via telephone and Internet communications;
  · Where and when the meetings are to be held, what the reports for the meetings will cover, etc.

② **Professional qualifications of the responsible person**
  · Professional qualifications of the person, who will actually perform the work as the local appraisal assistant

③ **Compensation and expenses**

④ **Schedule**
  · Specific schedule of the work, including meeting dates, progress report dates, and appraisal report submission deadlines.
  · Requirement to meet the deadlines.

⑤ **Scope of the local appraiser's responsibility**
  · Responsibility of the local appraiser with regard to users of the LREA's appraisal report, i.e., the client and third parties (which applies only to those portions of the appraisal reflecting the local appraisal assistant's work).

	現地鑑定補助方式	現地鑑定検証方式
不動産鑑定業者	①現地鑑定人の選任 ②鑑定評価書全体（品質管理）	①現地鑑定人の選任 ②鑑定評価書全体（品質管理）
不動産鑑定士	①現地基礎資料等の検証 ②鑑定評価書全体	①現地鑑定報告書の検証 ②現地鑑定報告書の鑑定評価検証報告書 ③現地鑑定報告書の日本語による翻訳文
現地鑑定人	①現地基礎資料等	①現地鑑定報告書

Ⅵ 現地鑑定人との連携・共同作業のための契約内容

(1) 現地鑑定補助方式

現地鑑定人との連携・共同作業を行うに当たっては、現地鑑定補助作業を行う者の資格・称号、現地鑑定補助作業の各段階における会議の開催、電話・インターネット通信等による意見交換、現地基礎資料等の作成要領及び提出期限、報酬等について契約を締結するものとする。その際の主な契約内容を例示すると次のとおりである。

① 業務委託の範囲
・現地鑑定補助作業の内容
・現地鑑定補助作業を行うに当たっての意見交換の方法（会議の開催、電話・インターネット通信等）
・会議資料の内容等

② 担当者の専門職業家としての資格
・現地鑑定補助作業を実際に担当する専門職業家の資格

③ 報酬及び費用

④ 日程
・会議の開催日、現地基礎資料等の説明を行う日、現地基礎資料等の提出日等連携・共同作業の具体的な日程
・期限厳守であること。

⑤ 現地鑑定人の責任範囲
・不動産鑑定士が作成する鑑定評価報告書（現地鑑定補助作業が反映された部分に限る。）の利用（依頼者等の利用）に対する現地鑑定人の責任の範囲

⑥ **Other issues**
 · Confidentiality of information, etc.
(2) **Verification of an appraisal performed by a local appraiser**
The contract specifies the qualifications and designation of the person, who will perform the appraisal, the appraisal plan, the method of communicating at each stage of the work through the exchange of views at meetings or via telephone and Internet, preparation guidelines and submission deadlines for the local appraiser's report, and the compensation for the appraisal. The following are examples of the main provisions of such a contract.
① **Scope of the contracted services, including**
 · That an appraisal of the subject property is to be performed in accordance with the approved or officially authorized real estate appraisal standards of the overseas country and other relevant laws, regulations, etc.
 · That the appraisal work is to be carried out based on the exchange of views in meetings held at each stage of the work and via telephone and Internet communications.
 · Where and when the meetings are to be held, what the reports for the meetings will cover, etc.
② **Professional qualifications of the responsible person**
 · Professional qualifications of the person, who will actually perform the appraisal in the overseas country
③ **Compensation and expenses**
④ **Schedule**
 · Specific schedule of the work, including the dates of meetings to review the appraisal work, dates for progress reports by the local appraiser, and other specific dates that apply to the collaboration.
 · Requirement to meet the deadlines.
⑤ **Scope of the local appraiser's responsibility**
 · Responsibility of the local appraiser with regard to the use of his appraisal report by the client and third parties.
⑥ **Other issues**
 · Confidentiality of information, etc.

The contract for collaborative work with the local appraiser overseas may include the following items:
(1) **Appraisal performed with a local assistant**
 ① **Scope of the contracted work**
  · Specific tasks to be undertaken by the local appraiser (such as gathering and providing basic information and data on the local market and supporting the appraisal work of the Japanese real estate appraiser, including the property inspection)
  · Identification of the real estate to be appraised
  · Recipient of the basic information and data (name and address) and number of copies to be sent
  · Ethical standards for reviewing the appraisal as specified by a real estate appraiser organization

⑥ その他
・情報の秘密保持等
(2) 現地鑑定検証方式
現地鑑定人との連携・共同作業を行うに当たっては、現地鑑定人の資格・称号、鑑定評価手法、作業の各段階における会議の開催、電話・インターネット通信等による意見交換、現地鑑定報告書の作成要領及び提出期限、鑑定評価の報酬等について契約を締結するものとする。その際の主な契約内容を例示すると次のとおりである。

① 業務委託の範囲
・対象不動産について、海外現地において認定又は公認された不動産の鑑定評価基準その他遵守すべき法令、規程等に基づき行う鑑定評価の内容
・鑑定評価を行うに当たっての作業の各段階における意見交換の方法（会議の開催、電話・インターネット通信等）
・会議資料の内容等

② 担当者の専門職業家としての資格
・鑑定評価を実際に担当する専門職業家の資格

③ 報酬及び費用
④ 日程
・会議の開催日、現地鑑定報告書の説明を行う日、現地鑑定報告書の提出日等連携・共同作業の具体的な日程
・期限厳守であること。

⑤ 現地鑑定人の責任範囲
・現地鑑定報告書の利用（依頼者等の利用）に対する現地鑑定人の責任の範囲
⑥ その他
・情報の秘密保持等

現地鑑定人との連携・共同作業のための契約に盛り込む具体的な事項については、例えば、以下のような内容が考えられる。
(1) 現地鑑定補助方式
【① 業務委託の範囲】
・現地鑑定補助作業の内容（現地基礎資料等の収集・提供及び実地調査を含む不動産鑑定士による鑑定評価の作業の補助等）
・対象不動産の特定
・現地基礎資料等の送付先（住所・名宛人）及び送付部数
・不動産鑑定人団体が定める鑑定評価を行う際の倫理（監督）基準
・現地鑑定人と不動産鑑定士との間で行う会議の開催方法
・会議の開催、電話・インターネット通信等による意見交換により作業を進めること。

- Method for holding meetings between the local appraiser and the Japanese real estate appraiser
- That the work shall proceed by exchanging views in meetings and though telephone and Internet communication

② **Specialist qualifications of the person in charge of the local appraisal support work**
- The person to perform the local appraisal support work must be a real estate appraiser with a license or designation authorized or officially recognized in the foreign country.

③ **Fees and expenses**
- The contract shall specify the total fees and expenses related to the local appraiser's support work and must include procedures for dealing with additional work or for changes in the report format and content.

④ **Schedule**
- Date for submitting the basic information and data
- Dates for briefings on the basic information and data
- Dates for meetings between the local appraiser and the Japanese real estate appraiser
- That strict observance of deadlines will be required

⑤ **Scope of responsibility of the local appraiser**
- The local appraiser shall be responsible for those sections of the appraisal report reflecting the local appraiser's support work (when the appraisal report is prepared by the Japanese real estate appraiser for use by the client and others).

⑥ **Other**
- Obligation to maintain confidentiality
- Measures to be taken should a conflict of interest arise
- Obligation to work for a resolution should a dispute arise over the contract

(2) **Verification of an appraisal performed by an local appraiser**
  ① **Scope of the contracted work**
  - Specific tasks in the collaborative work to be performed by the local appraiser (such as preparing an appraisal report including the results of the property inspection)
  - Identification of the real estate to be appraised
  - Recipient of the local appraisal report (name and address) and number of copies to be sent
  - Real estate appraisal standards that will apply to the appraisal (the three appraisal approaches should be used to the extent possible and a supplementary clause should be included on the application of appropriate appraisal methodology, such as the determination of highest and best use)
  - Ethical standards for reviewing the appraisal as specified by a real estate appraiser organization
  - Method for holding meetings between the local appraiser and the Japanese real estate appraiser (specific meeting materials to be provided, such as detailed maps of the location of the real estate to be appraised and the location of transactions supplying market data and a regional geographical analysis for comparing cap rates and rents)

【② 担当者の専門職業家としての資格】
・現地鑑定補助作業を行う者は、海外現地において不動産鑑定人として認定又は公認された資格・称号を有する者であること。

【③ 報酬及び費用】
・現地鑑定補助作業に係る報酬・費用の合計額であり、追加業務及びリポートの様式・内容変更の場合の対応を含むこと。

【④ 日程】
・現地基礎資料等の提出日
・現地基礎資料等の説明を行う日
・現地鑑定人と不動産鑑定士との間で行う会議の開催日
・期限厳守

【⑤ 現地鑑定人の責任範囲】
・不動産鑑定士が作成する鑑定評価報告書(現地鑑定補助作業の反映された部分に限る。)の利用(依頼者等の利用)に対し、現地鑑定人が責任を有すること。

【⑥ その他】
・守秘義務
・利益相反の発生への対応
・この契約に関する紛争が生じた場合の調整に関する努力義務

(2) 現地鑑定検証方式
【① 業務委託の範囲】
・現地鑑定人による連携・共同作業の内容(実地調査を含む現地鑑定報告書の作成等)
・対象不動産の特定
・現地鑑定報告書の送付先(住所・名宛人)及び送付部数
・鑑定評価に適用する不動産の鑑定評価基準(鑑定評価手法は可能な限り三手法とするほか、最有効使用の原則を適用するなど適切な鑑定評価手法を適用する旨必要に応じて補足すること。)
・不動産鑑定人団体が定める鑑定評価を行う際の倫理(監督)基準
・現地鑑定人と不動産鑑定士との間で行う会議の開催方法(対象不動産及び取引事例の地点の詳細地図、キャップレートや賃料比較に係る地域の地理的分析資料を用意すること等会議資料の内容)
・現地鑑定報告書には、対象不動産の権利を証明する書面を添付すること。
・会議の開催、電話・インターネット通信等による意見交換により作業を進めること。
・土壌汚染等の環境調査報告書の作成依頼を盛り込むこともあり得る。

- That a document certifying the title to the real estate to be appraised must be attached to the local appraiser's report
- That the work shall proceed by exchanging views in meetings and though telephone and Internet communication
- An additional clause may be included, such as a request for the preparation of an environmental assessment, including any evidence of soil pollution.

② **Specialist qualifications of the person in charge of local appraisal work**
- The person to perform the appraisal must be a real estate appraiser with a license or designation authorized or officially recognized in the foreign country.

③ **Fees and expenses**
- The contract shall specify the total fees and expenses related to the appraisal, and must include procedures for dealing with additional work or for changes in the report format and content.

④ **Schedule**
- Date for the local appraiser to submit the appraisal report
- Dates for briefings on the appraisal report of the local appraiser
- Dates for meetings between the local appraiser and the Japanese real estate appraiser
- That strict observance of deadlines will be required

⑤ **Scope of responsibility of the local appraiser**
- The local appraiser shall be responsible for the appraisal report (used by the client and others).

⑥ **Other**
- Obligation to maintain confidentiality
- Measures to be taken should a conflict of interest arise
- Obligation to work for a resolution should a dispute arise over the contract

---

Ⅶ. Verification of the information collected or the appraisal report submitted by the local appraiser, and any additional or supplemental investigation

(1) **Verification of the information collected or the appraisal report submitted by the local appraiser**

Regarding the information collected or the appraisal report submitted by the local appraiser, it is necessary for the LREA to verify that the basic information used in developing the appraisal, the appraisal methods applied, and the assumptions underlying the appraisal are appropriate and reasonable. Verification must be done for all of the following items.

① **An appraisal performed with a local assistant**
- The local appraiser's qualifications and designation.
- The date when the submitted information was prepared and the dates to which the information and data apply.
- The physical description of the subject property and the identification of relevant property rights.
- How the underlying assumptions were established based on the submitted data, and how the scope of investigation was determined.

【②　担当者の専門職業家としての資格】
　・鑑定評価を行う者は、海外現地において不動産鑑定人として認定又は公認された資格・称号を有する者であること。

【③　報酬及び費用】
　鑑定評価に係る報酬・費用の合計額であり、追加業務及びリポートの様式・内容変更の場合の対応を含むこと。

【④　日程】
　・現地鑑定報告書の提出日
　・現地鑑定報告書の説明を行う日
　・現地鑑定人と不動産鑑定士との間で行う会議の開催日
　・期限厳守

【⑤　現地鑑定人の責任範囲】
　・現地鑑定報告書の利用（依頼者等の利用）に対して現地鑑定人が責任を有すること。

【⑥　その他】
　・守秘義務
　・利益相反の発生への対応
　・この契約に関する紛争が生じた場合の調整に関する努力義務

Ⅶ　現地基礎資料等又は現地鑑定報告書の検証及び追加・補完調査

(1) 現地基礎資料等又は現地鑑定報告書の検証
現地基礎資料等又は現地鑑定報告書について、現地基礎資料等の内容又は鑑定評価手法その他の鑑定評価の内容の合理性及び鑑定評価額の適正性等につき、検証しなければならない。その際の検証は、少なくとも次の事項を含まなければならない。

① 現地基礎資料等の検証
　・現地鑑定人の資格・称号、所属する不動産鑑定人団体の確認
　・現地基礎資料等の作成された年月日及び資料データの時点の確認
　・対象不動産の物的事項、権利の態様等に関する事項の確認
　・現地基礎資料等の前提条件、調査範囲等の確認
　・資料データが明らかに不適切・不十分であると認められるかどうかの確認
　・資料データの出所の確認

- Whether the information and data are recognized to be complete, relevant and accurate..
- The source of the information and data.

② **Verification of an appraisal performed by a local appraiser**
- The local appraiser's qualifications and designation.
- The date on which the local appraiser's report was prepared and the date to which the appraisal report applies..
- The physical description of the subject property and the identification of relevant property rights.
- How the underlying assumptions and limiting conditions were established for the appraisal and how the scope of the investigation was determined.
- Whether the information and data are recognized to be complete, relevant and accurate.
- The source of the information and data.
- Whether the appraisal methods applied are in conformity with approved or officially authorized standards in the country where the subject property is located.
- That the factors determining prices are well understood and reasonable.
- That the appraisal has been reviewed and double-checked by other third-party local appraisers, where necessary.

(2) **Additional or supplemental investigation**

An additional or supplemental investigation is conducted if, on the basis of the verification of the information collected or the appraisal report submitted by the local appraiser, the LREA determines that it is necessary to develop a credible appraisal. The LREA can undertake this himself, or can suggest requiring it be done by the local appraiser.

It is necessary for the LREA to investigate and verify the local appraiser's report to determine that it is reasonable and appropriate in light of appraisal theory, including whether it complies with the approved or officially authorized real estate appraisal standards of the overseas country, and whether the analysis of pricing has been done in a logical and empirical manner.

Some maintain that the review performed by an LREA only needs to verify and explain the appraisal methods, and that the LREA has no responsibility regarding the data. However, this does not constitute an adequate verification by the LREA.

A supplemental investigation is performed if the LREA determines that it is necessary on the basis of his verification of the local appraiser's report and in light of the real estate appraisal standards of the overseas country. For example, this could entailenvironment-related investigations of soil contamination, asbestos, etc.

VIII. Determining the appraised value

(1) **An appraisal performed with a local assistant**

The LREA engages in collaboration with the local appraiser, as specified in sections I through VII above, and concludes that the appraised value is appropriate. Generally, the appraised value is stated in units of the currency of

② 現地鑑定報告書の検証
- ・現地鑑定人の資格・称号、所属する不動産鑑定人団体の確認
- ・現地鑑定報告書の作成された年月日及び鑑定評価の基準日の確認
- ・対象不動産の物的事項、権利の態様等に関する事項の確認
- ・鑑定評価の前提条件・制限的条件、調査範囲等の確認
- ・資料データが明らかに不適切・不十分であると認められるかどうかの確認
- ・資料データの出所の確認
- ・採用されている鑑定評価手法が、対象不動産が存する国又は地域において認定又は公認された不動産の鑑定評価基準に適合して行われているかの検証
- ・価格形成要因の理解と合理性の検証
- ・必要に応じて他の現地鑑定人による複数鑑定又は鑑定レビューなどによる検証

(2) 追加・補完調査
　現地基礎資料等又は現地鑑定報告書の検証を行い、その結果、適正な鑑定評価を行う上で必要があると認めるときは、追加・補完調査を行うものとする。この場合には、不動産鑑定士が行うほか、海外現地の他の専門職業家を選任して行うことも考えられる。

　現地鑑定報告書は、海外現地において認定又は公認されている不動産の鑑定評価基準に照らして適正な鑑定評価となっているか、価格形成要因を論理的かつ実証的に説明することが可能かなど鑑定理論に照らして合理性・妥当性を有しているかについて調査・検証することが必要である。

　なお、不動産鑑定士が行っている鑑定レビューの中には、単に鑑定評価手法のみを検証し、説明しているだけで、数値については一切責任を持たないとしているものも見受けられるが、これは、検証というには不十分である。
　また、現地鑑定報告書の検証を行い、日本の不動産鑑定評価基準（平成14年7月3日付け国土交通事務次官通知。以下単に「不動産鑑定評価基準」という。）に照らして必要があると認めるときは、追加・補完調査を行うものとする。例えば、土壌汚染、アスベスト等環境関連の調査などが想定される。

Ⅷ　鑑定評価額の決定等

(1) 現地鑑定補助方式
　不動産鑑定士は、ⅠからⅦまでに定めるところにより、現地鑑定人との連携・共同作業を行い、適正と判断される鑑定評価額を決定するものとする。
　鑑定評価額の表示は、原則として、海外現地の通貨の単位によるものとする。

the overseas country.

(2) **Verification of an appraisal performed by a local appraiser**
The LREA engages in collaboration with the local appraiser, as specified in sections I through VII above; and if the local appraiser's report is considered to be appropriate, the LREA accepts the appraised value. If the LREA does not agree with the opinion of value, the LREA then clearly states the reasons why, and concludes the appropriate value. (In some situations, the LREA may retain the services of a second local appraiser.)

Generally, the appraised value is stated in unit of the currency of the overseas country.

If a local assistant is engaged to work with the LREA on the appraisal, the appraised value is concluded by the LREA. If a local appraiser's report is submitted and verified by the LREA, the LREA accepts the appraised value. In either case, the LREA is responsible for the conclusion of the appraised value.

Ordinarily, it is probable that the LREA will accept the appraised value concluded by the local appraiser upon verification, since the LREA has been involved in the exchange of views at each stage of the local appraiser's work. However, if for any reason there is a difference of opinion about the appraised value, the LREA should than correct the appraisal report and conclude the appropriate appraised value, clearly stating the reasons for doing so.

Generally, the appraised value is stated in units of the currency of the overseas country, although this also depends on the wishes of the client. The appraisal report should also provide the exchange rate on the date to which the appraisal report applies and the conversion of the appraised value into Japanese currency (yen) at that exchange rate.

> (2) 現地鑑定検証方式
>   不動産鑑定士は、ⅠからⅦまでに定めるところにより、現地鑑定人との連携・共同作業を行い、現地鑑定報告書が適正なものであると判断する場合には鑑定評価額に同意するものとする。なお、同意しない場合には、その根拠を明らかにして適正と判断される鑑定評価額を決定するものとする。
>   鑑定評価額の表示は、原則として、海外現地の通貨の単位によるものとする。

　鑑定評価額は、現地鑑定補助方式の場合にあっては不動産鑑定士が決定し、現地鑑定検証方式である場合にあっては不動産鑑定士が同意することとなる。いずれの場合においても、鑑定評価額について、不動産鑑定士として責任を有することとなる。

　現地鑑定検証方式で行う場合の同意については、不動産鑑定士が現地鑑定人の鑑定評価の各作業段階において意見交換を行うなど鑑定評価の作業に関わるため、最終的な鑑定評価額に同意することとなるのが通常であると考えられるが、何らかの理由で鑑定評価額の意見に相違が生じた場合には、不動産鑑定士がその根拠を明記して鑑定評価額を修正し、決定するものとする。

　鑑定評価額の通貨の単位は、依頼者の意向にもよるが、原則的には、海外現地の通貨の単位によるものとし、鑑定評価報告書等には、本邦通貨（日本円）に換算した額での表示も併記するものとする。

> **IX. Preparation of the appraisal report, etc.**
>
> The appraisal report or the report on the appraisal verification is prepared by the LREA.
>
> (1) **An appraisal performed with a local assistant**
> The LREA carries out the appraisal and prepares the appraisal report based on the information submitted by the local appraiser.
>
> (2) **Verification of an appraisal performed by a local appraiser**
> The LREA verifies the content of the local appraiser's report in accordance with section VII above, and prepares a report on the appraisal verification. A Japanese language translation (or summary) of the local appraiser's report is prepared and the translation (or summary) is checked to ensure it accurately conveys the content of the original.
>
> The appraisal document is composed of the local appraiser's report (original language version) and a report on the appraisal verification (including any additional or supplemental investigations performed); a Japanese language translation (or summary) of the local appraiser's report is appended.

The Japanese real estate appraiser shall be responsible for preparing the appraisal report or the appraisal verification report. These will constitute the appraisal document that the real estate appraisal firm delivers to the client. When a Japanese appraiser verifies the appraisal of an overseas appraiser, the appraisal document shall consist of the appraisal verification report and the original appraisal report prepared by the local appraiser; and a Japanese translation of the local appraisal report shall be provided as an attachment. In this case, the scope of translation shall include, at the very least, all significant portions of the appraisal, and other portions may be provided in summary form in accordance with the client's wishes. Should a discrepancy arise between the original text and the Japanese translation, the original shall take precedence. The contract with the local appraiser shall include a clause to this effect, after the matter has been verified with the client, and the translation or other documents shall also include a statement to this effect.

> **X. Items included in the appraisal report, etc.**
>
> (1) **General principles as to what should be included**
> An effort should be made to include all items that are required by the Japanese Real Estate Appraisal Standards.
>
> If there are items that are considered necessary for inclusion under the Japanese Real Estate Appraisal Standards, but which are not considered essential in the real estate market of the overseas country and are not ordinarily included in appraisal reports by local appraisers, it is then acceptable to omit these items. However, in this case the reasons for their omission must be stated.
>
> (2) **Additional items to be included**
> The appraisal report or the report on the appraisal verification should indicate that the appraisal was performed in collaboration with a local appraiser. The

> **Ⅸ　鑑定評価報告書等の作成等**
>
> 　　鑑定評価報告書又は鑑定評価検証報告書は、不動産鑑定士が作成するものとする。
> (1)　現地鑑定補助方式
> 　　不動産鑑定士は、現地基礎資料等に基づき鑑定評価を行い、鑑定評価報告書を作成するものとする。また、現地基礎資料等（原文）を添付するものとする。
> (2)　現地鑑定検証方式
> 　　不動産鑑定士は、現地鑑定報告書をⅦに従ってその内容を検証し、鑑定評価検証報告書を作成するものとする。また、現地鑑定報告書の日本語による翻訳文を作成し、原文の内容が正確に翻訳されているかを確認するものとする。
> 　　鑑定評価書は、鑑定評価検証報告書（追加・補完調査を行った場合にあっては当該調査報告書を含む。）及び現地鑑定報告書（原文）により構成し、現地鑑定報告書の日本語による翻訳文を添付するものとする。

　鑑定評価報告書又は鑑定評価検証報告書の作成は、不動産鑑定士が責任をもって行う。これらは、不動産鑑定業者が依頼者に交付する鑑定評価書となるものであるが、現地鑑定検証方式の場合には、鑑定評価検証報告書及び現地鑑定報告書の原文により鑑定評価書を構成するものとし、現地鑑定報告書の日本語による翻訳文を附属資料として添付することとする。この場合において、翻訳する範囲については、少なくとも鑑定評価の重要な部分は行うものとし、依頼者の意向により、その他の部分については概要とすることも差し支えない。また、原文と翻訳文で内容が異なっていたときには、原文が優先されることとなる。このことについては、依頼者との間でも確認の上での現地鑑定人との契約事項であるとともに、翻訳文等にその旨記載しておくことが必要である。

> **Ⅹ　鑑定評価報告書等の記載事項等**
>
> (1)　記載事項の原則
> 　　不動産鑑定評価基準に照らして、必要な記載事項とされている内容をできる限り記載するものとする。
> 　　この場合において、不動産鑑定評価基準上記載すべき事項とされているものの、海外現地の不動産市場においては重視されず、現地鑑定評価報告書に記載されないことが通常である場合には記載しないこととして差し支えないが、その合理的理由を記載する必要がある。
>
> (2)　追加的記載事項
> 　　鑑定評価報告書又は鑑定評価検証報告書の記載事項については、不動産鑑定士が現地鑑定人と連携・共同作業により鑑定評価を行うこと、海外現地の不動

following items should also be included, since in many cases, the Japanese clients, investors, etc. may not have a thorough understanding of the conditions and trends in the real estate market of the overseas country.

① **Collaboration between the LREA and local appraiser**
The division of labor and specific duties undertaken by the LREA and the local appraiser in the appraisal should be clearly stated.

② **Trends in the real estate market and other value influences**
Keeping in mind that the appraisal report will be read by investors, the LREA should collect, analyze, and include sufficient information on the condition of the real estate market in the overseas country, including macroeconomic analyses of the market in the overseas country and the social, economic, fiscal and administrative factors affecting prices; and contract formats and customary practices in real estate transactions. Such information as is necessary serves to clarify those characteristics of the overseas market, which differ from the Japanese real estate market.

a. Trends in the real estate market of the overseas country;
Basic information on trends in the real estate market of the overseas country and the regional market for the property.

b. Legal and fiscal systems relating to the real estate market of the overseas country;
Differences in contracts, financial relationships, and taxation involving real estate in the overseas country.

c. Other required items;
Differences in customary practices in real estate transactions in the overseas country.

③ **Verification procedures for an appraisal performed by a local appraiser**
The report on the appraisal verification should include the verification procedures used to check the local appraiser's report. The verification procedures, reasons for accepting or rejecting the analyses and conclusions, and so on should be clearly stated for each of the items specified for verification under section VII above.

④ **Appraised value**
If the appraised value is to be stated in units of the currency of the overseas country, the report should then also include the exchange rate on the date to which the appraisal applies (the closing price of the currency on that date) and the appraised value should be converted into Japanese currency at that exchange rate.

(3) **Signature and seal**
The appraisal report should be signed and sealed by the LREA (the LREA's signature and seal affixed to the local appraiser's signed and sealed report).

The LREA is responsible for preparing the complete appraisal report or the report on the appraisal verification, which constitutes the basis for the appraisal delivered to the client. If there is any discrepancy between the items to be included in the report under the appraisal standards of the overseas country and under the Japanese Real Estate Appraisal

産市場の動向等について日本の投資家等が十分に把握していない場合が多いと考えられること等から、次の事項を追加的に記載するものとする。

① 不動産鑑定士及び現地鑑定人の連携・共同作業の役割分担
　当該鑑定評価に関する不動産鑑定士及び現地鑑定人のそれぞれの作業内容等役割分担について明記するものとする。

② 海外現地の不動産市場の動向に関する事項等
　鑑定評価書が投資家向けに開示されることも念頭に置き、海外現地における市場のマクロ的な経済分析、不動産取引の契約形態や慣行等の社会的・経済的・行政的な価格形成要因に関する次の事項について、日本の不動産市場と異なる特徴等を踏まえつつ、必要かつ十分な情報を収集・分析して記載するものとする。

　　ア　海外現地の不動産市場の動向に関する事項
　　　海外現地及びその周辺地域の不動産市場の動向を示す基礎資料等

　　イ　海外現地の不動産に関連する法制、税制等に関する事項
　　　海外現地における不動産の権利関係、不動産取引に係る契約内容及び税制の相違等

　　ウ　その他必要な事項
　　　海外現地における不動産取引に係る慣行の相違等

③ 現地鑑定検証方式における検証内容等
　鑑定評価検証報告書には、現地鑑定報告書の検証内容について記載するものとし、Ⅶに定める検証すべき事項について、それぞれの検証内容、根拠等を明記するものとする。

④ 鑑定評価額
　鑑定評価額を海外現地の通貨の単位で表示した場合においては、原則として、鑑定評価の基準日の為替レート（終値）及び当該レートにより換算した本邦通貨の単位での表示も併記するものとする。

(3) 署名押印
　鑑定評価書にあっては不動産鑑定士が、現地鑑定報告書にあっては現地鑑定人が署名押印するものとする。

　依頼者に交付する鑑定評価書の実質的な内容となる鑑定評価報告書又は鑑定評価検証報告書は、不動産鑑定士が責任をもって作成する。海外現地の不動産の鑑定評価基準で求められる記載事項と不動産鑑定評価基準で相違がある場合には、できる限り不動産鑑定評価基準に従って記載するものとする。

Standards, the report should be prepared according to the Japanese Real Estate Appraisal Standards to the extent possible. However, if there are items that are considered necessary for inclusion under the Japanese Real Estate Appraisal Standards, but which are not considered essential in the real estate market of the overseas country and are not ordinarily included in appraisal reports by appraisers in the overseas country, it is then acceptable for the LREA to omit these items, indicating the reasons for the omission.

For an appraisal performed by an overseas appraiser that has been verified by an LREA, the appraisal comprises both the overseas appraiser's report and the LREA's report on the appraisal verification. Those portions relating to the report on the appraisal verification are to be signed and sealed by the LREA (it is not necessary for the overseas appraiser to sign or seal the appraisal report or its Japanese translation). Documents such as the summary of the appraisal report are to be signed and sealed by the LREA and the overseas appraiser as joint endorsers.

XI. Other important matters

Overseas investment properties should be appraised according to the procedures specified in sections I through IX above. It is also essential that the overseas country have an adequate appraisal system in place to ensure the performance of credible appraisals, including the following:

① The availability of basic information on trends in the real estate market and factors that determine prices, information needed to confirm the physical description of and relevant property rights applying to the subject property, and the sales data needed to perform an appraisal.

② Qualifications and designations for approved or officially authorized real estate appraisers, and a real estate appraiser organization that sets such qualifications, confers designations, and provides training and education for real estate appraisers.

③ Approved or officially authorized real estate appraisal standards, which are enforced by the real estate appraiser organization through such means as the suspension or abrogation of designations in cases involving improper professional conduct, including violation of those standards.

However, even in a country where the circumstances at [2] and [3] do not fully prevail, it is still possible to engage in collaboration on a real estate appraisal based on these guidelines, provided the local appraiser is a person, who has demonstrated the proper qualifications and has obtained a designation in another country, where these circumstances do prevail.

It is generally difficult to accept a request to perform an appraisal of an overseas property in a country where the above circumstances do not prevail, and the LREA should consider turning down such a request.

A separate appendix at the end lists countries with appraisal systems that to date meet the conditions of XI 1, 2, and 3 above as evaluated by the Ministry of Land, Infrastructure,

ただし、不動産鑑定評価基準では記載事項とされているものであっても、海外現地の不動産市場において重視されず、海外現地の鑑定評価書においては記載されないことが通常である場合には、その合理的理由を記載し、省略することとしても差し支えない。

鑑定評価額は、海外現地の通貨の単位とし、鑑定評価の基準日の為替レート（終値）及び当該レートにより換算した本邦通貨（日本円）での表示も併記することを原則とするが、本邦通貨への換算は鑑定評価の基準日の為替レート（終値）以外の為替レートや一定期間を決めて平均化した為替レートを使用するなど依頼者の意向により変更して差し支えない。

現地鑑定検証方式における署名押印は、鑑定評価書のうち、鑑定評価検証報告書に係る部分に署名押印するものとする（現地鑑定評価報告書及びその日本語による翻訳文に署名押印する必要はない。）。

なお、これらに加えて、鑑定評価書の概要（いわゆるサマリー）が作成される場合には、不動産鑑定士及び現地鑑定人の連名による署名押印をしているものも見られるが、サマリーへの署名押印の方法については、不動産鑑定業者と依頼者及び現地鑑定人との合意に基づき行うものとする。また、現地鑑定人の署名押印は、海外現地において、通常、署名のみで行われている場合には、署名のみで差し支えない。

XI　その他留意事項

海外不動産の鑑定評価に当たっては、ⅠからⅩまでに定める手続きにより実施されるべきであり、その際には、海外現地の国又は地域において、

① 鑑定評価を行うために必要となる事例資料、対象不動産の物的確認及び権利の態様等の確認に必要となる資料並びに価格形成要因に照応する資料その他不動産市場の動向を示す基礎資料があること。

② 認定又は公認された不動産鑑定人の資格・称号を付与し、かつ、不動産鑑定人を指導育成する不動産鑑定人団体が存在していること。

③ 認定又は公認された不動産の鑑定評価基準を有し、これに逸脱するなど不正又は不当な鑑定評価が行われた場合には、不動産鑑定人団体により不動産鑑定人の資格・称号の使用停止・剥奪等の指導監督が行われること。

など適正な鑑定評価が行われるための制度が十分に整っていることが必要である。

ただし、これらの要件のうち②又は③の要件が十分に整っていない国又は地域においても、これらの要件が整った他の国又は地域の資格・称号を有している者が現地鑑定人となる場合には、本ガイドラインに基づく不動産鑑定評価の連携・共同作業を推進することが可能である。

以上の要件が満たされない海外不動産の鑑定評価については、鑑定評価の依頼を受けることは一般的には困難と考えられ、依頼の拒否も検討すべきである。

XI ①②③の要件を備える国又は地域における鑑定評価制度については、国土交通省においてこれまで調査してきた範囲で例示すると、別表のとおりである。

Transport and Tourism. Given that there may be countries not listed in the table that have adequate systems for real estate appraisal, we continue to study and evaluate foreign appraisal systems, bearing in mind the evolving demands of investors in foreign real estate, and will add those countries to the list with similar appraisal systems in place as we become aware of them.

> ## XII. Relationship between the guidelines and the Real Estate Appraisal Standards
>
> The guidelines specify standard procedures for performing appraisals, including appraisal methods, and principles concerning collaboration with local appraisers overseas. The objective of the guidelines is to ensure credible appraisals that provide for investor protection when a LREA performs an appraisal of an overseas investment property.
>
> If Japanese private funds begin to include overseas properties in their investment portfolios, or if in the future the listing rules of Japanese securities exchanges are revised so that J-REITs can include overseas investment properties in their asset portfolios, real estate in Japan and real estate overseas will be more integrated into the global real estate market; and real estate appraisal by a LREA is mandated for J-REITs in the Japanese regulations. Therefore, appraisal of these overseas properties will also fall under the regulation of the Real Estate Appraisal Act(Act No.152 of 1963).
>
> In such appraisals, the procedures and principles specified in the guidelines will be incorporated into the Japanese Real Estate Appraisal Standards and any appraiser failing to comply with the guidelines would be subject to disciplinary measures such as further instruction and guidance under the Real Estate Appraisal Act.

If Japanese private funds begin to invest in foreign real estate and if it also becomes possible for J-REITs to invest in foreign real estate, a single real estate market will be created out of overseas and domestic properties. In this situation, it will be undesirable for appraisal procedures and accuracy to vary, depending on whether the real estate to be appraised is located in Japan or overseas, since this could lead to disorder in the domestic real estate market.

Furthermore, given that appraisals by Japanese real estate appraisers are required for J-REITs under the Law on Investment Trusts and Investment Companies (Law No. 198 of 1951) and the Law for the Securitization of Assets (Law No.105 of 1998), such appraisals by Japanese real estate appraisers should be subject to guidance and supervision under the Law on Real Estate Appraisal.

Therefore, for all appraisals to which the above laws apply, the guidelines shall have the same significance as the Real Estate Appraisal Standards of Japan.

別表に掲げる国又は地域以外においても不動産鑑定評価制度が十分に整っている国又は地域があることも想定されることから、今後、海外不動産投資の需要動向等を勘案しつつ、海外の鑑定評価制度について調査・検討し、これらと同程度の水準の制度が整っている国又は地域を追加していくこととする。

> **XII　本ガイドラインの位置づけ**
>
> 　本ガイドラインは、海外不動産への投資を行う際に不動産鑑定士が鑑定評価を行う場合において、投資家保護及び鑑定評価の信頼性の向上の観点から適正な鑑定評価が行われるよう、現地鑑定人との連携・共同作業のあり方、鑑定評価の手法等鑑定評価の標準的手法について示すものである。
> 　一方、日本のプライベートファンドが海外不動産を組み入れる場合や、今後、Ｊリートによる海外不動産の組み入れが可能となった場合には、海外不動産と本邦不動産とで一つの不動産市場が形成されること、Ｊリートについては不動産鑑定士による鑑定評価が義務づけられていること等にかんがみ、不動産鑑定士が行うこれらの海外不動産の鑑定評価については、不動産の鑑定評価に関する法律（昭和38年法律第152号）に基づく指導監督を行うことが必要である。
> 　したがって、これらの鑑定評価については、本ガイドラインの内容は不動産鑑定評価基準と同等の位置づけとして取り扱うこととし、本ガイドラインを逸脱することにより不当な鑑定評価が行われた場合には、同法に基づく指導監督を行うものとする。

　日本のプライベートファンドが海外不動産を組み入れる場合や、今後、Ｊリートの運用対象資産に海外不動産が組み入れられることとなった場合、海外不動産と日本の不動産とで一つの不動産市場が形成されることとなる。こうした場合において、不動産の鑑定評価が対象不動産の国内外の区別によって鑑定評価手法、精度等に差が生じることとなれば、国内不動産市場に混乱を招くことにもなり望ましくない。

　また、Ｊリート等については、投資信託及び投資法人に関する法律（昭和26年法律第198号）及び資産の流動化に関する法律（平成10年法律第105号）において不動産鑑定士による鑑定評価が義務づけられていること等にかんがみれば、不動産鑑定士が行うこれらの鑑定評価については、不動産の鑑定評価に関する法律の指導監督の対象とする必要がある。

　したがって、これらの場合の鑑定評価については、本ガイドラインの内容は不動産鑑定評価基準と同等の位置づけとして取り扱うものである。

Appendix

	USA	UK	Australia	Singapore
Designations & Qualifications	①State Certified Apprasider/State Licensed Appraiser ②MAI (Commercial・Residential・Indutrial), SRPA (Commercial・Residential・Industrial), SRA (Residential)	MRICS (Member) FRICS (Fellow)	Certified Practising Valuer (CPV)	Singapore Institute of Valuers (SIV)
Organizations	①State Regulatory Agency (50 States) ②Appraisal Institute	Royal Institution Of Chartered Surveyors (RICS)	Australian Property Institute (composed of API members)	Singapore Institute of Surveyors and Valuers
Constituents	See above.	See above.	See above.	See above.
Membership	①Approx.95,000 ②Approx.6,000	Approx. 130,000 (121countries)	Approx. 7,500	Approx. 1,800
Appraisal Standards	US USPAP (Appraisal Foundation)	RICS Appraisal and Valuation Standards (RICS)	Professional Practice Standards (API/PINZ)	SISV Valuation Standards and Guidelines(SISV)

〔別表〕

	アメリカ合衆国	英国	オーストラリア	シンガポール
資格・称号	①州公証・公認鑑定人 ②MAI（商・住・工），SRPA（商・住・工），SRA（住）	MRICS（member） FRICS（fellow）	CPV Certified Practising Valuer	SIV Singapore Institute Of Valuers
登録機関	①州不動産鑑定評価委員会(50州) ②不動産鑑定協会（Appraisal Institute）	RICS Royal Institution of Chartered Surveyor	①州不動産鑑定評価委員会（APIのmemberから登録） ②API Australian Property Institute	Singapore Institute of Surveyors and Valuers
所属団体	同上	同上	同上	同上
人数	①約9万5千人 ②約6千人	約13万人（121カ国）	約7千5百人	約1千8百人
鑑定評価基準（基準作成団体）	USPAP(Appraisal Foundation)	RICS Appraisal and Valuation Standards（RICS）	Professional Practice Standards（API/PINZ）	SISV Valuation Standards and Guidelines(SISV)

Appendix

	Taiwan	Korea	Germany	Hong Kong
Designations & Qualifications	State Certified Real Estate Appraiser	Property Appraiser	Property Valuation Expert	MHKIS (Member) FHKIS (Fellow)
Organizations	Dept. of Land Administration	The Ministry Of Construction and Transportation (MOCT)	IfS-ZERT	Hong Kong Institute of Surveyors
Constituents	The Real Estate Appraiser's Association of the Republic of China	Korea Association of property (KAPA)	BVS (Association of Publicly appointed and Sworn Experts by chamber of commerce and court) BDGS (Munich)	See above.
Membership	Approx. 200	Approx. 2,500	Approx. 1,000	Approx. 1,400
Appraisal Standards	Regulations on Real Estate Appraisal (Dept. of Land Administration, Ministry of the Interior, Central Government)	The laws on Public Notice relating to Real Estate Pricing and Appraisal /The Ministerial Ordinances on Appraisal (MOCT)	WERTV (IFS-ZERT)	The HKIS Valuation Standards On Properties

〔別表〕

	台湾	大韓民国	ドイツ	香港
資格・称号	不動産估價師	鑑定評価士	Property Valuation Expert	MHKIS（member） FHKIS（fellow）
登録機関	市（地政局等）	国（建設交通部）	IfS-ZERT	Hong Kong Institute of Surveyors
所属団体	台北市（高雄市・台中市）不動産估價師公會・中華民國不動産估價師公會全國聯合會	韓国鑑定評価協会	BVS（地方商工会議所・裁判所指定鑑定人協会） BDGS（ミュンヘン）等	同上
人数	約2百人	約2千5百人	約1千人	約1千4百人
鑑定評価基準（基準作成団体）	不動産估價技術規則（中央政府内政部地政司）	不動産価格公示および鑑定評価に関する法令 鑑定評価に関する規則（建設交通部）	WERTV（IfS-ZERT）	the HKIS Valuation Standards on Properties（HKIS）

INDEX（英和索引）

> ⊛…米国、⊛…英国、⊘…オーストラリア、⊕…中国、⊛…国際評価基準を示す。
> 複数の個所に出てくる用語については、とくに主な説明がなされている個所について頁数をゴチック体で示した。

A

accrued depreciation（減価修正） ……………………………………………… 194
actual nominal rent（実際支払賃料） ……………………………………………… 214
actual real rent（実際実質賃料） …………………………………… 212、214、246、340
adjustment for conditions of sale（事情補正） ……………………………… 188、**306**
agricultural area（農地地域） ……………………………………………… 146、156
agricultural land（農地） ……………………………………… 148、160、180、**240**
allocation method（配分法） ……………………………………………… 198
allowance for collection loss（貸倒れ準備費） ……………………………………… 212
amounts paid for consent to change the lease terms（条件変更承諾料） ………… 254
anticipated yield（期待利回り） ……………………………………………… 210
appraisal document（鑑定評価書） ……………………………………… 226、364
Appraisal Foundation（鑑定財団⊛） …………………………………… 6、**36**、46
Appraisal Institute（不動産鑑定協会⊛） ……………………………… 6、**36**、46
appraisal method（鑑定評価の方式） …………………………… **186**、222、304
appraisal of assemblage value（併合鑑定評価） ………………………………… 170
appraisal of component value（分割鑑定評価） ………………………………… 170
appraisal of overseas investment properties（海外投資不動産の鑑定評価） …… 28、30
appraisal of securitization-properties（証券化対象不動産の鑑定評価） ……… 28、**256**、342
appraisal of severance value（部分鑑定評価） ………………………………… 168
appraisal of site value as if vacant（独立鑑定評価） ………………………… 168
appraisal performed with a local assistant（現地鑑定補助方式） …… 362、364、372
appraisal process（鑑定評価の手順） ……………………………… **218**、328
appraisal report（鑑定評価報告書） …………………… **226**、230、260、376
arbitration（調停） ……………………………………………………………… 308
area-specific value influences（地域要因） ……………………………… 154、188
asking price（売り希望価格） ……………………………………… 302、**306**、308
Asset Liquidation Law（資産の流動化に関する法律） ………… 26、172、**294**
assumptions and limiting conditions（想定上の条件） ………… 170、226、290
auction sale（競売） ……………………………………………………………… 308
Australian Property Institute（API）（オーストラリア・プロパティ協会（API）） …… 66

B

bankruptcy（倒産） ……………………………………………………………… 308
base value（基礎価格） ………………………………………… 210、326、340
basic appraisal problem（鑑定評価の基本的事項） ………… **168**、218、290
Basic Land Act（土地基本法） ……………………………………………… 142
bubble（バブル） ……………………………………………………………… 4、16

building demolition cost（建物等の撤去費） ······································314、316
building document（設計図書） ··338
building drawing（建物図面） ··338
building residual technique（建物残余法） ···312
building site（宅地） ·····················148、158、178、232、252、330、340
building site area（宅地地域） ···**146**、154
building sites with an interim use（宅地見込地） ·····················**148**、240
buildings on leased land（借地権付建物） ··································150、**244**
Building Standards Act（建築基準法） ··288
built-up property（建物及びその敷地／複合不動産） ···**150**、162、180、204、242、254、338、340
buried cultural assets（埋蔵文化財） ···286

c

capital expenditures（資本的支出） ··**268**、274
capital investment（元本） ···140
capitalization over a definite term（有期還元法） ··································312
capitalization rate（還元利回り） ·····························200、**204**、308、316
category of land（地目） ··228
central commercial area（準高度商業地域） ··282
city planning tax（都市計画税） ··204、212
Civil Rehabilitation Law（民事再生法） ·······························26、174、**294**
collection losses allowance（貸倒れ損失） ··································**266**、274
commercial area（商業地域） ···154、**282**
commercial land（商業地） ···158、**178**
common area（共用部分） ···150、**338**
common area charges（共益費） ···208、**266**
comparable data（事例資料） ···220
comparison method（比較方式） ···58
compatibility between building and site（建物と敷地の適応） ····**162**、194
compulsory sale（公売） ··308
condominium unit（区分所有建物（及びその敷地）） ·············150、**244**、338
confidentiality（秘密を守る義務） ···120
configuration of real estate（不動産のあり方） ·····································138
conflict of interest（利害関係） ···230
co-ownership（共有持分） ···150、**338**
corner lot（角地） ···158
Corporate Reorganization Law（会社更生法） ·································174、**296**
cost approach（原価法／原価方式） ·······················26、44、76、102、**190**
cost of replacement method（コストに基づいて価値を求める方式㊈） ·········60
cost of tenant removal（立退料） ··308
cultural assets（文化財） ··174
Cultural Properties Protection Law（文化財保護法） ·····························286

current rent（現行賃料） ……………………………………………………………216
current value opinion（現在時点の鑑定評価） ………………………………170

D

data management process（データ管理システム㊇） ……………………10
data on value influences（要因資料） ………………………………………220
date of the appraisal report（鑑定評価を行った年月日） ………**228**、292
date of the property inspection（実査日） …………………………………228
date of the value opinion（価格時点） ……………………170、228、**292**
debt service coverage ratio（借入金償還余裕率） …………………………320
declining balance method（定率法） …………………………………………194
depreciable property component（償却資産） ………………………………308
depreciated replacement cost（DRC）（特別な積算価格㊇㊀） ……56、100
depreciation（減価償却費） ……………………………204、210、308、320
depreciation over a period（耐用年数） ……………………………………194
depth（奥行） ……………………………………………………………………158
designated area（指定区域〈土壌汚染対策法〉） ……………………………288
deterioration（老朽化） …………………………………………………………194
difference between market rent and contract rent（賃料差額） …………236
difference between the two NOIs（差額純収益） …………………………334
direct capitalization method（直接還元法） …………………………200、**308**
disciplinary measure（懲戒処分） …………………………………………32、**122**
Discounted Cash Flow Method（割引キャッシュフロー法／DCF法） ……200、**264**、320、344
discount rate（割引率〈収益還元法〉／投下資本収益率〈開発法〉） ……200、**204**、322、330
distribution factor（配分率） …………………………………………………246
durability（永続性（不変性）） ………………………………………………138

E

earthquake resistance of a building（耐震性） ……………………………288
earthquake resistance standards（耐震基準） ………………………………288
easement（地役権） ……………………………………………………………174
economic obsolescence（経済的要因〈経済的陳腐化〉） ……………………194
economic value influences（経済的要因〈一般的要因〉） …………………152
effective demand（有効需要） …………………………………………………138
effective gross income（運営収益） ……………………………………**266**、274
engineering report（エンジニアリング・レポート） ……258、**262**、342、360
excavation survey（発掘調査） ………………………………………………286
Excessive liquidity（過剰流動性） ……………………………………………8
exclusively owned area（専有部分） …………………………150、246、338
existing use value（EUV）（現行用途前提の市場価値㊇㊁） ……………56、74
exposure time（市場公開期間㊇㊀） …………………………………42、100

F

factory or business facility that uses harmful substances（有害物質使用特定施設） ……………286
fair value（公正価値㊍㊺㊱） ……………………………………………………………56、74、100
final opinion of value／appraised value（鑑定評価額） ………………**222**、226、228、372
finite nature of supply（不増性） ……………………………………………………………138
fixity（固定性） ………………………………………………………………………………138
floor loads（床荷重） …………………………………………………………………………288
forestland（林地） …………………………………………………………146、160、180、**240**
forestland area（林地地域） ……………………………………………………………146、156
freehold／fee simple（フリーホールド㊗㊍㊱㊁） …………………………………40、52、70
functional obsolescence（機能的要因） ………………………………………………………194
function of the appraisal（鑑定評価の依頼目的） …………………………………………228

G

general value influences（一般的要因） ……………………………………………………152
Global Investment Performance Standards（GIPS）（グローバル投資実績基準（GIPS）㊗） …………48
governmental value influences（行政的要因） ……………………………………………154
government sale of land usage rights（払い下げ式の土地使用権（出譲）㊁） ……………84
gross income（総収益） ……………………………………………………202、266、**320**
Ground Lease Law（借地法） ………………………………………………………………236
ground rent（地代） …………………………………………………………………………326
Guidance Notes on the Real Estate Appraisal Standards
　（不動産鑑定評価基準運用上の留意事項） ………………………………………………279
Guidelines for the Appraisal of Overseas Investment Properties
　（海外投資不動産鑑定評価ガイドライン） ………………………………………………347

H

highest and best use（HABU）（最有効使用） ……………24、42、56、72、100、164、**182**、228、302
holding period（保有期間） ……………………………………………………………200、324
Hoskold method（ホスコルド式） …………………………………………………………314
house number（家屋番号） ……………………………………………………………………228
Housing Quality Assurance Law（住宅の品質確保の促進等に関する法律） ………………288

I

identification of ownership and interests（権利の態様の確認） …………………………218
identification of the physical characteristics（物的確認） ………………………………218
identification of the subject property（対象不動産の確定（確認）） ……………168、**218**、290
immovability（不動性（非移動性）） ………………………………………………………138
improvements（定着物） ……………………………………………………………………138

INDEX(英和索引)

incidental expenses(付帯費用) ································330
income analysis approach(収益分析法) ····························212
income capitalization approach(収益還元法／収益方式) ··············28、44、76、102、**198**、308
indicated rent(試算賃料) ···222
indicated value(試算価格) ··222
industrial area(工業地域) ··156
industrial land(工業地) ·····································160、178
installment payment(割賦払い) ····································308
insurance premium(損害保険料) ································204、212
interior finish(内装) ··288
International Valuation Standards(IVS)(国際評価基準) ···············14、**94**
investment method(投資方式) ······································58
Investment Trust and Investment Corporation Law
　(投資信託及び投資法人に関する法律) ·······················172、294
investment value／worth(投資価値㊤㊥㊦㊜) ··········26、44、58、74、102
Inwood method(インウッド式) ·····································314

J

Japan Home Performance Standards(日本住宅性能表示基準) ············288
J−REITs(不動産投資信託(Jリート)) ·······························352

L

land in a transitional area(移行地) ·····························180
Land Lease and Building Lease Law(借地借家法) ·············148、236、248
land portion of built−up property(建付地) ···················148、**234**
Land Price Publication Act(地価公示法) ···························224
land residual technique(土地残余法) ·························232、**312**
land use regulation(土地利用規制) ································300
large−scale repair expenses(大規模修繕費) ····················204、322
large−scale repair project(大規模修繕に係る修繕計画) ·············288
Law for Unit Ownership, etc. of Building／Law for Condominium
　(建物の区分所有等に関する法律) ·································150
lease−based property(賃貸用不動産) ·························198、202
lease contract(賃貸借契約) ·······································162
leased fee interest in land(底地) ···························148、**238**
leasehold(リースホールド㊤㊥㊦㊜) ·······················40、52、70
leasehold interest in land(借地権) ·····················148、**236**、330
lease term(契約期間) ··236、326
Licensed Real Estate Appraiser(LREA)(不動産鑑定士) ········22、**114**、138、142、354
liquidation(清算) ···308
liquidity crisis(流動性危機) ······································18

local appraiser（現地鑑定人） ……………………………………………………………358
lot in a transitional area（移行地） ……………………………………………**148**、162
lot width（間口） …………………………………………………………………158、160

M

maintenance and management fee（維持管理費） ………………………………204、210
management bylaws（管理規約） ………………………………………………………288
management fee（管理費） ………………………………………………………210、338
marketable real estate（市場性を有する不動産） …………………………………170、**172**
market area（同一需給圏） ………………………………………………………**178**、300
market area analysis（地域分析） ………………………………………………**176**、298
market area category（用途的地域） ……………………………………………………176
market-derived capitalization rate（取引利回り） ………………………206、210、316
market exposure time（市場公開期間） …………………………………………24、**292**
marketing period（市場公開期間㊥㊐） ……………………………………………56、72
market rent（正常賃料） ……………………………………**174**、214、226、252、340
market rent under new lease（新規賃料） …………………………**174**、210、252、254、340
market value（正常価格／市場価値） ………24、42、56、72、86、98、**170**、226、292
methods based on observation（観察減価法） …………………………………………196
methods of estimating accrued depreciation over a period（耐用年数に基づく方法） ……………194
monitoring／monitor（監視検証） ……………………………………………………10、**32**

N

neighborhood commercial area（近隣商業地域） ………………………………………284
net cash flow（NCF）／Adjusted Net Operating Income
　（純収益） ………………………………198、**200**、202、**268**、274、308、320、344
net income（収益純賃料） ………………………………………………………………212
net operating income（NOI）（運営純収益） …………………………………268、274、344
net rent（純賃料） ………………………………………………………………………208
nominal rent（支払賃料） …………………………………………………………208、226
non-conformity（不適合） ………………………………………………………………194
non-fungibility（個別性（非同質性、非代替性）） ……………………………………138
non-refundable deposit（権利金／礼金） ………………………………………………208

O

offering price（買い希望価格） …………………………………………………………302
operating expenses（必要諸経費／運営費用） ……………………………208、**210**、266、274
ordinary level annuity factor（複利年金現価率） ………………………………………314
owner-occupied building and its site（自用の建物及びその敷地） ……………………150、**242**
owner-occupied property for business operation（賃貸以外の事業に供する不動産） ………198、202
ownership and interests（権利） ………………………………………………………218

INDEX(英和索引)

P

periodic building lease(定期建物賃貸借)	242
periodic leasehold interest in land(定期借地権)	236
physical deterioration(物理的要因)	194
physical development & title category(類型)	**146**、148、282
plottage value(併合価値㊟)	44
potential gross income(貸室賃料収入)	**266**、274
prepayment of rent(賃料の前払い)	330
previous appraisal value(鑑定評価先例価格)	220
price level(価格水準)	190
prime area of retail/office mix(複合高度商業地域)	282
prime commercial area(高度商業地域)	282
prime office area(業務高度商業地域)	282
prime retail area(一般高度商業地域)	282
principle of anticipation(予測の原則)	166
principle of balance(均衡の原則)	166
principle of change(変動の原則)	164
principle of competition(競争の原則)	166
principle of conformity(適合の原則)	166
principle of contribution(寄与の原則)	166
principle of income allocation(収益配分の原則)	166
principle of increasing or decreasing returns(収益逓増及び逓減の原則)	166
principle of substitution(代替の原則)	164
principle of supply and demand(需要と供給の原則)	164
profits method㊟(利益に基づいて価格を求める方式)	60
property analysis(個別分析)	**182**、302
property identification data(確認資料)	220
property inspection(実地調査)	**260**、358
property-specific value influences(個別的要因)	**158**、182、286、302
property-specific value influences on building(建物に関する個別的要因)	**162**、288
property-specific value influences on built-up property(建物及びその敷地に関する個別的要因)	**162**、288
property-specific value influences on land(土地に関する個別的要因)	**158**、286
property taxes(固定資産税)	**204**、212
prospective value opinion(将来時点の鑑定評価)	**170**、292
published land price(公示価格)	224

Q

quick sale(早期売却)	**172**、296

R

rate of growth（変動率）……198
raw land（素地）……192
real estate appraisal（不動産の鑑定評価）……112、**142**
Real Estate Appraisal Act（不動産の鑑定評価に関する法律）……6、**109**、142、382
real estate appraisal business（不動産鑑定業）……**112**、118
real estate appraisal business operator／real estate appraisal firm（不動産鑑定業者）……**112**、356
Real Estate Appraisal Standards（不動産鑑定評価基準）……8、20、**133**
real estate securitization（不動産証券化）……10、256、352
real estate taxes（公租公課）……204、212
real rent（実質賃料）……208
reconciliation of the indicated values（試算価格の調整）……222
Red Book（RICS鑑定評価業務基準®）……4、**50**
refundable security deposit（敷金／保証金）……208
registration（登録）……118
registration／registry book（登記（簿））……22、218、220
regulations stipulated in public laws（公法上の規制）……158
reliability（信頼性）……4、8
remaining economic life（経済的残存耐用年数）……194
renewal charge／renewal fee（更新料）……252、254
rent（賃料）……252、326、340
rental data comparison approach（賃貸事例比較法）……**212**、216、326
rental disparity analysis approach（差額配分法）……214
rental value（賃料）……**174**、208
rent indicated by the income analysis approach（収益賃料）……212
rent indicated by the rental data comparison approach（比準賃料）……212
rent indicated by the summation approach（積算賃料）……210
rent under renewed lease（継続賃料）……174、**214**、252、254
repair expenses（修繕費）……204、**266**、274
replacement cost（置換原価（価格））……74、190
reproduction cost（再調達原価（価格））……74、190
residential area（住宅地域）……154、282
residential land（住宅地）……158、178
residual method（残余方式®）……60
retrospective value opinion（過去時点の鑑定評価）……170、**292**
reversionary value（復帰価格）……200、**324**
right of superficies（地上権）……148
Royal Institution of Chartered Surveyors（RICS）（王立勅認サーベイヤー協会（RICS）®）……4、**50**

S

safe rate（蓄積利回り）……316

INDEX（英和索引）

sales comparison approach（取引事例比較法／比較方式） ……………26、44、76、102、**196**、306
sales data（取引事例）……………………………………………………………………186
salvage value（残材価額）………………………………………………………………194
sanctions（罰則）…………………………………………………………………………128
scope of work（業務の範囲㊟）………………………………………………………22、**40**
second-tier commercial area（普通商業地域）………………………………………284
sectional superficies(air/underground rights)（区分地上権）……………148、**238**、330
securitization-properties（証券化対象不動産）………………………………256、**342**
similar or comparable neighborhood（類似地域）……………………………………176
sinking fund factor（償還基金率）………………………………………………………310
site preparation（造成）……………………………………………………………190、330
sites with interim use（見込地）………………………………………………148、162、180
skeleton lease（スケルトン貸し）………………………………………………………340
social value influences（社会的要因）…………………………………………………152
Soil Contamination Measures Law（土壌汚染対策法）……………………………286、336
special grant of land usage rights（割り当て式の土地使用権㊥）…………………………86
special rent（限定賃料）……………………………………………………………174、226
special value（限定価格／特殊価値）……………………26、58、74、102、**172**、226
standing tree and bamboo（立木竹）…………………………………………………148
straight-line method（定額法）…………………………………………………………194
subdivision development analysis（開発法）………………………………186、232、**330**
subject neighborhood（近隣地域）……………………………………………………**176**、298
subject property（対象不動産）…………………………………………………168、290
sub-prime home mortgages（低所得者向け（サブプライム）住宅ローン㊟）……………18
suburban roadside commercial area（郊外路線商業地域）…………………………284
summation approach（積算法）………………………………………………………**210**、326
survey drawing（実測図）…………………………………………………………………338
synergistic value（シナジー価値㊥）……………………………………………………102

T

tenant-occupied building and its site（貸家及びその敷地）………………150、**242**、338
tenant's right(leasehold interest in building only)（借家権）………………244、**248**
terminal capitalization rate（最終還元利回り）………………………………200、**324**
time adjustment（時点修正）……………………………………………………188、196、**308**
topography（地勢）…………………………………………………………………………152
total expenses（総費用）……………………………………………………202、204、322
total rentable area（総賃貸可能床面積）………………………………………………288
transfer agreement fee（名義書替料）…………………………………………………234
transparency（透明性）……………………………………………………………………4、8
trend approach（スライド法）……………………………………………………………216
typical transaction pattern（取引慣行）…………………………………………………238

U

UK-REIT（英国リート）……………………………………………………………64
Uniform Standards of Professional Appraisal Practice（USPAP）
　（鑑定評価業務統一基準（USPAP）㊇）………………………………………36
use category（種別）……………………………………………**146**、232、282
utility ratio for each floor of the building（階層別効用比率）………………246
utility ratio for each location on each floor（位置別効用比率）……………246

V

vacancy allowance（空室等による（損失相当額））……………212、**266**、274
vacant land（更地）……………………………………………148、**232**、330
value for regulated purpose（VRP）（特定価格）………24、**172**、228、294
value indicated by the cost approach（積算価格）………………………………190
value indicated by the income approach（収益価格）…………………………200
value indicated by the sales comparison approach（比準価格）………………196
value in use／use value（使用価値㊇㊈㊉㊄）………………44、58、74、100
value of special-purpose property（特殊価格）………26、44、**174**、228、248
value other than market value（市場価値以外の価値）………………74、88、100
verification of an appraisal performed by a local appraiser（現地鑑定検証方式）……**362**、366、374
vertical allotment ratio（立体利用率）……………………………………240、334

W

worth／investment value（投資価値㊇㊈㊉㊄）………26、44、58、74、102

Y

yield approach（利回り法）………………………………………………………214

和英索引（INDEX）

※…米国、※…英国、※…オーストラリア、※…中国、※…国際評価基準を示す。
複数の個所に出てくる用語については、とくに主な説明がなされている個所について頁数をゴチック体で示した。

あ

RICS鑑定評価業務基準※（Red Book） …… 5、**51**

い

移行地（land in a transitional area／lot in a transitional area） …… **149**、163、181
維持管理費（maintenance and management fee） …… 205、211
位置別効用比率（utility ratio for each location on each floor） …… 247
一般高度商業地域（prime retail area） …… 283
一般的要因（general value influences） …… 153
インウッド式（Inwood method） …… 315

う

売り希望価格（asking price） …… 303、307、309
運営収益（effective gross income） …… **267**、276
運営純収益（net operating income（NOI）） …… **269**、276、345
運営費用（operating expenses） …… 267、276

え

英国リート（UK-REIT） …… 65
永続性（不変性）（durability） …… 139
エンジニアリング・レポート（engineering report） …… 259、**263**、343、361

お

王立勅認サーベイヤー協会（RICS）※（Royal Institution of Chartered Surveyors（RICS）） …… 5、**51**
オーストラリア・プロパティ協会（API）（Australian Property Institute（API）） …… 67
奥行（depth） …… 159

か

海外投資不動産鑑定評価ガイドライン（Guidelines for the Appraisal of Overseas Investment Properties） …… **347**
海外投資不動産の鑑定評価（appraisal of overseas investment properties） …… 29、31
買い希望価格（offering price） …… 303
会社更生法（Corporate Reorganization Law） …… 173、**297**
階層別効用比率（utility ratio for each floor of the building） …… 247

開発法（subdivision development analysis）……………………………………187、233、**331**
家屋番号（house number）……………………………………………………………………229
価格時点（date of the value opinion）………………………………………171、229、**293**
価格水準（price level）…………………………………………………………………………191
確認資料（property identification data）……………………………………………………221
過去時点の鑑定評価（retrospective value opinion）……………………………171、**293**
貸室賃料収入（potential gross income）…………………………………………**267**、276
貸倒れ損失（collection losses allowance）………………………………………**267**、276
貸家及びその敷地（tenant-occupied building and its site）……………151、**243**、339
過剰流動性（Excessive liquidity）………………………………………………………………9
割賦払い（installment payment）……………………………………………………………307
角地（corner lot）………………………………………………………………………………159
借入金償還余裕率（debt service coverage ratio）…………………………………………321
還元利回り（capitalization rate）……………………………………201、**205**、309、317
観察減価法（methods based on observation）……………………………………………197
監視検証（monitoring／monitor）………………………………………………………11、**33**
鑑定業者（real estate appraisal firm／real estate appraisal business operator）………113、227、357
鑑定財団㊧（Appraisal Foundation）…………………………………………7、**37**、47
鑑定評価額（final opinion of value／appraised value）…………223、227、229、373
鑑定評価業務統一基準
　（USPAP）㊧（Uniform Standards of Professional Appraisal Practice（USPAP））……………37
鑑定評価書（appraisal document）………………………………………………227、365
鑑定評価先例価格（previous appraisal value）……………………………………………221
鑑定評価の依頼目的（function of the appraisal）…………………………………………229
鑑定評価の基本的事項（basic appraisal problem）………………………**169**、219、291
鑑定評価の手順（appraisal process）………………………………………………**219**、329
鑑定評価の方式（appraisal method）……………………………………187、**223**、305
鑑定評価報告書（appraisal report）………………………………**227**、231、261、377
鑑定評価を行った年月日（date of the appraisal report）………………………**229**、293
元本（capital investment）……………………………………………………………………141
管理規約（management bylaws）……………………………………………………………289
管理費（management fee）…………………………………………………………211、339

き

基礎価格（base value）………………………………………………………211、327、341
期待利回り（anticipated yield）………………………………………………………………211
機能的要因（functional obsolescence）……………………………………………………195
共益費（common area charges）…………………………………………………209、267
行政的要因（governmental value influences）……………………………………………155
競争の原則（principle of competition）……………………………………………………167
業務高度商業地域（prime office area）……………………………………………………283
業務の範囲㊧（scope of work）…………………………………………………………23、**41**

399

和英索引(INDEX)

共有持分(co-ownership) ……………………………………………………151、**339**
共用部分(common area) ……………………………………………………151、**339**
寄与の原則(principle of contribution) ……………………………………………167
均衡の原則(principle of balance) …………………………………………………167
近隣商業地域(neighborhood commercial area) …………………………………285
近隣地域(subject neighborhood) …………………………………………**177**、299

く

空室等による損失(相当額)(vacancy allowance) ………………………213、**267**、276
区分所有建物(及びその敷地)(condominium unit) ………………151、**245**、339
区分地上権(sectional superficies(air/underground right)) …………149、**239**、331
グローバル投資実績基準(GIPS)®(Global Investment Performance Standards(GIPS)) …………49

け

経済的残存耐用年数(remaining economic life) ………………………………………195
経済的要因〈一般的要因〉(economic value influences) ……………………………153
経済的要因〈経済的陳腐化〉(economic obsolescence) ……………………………195
継続賃料(rent under renewed lease) ……………………………175、**215**、253、255
競売(auction sale) ……………………………………………………………………309
契約期間(lease term) ……………………………………………………………237、327
減価修正(accrued depreciation) ……………………………………………………195
減価償却費(depreciation) …………………………………………205、211、309、321
原価法/原価方式(cost approach) ………………………………27、45、77、103、**191**
現行賃料(current rent) ………………………………………………………………217
現行用途前提の市場価値®⑦(existing use value(EUV)) …………………………57、75
現在時点の鑑定評価(current value opinion) …………………………………………171
現地鑑定検証方式(verification of an appraisal performed by a local appraiser) ……**363**、367、375
現地鑑定人(local appraiser) …………………………………………………………359
現地鑑定補助方式(appraisal performed with a local assistant) ………**363**、365、373
建築基準法(Building Standards Act) ………………………………………………289
限定価格(special value) ………………………………………………………27、**173**、227
限定賃料(special rent) ……………………………………………………………175、227
権利(ownership and interests) ………………………………………………………219
権利金(non-refundable deposit) ……………………………………………………209
権利の態様の確認(identification of ownership and interests) ……………………219

こ

郊外路線商業地域(suburban roadside commercial area) …………………………285
工業地(industrial land) …………………………………………………………161、179
工業地域(industrial area) ……………………………………………………………157

和英索引(INDEX)

公示価格(published land price) ……225
更新料(renewal charge／renewal fee) ……253
公正価値㊞㋐㊌(fair value) ……57、73、101
公租公課(real estate taxes) ……205、211
高度商業地域(prime commercial area) ……283
公売(compulsory sale) ……309
公法上の規制(regulations stipulated in public laws) ……159
国際評価基準(International Valuation Standards(IVS)) ……15、**95**
コストに基づいて価値を求める方式㊞(cost of replacement method) ……61
固定資産税(property taxes) ……205、211
固定性(fixity) ……139
個別性(非同質性、非代替性)(non-fungibility) ……139
個別的要因(property-specific value influences) ……**159**、183、287、303
個別分析(property analysis) ……**183**、303

さ

最終還元利回り(terminal capitalization rate) ……201、**325**
再調達価格／再調達原価(reproduction cost) ……75、**191**
最有効使用(highest and best use(HABU)) ……25、43、57、73、101、165、**183**、229、303
差額純収益(difference between the two NOIs) ……335
差額配分法(rental disparity analysis approach) ……215
更地(vacant land) ……149、**233**、331
残材価額(salvage value) ……195
残余方式㊞(residual method) ……59

し

敷金(refundable security deposit) ……209
試算価格(indicated value) ……223
試算価格の調整(reconciliation of the indicated values) ……223
試算賃料(indicated rent) ……223
資産の流動化に関する法律(Asset Liquidation Law) ……27、173、**295**
市場価値(market value) ……25、43、57、73、87、99、**171**、293
市場価値以外の価値(value other than market value) ……75、89、101
市場公開期間(market exposure time／exposure time／marketing period) ……25、43、57、73、101、**293**
市場性を有する不動産(marketable real estate) ……171、**173**
事情補正(adjustment for conditions of sale) ……189、**307**
実際実質賃料(actual real rent) ……**213**、215、247、341
実際支払賃料(actual nominal rent) ……215
実査日(date of the property inspection) ……229
実質賃料(real rent) ……209

401

和英索引（INDEX）

実測図（survey drawing） ……………………………………………………………339
実地調査（property inspection） ……………………………………………261、359
指定区域〈土壌汚染対策法〉（designated area） ………………………………287
時点修正（time adjustment） ………………………………………189、197、**309**
シナジー価値⑲（synergistic value） ……………………………………………103
支払賃料（nominal rent） …………………………………………………**209**、227
資本的支出（capital expenditures） ………………………………………**269**、276
社会的要因（social value influences） …………………………………………153
借地権（leasehold interest in land） ……………………………149、**237**、331
借地権付建物（buildings on leased land） …………………………………151、**245**
借地借家法（Land Lease and Building Lease Law）………………149、**237**、249
借地法（Ground Lease Law） ……………………………………………………**237**
借家権（tenant's right（leasehold interest in building only））……………243、**249**
収益価格（value indicated by the income approach） ……………………………201
収益還元法／収益方式（income capitalization approach） ……27、45、77、103、**199**、309
収益純賃料（net income） …………………………………………………………213
収益賃料（rent indicated by the income analysis approach）…………………213
収益逓増及び逓減の原則（principle of increasing or decreasing returns） …………167
収益配分の原則（principle of income allocation） ……………………………167
収益分析法（income analysis approach）…………………………………………213
修繕費（repair expenses） …………………………………………205、**267**、276
住宅地（residential land） …………………………………………………159、179
住宅地域（residential area） ………………………………………………155、283
住宅の品質確保の促進等に関する法律（Housing Quality Assurance Law） ……289
種別（use category） ………………………………………………**147**、233、283
需要と供給の原則（principle of supply and demand） …………………………165
準高度商業地域（central commercial area） ……………………………………283
純収益（net cash flow（NCF）
　　／Adjusted Net Operating Income）……………199、**201**、203、**269**、276、309、321、345
純賃料（net rent） …………………………………………………………………209
使用価値㊗㊥㊆⑲（value in use／use value） ………………………45、59、75、101
償還基金率（sinking fund factor） ………………………………………………311
償却資産（depreciable property component）……………………………………309
商業地（commercial land） …………………………………………………159、179
商業地域（commercial area） ………………………………………………155、**283**
証券化対象不動産（securitization-properties） …………………………257、**343**
証券化対象不動産の鑑定評価（appraisal of securitization-properties）………29、**257**、343
条件変更承諾料（amounts paid for consent to change the lease terms）………255
自用の建物及びその敷地（owner-occupied building and its sites）………151、**243**
将来時点の鑑定評価（prospective value opinion） ……………………171、293
事例資料（comparable data）………………………………………………………221
新規賃料（market rent under new lease） …………………175、**211**、253、255、341
信頼性（reliability） …………………………………………………………………5、9

す

スケルトン貸し（skeleton lease） ……………………………………………………………341
スライド法（trend approach） ……………………………………………………………217

せ

清算（liquidation） …………………………………………………………………………309
正常価格（market value） ………………………………………………25、**171**、227、293
正常賃料（market rent） …………………………………**175**、215、227、253、341
積算価格（value indicated by the cost approach） …………………………………191
積算賃料（rent indicated by the summation approach） …………………………211
積算法（summation approach） …………………………………………**211**、327
設計図書（building document） …………………………………………………………339
専有部分（exclusively owned area） …………………………………151、247、339

そ

早期売却（quick sale） ………………………………………………………173、297
総収益（gross income） ……………………………………**203**、267、321
造成（site preparation） ………………………………………………………191、331
総賃貸可能床面積（total rentable area） ………………………………………………289
想定上の条件（assumptions and limiting conditions） ……………171、227、291
総費用（total expenses） ………………………………………………203、205、323
底地（leased fee interest in land） ……………………………………………149、239
素地（raw land） ……………………………………………………………………………193
損害保険料（insurance premium） …………………………………………205、213

た

大規模修繕に係る修繕計画（large-scale repair project） ……………………………289
大規模修繕費（large-scale repair expenses） …………………………205、323
対象不動産（subject property） …………………………………………………169、291
対象不動産の確定（確認）（identification of the subject property） ………169、219、291
耐震基準（earthquake resistance standards） ………………………………………289
耐震性（earthquake resistance of a building） ………………………………………289
代替の原則（principle of substitution） ……………………………………………165
耐用年数（depreciation over a period） ……………………………………………195
耐用年数に基づく方法（methods of estimating accrued depreciation over a period） ……195
宅地（building site） ………………………………**149**、159、179、233、253、331、341
宅地地域（building site area） ……………………………………………………147、155
宅地見込地（building sites with an interim use） ……………………………149、241
立退料（cost of tenant removal） ……………………………………………………307

和英索引（INDEX）

建付地（land portion of built-up property） ……………………………149、**235**
建物及びその敷地（built-up property） ……………**151**、163、181、243、255、339、341
建物及びその敷地に関する個別的要因
　（property-specific value influences on built-up property） ………………**163**、289
建物残余法（building residual technique） ………………………………………313
建物図面（building drawing） ……………………………………………………339
建物等の撤去費（building demolition cost） ………………………………315、317
建物と敷地の適応（compatibility between building and site） ……………**163**、195
建物に関する個別的要因（property-specific value influences on building） ……**163**、289
建物の区分所有等に関する法律
　（Law for Unit Ownership, etc. of Building／Law for Condominium） ………151

ち

地域分析（market area analysis） …………………………………………**177**、299
地域要因（area-specific value influences） ………………………………**155**、189
地役権（easement） ………………………………………………………………175
地価公示法（Land Price Publication Act） ……………………………………225
置換原価／置換価格（replacement cost） ……………………………………75、191
蓄積利回り（safe rate） ……………………………………………………………317
地上権（right of superficies） ……………………………………………………149
地勢（topography） ………………………………………………………………153
地代（ground rent） ………………………………………………………………327
地目（category of land） …………………………………………………………229
懲戒処分（disciplinary measure） …………………………………………31、**123**
調停（arbitration） ………………………………………………………………**309**
直接還元法（direct capitalization method） ………………………………201、309
賃貸以外の事業に供する不動産（owner-occupied property for business operation） ………199、203
賃貸借契約（lease contract） ……………………………………………………163
賃貸事例比較法（rental data comparison approach） ……………**213**、217、327
賃貸用不動産（lease-based property） …………………………………199、203
賃料（rent／rental value） ……………………………175、209、253、327、341
賃料差額（difference between market rent and contract rent） ………………237
賃料の前払い（prepayment of rent） ……………………………………………331

て

定額法（straight-line method） …………………………………………………195
定期借地権（periodic leasehold interest in land） ……………………………237
定期建物賃貸借（periodic building lease） ……………………………………243
低所得者向け（サブプライム）住宅ローン※（sub-prime home mortgages） ………17
定着物（improvements） …………………………………………………………139
定率法（declining balance method） ……………………………………………195

和英索引(INDEX)

データ管理システム㉘(data management process) ・・・・・・・・・・・・・・・・・・・・・・・・・・・・・・・・・・・・11
適合の原則(principle of conformity) ・・・167

と

同一需給圏(market area) ・・**179**、301
投下資本収益率〈開発法〉(discount rate) ・・・・・・・・・・・・・・・・・・・・・・・・・・・・・・・・・・・・・・331
登記(簿)(registration／registry book) ・・・・・・・・・・・・・・・・・・・・・・・・・・・・・23、219、221
倒産(bankruptcy) ・・309
投資価値㉘㉙㉗㉖(investment value／worth) ・・・・・・・・・・・・・・・・・・27、45、59、75、103
投資信託及び投資法人に関する法律
　　(Investment Trust and Investment Corporation Law) ・・・・・・・・・・・・・173、295
投資方式(investment method) ・・59
透明性(transparency) ・・5、9
登録(registration) ・・119
特殊価格(value of special-purpose property) ・・・・・・・・・・・・・・・27、45、**175**、229、249
特殊価値(special value) ・・59、75、103
特定価格(value for regulated purpose(VRP)) ・・・・・・・・・・・・・・・・・25、**173**、229、295
特別な積算価格㉙㉖(depreciated replacement cost(DRC)) ・・・・・・・・・・・・・・・・57、101
独立鑑定評価(appraisal of site value as if vacant) ・・・・・・・・・・・・・・・・・・・・・・・・・・・・・169
都市計画税(city planning tax) ・・・205、211
土壌汚染対策法(Soil Contamination Measures Law) ・・・・・・・・・・・・・・・・・・・287、337
土地基本法(Basic Land Act) ・・143
土地残余法(land residual technique) ・・・・・・・・・・・・・・・・・・・・・・・・・・・・・・・・・・233、**313**
土地に関する個別的要因(property-specific value influences on land) ・・・・・159、287
土地利用規制(land use regulations) ・・・301
取引慣行(typical transaction pattern) ・・237
取引事例(sales data) ・・・187
取引事例比較法／比較方式(sales comparison approach) ・・・・・・・・27、45、77、103、**197**、307
取引利回り(market-derived capitalization rate) ・・・・・・・・・・・・・・・・・・**207**、211、317

な

内装(interior finish) ・・・289

に

日本住宅性能表示基準(Japan Home Performance Standards) ・・・・・・・・・・・・・・・・289

の

農地(agricultural land) ・・・・・・・・・・・・・・・・・・・・・・・・・・・・・・・・・・・・・・149、161、181、**241**
農地地域(agricultural area) ・・・147、157

和英索引(INDEX)

は

配分法(allocation method) ……199
配分率(distribution factor) ……247
発掘調査(excavation survey) ……287
罰則(sanctions) ……129
バブル(bubble) ……5、17
払い下げ式の土地使用権(出譲)⊕(government sale of land usage rights) ……85

ひ

比較方式(comparison method) ……59
比準価格(value indicated by the sales comparison approach) ……197
比準賃料(rent indicated by the rental data comparison approach) ……213
必要諸経費(operating expenses) ……209、**211**
秘密を守る義務(confidentiality) ……121

ふ

複合高度商業地域(prime area of retail/office mix) ……283
複合不動産(built-up property) ……205、341
複利年金現価率(ordinary level annuity factor) ……315
不増性(finite nature of supply) ……139
付帯費用(incidental expenses) ……331
普通商業地域(second-tier commercial area) ……285
復帰価格(reversionary value) ……201、**325**
物的確認(identification of the physical characteristics) ……219
物理的要因(physical deterioration) ……195
不適合(non-conformity) ……195
不動産鑑定業(real estate appraisal business) ……113、119
不動産鑑定協会⊕(Appraisal Institute) ……7、37、47
不動産鑑定業者(real estate appraisal business operator/real estate appraisal firm) ……113、357
不動産鑑定士(Licensed Real Estate Appraiser (LREA)) ……23、**115**、139、143、353
不動産鑑定評価基準(Real Estate Appraisal Standards) ……7、21、**133**
不動産鑑定評価基準運用上の留意事項
　(Guidance Notes on the Real Estate Appraisal Standards) ……279
不動産証券化(real estate securitization) ……11、257、351
不動産投資信託(Jリート)(J-REITs) ……353
不動産のあり方(configuration of real estate) ……139
不動産の鑑定評価(real estate appraisal) ……113、**143**
不動産の鑑定評価に関する法律(Real Estate Appraisal Act) ……7、**109**、143、383
不動性(非移動性)(immovability) ……139
部分鑑定評価(appraisal of severance value) ……169

フリーホールド㊗㊥㉔㊿(freehold／fee simple) ··41、53、71、99
文化財(cultural assets) ···175
文化財保護法(Cultural Properties Protection Law) ·······································287
分割鑑定評価(appraisal of component value) ··169

へ

併合価値㊗(plottage value) ···45
併合鑑定評価(appraisal of assemblage value) ··169
変動の原則(principle of change) ···165
変動率(rate of growth)···199

ほ

保証金(refundable security deposit) ··209
ホスコルド式(Hoskold method) ···315
保有期間(holding period) ···201、325

ま

埋蔵文化財(buried cultural assets) ···287
間口(lot width)···159、161

み

見込地(sites with interim use) ··149、163、181
民事再生法(Civil Rehabilitation Law)···27、173、**295**

め

名義書替料(transfer agreement fee) ··235

ゆ

有害物質使用特定施設(factory or business facility that uses harmful substances) ················287
有期還元法(capitalization over a definite term) ··313
有効需要(effective demand) ··139
床荷重(floor loads) ···289

よ

要因資料(data on value influences) ··221
用途的地域(market area category) ···177

407

和英索引(INDEX)

予測の原則(principle of anticipation) ……………………………………………………167

り

リースホールド㊗㊥㋕㊻(leasehold) …………………………………………41、53、71、99
利益に基づいて価格を求める方式㊥(profits method) ………………………………61
利害関係(conflict of interest) …………………………………………………………231
立体利用率(vertical allotment ratio) ……………………………………………241、335
利回り法(yield approach) ………………………………………………………………215
流動性危機(liquidity crisis) ………………………………………………………………17
立木竹(standing tree and bamboo) …………………………………………………149
林地(forestland) ………………………………………………………147、161、181、**241**
林地地域(forestland area) ………………………………………………………147、157

る

類型(physical development & title category) ……………………………**147**、149、283
類似地域(similar or comparable neighborhood) ……………………………………177

ろ

老朽化(deterioration) ……………………………………………………………………195

わ

割り当て式の土地使用権㊻(special grant of land usage rights) ……………………87
割引キャッシュフロー法／DCF法(Discounted Cash Flow Method)……201、**265**、321、345
割引率〈収益還元法〉(discount rate) …………………………………………201、**205**、323

Copyright reserved by the **JAPAN REAL ESTATE INSTITUTE**
Kangin-Fujiya Bldg., 1-3-2, Toranomon Minato-ku Tokyo
105-8485, Japan　　　　　　　　　　　Tel：03(3503)5335
　　　　　　　　　　　　　　　URL http://www.reinet.or.jp

Published by **JUTAKU-SHIMPOSHA, INC.**
TAM Bldg., 1-4-9, Nishishimbashi Minato-ku Tokyo 105-0003, Japan

【執筆者紹介】

> 渡辺　卓美（Takumi WATANABE）
> 1945年、長野県生まれ
> 財団法人日本不動産研究所　研究部・国際業務担当上席主幹
> 不動産鑑定士（LREA）、CRE（USA）、FRICS（UK）
> ㈶日本不動産研究所のクロス・ボーダー評価において、長く責任者として従事。主な著書に「現代の都市法」（共著、東京大学出版会。日本不動産学会賞受賞）、「日本の都市法Ⅱ」（共著、東京大学出版会）などがある。

※本書は、『英語で読む不動産鑑定評価基準』（2003年7月初版発行）を増補・改訂し、改題版として発行したものです。

Japan Real Estate Appraisal in a Global Context
～不動産鑑定評価の国際化～

2003年7月31日　　初版発行
2008年9月9日　　改題版第1刷発行

編著者	㈶日本不動産研究所	
発行者	中　野　博　義	
発行所	㈱住宅新報社	

編集部	〒105-0003	東京都港区西新橋1-4-9（TAMビル）
		電話（03）3504-0361
出版販売部	〒105-0003	東京都港区西新橋1-4-9（TAMビル）
		電話（03）3502-4151
大阪支社	〒530-0005	大阪市北区中之島3-2-4（大阪朝日ビル）
		電話（06）6202-8541㈹
	ウェブサイト	http://www.jutaku-s.com/

©2008　JAPAN REAL ESTATE INSTITUTE
Printed in Japan　ISBN978-4-7892-2788-9　C2030
印刷・製本／亜細亜印刷
定価はカバーに表示してあります。落丁本・乱丁本はお取り替えいたします。

> 本書の全部または一部を無断で複写複製（コピー）することは、著作権法上での例外を除き、禁じられています。